Sefer HaYovel
of Yeshivat Har Etzion

Sefer HaYovel
of Yeshivat Har Etzion

Edited by

Rabbi Yonatan Shai Freedman
Rabbi Yair Kahn
Rabbi Elyakim Krumbein
Rabbi Tzvi Sinensky

Copyright © 2019 by Yeshivat Har Etzion

978-1-947857-28-5
All Rights Reserved

All rights reserved. Except for brief quotations in printed reviews, no part of this publication may be reproduced, stored in a retrieval system, or transmitted in any form or by any means (printed, written, photocopied, visual electronic, audio, or otherwise) without the prior permissions of the publisher.

Editorial Committee:

Rabbi Yonatan Shai Freedman
Rabbi Yair Kahn
Rabbi Elyakim Krumbein
Rabbi Tzvi Sinensky

Copyeditor:

Jonny Brull

Production:

Rabbi Yonatan Shai Freedman
Yoel Weiss

Cover image © 2019 Shachar Gesundheit

Yeshivat Har Etzion
Alon Shevut 9043300, Israel

Published & Distributed by

Kodesh Press L.L.C.
New York, NY
www.KodeshPress.com
kodeshpress@gmail.com

שמע בני מוסר אביך
ואל תטוש תורת אמך

In loving memory of

Yitzchak & Sheva Shayndel Schwartz

Dedicated by Avraham & Sarah Schwartz

Table of Contents

Introduction 13
Editor's Foreword 15

Founding *Rashei Yeshiva zt"l*

HaRav Yehuda Amital *zt"l*
Remarks at the Dedication of the Beit Midrash of Yeshivat Har Etzion . . 17

HaRav Aharon Lichtenstein *zt"l*
"And to Serve Him" – This is Talmud Torah 19

Rashei Yeshiva

HaRav Baruch Gigi
A Talmid Should Not Give a Halakhic
    Decision in the Place Where His Rav Resides 41

HaRav Mosheh Lichtenstein
On the Yeshiva Rabbinate 59

HaRav Yaakov Medan
A Note on the Order of the Chapters and the Mishnayot in Masekhet Gittin . 83

Alumni

DIVREI HESPED

Rabbi Dr. Michael Rosensweig '73
A Rebbe as a Father: Divrei Hesped for HaRav Aharon Lichtenstein *zt"l* . 89

Terry Novetsky '80
HaRav Aharon Lichtenstein *zt"l*: A Talmid's Remembrance 101

IYYUN AND HALAKHA

Rabbi Yitzchak Etshalom '83
"Lo Tevashel Gedi": The Thrice-Banned Mixture 107

Rabbi David Brofsky '90
Brit Mila: The Father's Obligation 121

Rabbi Dr. Moti Novick '92
The Prohibition of Withholding Wages 133

Rabbi Yehoshua Grunstein '95
Kiddush on Wine: Welcoming the Challenge 145

Rabbi David Nachbar '96
*The Dynamic Relationship Between Kevod Ha-Av
and Kevod Ha-Rav in Rambam's View* 159

Rabbi Dr. Shlomo Brody '98
Halakhic Dilemmas of the "Knife Intifada" 175

PHILOSOPHY AND ETHICS

Rabbi Joel Finkelstein '81
The Interplay of the Interpersonal and Divine Commandments 189

Rabbi Nathaniel Helfgot '81
*Decision-Making on Matters of Halakhic
Public Policy or Meta-Halakhic Issues: Some Tentative Thoughts* . . 199

Rabbi Dr. Yossef Slotnik '83
*Disdain, Fear and Harmony: Themes in
the Relationships Between Jews and Non-Jews* 215

Rabbi Reuven Ziegler '86
The Meaning of Prayer: Three Themes in Rav Soloveitchik's Writings . . 237

Rabbi Mark Smilowitz '88
Understanding Rambam's "Necessary Belief" in God's Emotions . . . 255

Rabbi Dr. Shlomo Dov Rosen '93
*Planning and Engaging Life: Globalization,
Egalitarianism, Agency, and Chesed* 269

Rabbi Rafi Eis '98
The Shofar and the Jewish Future 281

Rabbi Dr. Yaakov Jaffe '98
The Ethics of Testimony 289

Rabbi Tzvi Sinensky '98
Derekh Eretz as Rabbinic Natural Morality 305

Rabbi Dr. Aaron Segal '99
If This World is an Anteroom, Why Be This-Worldly? 319

Rabbi Shlomo Zuckier '05
Leavings of Sin: HaRav Aharon Lichtenstein zt"l on Teshuva 333

TALMUD TORAH
Rabbi Michael Taubes '77
The Obligation to Teach Torah to One's Post-Bar Mitzva Child 345

Rabbi Ari Kahn '80
The Arrival of Rabbi Akiva 357

Rabbi Moshe Taragin '83
A Divine Torah Delivered to Human Beings 371

Rabbi Nasanayl Braun '92
Soul Food: The Profound Impact of Talmud Torah 385

Rabbi Dovid Gottlieb '09
The 48 Kinyenei Torah: An Introduction 395

TANAKH
Rabbi Dr. Michael Berger '80
Berakhot and Bilam 407

Gidon Rothstein '82
Success is Hard-Fought, For Our Greatest 419

Rabbi Dr. Ezra Frazer '96
Father Knows Best? Understanding Yitzchak's Love of Eisav 429

Rabbi Elie Weissman '96
The Days and Nights of Shir Hashirim 437

Rabbi Daniel Fridman '02
*In the Presence of the Almighty: The Compromise
    Between Moshe and the Tribes of Gad and Re'uven* 443

About the Authors 451

Introduction

In *Parashat Tetzaveh* (27:20), Aharon and his sons are commanded *"leha'alot ner tamid"* (to light a lamp that burns continually). The *Gemara* (*Shabbat* 21a) states that this means that the flame ascends of itself once it is kindled. In *Mishlei* (6:23) we are told *"ki ner mitzva ve-Torah or"* (the *mitzvot* are a lamp and the Torah is a light). Just as the light in the *Mikdash* needs to be able to share its light on its own, proper Torah education means educating a student to be able to live a life of Torah, who in turn is able to pass on its message to others.

For more than four decades, Yeshivat Har Etzion was led by its founding *Rashei Yeshiva zt"l*. Those fortunate enough to be their *talmidim* learned first-hand the importance of *talmud Torah*, diligence in learning, love of the Land and People of Israel, and proper ethics and *middot*. They inculcated these values in their *talmidim* and lived these values by example. They were successful in educating generations of *talmidim* who are in turn educating another generation with these values, passing on these values to those who did not merit to learn from them directly. This year the 51st *machzor* of the Yeshiva has begun learning from *Rashei Yeshiva* and *Ramim* who are carrying on the legacy of the founding *Rashei Yeshiva zt"l*, a sure sign of their educational success.

In honor of the Yeshiva's 50th anniversary, many of the Yeshiva's Rabbinic alumni were asked to submit a Torah article on values close to the Yeshiva, such as on *talmud Torah*, *ahavat Yisrael*, ethics, or *Tziyonut*. This volume would not be complete without the Torah of the founding *Rashei Yeshiva*, but it stresses the contributions and submissions of the current *Rashei Yeshiva* and alumni educators who are currently sharing Torah of the Yeshiva around the world. We are grateful to those who submitted articles and are especially appreciative of the dedicated editors who helped bring this project to fruition.

The contributors to this volume represent only a small sample of the breadth of our Rabbinic alumni base. Hundreds of Rabbinic alumni on six continents play pivotal roles in Jewish education across the globe sharing the Yeshiva's vision, values, and Torah from the pulpit, in schools, on college campuses, and to the Jewish community at large.

יהי רצון שיזכו להגדיל תורה ולהאדירה

Rabbi Yonatan Shai Freedman
Overseas Alumni Coordinator

Hillel Silvera
President

Yoel Weiss
Executive Vice President

Editor's Foreword

Shivim panim la-Torah: there are seventy faces to the Torah; and as with the Torah in general, so too with *Torat Har Etzion*. This book contains an assortment of articles on a variety of topics, each composed in its own unique style as per the writer. The diversity of the various essays included herein, both in terms of style as well as subject, is testament to the success of Yeshivat Har Etzion in its ability to produce alumni excelling in many areas of Torah, from *machshava* and *Tanakh* to *halakha* and *iyyun*, and the individuality that they acquire in doing so.

It is the nature of any work with multiple contributors, such as this, to pose difficulties before its editors in their attempt to generate some form of consistency without detracting from the individuality of the writers. It is our hope that we have achieved the correct balance here. My editing was, for the most part, purely technical, in my efforts to create a sense of uniformity among the articles and their terminology, without compromising the integrity of the particular essay at hand (and I apologize profusely if I have failed in doing so). This balance between distinctiveness and similitude surely reflects the mandate that we received at Yeshivat Har Etzion: to encourage and inspire individuality in Torah, stemming from a united front whereby we are charged with the task of unwavering loyalty to *Torat Hashem*. As I once heard *Moreinu* HaRav Aharon Lichtenstein *zt"l* state in a *sicha* on Shavu'ot night: On the one hand, it is "*Torat Hashem*" (*Tehillim* 1:2), God's Torah; but it is also "*Torato*" (ibid.), the Torah of the individual who studies it – and it is our mission to transform *Torat Hashem* into *Torateinu*, to make it our own.

The *Gemara* states:

Rabbi Yochanan said: An unnamed *mishna* is credited to Rabbi Me'ir; an unnamed *tosefta* is credited to Rabbi Nechemya; an unnamed *Sifra* is credited to Rabbi Yehuda; and an unnamed *Sifrei* is credited to Rabbi Shimon – but they all stem from Rabbi Akiva. (*Sanhedrin* 86a)

So too, each of these articles is to the credit of its writer – but they all stem from *Torat Har Etzion*.

May we merit "*lehagdil Torah u-lha'adirah*": to make Torah great and glorious,

Jonny Brull ('11)

Remarks at the Dedication of the *Beit Midrash* of Yeshivat Har Etzion*

HaRav Yehuda Amital *zt"l*

The stones that were incorporated into this structure are *avnei chefetz*, desired stones, for indeed much desire and heart went into this building on the part of the doers and the movers, the planners and the builders.

For the stone shall cry out of the wall; it shall speak and answer.

The content of this building is symbolized by its structure, its design and its form. Its broad base that spreads out and entrenches itself along the edges of the rocky hill, in contrast to its narrowing top, which brings to mind the verse "though firm be your dwelling-place, and though your nest be set in the rock" (*Bamidbar* 24:21), expresses first and foremost our firm hold on the place, not a weak hold, but one that is firm, full and deeply rooted. "This is My resting-place forever; here will I dwell, for I have desired it" (*Tehillim* 132:14) – this place, and many others.

This building will not produce intellectuals who are detached from reality and spin around themselves in an egocentric circle. From here will emerge, with God's help, Torah scholars whose minds reach the highest levels of the Torah, but who are nevertheless deeply involved in Jewish spiritual, social, political and historical reality. Torah scholars who are involved with the people and fully aware of everything that is happening in Jewish society to its very margins.

From this broad base the building tapers upward. All of its diagonal lines from every direction strive to reach on high, as if they were searching for some point somewhere up above.

I pray that all the striving in this building be aimed exclusively upward; not toward degrees, or certificates, or positions, but to spiritual elevation, in the spirit of (*Eikha* 3:41): "Let us lift up our heart with our hands unto God in the heavens." This building, which rises on high and is visible from afar with its striking strength and rule over the neighboring mountains and valleys and which expresses the dominance of the renewed Jewish settlement in this region, points to the supremacy of the *Beit Midrash* in our physical and spiritual existence in the Holy Land.

This building can be seen from great distances, rising up and standing out in its aristocratic solitude, but as one draws near and enters into it, one is struck by the warmth that permeates it, by the cohesion of the students studying in it. Each individual sitting in study fills up, as it were, its entire space. There is no sense of nullity, of a dumbfounded particle lost in a threatening cavern, but rather a feeling of sitting in the tent of Torah, enjoying its warmth, modesty and collegiality.

The wings of the building projecting from the area of the Torah Ark, which turn to the sides while slanting upwards, wish to express the openness to understand and feel the stirrings of the hearts of students coming from all different sectors and circles, and the aspiration not to withdraw from society, but rather to go out, to take the Torah out to the streets of the city, to bring the word of God to those who thirst for it, even if they are not yet aware of how thirsty they are. Like a king, who had two Torah scrolls, one that he kept in his treasury, and one that he kept at his side at all times, even when he went out to war.

Congratulations to the architects who strove to reach inward, to the soul.

* Translated by David Strauss

"And to Serve Him" – This is *Talmud Torah** [1]

HaRav Aharon Lichtenstein *zt"l*

Introduction

"All depends on luck," asserts the *Zohar*, "even a *Sefer Torah* in the *Heikhal*."[2] Two parallel, almost identical, statements entered the *Heikhal* of halakhic literature. One enjoyed good fortune, the other not. A *beraita* proposes several interpretations of the phrase, "And to serve Him with all your heart," in the opening verse of the middle section of *Shema* (*Devarim* 11:13):

> "And to serve Him (*le-ovdo*) with all your heart" – this is *talmud Torah*.[3] You might say this refers to actual *avoda* [i.e. sacrificial service]. When it says: "And the Lord took the man, and put him into the Garden of Eden to work it (*le-ovdah*) and to keep it" (*Bereishit* 2:15) – what work was there in former days and what keeping was there in former days? Thus, you learn: "To work it" – this is *talmud Torah*; "and to keep it" – this is observance of the *mitzvot*. And just as sacrificial service at the *mizbei'ach* is called *avoda*, so is *talmud Torah* called *avoda*.
>
> Another explanation: "And to serve Him" – this is *tefilla*, prayer. You might say that this refers to actual *avoda* [i.e. sacrificial

---

1. This article was originally published in Hebrew: *"U-l'ovdo – Zeh Talmud,"* *Darkhei Shalom: Iyyunim Ba-Hagut Ha-Yehudit, Muggashim Le-Shalom Rosenberg*, Binyamin Ish-Shalom (ed.), Jerusalem 5767, pp. 181-191.
2. *Zohar Parashat Naso* (ed. Margoliyot, p. 134).
3. Editor's note: Although the actual words of the *Sifrei* here are *"zeh talmud,"* the *Sifrei* is referring to *"talmud Torah"* (and not *"Gemara"*), and therefore we have rendered it thus throughout this essay.

service]. Therefore, the verse states: "with all your heart." Is there service in the heart (*avoda sheba-lev*)? Thus, the verse teaches: "And to serve Him with all your heart" – this is *tefilla*. And it is similarly stated with David: "Let my prayer be set forth as incense before You, the lifting up of my hands as the evening sacrifice" (*Tehillim* 141:2). And Daniel says: "And when Daniel knew that the writing was signed, he went into his house – now his windows were open in his upper chamber toward *Yerushalayim* – and he kneeled upon his knees three times a day, and prayed, and gave thanks before his God, as he did aforetime" (Daniel 6:11)... Now was there sacrificial service in *Bavel*? Thus, the verse teaches: "And to serve Him" – this is *tefilla*. Just as sacrificial service at the *mizbei'ach* is called *avoda*, so is *tefilla* called *avoda*. (*Sifrei Parashat Eikev*)[4]

The identification of *tefilla* with *avoda* in general, and with *avoda sheba-lev* in particular, has had the good fortune of constant rejuvenation. It long ago penetrated the consciousness of *talmidei chakhamim* via several lines at the beginning of *Ta'anit*,[5] and the stream of books focusing on this topic has not stopped.[6] In contrast, the determination that "to serve Him" refers to *talmud Torah* has remained relatively forlorn. Of course, the issue of *talmud Torah* was never removed from the agenda, and echoes of this assertion, with all its halakhic, philosophic, theological and methodological ramifications, burst forth and are sounded in many different sources and contexts. However, it has certainly not taken center stage. The *rishonim* make several references to it. Rambam mentions it in his *Sefer Ha-Mitzvot*,[7] and so too Ramban in his *hasagot* there and in his Commentary to the Torah. This is the way

---

4. On *Devarim* 11:13 (ed. *Netziv*, no. 5).
5. *Ta'anit* 2a: "As it was taught: 'To love the Lord your God, and to serve Him with all your heart' – what is service of the heart? You must say *tefilla*."
6. I will note only two recent works: Rav J. B. Soloveitchik, *Worship of the Heart, Essays on Jewish Prayer*, S. Carmy (ed.), New York 2003; Rav Shlomo Engel, *Avoda Sheba-Lev – Zo Tefilla*, Jerusalem 2003.
7. Rambam *Sefer Ha-Mitzvot* positive 5.

Yerei'im explains the mitzva of *avoda*/service,[8] and in the continuation he cites both components of the *Sifrei*'s remark. Rokei'ach cites the statement as one of several sources noted in *Hilkhot Chasidut* at the beginning of the book.[9] But by any measure, this is an exceedingly meager yield, even if we assume that there are additional citations that have escaped me. This fact is good cause for presenting a discussion that does not pretend to exhaust the issue, but will try at least to raise it, if only in brief summary, in our hearts.

To do our job properly, we must act on two planes: On the one hand, we must conduct a focused analysis of the *Sifrei*'s statement and its context; on the other hand, we must clarify the topic in relation to other areas and sources. The textual discussion itself divides into two issues: First, we must understand the structure of the passage, and the way it reaches its conclusion; second, we must examine the content of that conclusion.

The Course of the *Sifrei*'s Discussion

The *Sifrei*'s discussion includes an examination of different senses of *avodat Hashem*. It first suggests the clearest and simplest of them ("actual *avoda*"), which refers to observance of the *mitzvot* in general, and the sacrificial service in particular. In the continuation it rejects this sense. While it is clear that this is indeed the meaning in many verses, it should not be accepted here because it does not fit into every context, for we find a place where it is difficult to adopt it (*Bereishit* 2:15). Thus, the conclusion is that in our verse we should prefer a different understanding, which though it is not the usual understanding, it is most appropriate for the verse under discussion.

The difficulties in this argument are glaring. The *tanna* is well aware that at first glance the most available and reasonable explanation is "actual *avoda*" (i.e. sacrificial service). And in contrast to what is common in the halakhic *midrashim* and in the *Gemara*, this explanation is rejected not because it is already included in some other verse, but because somewhere

---

8. *Sefer Yerei'im* no. 406: "To serve God, 'And you shall fear your God' (*Vayikra* 25:17 and elsewhere), He commanded that Israel study the Torah, toil with it and pray before Him." See *To'afot Re'eim*, who discusses the suggestion that this should read "serve (*ya'avdu*)" instead of "toil (*ya'amlu*)."
9. *Sefer Ha-Rokei'ach Ha-Gadol*, Warsaw 1880, 5a.

else in the Torah this explanation is unreasonable and a different understanding is necessary, and based on this we conclude that here too we should adopt this alternative explanation. However, the entire course of this discussion is puzzling. Is it reasonable that because the explanation of "actual *avoda*" does not fit in a different context, or even in several different contexts, we should replace it here with a different explanation that is unsuitable in an even greater number of contexts? What is more, in the story of Adam in *Gan Eden*, where the understanding of "actual *avoda*" is rejected,[10] the identification of the "*le-ovdah*" with *talmud Torah* is possible only if we disregard the plain sense (*peshat*) of the text, which clearly deals with tending and cultivating the garden, that is to say, "actual *avoda*." Did any commentary ever consider connecting the prohibition: "You shall not bow down to them, nor serve them" (*Shemot* 20:4), or the question: "What is this service to you" (*Shemot* 12:26), to *talmud Torah*? If so, what is the concern if we distinguish between "to serve Him with all your heart" and "to work it and to keep it?" And furthermore, does the rejection of "actual *avoda*" as an option for understanding the verse necessarily bring us to adopt the understanding that "to serve Him" refers specifically to *talmud Torah*? Is there no room for a third possibility?

The exegetical difficulties are, indeed, daunting. But this is precisely what clarifies and emphasizes the principled position that underlies the midrashic exposition. There is almost no escaping the feeling that in this case the awareness of the unique and existential significance of *talmud Torah* as an integral aspect of *avodat Hashem*, and the understanding of its importance as drawing from the roots and foundations of that *avoda*, and even nurturing them, are so deep and strong, that they have encouraged the proposal of an interpretation designed to inculcate clear messages, even though it does not accord with the plain sense of Scripture, nor even with the plain understanding commonly found in the *Midreshei Halakha*. It is possible

---

10. In contrast to the famous *midrash* in *Bereishit Rabba* 16:8: "Another explanation: 'To work it and to keep it' – this refers to the *korbanot*, as it is stated: 'You shall serve God' (*Shemot* 3:12)." See Rabbeinu Hillel's commentary to the *Sifrei*, *Devarim* 11:13 p. 32, where he raises an objection from this *midrash* to the *Sifrei*'s rejection of the understanding of "actual *avoda*," because there was no such service in ancient times, and he leaves the objection unresolved.

that somebody might see this assessment as a belittlement of the exposition and an erosion of its halakhic standing, to the point of defining it as a mere *asmakhta*, but this does not suffice to reject it. First of all, we have it from the school of Ramban that this is not a rare phenomenon, and "such *beraitot* are misleading, and should not be written in their plain sense."[11] Second, while we are dealing with this issue in connection with *talmud Torah*, there is a large group of *rishonim* who understood that the exposition: "'To serve Him' – this is *tefilla*," is only an *asmakhta*, seeing that they maintain that *tefilla* is only a Rabbinic obligation.[12] Third, even if we assume that this suggestion weakens the connection between *talmud Torah* and *avodat Hashem* in terms of the Biblical verses, it confirms and strengthens this connection on the level of Chazal's attitude toward *talmud Torah*, and it is from their mouths that we live and their waters that we drink. If it is true that to a certain degree they strove – and perhaps even took the initiative – to deepen and strengthen the dimension of *avodat Hashem* in *talmud Torah*, their aspiration supports our existential awareness in this regard.

The *Sifrei*'s Conclusion

The second textual issue relates to the content of the conclusion, and it raises more of a doubt than a difficulty. There is a striking difference between the two parts of the *Sifrei* passage: In the first part, which assumes that the "*avoda*" under discussion is *talmud Torah*, the understanding of "actual *avoda*" is rejected because it does not accord with an external source (*Bereishit* 2:15). In the second part, which assumes that the "*avoda*" is *tefilla*, the understanding of "actual *avoda*" is rejected because it does not sufficiently accord with the verse itself that is under discussion – "and to serve Him with all your heart" – for only *tefilla* fits this description. What is the meaning of this discrimination? Does it mean that the requirement "to serve Him with all your heart" is more appropriate for *tefilla* than for

---

11. Ramban on *Shemot* 12:16, who argues with Rashi who cited as is the *Mekhilta*'s exposition regarding work performed through the agency of others on *Yom Tov*.
12. Based on *Sukka* 38a; *Shabbat* 11a; *Berakhot* 21a. See Ramban's *hasagot* to Rambam's *Sefer Ha-Mitzvot* (positive 5). See also *Sha'agat Aryeh* no. 14; and *Mishkenot Ya'akov* OC 90.

talmud Torah, because regarding *tefilla* an aspect of its fulfillment, and perhaps even the act of *tefilla* itself, is in the heart, which is not the case regarding *talmud Torah* (except, of course, for that level that is required in every mitzva, in the sense of "God seeks the heart")? Or perhaps this means that at most the requirement of "*avoda sheba-lev*" with respect to *talmud Torah* parallels the level of intention and experience that is supposed to characterize the sacrificial *avoda*-service, and not more than that?

It seems to me that any conclusion that totally uproots the dimension of *avoda sheba-lev* from *talmud Torah* would be overly hasty and fundamentally mistaken. It is true that it may be inferred from the *Sifrei*'s discussion that in choosing between the sacrificial *avoda*-service and *talmud Torah* for understanding the content of "to serve Him with all your heart," the matter should not be decided on the basis of a difference in the relationship of these two possibilities to the level of "with all your heart," but rather an external proof must be enlisted. However, after the matter has been decided, for whatever reason and based on whatever source, the result is that the full formulation in the verse, including the component of "heart," applies to *talmud Torah*. From here it follows that, based on the first exposition in the *Sifrei*, *talmud Torah* should be defined as *avoda sheba-lev*, parallel to the definition of *tefilla* as such based on the second exposition.

It would seem that this is precisely the novelty of the *Sifrei* passage. The very connection that it creates between *talmud Torah* and *avoda*, over and beyond the general idea of accepting the yoke of Heaven and doing God's will, is noted in the *Sifrei*, apparently based on a logical argument brought in a different context. Regarding the verse: "After the Lord your God shall you walk, and Him shall you fear, and His commandments shall you keep, and unto His voice shall you hearken, and Him shall you serve, and unto Him shall you cleave" (*Devarim* 13:5), it is stated there in the *Sifrei*: "'And Him shall you serve' – you shall serve Him with His Torah and in His Temple."[13] It is true that the Vilna Ga'on does not read: "with His Torah," and thus he restricts the phrase to the *avoda* in the *Beit Ha-Mikdash*, but the more common reading has firm foundations, and is found in the words

---

13. *Sifrei Parashat Re'eh* on *Devarim* 13:5 (ed. Netziv, no. 33), and see *Emek Ha-Netziv*, ad loc.

"And to Serve Him" – This is *Talmud Torah* | 25

of several of the most prominent *rishonim*.[14] If so, the novelty in our passage is the aspect of "heart" in *talmud Torah*.

The Difference Between *Tefilla* and
Talmud Torah* Regarding *Avoda Sheba-Lev
Clearly there is a difference regarding the meaning of "heart" between *tefilla* and *talmud Torah*. With regard to *tefilla*, the aspect of "of the heart" is indispensable. The Rav *zt"l*, based on Rambam and the explanation offered by Rav Chayyim,[15] would often note that the *kavana* (intention) that is required for *tefilla* is not the same as the *kavana* required for the *mitzvot* in general. Regarding the other *mitzvot*, the content of the *kavana* is intention to fulfill one's obligation; it is an external condition that must be met in order to fulfill the mitzva, or at most in order to define the action as the act of a mitzva.[16] In contrast, *kavana* regarding *tefilla* relates not to the result (*totza'a*) – fulfillment of one's obligation – but rather to the act (*ma'aseh*), to the consciousness of the petitioner standing before the King. This consciousness is what characterizes *tefilla* and distinguishes it from mere declaration and pronouncement; without it the words lack the nature and designation of *tefilla*. In the worst case they are an abomination: "A person who is drunk should not pray, because he cannot have proper *kavana*. If he does pray, his *tefilla* is an abomination."[17] In the best case, it is a neutral act. The root of this determination lies in the matter we are discussing.

---

14. Rambam cites this reading in his *Sefer Ha-Mitzvot* (positive 5), and Ramban notes it and uses it in his explanation of the verse in *Va'etchanan*: "You shall fear the Lord your God; and Him shall you serve, and by His Name shall you swear" (*Devarim* 6:13): "And they further expounded: You shall serve Him with your Torah, by studying Torah and meditating upon it, this too being His *avoda*." And similarly, in the commentary of Rabbeinu Hillel to the *Sifrei*, ad loc.: "'And Him shall you serve' – this is written without specification, implying both *avoda* with the Torah, that is, occupation in *talmud Torah*, and *avoda* in the *Mikdash*."
15. See *Chiddushei Rabbeinu Chayyim Ha-Levi al Ha-Rambam, Hilkhot Tefilla* 4:1.
16. The connection that the *Gemara* (*Rosh Ha-Shana* 28b; *Eiruvin* 96a) draws between *kavana* in *mitzvot* and the prohibition of *bal tosif*, and not only in connection with fulfilling one's obligation, implies that according to the opinion that *mitzvot* require *kavana*, the absence of *kavana* not only hinders fulfillment of the mitzva, but removes from the action the status of an act of a mitzva.
17. Rambam *Hilkhot Tefilla* 4:17; see also *Chiddushei Ha-Ramban Berakhot* 22a, who suggests that the disqualification of a drunkard is limited to *tefilla* in its narrow sense, but does not apply to the *Shema* or to other *berakhot*.

This is the way that Rambam explains the matter when he lists the things that prevent one from praying: "Proper *kavana*: What is implied? Any *tefilla* that is not recited with proper *kavana* is not *tefilla*."[18] In contrast to external factors that prevent one from praying, e.g. the purification of one's hands, the covering of nakedness, and the purity of the place of *tefilla*,[19] regarding which Rambam merely states that they disqualify the *tefilla*, here he resolutely asserts: "Any *tefilla* that is not recited with proper *kavana* is not *tefilla*."

In contrast, the situation regarding *talmud Torah* is altogether different. As was emphasized by Ba'al Ha-Tanya,[20] there are two aspects to this mitzva – study and knowledge. Side by side stand the intellectual occupation that constitutes both the act (*ma'aseh*) and the fulfillment (*kiyyum*) of the mitzva, and the cognitive reality of amassing Torah knowledge, "that the words of the Torah shall be clear-cut in your mouth, so that if anyone asks you something, you should not show doubt."[21] It seems to me that regarding these two aspects of *talmud Torah*, the dimension of "'and to serve Him' – this is *talmud Torah*" does not hinder fulfillment. That is to say, it is not a categorical condition for defining study that lacks the dimension of "with the heart" as the act of a mitzva, and in this way *talmud Torah* is different to *tefilla*. It is true that *talmud Torah* that lacks the foundation of obligation and faith is banished from the circle of the mitzva and is even regarded as a negative phenomenon.[22] But once a person gets beyond this obstacle,

---

18. *Hilkhot Tefilla* 4:15.
19. See what he writes later in the chapter. Further examination is required regarding "things that might bother and distract one," a factor located somewhere between the external matters and the world of *kavana*.
20. See *Shulchan Arukh Ha-Rav, Talmud Torah* ch. 2. And see Rav Sh. Zevin, *Talmud Torah Vi-Ydi'atah*, in his *Le-Or Ha-Halakha*, Tel Aviv 1957, pp. 204-212.
21. *Kiddushin* 30a. See also Ran on *Nedarim* 8a s.v. *ha ka mashma lan*.
22. As is cited in the *Yerushalmi* (*Shabbat* 1:2): "Rabbi Yochanan said: If one studies not in order to observe, it would have been better for him had the afterbirth in which he lay turned over his face, and he not entered the world;" and the *Bavli* (*Yoma* 72b) cites statements no less harsh in the names of other *amora'im*: "Rabbi Yehoshu'a ben Levi said: What is the meaning of the verse: 'And this is the law that Moshe set before the Children of Israel?' If he is meritorious it becomes for him a medicine of life; if not – a deadly poison. This is what Rava meant when he said: If he uses it the right way, it is a medicine of life to him; he who does not use it

he does not encounter any additional hurdles the surmounting of which is indispensable for his study to be regarded as the act of a mitzva. To the best of my knowledge, there is no formulation similar to that coined by Rambam regarding *tefilla* that asserts that "any *talmud Torah* that is not undertaken with proper intention is not *talmud Torah*."

It is easy to locate the reason for this difference. The obligation of *tefilla* has but one source: "And to serve Him with all your heart." Of course, testimony to the standing of *tefilla* as a positive and foundational spiritual phenomenon is not lacking in the Torah. *Tefilla* is recognized as a universal channel of *avodat Hashem*: "Hear You in heaven, Your dwelling place, and do according to all that the stranger calls to You for" (*Melakhim Alef* 8:43), and there is no shortage of citations of the *tefillot* offered by the fathers and leaders of the nation. It also fits in together with other key *mitzvot* that shape man's relationship with his Creator – love, fear, cleaving – and even advances their realization. Even according to those who say that the obligation of *tefilla* is Rabbinic, it is very possible that *tefilla* involves the fulfillment of an independent mitzva. But as for the command that establishes *tefilla* as a normative action, whether by Torah law or by Rabbinic decree, and thereby defines its nature and content, there is only one "to serve Him with all your heart." Thus, *tefilla* that does not meet the

---

the right way, it is a deadly poison" (and compare *Shabbat* 31a). So too Rabbeinu Bachya expresses readiness to load this motif onto *Devarim* 30:15, which is one of the key sources for the principle of free will: "Alternatively, 'life and good and death and evil' refer to the Torah itself, as it is stated: 'I also gave them statutes that were not good, and ordinances whereby they should not live' (*Yechezkel* 20:25), for the Torah is life for the righteous person and death and evil for the wicked." The *mishna* in *Avot* 4:5 states: "Rabbi Yishma'el said: He who learns in order to teach, they afford him adequate means to learn and to teach; and he who learns in order to practice, they afford him adequate means to learn and to teach and to practice." This implies that even study that is not undertaken in order to practice has value and is considered a fulfillment of the mitzva of *talmud Torah*. But it is clear, and thus it follows from the words of the commentaries ad loc., that the first clause is dealing not with a person who does not accept halakhic obligation, but rather with one who does not appoint himself on the plane of implementation to advance the Torah system.

requirements of this one solitary verse, *tefilla* that lacks the dimension of "your heart" or that lacks the character of "*avoda*" in general, is not *tefilla*.

Regarding *talmud Torah*, on the other hand, there are several verses that obligate it, without mentioning "*avoda*" or connecting it to "the heart": "And you shall teach them diligently to your children" (*Devarim* 6:7); "That you may learn them, and observe to do them" (*Devarim* 5:1); "This book of the law shall not depart out of your mouth, but you shall meditate therein day and night" (*Yehoshu'a* 1:8). These obligations determine a standard for *talmud Torah* and shape its foundation, but do not set *avoda sheba-lev* as a necessary requirement. According to these sources, in order to fulfill one's obligation, study and meditation that are detached from "*avoda*" suffice, provided, as stated earlier, that they are founded on faith in the source of the Torah that is being studied, and acceptance of its authority and commands.

The Relationship Between *Talmud Torah* and *Avodat Hashem*

Does this mean that there is a disconnection between *talmud Torah* and *avodat Hashem* in general, and *avoda sheba-lev* in particular? Not at all. It is true that the term "*avoda*" has a double meaning, both with regard to idol worship – "*avoda zara*" – and, *mutatis mutandis*, with regard to God – "*avodat Hashem*" – for in the narrow sense we are dealing with a ritual practice focused specifically on the offering of sacrifices. The Torah distinguishes between different aspects of the ritual, and this distinction is reflected also in *halakha* with special halakhic emphasis on *avoda* performed in the usual manner of serving that deity: "You shall not bow down to them, nor shall you serve them."[23] Parallel to this, *avodat Hashem* also focuses on this sense – in the *mishna* (*Avot* 1:2) that lists the three things upon which the world stands,[24] and in the content of *Sefer Avoda* in Rambam's *Mishneh Torah* – in the operation of the *Mikdash* with all of its components.

This being the case, *talmud Torah* has no special connection to the sense of "*avoda*" on the plane of the sacrificial service, not even on the level

---

23. As opposed to performing one of the four *avodot ha-Mikdash* to an alien entity. See *Sanhedrin* 60b, and Rambam *Hilkhot Avodat Kokhavim* 3:1-2.
24. See Rambam *Hilkhot Avodat Kokhavim* 1:18.

that exists, if only in the borrowed sense, with *tefilla*. At the same time, however, there is a more comprehensive sense of "*avoda*," namely, *avodat Hashem* that includes an existential and practical relationship between the servant and the One being served, and involves the determination of the fundamental standing and acceptance of authority on the part of the believer, in an experiential system and in the realization of desires. In this broad sense of "*avoda*," *talmud Torah* most definitely has a special connection, far beyond that which is expressed in the fulfillment of an ordinary mitzva or in recoiling from some transgression.

This connection, which, as stated, is not indispensable at the minimal level, is at the optimal levels two-directional from a halakhic perspective. On the one hand, perfect *avoda* requires study; *halakha* that directs one's steps in all of a person's ways certainly does not skip over his intellectual pursuits. Even one who does not accept Rambam's view that the focus of the image of God lies in reason[25] nonetheless recognizes mental capacity as one of the pillars of man's identity (*homo sapiens*). Judaism bestows distinguished standing upon a person's intellectual activity far beyond what is found in the world in general, in that *avodat Hashem* does not express itself only in recognizing the Creator and understanding His will, but also in the study and clarification of His Torah.

On the other hand, *talmud Torah* is imperfect when "*avoda*" is not one of its fundamental components; and not just any *avoda*, but "*avoda sheba-lev*," with all that this implies on the most basic level. This being the case, the clearest expression of this is the perception of the experience of *talmud Torah* as an encounter with its Giver. This encounter in and of itself is two-directional: On the one hand, *talmud Torah* reflects the person's desire to know God who spoke and brought the world into existence, in the sense of "Know the God of your father" (*Divrei Hayamim Alef* 28:9), while on the other hand, *talmud Torah* enables the *Shekhina* to enter the person's soul. The first direction is when, with an integrated effort, cognitive and principled, the Torah student strives to realize the ideal of deepening his knowledge of the Creator in itself, and intensifying the existential and

---

25. See *Moreh Ha-Nevukhim* part 1 ch. 2.

moral level, as in Yirmeyahu's famous prophecy: "But let him that glories in this, that he understands and knows Me, that I am the Lord who exercises mercy, justice, and righteousness, in the earth; for in these things I delight, says the Lord."[26] Beyond this, *talmud Torah* serves as a means to intensify one's love of God, in the spirit of Rambam's assertion: "One can love God only as an outgrowth of the knowledge that he knows Him. The nature of one's love depends on the nature of one's knowledge. A small amount of knowledge arouses a lesser love. A greater amount of knowledge arouses a greater love."[27] The process of courtship and study, the integration of the absorption of the lessons and contents, and the knowledge of God whose voice bursts forth from the words and whose presence pokes out from between the lines – draws the Torah student close to the Rock from which he was hewn.

However, it is not only man's striving and his aspiration to know his Creator that is reflected in the study encounter. From the other side, and in parallel, the *Shekhina* descends to the miniature sanctuary that is the student's soul:

> But when two sit together and there are words of Torah spoken between them, the *Shekhina* abides among them, as it is stated (*Malakhi* 3:16): "Then they that feared the Lord spoke one with the other; and the Lord hearkened and heard, and a book of

---

26. *Yirmeyahu* 9:23. We must understand the significance of the fact that Rambam, who throughout his *Moreh Ha-Nevukhim* emphasizes and glorifies the standing of knowledge and reason, cites this verse, which integrates study and implementation, in the final chapter of the book.

27. *Hilkhot Teshuva* 10:6. Though Rambam's words in the continuation, at the end of *Sefer Madda*, imply that the conclusion from this is delving into the realms of philosophy and metaphysics, as opposed to the halakhic contents to which the vast majority of the *Mishneh Torah* is dedicated – from the *Sifrei* it may be understood that the very occupation with God's Torah, and examination of His desire as it is reflected in His *mitzvot*, yields both knowledge and love: "'And these words which I command you today shall be in your heart' – why was this said? Since it says: 'And you shall love the Lord your God with all your heart,' I do not know how one is to love God. Therefore, the verse states: 'And these words which I command you today shall be in your heart.' For in that way you come to know God and cleave to His ways" (*Sifrei Parashat Va'etchanan* on *Devarim* 6:5, *Netziv* ed., sec. 8).

remembrance was written before Him, for them that feared the Lord and that thought upon His Name." I have no Scriptural proof for the presence of the *Shekhina* except among two. From where is there proof that even where there is only one person, the Holy One, blessed be He, appoints unto him a reward? Since it is stated (*Eikha* 3:28): "He sits alone and meditates in stillness, yet he takes a reward unto himself." (*Avot* 3:3)

The *mishna* might be dealing also with future reward. But even without that the student is rewarded by the very encounter with the *Shekhina* that stands before him and hovers above his head.

If so, the dialectical encounter serves as an incentive to study. This idea is strengthened by a different aspect, man's standing before God. As was emphasized by Maharal,[28] *avoda*, service, is connected to *avdut*, servitude. The purpose of *Yetziat Mitzrayim* was: "You shall serve God upon this mountain" (*Shemot* 3:12). The entire process of leaving *Mitzrayim* was founded on the previous *avdut* of the people who descended from the *avot*, which gave rise to a new *avdut*: "They are My servants whom I have brought forth out of Egypt" (*Vayikra* 25:55). Because of this, *talmud Torah* is energized by *avoda* in the sense of *avdut* – obedience to command and to Him who commands. Ramban notes: "'And Him shall you serve' – to do everything that He has commanded you, as a servant who fulfills his master's commands."[29] To the extent that we have been commanded to study Torah, our consciousness of this mitzva encourages and inspires that study. While it is true that a well-rooted Jew studies Torah not only because he is commanded, but because he desires to do so, out of love for Torah and recognition of its value, nevertheless, "superior is he who acts after being commanded."

"*Avoda*" serves, then, not just as a motivation for study, but also as its goal. It is true that according to the tradition of *Volozhin* and *Brisk* it is not the only goal, for according to them "Torah for its own sake (*li-shmah*)" means Torah for the sake of the Torah itself, and not for the sake of other

---

28. *Netivot Olam, Netiv Ha-Avoda* ch. 1.
29. In his commentary to *Devarim* 10:13.

spiritual objectives, lofty as they may be. But according to other traditions, e.g. that of Rabbeinu Bachya[30] in his commentary to the words of the *mishna* ("Study is not the most important thing, but deed") at the end of the first chapter of *Avot* (1:17): "That is to say, the objective of knowing and toiling in Torah is not that one should study much Torah. Rather, the goal is that the study bring one to deed. This is what is written: 'That you may learn them, and observe to do them' (*Devarim* 5:1), that is, that the objective of *talmud Torah* is that one observe the Torah."[31] In any event, even those who emphasize the idea of Torah for its own sake assign a distinguished place to enhancing the level of *avoda* among the objectives of *talmud Torah*. Thus writes Rav Yosef Baer, in his introduction to his *Beit Ha-Levi*: "It is well-known that there are two aspects to *talmud Torah*: the first, that one should know what to do, for if one does not study, how is he to fulfill the *mitzvot*, and an ignorant person is not pious."[32] Beyond the need for knowledge in order to fulfill the *mitzvot* in a precise and perfect manner, there is an additional aspect to the assertion that an ignorant person is not pious ("*lo am ha-aretz chasid*"). Among other things, the path that leads to piety winds its way through *talmud Torah*. On the localized level, the connection is created with respect to the realm being studied. The level of commitment and realization that Ramchal presents in the second half of his *Mesillat Yesharim* as characteristic of the pious person is reflected in the way that each and every mitzva is fulfilled, and it is partially attained by way of identification with each realm in itself that follows from the clarification of its contents to its minutest details. Alongside this there is general piety, as a character trait implanted in a person and his service of God, which is also connected to Torah, which refines, sanctifies and elevates him.

---

30. Editor's note: This reference is to Rabbeinu Bachya ben Asher, best known for his commentary on *Chumash*; not to be confused with Rabbeinu Bachya ibn Pakuda, author of *Chovot Ha-Levavot*, quoted later on in the article.
31. In his commentary to *Avot* 1:17, in *Kitvei Rabbeinu Bachya* (ed. Chavel) p. 548.
32. See *Beit Ha-Levi*, Jerusalem 1997, beginning of *Parashat Mishpatim*. He, however, inclines to see the practical side of *talmud Torah* as preparatory work for fulfilling a mitzva, and not, as I understand it, as one of the fulfillments of the mitzva itself.

Avoda as Submission

If so, the aspect of *avoda* in *talmud Torah* serves not only as a motivation for study and as its goal, but it also impacts on its nature. Its primary expression is the quality that Rabbeinu Bachya (ibn Pakuda) sets at the heart of *Sha'ar Avodat Hashem* in his *Chovot Ha-Levavot*. In contrast to Ramban, who spoke, as noted earlier, about obedience that finds expression in the observance of the *mitzvot*, Rabbeinu Bachya emphasizes a more comprehensive quality – submission: "*Avoda* may be defined as a beneficiary's submission to his benefactor, expressed in rendering good that is within his power to the latter in return for the favor received." He divides up submission according to its roots and foundations:

> This submission is of two kinds: The first is submission induced by fear, hope, necessity or compulsion. The second is submission arising from a sense of duty, from the conviction that it is right to aggrandize and exalt the person to whom submission is rendered. Of the first kind is that submission to God that has been induced by an external stimulus (the Torah), as we have mentioned, and the obligation of which arises from hope of reward or fear of punishment in this world and the next. But the second kind is the submission that arises from an inward urge in the intellect (conscience), innate in the nature of a human being in whom body and soul are joined together. Both kinds of submission are praiseworthy and lead to salvation in the life hereafter, the World of Eternal Rest. But one of these leads to the other and is a step by which we ascend to it. The former is the submission induced by the study of Torah. The [latter] submission that is induced by the urge of the understanding and based on rational demonstrations, is nearer to God and more acceptable on seven grounds. (*Chovot Ha-Levavot*, Avodat Hashem ch. 3)

In the continuation there, Rabbeinu Bachya lists and clarifies these seven grounds. To those accustomed to a more modern religious consciousness, his detailed discussion is of an overly rationalistic nature and tends to ignore the existential and essential foundation that dictates man's submission to his Creator. This foundation is man's very standing as a created and dependent being: on the one hand, "Should the axe boast itself against him that hews therewith? Should the saw magnify itself against him that moves it?" (*Yeshayahu* 10:15), and, on the other hand, God's perfection and uniqueness.

For our purposes, we shall divide the discussion according to areas of application, for submission in *talmud Torah* has two dimensions: intellectual and existential. The intellectual dimension is theological; it determines assumptions and impacts upon conclusions, sets methodological and substantive boundaries for the activity of the student or scholar in order to block enticing lines of thought, sometimes by loading data that is difficult for logical digestion. The complicated question of the relationship between faith and knowledge, both in our world and in the world in general is an ancient and well-known matter, and this is not the place to investigate it. Let us suffice with the safe assertion that while Judaism does not advocate fideism that glorifies the absurd, it also does not bestow absolute sovereignty to the rule of individual reasoning. In practice it binds the believing student twice: it sets him, for example, before verbal analogies that do not accord with his scholarly habits, and then binds him not only from suggesting his own verbal analogy, but even from drawing certain conclusions that he finds rationally persuasive. In our context, let us suffice with the simple fact that the struggle with this sensitive issue is clearly connected to the aspect of *avoda* in *talmud Torah* as *submission*; that aspect that demands not only honor and esteem that Ramban discusses in a different context,[33] but also the submission emphasized by Rabbeinu Bachya.

The second dimension of submission belongs to the existential level of *talmud Torah*. On the one hand, *talmud Torah* is padded with a noetic character that makes skillful use of cognitive tools for the purpose of deciphering texts, clarifying concepts, and building conceptual systems.

---

33. Ramban on *Shemot* 23:24: "Service is the honor that the servant shows his master." The verse deals with the prohibition of *avoda zara*, but Ramban's definition is comprehensive.

For this purpose, the traits of level-headedness and emotional distance are perceived as legitimate, and according to many even recommended. It is clear, however, that emotional distance and *avodat Hashem* are contradictory, and that, at the root of the experience, level-headedness and the realization of "'and to serve Him' – this is *talmud Torah*" cannot coexist. Is existential distance possible when one stands before his Maker? There is, of course, room and even a necessity for a certain distance in that situation, but the gap that follows from fear and trembling – "When he continues to reflect on these same matters, he will immediately recoil in awe and fear, appreciating how he is a tiny, lowly, and dark creature, standing with his flimsy, limited wisdom before He who is of perfect knowledge"[34] – is not the same as emotional standstill and calm imperviousness.

The Experience of *Talmud Torah* as *Avoda Sheba-Lev*

The service of *talmud Torah* is a spiritual experience. It is clear that over the course of such study, when a person deciphers an obscure passage in the *Yerushalmi*, contends with a contradiction in Rambam, or strives to resolve a difficulty raised by Rav Akiva Eiger – his focus is concentrated on the sources and their contents and he does not wander about in the heavenly worlds. He is occupied with his localized mission and he girds his loins in order to succeed in the intellectual task. But all this takes place with the feeling of one who received the Torah standing before Him who gave it, and this atmosphere, even when his attention is drawn away from it, does not leave the *talmid*'s consciousness. Torah should not only make the simple wise, but also restore the soul and gladden the heart; we study it out of the faith that the first goal even depends on the second. As is appropriate for *avoda*, the experience itself is twofold: on the one hand, it is padded with a feeling of joy and uplifting, based on an awareness of the fortune of one who merits to be among those who sit in the *Beit Midrash*, and on the elation connected to joy that is accompanied by drawing near to God; on the other hand, it is filled with the holy trembling connected both to the greatness of the responsibility and the emotional load of the very encounter with Torah and its Giver, as is described in the *Bavli*:

---

34. Rambam *Hilkhot Yesodei Ha-Torah* 2:2.

> Moshe went up in a cloud, was covered by the cloud, and was sanctified by the cloud in order that he might receive the Torah for Israel in sanctity, as it is written (*Shemot* 24:16): "And the glory of the Lord abode upon *Har Sinai*" … Rabbi Matya ben Cheresh says: The purpose of Scripture here was to inspire him with awe, so that the Torah be given with awe, with dread, with trembling, as it is stated (*Tehillim* 2:11): "Serve the Lord with fear and rejoice with trembling." (*Yoma* 4b)[35]

Thus, at the time of the giving of the Torah itself, and thus in daily *talmud Torah*:

> As it has been taught: "And you shall make them known to your children and your children's children," and it is written immediately afterwards: "The day on which you did stand before the Lord your God in *Chorev*." Just as there it was in dread and fear and trembling and quaking, so in this case it must be in dread and fear and trembling and quaking. (*Berakhot* 22b)[36]

This applies to all, great and small; from the most supreme of the human race to the most mediocre of Torah students.

"And to Serve Him" – This is Both *Talmud Torah* and *Tefilla*

The words, "And rejoice with trembling," connect the world of Torah to the world of *tefilla*, to which this verse is associated as well. The *Gemara*, relating to the *mishna* that states: "One should not stand up to recite *tefilla* save in a reverent frame of mind," states: "What is the Scriptural source of this rule… Rather Rav Nachman bar Yitzchak said: We learn it from here: 'Serve the Lord with fear and rejoice with trembling.' What is meant by

---

35. Compare *Avot De-Rabbi Natan* 1:1.
36. This point appears there as the basis of the prohibition of a *ba'al keri* to occupy himself with words of Torah. In the continuation of the passage it becomes clear that this prohibition was not accepted in actual practice. However, this is only because of the rejection of the practical conclusion. The fundamental perception regarding the nature of the assembly at *Har Sinai* remains firmly in place.

'rejoice with trembling?' Rav Adda bar Matana said in the name of Rav: In the place where there is rejoicing there should also be trembling" (*Berakhot* 30b). The common denominator is, of course, *avoda*, and in this context not mere *avoda*, but *avoda sheba-lev*, as an experiential and emotional initiative. But we are not dealing merely with a common denominator, but with an integration between the two. While it is clear that on the level of the activity that is taking place, "the times for *tefilla* and *talmud Torah* are distinct from each other"[37] – there are nevertheless points of contact in the field. It was not for naught that Chazal established, and their position was adopted by Rambam, that "one should not stand to pray… but rather in the midst of words of Torah."[38] The strongest halakhic connection relates to the place of *tefilla*, as is mentioned in the *Gemara* in *Berakhot*:

> Abbayei said: At first I used to study in my house and pray in the Synagogue. Since I heard the saying of Rabbi Chiyya bar Ami in the name of Ulla: "Since the day that the *Beit Ha-Mikdash* was destroyed, the Holy One, blessed be He, has nothing in His world but the four cubits of *halakha* alone," I pray only in the place where I study. Rabbi Ami and Rabbi Assi, though they had thirteen Synagogues in *Teveri'a*, prayed only between the pillars where they used to study. (*Berakhot* 8a)

The *rishonim* disagree on the issue of setting aside *tefilla be-tzibbur* in favor of praying "between the pillars where they used to study" (the place of study).[39] But regarding the principle of overlap in itself there is no dispute, and so too regarding the conceptual principle reflected in it. The two statements in the *Sifrei* are different and parallel each other, but they are not contradictory. Perfect fulfillment of "and to serve Him with all your heart" dictates joining the two of them together – *tefilla* and *talmud Torah*.

---

37. *Shabbat* 10a. This statement appears as a response to Rava's critique of one who prayed at excessive length, thus forsaking the eternal life of *talmud Torah* in favor of petitioning for his temporal needs through *tefilla*.
38. Rambam *Hilkhot Tefilla* 4:18; and see in the *Gemara, Berakhot* 31a.
39. See the commentary of Talmidei Rabbeinu Yona on Rif, 4a in the *Alfas* s.v. *ela beini*.

The spirit of Rabbi Ami and Rabbi Assi has excited the Torah world from time immemorial, and it is the tradition of the *yeshivot*. There is no physical detachment between the *Batei Midrash* and *tefilla*. Both the song of *talmud Torah* and the voice of *tefilla* are heard together in one central room. Torah is studied between the pillars where they used to pray, and *tefilla* is sounded between the pillars where they used to study, and there is no fundamental gap between the two realms. A parallel and integrated striving for the personal and institutional realization of the various dimensions of "and to serve Him with all your heart" is found in every *yeshiva*, each one finding the balance appropriate for it.

Today, however, there is room for concern that this tradition has become exposed to erosion from various and contradictory directions. On the one hand, in certain academic circles – some of which glorify existential restraint and emotional clarity, while others have reconciled themselves to it – the dimension of *avoda*, in all of its facets, has been seriously eroded, and its connection to the Torah, and perhaps even to its Giver, has been impaired. On the other hand, in other circles, the *result* of the *avoda* of *talmud Torah* is highly praised, but they do not esteem, neither ideologically nor practically, the component of *study* in that *avoda* – the effort and toil, the examination and the clarification, the striving and the knowledge, the war of Torah in its full strength and its full scope.

Both of these perceptions undermine the principle of "'and to serve Him' – this is *talmud Torah*," though not to the same degree. We are called to strive to realize the vision and ideal that should be the wish of every *ben Torah*, every Torah institution, and of the Torah world in general, at all levels and in all branches. That is what we aspire to preserve. It is our obligation and desire to integrate our *talmud Torah* into our *avoda*, to characterize it as one of its components, to fill it with its contents. At the same time, it is our responsibility to ensure that this integrated Torah will also remain at the proper intellectual level, and not only at the existential level; that it require serious investment, that it promote both clarification and command; that it accord with the spirit of Rambam's definition: "Understanding and conceptualizing the ultimate derivation of a concept from its roots, inferring one concept from another and comparing concepts, understanding the Torah based on the principles of Biblical exegesis, until one appreciates the essence of those principles and how the prohibitions and the other decisions that one received according to the oral traditions can be derived using them. The latter topic is called *talmud*."[40] This effort will be our contribution, like a stirring from below to the stirring up above, for which we pour our hearts in supplication every day before He who examines all men's hearts:

> Inspire us (*ve-tein be-**libbeinu***) to understand and to discern, to perceive, learn and teach, to observe, do and fulfill all the instructions of Your Torah, with love.

* Translated by David Strauss

---

40. *Hilkhot Talmud Torah* 1:11. In the *Vilna* edition, and those that followed in its wake, it reads: "is called *Gemara*." However, in the Frankel edition which is based on manuscripts, the reading is as I have cited it. In any event, if we wish to be precise about the relationship between the two terms, we must be careful not to impose modern day contexts and associations upon the sources in Chazal.

A *Talmid* Should Not Give a Halakhic Decision in the Place Where His *Rav* Resides*

HaRav Baruch Gigi

I. The Prohibitions and Their Scope

Two *halakhot* are taught in two *beraitot* in *Sanhedrin* 5b: 1) "A *talmid* (disciple) should not give a halakhic decision in the place where his *Rav* resides, unless there is a distance of three parasangs, the space occupied by the camp of Israel, between them." 2) "There and then it was decreed that a *talmid* should not give a halakhic decision unless he was granted permission by his *Rav*." The first *beraita* prohibits giving a halakhic decision in "the place" where his *Rav* resides, and we must define what that "place" includes, and the second *beraita* prohibits such a decision even outside his "place," unless the *talmid* was granted permission by his *Rav*.

It appears from the *Gemara* that the prohibition to give a halakhic decision in the place of one's *Rav* is only within a distance of three parasangs, but outside three parasangs this is fully permitted. But in the days of Rabbi Yehuda Ha-Nasi it was decreed that a *talmid* should not give a halakhic decision even outside of three parasangs, unless he was granted permission from his *Rav*, this out of concern for a mistake following from a misunderstanding of the ruling. The assumption is that the *Rav* will permit his *talmid* to issue halakhic rulings, only after he is sure that the *talmid* will be precise in his rulings, so that they not lead to any misunderstandings.

There is room to ask about the decree of Rabbi Yehuda Ha-Nasi whether it stems in any way from concern for the *Rav*'s honor, or whether it is wholly based on concern about misunderstandings.

In the *Gemara* in *Eiruvin*, a distinction is made between two situations of halakhic decision-making: in the presence of one's *Rav* and not in the presence of one's *Rav*:

> Rava ruled: In the presence of one's *Rav* it is forbidden [to give a legal decision] under the penalty of death; in his absence this is forbidden but the penalty of death is not incurred. Is then no penalty of death incurred in his absence? Was it not in fact taught: Rabbi Eli'ezer ben Ya'akov stated: The sons of Aharon died only because they gave a legal decision in the presence of their *Rav* Moshe… Rabbi Eli'ezer, furthermore, had a *talmid* who once gave a legal decision in his presence. Rabbi Eli'ezer said to his wife, Imma Shalom, "I wonder whether this man will live through the year;" and he actually did not live through the year. She asked him, "Are you a prophet?" He replied, "I am neither a prophet nor the son of a prophet, but I have this tradition: Whosoever gives a legal decision in the presence of his *Rav* incurs the penalty of death." Now, in connection with this incident, Rabba bar Bar Chana related in the name of Rabbi Yochanan: That *talmid*'s name was Yehuda ben Gurya and he was three parasangs distant from his *Rav*. He was in his presence. But was it not stated that he was three parasangs distant? And according to your conception what need was there for the mention of his name and the name of his father? But the fact is that all the details were given in order that it be not said that the whole story was a fable. (*Eiruvin* 63a)

According to many *rishonim* in the wake of Tosafot, it turns out that "in his presence" does not necessarily mean in his actual presence; even if he is within three parasangs this is considered "in his presence," and he is liable for the death penalty. "In his absence" where issuing a ruling is forbidden but the penalty of death is not incurred, is outside of three parasangs. According to the simple understanding, this means that it is forbidden in all places, even at the far end of the world. According to this, in light of the conclusion that may be drawn from the *Gemara* in *Sanhedrin* that fundamentally it is not necessary to receive permission to rule, and that this is necessary only because of the decree issued in the days of Rabbi Yehuda Ha-Nasi in the wake of imprecise rulings and the concern about misunderstandings, we must say that the prohibition to issue rulings even not in the presence of one's *Rav* that is mentioned in *Eiruvin* is precisely for this reason of imprecision, and receiving permission removes this prohibition. This, however, is difficult, for the *Gemara* there implies that the prohibition is not concern for the *Rav*'s honor, but rather concern about imprecision. Perhaps it may be argued that even though the reason for the decree was concern about imprecision, when they issued the decree, they did so by expanding the prohibition to issue halakhic rulings out of concern for the honor of the *Rav*.

Alternatively, we can adopt the position of Riva who limits the prohibition beyond three parasangs, as is mentioned in his name in *Mordekhai* (*Eiruvin* 510): "That is to say, only in a place where the *Rav* comes at regular times, e.g. on the market day, or on Mondays and Thursdays. But in a place not regularly visited by the *Rav*, but only occasionally, it is permitted." Similarly, Ritva there writes[1] that the prohibition outside three parasangs is limited to the *Rav*'s province or places that the *Rav* frequently visits or the like, but totally outside the *Rav*'s area of control there is no problem whatsoever stemming from the honor due to the *Rav*, and it is necessary to receive permission there only because of the concern regarding imprecision, this being the decree of Rabbi Yehuda Ha-Nasi. Many *rishonim*, however, emphasize that in the position of Tosafot the prohibition stemming from concern for the *Rav*'s honor is not limited to a particular place. See Rashba, Ritva, and Ran in *Eiruvin*, ad loc., regarding the view of Tosafot.

For this reason, Tosafot in *Eiruvin* write that a distinction must be made between a full-fledged *talmid* and a *talmid chaver*, a disciple-colleague. A full-fledged *talmid* must not issue a halakhic ruling within three parasangs, under the penalty of death, and outside three parasangs this is prohibited

---

1. *Eiruvin* 63a s.v. *gam ma she-katav*.

in all places, but the death penalty is not incurred. But a *talmid chaver*[2] is permitted to issue a halakhic ruling outside three parasangs. According to this opinion, we must say that this means that a *talmid chaver* is permitted to issue a ruling, and therefore he need not receive permission, and that which is stated in the *Gemara* that he must nevertheless receive permission is because of the incident reported there. This is what Ran in *Sanhedrin* writes: "Tosafot have a different opinion, and they explain that in his presence he is liable for the death penalty, this being within three parasangs, and in his absence, which is outside three parasangs, it is prohibited by Torah law." According to them it is difficult: Why was it necessary to decree here that a *talmid* must not issue a halakhic ruling unless he received permission from his *Rav*, for even without this decree there is a Torah prohibition? And they were forced to explain this decree as referring to a *talmid chaver*, regarding whom within three parasangs there is a prohibition, and outside three parasangs it is permitted, and because of this decree there is a prohibition even outside three parasangs, unless he received permission.

Rashba has a different understanding. "In his presence" – means in his actual presence,[3] and this carries the death penalty. "In his absence" – means within three parasangs, where there is a prohibition. But outside three parasangs there is no prohibition whatsoever stemming from the honor due to one's *Rav*, and the only prohibition is the decree of Rabbi Yehuda Ha-Nasi.

Let us now examine the position of Rambam:

What is meant by disputing the authority of one's *Rav*? A person who establishes a house of study [where] he sits, explains, and

---

2. Ritva also makes the distinction made by Tosafot between a full-fledged *talmid* and a *talmid chaver*, but in his opinion, this means that a *talmid chaver* can issue rulings outside three parasangs, even if it is the *Rav*'s province, something that is forbidden to a full-fledged *talmid*.

3. It is not clear according to Rashba whether the *talmid* is liable for the death penalty only if he issued his ruling in his *Rav*'s actual presence, or even in a larger area. In a responsum (*siman* 111) he explicitly writes that he is liable even in his place or within the limits of his city: "In his presence means in his actual presence, or in his place and in his city."

teaches without his *Rav*'s permission in his *Rav*'s lifetime. [This applies] even when one's *Rav* is in another country.

It is forbidden to ever render a halakhic judgment in the presence of one's *Rav*. Whoever renders a halakhic judgment in his *Rav*'s presence is worthy of death.

If a person asked [a *talmid*] regarding a halakhic question and there were twelve *mil* between him and his *Rav*, he is permitted to answer. [Furthermore,] to prevent a transgression, it is permitted to give a halakhic judgment even in the presence of one's *Rav*.

What does the above imply? For example, if one saw a person perform a forbidden act because he was unaware of the prohibition or because of his perversity, he should [try to] prevent him [by] telling him: This is forbidden. [This] applies even in his *Rav*'s presence and even though one's *Rav* had not given him permission. Wherever the desecration of God's Name is involved, no deference is paid to a *Rav*'s honor.

When does the above apply? With regard to a matter that came up incidentally. However, establishing oneself as a halakhic authority to sit and reply to all who ask concerning halakhic matters is forbidden, even if [the *talmid*] is at one end of the world and the *Rav* at the other, until either: a) the *Rav* dies; or b) the *talmid* receives permission from his *Rav*. Not everyone whose *Rav* dies is permitted to sit and render judgment concerning Torah law; only one who is a *talmid* worthy of rendering judgment. (*Hilkhot Talmud Torah* 5:2-3)

According to Rambam, in the *Rav*'s actual presence, there is a prohibition under the penalty of death; in his absence, within three parasangs, issuing a ruling is prohibited but the death penalty is not incurred (this is according to the explanation of Rivash (*siman* 271), but there is room to explain that within three parasangs is considered in the *Rav*'s presence, which is under the penalty of death). And outside three parasangs an incidental ruling is permitted but regular rulings are prohibited, unless the *talmid* received permission from his *Rav*. According to Rivash it would seem that this prohibition is the decree of Rabbi Yehuda Ha-Nasi, but according to the second possibility this too is part of the prohibition of the *Gemara* in *Eiruvin* in the words of Rava that in the *Rav*'s absence it is prohibited, but the death penalty is not incurred, and it is about this that Rambam writes that receiving permission helps regarding the issue of the *Rav*'s honor. But according to this, what was the decree of Rabbi Yehuda Ha-Nasi and where does it find expression? Even though there is an opinion that Rambam did not codify the decree of Rabbi Yehuda Ha-Nasi, it seems more convincing to me to say like Rivash that Rambam's ruling regarding incidental and regular rulings is taken from the *Gemara* in *Sanhedrin,* and there one who has not been authorized to issue rulings is forbidden to issue regular rulings, even at the end of the world, and the prohibition to issue rulings within three parasangs of one's *Rav* refers to incidental rulings. According to this we can understand the difference between regular and incidental rulings, and we can also understand the allowance to issue rulings after the *Rav*'s death. It would appear from the words of Rambam that the requirement to receive permission from one's *Rav* in order to issue rulings was meant to bestow upon him the status of one who has reached the level of issuing rulings. After the *Rav* has died, there is no longer anyone from whom to receive permission, and therefore he can issue rulings if he knows about himself that he has reached that level.

II. The Parameters of the Prohibition to Issue Rulings in the Place of One's *Rav*

The simple understanding is that this prohibition stems from the *halakha* that one must honor one's *Rav*. Since a person is obligated to honor his *Rav*, he must demonstrate that honor by directing to him any question that came his way. One who issues a ruling in the place of his *Rav* is guilty of irreverence. This is what is implied by the *Gemara* in *Eiruvin* where it speaks of preventing a person from committing a transgression:

Rava ruled: When it is a question of preventing one from committing a transgression it is quite proper [for a *talmid* to give a legal decision] even in his *Rav*'s presence. Ravina once sat in the presence of Rav Ashi when he observed that a certain person was tying his ass to a palm tree on *Shabbat*. He called out to him but the other took no notice. He said to him: Let this man be placed under the ban. [Ravina] said to him: Does such an act as mine appear as irreverence? [Rav Ashi responded:] "There is no wisdom for understanding nor counsel against the Lord" (*Mishlei* 21:30); wherever the Divine Name is being profaned no respect is to be shown to one's *Rav*. (*Eiruvin* 63a)

And as Rashi writes there at the beginning of the passage (63a): "Is it then permitted to a *talmid* to give a ruling accordingly in a district that is under the jurisdiction of his *Rav* – since it does not depend on logical reasoning and it is an obvious matter, it is permitted; or perhaps, this is irreverence." The two sides of the *Gemara*'s uncertainty are: Since the matter is obvious, there is no prohibition whatsoever, because there is no insult here to the *Rav*, or perhaps, nevertheless, issuing a ruling in a place that is under the jurisdiction of one's *Rav* is an act of impertinence. And the *Gemara*'s answer is that this too is prohibited. From here we see that according to Rashi, even a simple ruling involves impertinence towards one's *Rav*, and so it also follows from the words of several other *rishonim*, as well as from the plain meaning of the *Gemara*.

But Tosafot write:

Ri says: This applies only to a matter that appears to be a novelty for the person asking the question; even the question of the permissibility of eating an egg with *kutcha* and the question regarding *Megillat Ta'anit* refer to such matters. These are mentioned to teach us only that even regarding matters that the *talmid* himself knows that he is not wrong, he is forbidden to issue a ruling. But regarding a matter that the person asking the question knows is well-known, like the laws of the taste of prohibited foods, or the like, so that when he issues him an allowance, it does not appear to him to be a novelty, it is permitted. (Tosafot *Eiruvin* 62b)

The words of Tosafot suggest that they maintain that regarding an absolutely simple matter there is no prohibition. It may be understood that according to them in the case of a simple ruling there is no insult to the honor of the *Rav*, because something that does not appear novel to the questioner does not involve an inappropriate seizure of authority.

The focus of the difference between Rashi and Tosafot lies in the definition of honoring one's *Rav* in our context. According to Tosafot, the problem lies in assuming authority in the place of one's *Rav*, taking the authority to decide matters, and therefore when there is no novelty for the questioner, there is no insult. According to Rashi, on the other hand, a person is obligated to actively honor his *Rav*, and therefore, even regarding the simplest matter, he is obligated to refer the questioner to his *Rav*.

It is possible to read this into the words of Tosafot in the continuation: "And Ravina who examined the slaughterer's knife in *Bavel*, this was sort of a novel matter that involved a seizure of authority, as we said (*Chullin* 17b): 'The ruling that one must present the knife to a *chakham* (sage) for examination was laid down only out of respect to the *chakham*.'" It appears from the words of Tosafot that the problem is seizing authority in the place of one's *Rav*, and this occurs in one of two situations: examining a slaughterer's knife in the place of one's *Rav* involves the seizure of authority, because it is like a novel ruling, and issuing a novel ruling involves the seizure of authority, and is therefore prohibited.

Rosh on this passage takes the issue in another direction:

It seems that this applies only to a matter that appears to involve a novelty for the questioner; even the question of the permissibility of eating an egg with *kutcha* and the question regarding *Megillat Ta'anit* refer to such matters. These are mentioned to teach us only that even regarding matters that the *talmid* himself knows with certainty that he is not wrong, he is forbidden to issue a ruling. But regarding a matter that the questioner knows is simple, like the laws of the taste of prohibited foods, or a prohibited food that became intermingled with permitted food that it is neutralized in sixty parts of the permitted food, and the like, so that when he issues him an allowance, it does not appear to him to be a novelty, because he already heard that this ruling is simple for all of Israel, it is permitted. And as for Ravina who examined the knife of a slaughterer in *Bavel*, this was not a ruling, but only a show of respect for the *chakham*, as it is stated: The rule that one must present the knife to a *chakham* for examination was laid down only out of respect to the *chakham*. And it is inappropriate for a *talmid chakham* to seize authority before his *Rav* unless he received permission to do so from his *Rav*. (Rosh *Eiruvin* 6:2)

Rosh distinguishes between issuing a ruling and examining a knife. Unlike Tosafot who see the entire problem on the continuum of seizing authority, and maintain that any matter that appears to be a novelty involves the seizing of authority, Rosh clearly defines two different realms: issuing a ruling and examining a knife. According to Rosh, examining a knife does not involve a ruling, and is forbidden because it involves the seizure of authority in the place of one's *Rav*, and the essence of the prohibition is because of the honor that must be shown one's *Rav*. Issuing a ruling, however, involves a different prohibition, namely, that a *talmid* is forbidden to rule in the place of his *Rav*, because the sole authority to issue rulings is the authority of the *Rav*, as we learned from Moshe. This new definition of the prohibition to issue rulings, which is not directly connected to the honor that is due one's *Rav*, but rather to the authority to pass down the Torah, seems to parallel the definition of issuing rulings in other areas, e.g. issuing a ruling with regard to a communal sin-offering (*par he'elem davar shel tzibbur*) or issuing a ruling with regard to a *zakein mamrei* (rebellious elder).

Ramban in his commentary to *Parashat Beha'alotekha* writes:

> But it appears from the words of our Rabbis, that it was the customary practice in Israel that a person would not prophesy about the future in a place where there was a prophet greater than him, but rather he would follow after him as one of his *talmidim* who were called "the sons of the prophets," for this would be like issuing a ruling in the place where one's *Rav* resides. (Ramban *Bamidbar* 11:28)

I wish to argue that a *talmid* is bound by a prohibition to issue rulings in the place of his *Rav* that is similar to the prohibition applying to a *zakein mamrei* before the *Beit Din Ha-Gadol* (High Court). The *Rav* in relation to his *talmidim* is treated like the *Beit Din Ha-Gadol*, from which teaching and instruction go out to all of Israel. According to this it is not the seizure of authority that is the problem, but the issuing of a ruling itself.

According to what we have said, that the basic principle is the prohibition to issue rulings, we can learn from there another limitation that is mentioned by the *rishonim*, namely, that the prohibition only applies to a ruling that was given in response to a practical question, and not to a theoretical question. Of course, this can be connected to the issue of the *Rav*'s honor, that when one issues a practical ruling in the place of his *Rav*, he seizes authority. But here too there are *rishonim* who base their opinion on the passages in *Horayot* and *Sanhedrin* that a *Beit Din* or a *chakham* is liable only when they issue a practical ruling, and regarding a *zakein mamrei* it says that he is liable only if he acted in accordance with his ruling or instructed others to do so.

The limitation of a ruling that involves a novelty for the questioner seems to draw also from the passages in *Horayot* and *Sanhedrin*. The *Gemara* in *Horayot* says:

> Rav Yehuda said in the name of Shmu'el: The court is liable only when they ruled concerning a prohibition that the Sadducees do

not admit, but if concerning a prohibition that the Sadducees admit, they are exempt. What is the reason? It is a matter that anyone can learn at school. (*Horayot* 4a)

And in *Sanhedrin* it says that a *zakein mamrei* is not liable if he says that there is no mitzva of *tefillin* or the like (*Sanhedrin* 88a), and Rashi (ad loc.) explains: "If he says there is no mitzva of *tefillin*, he is exempt – as this is not a ruling, for it is a matter that anyone can learn in school."

According to what we have said, we can understand the continuation of Rosh's comments in *Eiruvin*:

> If the members of the *talmid*'s household were in need of a ruling, and they asked him the question, the matter is uncertain. Perhaps he is permitted to rule for them, similar to what is stated that a young *talmid chakham* ("*tzurba mei-rabbanan*") may examine a knife for himself. Or perhaps this applies only to the examination of a knife, which must be shown to a *chakham* only out of respect to the *chakham*, and in such a case he waives his honor so as not to bother the young *talmid chakham* to come to him. But whether something is permitted or prohibited he may not rule even for himself in the place of his *Rav*. I am inclined to prohibit. (Rosh *Eiruvin* 6:2)

In the *Gemara* there, they permit a *chakham* to examine a knife for himself, and based on this ruling, *Chavot Ya'ir* rules that he is permitted also to rule on halakhic questions that arise in his household:

> Which is not the case regarding other rulings whether something is permitted or prohibited, or ritually pure or impure, a person is permitted to rule on these matters if he is qualified to do so, as is implied by the aforementioned Tosafot. And so writes Rash there. This applies even in the place of his *Rav*, as we find in *Eiruvin*, the beginning of Chapter *Hadar*, that a young *talmid chakham* may

rule for himself. (Only for himself is he permitted to rule, but not for his father or his brother; but if he has an interest in that ruling, even the slightest interest, he is permitted.) (*Chavot Ya'ir* 122)

Chavot Ya'ir's ruling is cited in *Pitchei Teshuva* (YD 242:5). But Rosh was in doubt about the matter, and he was inclined to prohibit it, because he distinguished between a halakhic ruling and the examination of a knife, which is not considered a halakhic ruling, and the whole ruling that one must present the knife to a *chakham* for examination was laid down only out of respect to the *chakham*, and here his *Rav* waives his honor. But as for issuing a ruling, he was in doubt whether a ruling that a person issues for himself falls into the category of a halakhic ruling. It does not appear that he was in doubt whether a *chakham* waives his honor with regard to issuing rulings. Rosh's *talmid*, Rabbeinu Yerucham, writes:

> Rosh writes that an uncertainty arises in a case where the members of a *talmid*'s household were in need of a ruling, and they asked him the question – is he permitted to issue a ruling, as we said about examining a knife for himself, or do we say that this is different, for perhaps this applies only to a knife, which must be shown to a *chakham* only out of respect to the *chakham*, and in such a case he waives his respect so as not to bother the young *talmid chakham* to come to him. But as for issuing a ruling, even for himself, this is prohibited in the place of one's *Rav*. It stands to reason that is prohibited. This seems to be clear and evident in the *Gemara* in *Eiruvin*.

It would appear that Rabbeinu Yerucham's ruling is based on the source of the matter that is learned from Moshe, for Nadav and Avihu ruled for themselves. And certainly, if we connect this to the *halakhot* pertaining to a *zakein mamrei* it is obvious, for it is stated there that he is liable only if he ruled for others or acted himself in accordance with his ruling.

It seems that additional proof for this understanding of ruling in the place of one's *Rav* as an expression of rebellious ruling can be derived from the *Yerushalmi* in *Avoda Zara* regarding the ban on non-Jewish oil that Rabbi Yehuda Ha-Nasi lifted:

> Yitzchak bar Shmu'el bar Marta went down to *Netzivin*, where he found Simlai Ha-Deromi. He sat and expounded: Rabbi Yehuda Ha-Nasi and his *Beit Din* permitted [non-Jewish] oil. Shmu'el said: But Rav did not accept upon himself to eat it. Shmu'el said to him: Eat it, or else I will write about you that you are a *zakein mamrei*. (*Yerushalmi Avoda Zara* 2:8)

And similarly, in the *Yerushalmi* in *Yevamot*:

> Rabbi Yirmeya said: This one performs *chalitza* and this one keeps her as his wife. Rabbi Yuda bar Pazi said in the name of Rabbi Yochanan: She must leave. Rabbi Yosei said in the name of Rabbi Hila: She must leave. Rabbi Yosei asked Rabbi Pinchas: What does Rabbi Yehuda Ha-Nasi say? He said to him: Like Rabbi Yirmeya. He said to him: Retract, or else I will write about you that you are a *zakein mamrei*. (*Yerushalmi Yevamot* 10:4)

And see what Rav Elchanan Wasserman says about this passage in the *Yerushalmi* in *Kunteres Divrei Soferim* (*siman* 2, 7). He understood these words literally that the reference was to the actual *halakha* of *zakein mamrei*, which brought him to several novel ideas about the matter. But according to what we have suggested, the reference is to the ruling of a *talmid* in the place of his *Rav*, who is treated like a *zakein mamrei*. In the two cases, we are dealing with two types of ruling: one type of ruling for others, and Rav regarding non-Jewish oil ruled for himself, even though there he merely refrained from eating the oil. We wish to emphasize that even according to what we are saying we are dealing with a borrowed term. But it is easier if we understand that the prohibition is connected to the ruling itself.

Yerushalmi Shevi'it 6:1 states that if a *talmid* issued a ruling, his ruling is not a ruling. Now, if the problem lies in the honor that is due to the *Rav*, why is the *talmid*'s ruling not a ruling? But if the problem lies in the ruling itself, we can understand that such a ruling in the place of one's *Rav* is not a ruling. There is a practical difference regarding the case of a ruling that follows another ruling, that a *chakham* should not rule on a matter that was already ruled upon by others.

According to what we have said, it is clear that we can hang the dispute among the *rishonim* whether permission or waiver removes the prohibition to issue a ruling in the place of one's *Rav* on the question of whether the prohibition stems from the honor that is due one's *Rav* or if it depends on the parameters of issuing rulings. We saw that Rosh maintains that permission or waiver helps only regarding the examination of a slaughterer's knife, which is a *halakha* connected to the *chakham*'s honor and not to issuing rulings. This accords with what we have said,[4] and goes against what *Arukh Ha-Shulchan* (24:12) inferred from his words. So too it would appear from Tosafot in *Sanhedrin* 5b and from Rambam that a waiver does not help within three parasangs. However, Rashba and Ra'avad maintain that a waiver helps (see *Shut Ha-Rashba* 1:111), and it seems that the dispute can be understood as depending on the question mentioned above.

See also Ran on *Sanhedrin* who writes:

> It seems to Rabbeinu David that [a ruling] regarding something forbidden by Torah law is prohibited even after receiving permission… But I don't have a proof… In fact I can say to you that with permission, it is permitted. And the reason is that since it is because of the honor due to one's *Rav*, he can waive it, for we maintain that if a *Rav* waives his honor, his honor is waived. (*Chiddushei Ha-Ran Sanhedrin* 5b)

---

4. It stands to reason that if the focus is the ruling, the *Rav*'s waiver will not help. But there is room to disagree, for even in the case of a *zakein mamrei*, the *tanna'im* disagree whether a waiver helps, as is mentioned below. Indeed, Ramban in his commentary to the Torah says that a waiver helps. Therefore, it seems to me that the opinion that allows for a waiver can be understood in two ways, but the opinion that does not allow for a waiver is more understandable if this is a matter of issuing rulings, that there is no room for other rulings in the place of the *Rav*.

It should be noted that also in the matter of a *zakein mamrei*, the *tanna'im* disagree as to whether a waiver helps, because essentially even the prohibition of issuing a ruling is a matter of honoring one's *Rav*. In the end, the *halakha* was decided that, in the case of a *zakein mamrei*, a waiver does not help, because it was God's desire that the Torah be decided by the *Beit Din Ha-Gadol* and that there be no disputes in Israel. If so, the same applies to the matter under discussion, that the channel of handing down the Torah must go through the *Rav*, and therefore we are not dealing with the personal honor of the *Rav*, but rather with the honor and continuity of the Torah.

The *Gemara* says: "Rava ruled: In the presence of one's *Rav* it is forbidden [to give a legal decision] under the penalty of death; in his absence this is forbidden but the penalty of death is not incurred." The *rishonim* disagree about how to understand "in his presence" and "in his absence," but all agree that there are two levels of prohibition. It may be explained that the level of the prohibition depends on the level of the insult to the *Rav*'s honor; in his presence, the insult is greater, and issuing a ruling carries the death penalty. Perhaps it may even be argued that in his presence there is insult, but in his absence there is no insult, but only an obligation to show honor. But it is possible to suggest another reason for the distinction, namely, that in the *Rav*'s presence the prohibition stems from the matter of issuing rulings, that is, that in the place of one's *Rav*, the *Rav* must be the source of rulings, and only he is permitted to issue rulings; whereas in his absence the prohibition stems from the insult to the *Rav*'s honor when the *talmid* seizes authority, and in this matter there is room for receiving permission. If what we have said is correct, we can explain the position of Rambam. Rambam discusses these *halakhot* in two places: in *Hilkhot Talmud Torah* in the context of the honor due to one's *Rav* and to a *talmid chakham*, and in *Hilkhot Sanhedrin* in the context of the *halakhot* governing a *talmid* who has reached the level that he is fit to issue rulings. In *Hilkhot Sanhedrin* he mentions only the prohibition to issue rulings within three parasangs of one's *Rav*, and no more, whereas in *Hilkhot Talmud* Torah he mentions also the prohibition of issuing rulings outside three parasangs. It seems to me that in the context of the *halakhot* of issuing rulings the prohibition is limited to three parasangs as is learned from Moshe; the prohibition outside three parasangs stems from the honor due to one's *Rav*, and its place is in *Hilkhot Talmud Torah*, and not in *Hilkhot Sanhedrin*.

And finally, we come to the passage in *Ketubbot* 60b that clearly implies that there is another reason for the prohibition to issue a ruling in the place of one's *Rav*, namely, that the *talmid* would have no success in dealing with the matter. This might be understood as a technical problem, that owing to the honor that is due to one's *Rav*, the *talmid* will not merit Divine assistance in his ruling. However, it is evident from Tosafot that they are of the opinion that even if the *talmid* received permission or if the *Rav* waived his honor, the *talmid* will not have success in dealing with the matter. Their words suggest that the *talmid* is absolutely prohibited from issuing a ruling in the place of his *Rav*. This is also *Beit Yosef's* understanding of Tosafot:

> It seems from the words of Tosafot in the first chapter of *Sanhedrin* (5b s.v. *ela*) that even if the *talmid* received permission from his *Rav*, issuing a ruling within three parasangs is prohibited. This is also the implication of what is stated in *Ketubbot* 60b: "Abbayei's tenant once came to Abbayei and asked him: Is it permissible to betroth [a nursing woman] fifteen months after [her child's birth]? He said to him: In the first place [whenever there is disagreement] between Rabbi Me'ir and Rabbi Yehuda the *halakha* is in agreement with the view of Rabbi Yehuda…. When he came to Rav Yosef the latter told him: Both Rav and Shmu'el ruled that [a nursing woman] must wait twenty-four months…. Abbayei said: The statement made by the Rabbis that even [a question about the permissibility of eating] an egg with *kutcha* a man shall not decide in a district [which is under the jurisdiction] of his *Rav* was not due [to the view that this might] appear as an act of irreverence, but to the reason that [a *talmid*] would have no success in dealing with the matter. For I have in fact learned the tradition of Rav and Shmu'el and yet I did not get the opportunity of applying it." And Rashi explained that

he would have no success in dealing with the matter and ruling correctly. And Tosafot write that there is a practical difference in the case where the *Rav* waives his honor, which is permitted, but even so the *talmid* should not issue a ruling because he will not succeed in dealing with the matter because his *Rav* is there. The implication is that anywhere within three parasangs is considered that his *Rav* is there and he must not issue a ruling. That which they write that it is permitted means that there is no issue of honor due to the *Rav* because he waived his honor. So writes Maharik in *shoresh* 171, that permission helps only outside of three parasangs, but not within three parasangs. (*Beit Yosef* YD 242)

It seems clear that the issue is that Divine assistance is extended only to the *Rav* and not to the *talmid*. Just as we find with the *Beit Din Ha-Gadol* that the place where it convenes causes the *Shekhina* to rest there, so too with every *Rav* who issues rulings. Hence the *talmid* must not issue rulings in that place because the *Shekhina* rests on the channel that is designated for the handing down of the Torah, on the *Rav*.

* Translated by David Strauss

On the *Yeshiva* Rabbinate* [1]

HaRav Mosheh Lichtenstein

I

To the outside observer, it might seem that there is nothing better than being a Rabbi in a *yeshiva*. He sits in the *Beit Midrash*, with a crown on his head, surrounded by *talmidim* (students) who thirst for his Torah and wait for the words that issue from his mouth. Far from the tumult of life, and like a shield that protects from its unsightliness, the *yeshiva* is a nature reserve in which the *Rav* and his *talmidim* gather to meditate on the Torah's words of wisdom, to debate the matters in dispute between Abbayei and Rava, and to share the experience of *Shabbat* and the *chaggim* (festivals), tightly bound by spiritual connections and the ties of love. If many of the *yeshiva*'s graduates define their years of study as significant and formative, and one of the best periods of their lives, the *Rav* who enjoys this his entire life and is never forced to leave the tent of Torah should be the happiest person in the world. He dwells in the house of God all the days of his life, beholding the graciousness of God and enjoying His Torah.

Indeed, it must be admitted that in its finest hours, the *Yeshiva* Rabbinate looks just like this. Both in moments of climactic exaltation and in the hours of day-to-day perseverance in study, there is *me'ein Olam Ha-*

---

1. This article was originally written in Hebrew fifteen years ago and published ten years ago. Therefore, the contemporary trends mentioned herein reflect an Israeli perspective of a decade ago. However, the issues raised in the contemporary, as well as the theoretical, parts of this article remain relevant as they are inherent to the institutional framework; this being said, some of the trends mentioned here and the suggested application must be understood in their context.

ba, a quasi-sense of the World to Come. When *talmidim* show their love, when the words of the Torah inspire the kind of joy that abounded when it was first given, when the feelings of novelty and flight surge through the seats in the *Beit Midrash*, the *Rav* feels himself uplifted and blessed. When a student bears his soul before his teacher and lays out before him his troubles, his worries, and his aspirations, there is a thrilling existential encounter between two souls that cleave tightly one to the other.

However, it cannot be denied that this is not the usual case. All too frequently, a *yeshiva* Rabbi finds himself in a constant state of personal tension, his heart filled with frustration and disappointment, uncertainty and fear. In part, these are natural feelings of missed opportunity and failure with regard to one *talmid* or another. As the *mishna* attests in *Avot*, time is short and the workers are lazy, but the pressing of the Master does not always help. In addition, there is often dissatisfaction with a *shi'ur* that was given on one topic or another. In sum, the disappointment of "having a hundred but wanting two hundred" that lurks in the heart of every person with spiritual ambition, constantly pursues the educator. However, apart from the feelings that stem from a lack of skill or the natural desire for success – feelings that characterize every profession and are familiar to anyone in a position of responsibility – there are also inherent tensions that arise from the very definition of the Rabbinic role. It is to these that I wish to relate in the following lines.

In the *yeshivot* in Israel it is customary to refer to one who delivers a *shi'ur* by the title "*Ram*." Originally, the expression was an acronym for the Aramaic term "*Reish Metivta*" (head of the Academy), an appendage of Rabbinic language common in the *yeshiva* world. However, when people from the general public ask me to explain my work, I answer that I am a *Ram*, a "*Rav Mechannekh*" (Rabbi-educator). This linguistic difference is not only a convenient solution to the difficult task of explaining an obscure Aramaic acronym to those who are far from *yeshiva* discourse; it also contains within it the basic tension that lies at the door of the *Yeshiva* Rabbinate.

Chazal, in a famous *midrash*, which is the basis for any discussion concerning the *Rav-talmid* relationship, use the metaphor of father and son to define the relationship between a Rabbi and his disciple: "'And you shall teach them diligently to your sons' (*Devarim* 6:7) – these are the disciples."[2] A father's standing in relationship to his son is based on love, embraces authority, and casts responsibility upon the father to take care of the son's needs. A son is the aspiration of his father's life and his successor in this world, on Earth, and the father must do everything he can to ensure that the son will follow in the path of the good and preserve the ways of the righteous. All of the father's strengths, energy, and time are dedicated to this end to which he is bound. It is not by chance that the *halakha* (*Kiddushin* 29a) coined the phrase "obligations of the son upon the father." This mission clearly requires time and resources, and these should be given willingly and with love. If Chazal saw a *Rav* as a father, and his *talmid* as a son, the expectation from the *Rav* is that he see himself as his *talmidim*'s father. From their perspective, a *Rav* should bestow upon his *talmidim* warmth and love; he should invest all of his energy in them and see them as his future. On the other hand, the *talmid* is expected to respond in the same currency and see his *Rav* as his spiritual father with everything that entails.

This understanding is critical for the meaning of the Rabbi's work. It imposes great duties and heavy responsibility upon him, but also opens the door to deep emotional and existential ties with his *talmidim*. The mystery of "whoever teaches the son of his neighbor Torah, Scripture assigns it to him as if he had begotten him" (*Sanhedrin* 19b) relates the *talmid* to the teacher and sees the two as sharing one existence and being, similar to the model of ordinary parenting. The privilege of seeing many sons continuing in his path and continuing him and his enterprise uplifts the *Rav* and draws a thread of grace over his educational activity. His legacy is not limited to the novel insights that he reached and the writings that he published, but includes also the *talmidim* whom he mentored. They became part of his life work, also because they are Torah scholars who continue his scholarly approach, but first and foremost because they are souls whom he molded spiritually. The *Rav* has merited that in him is fulfilled the idea that "whoever preserves a single soul, Scripture ascribes merit to him as though he had preserved a complete world" (*Sanhedrin* 37a).

---

2. *Sifrei Devarim* 34; cited also in Rashi's commentary, ad loc.

As long as this lofty and elevated vision stands before his eyes, and encourages and motivates him, it also casts a great burden and tension on the *Ram*, by virtue of the very definition of his role as the *Rav* of the *talmidim* who attend his *yeshiva*. He has the great advantage that his primary occupation is with young men, who in large measure are still at the stage of shaping their spiritual world. The formative period of their lives, defined by the *mishna* in *Avot* as a blank piece of paper, has not yet passed, and they have not yet reached the stage of erased paper, writing on which is difficult and exhausting. The personality that is shaped during these years will continue in the way it has chosen for years to come. The influence and success of *Rashei Yeshiva* regarding their *talmidim* is attested to by all those *yeshiva bogrim* (alumni) who regularly turn to their teachers for counsel and support at critical points in their lives. The full strength of their impact is also evident from all those who ask themselves: What would my *Rav* say, or how would he guide me in these circumstances, and what would he expect of me?

However, the *yeshiva* framework creates difficulties from other directions. The *yeshiva* of the late twentieth century is an institution of a completely different size than its Eastern European predecessor. Its *talmidim* are in constant contact with their families and with the society from which they come (in the wake of the technological developments in the field of transportation and communications). The age of the *talmidim* and the duration of their study are also not the same as they were in the past. Unlike the community Rabbi, who accompanies the families in his community over many years, is together with them in the life cycle that extends over all stages of life, and meets with them in their homes, a *yeshiva Ram* teaches a young man for a year or two, until the curriculum advances him to the next level. Moreover, the encounter is limited not only in time but also in circumstances. Entire aspects of the *talmid*'s world and experience are outside the realm of the shared encounter between the *Rav* and the *talmid*. The *talmid*'s nuclear and extended family, his mundane world, his leisure pastimes, and even some of the *chaggim* find no expression in his stay in the *yeshiva*. The *Rav* is not necessarily familiar with these worlds, and even if he is well informed about what is happening in them, there is no guarantee that he will be able to influence them. Not everyone is privileged to cast his net in Jerusalem when he is living in Netzivin. And even if the *talmid* draws on the values and ways of the *yeshiva* when he is outside it, his *Rav* does not enjoy the existential partnership of a *Rav* and his *talmid*, because he does not share the same world. Thus, the *talmid*'s behavior in the *yeshiva* is evident to the *Rav*, influenced by his guidance, and experiences his partnership, but what about his conduct outside the walls of the *Beit Midrash*, that which does not enter into this covenant?

The conclusion, therefore, is that the primary satisfaction derived from the sacred work that is carried out in a *yeshiva* involves the exciting existential encounter that takes place within the walls of the institution, but this achievement is not regularly attained.

II

In my remarks so far, I pointed to the inherent difficulties of the *Yeshiva* Rabbinate from the perspective of the personal, educational role that it fills. The truth is that we are dealing with advantages and disadvantages stemming from the very definition of the role and from the changing social reality of each generation, and they are the challenges that face every educator. From this point on, I would like to deal with a more basic tension inherent to the role of *Ram* by the very duality that it embodies. We are not dealing with the educational challenges in themselves, but with the clash between the educational focus and the creative focus of his work.

Chazal define a *Beit Midrash* as "a place where the Torah is magnified" (*Megilla* 27a), not only because of the many *talmidim* found there, but because it is a place designed for the development and perfection of the Torah enterprise. In other words, a *Beit Midrash* is meant not only to spread Torah, but also to develop it. In recent generations, the institution of the *yeshiva* has assumed this role and has become a center of novel Torah insights. New approaches emerged from within the walls of the *Beit Midrash*, and scholarly revolutions took place within the *yeshivot*. From the time of the rise of the *yeshiva* world at the beginning of the nineteenth century and until today, we have been witness to a continuous process of shifting the center of gravity of the creative Torah enterprise from the world of the Community Rabbinate to the world of the *yeshivot*.

The ideological justification assigned by Rav Chayyim *Mi-Volozhin* – the founder of the modern *yeshiva* and the father of the Lithuanian *yeshiva* world, which serves as a prototype for most contemporary *yeshivot* – to the centrality of the mitzva of Torah study lies in the benefit that will rise from it for the Torah discipline itself. The institution of the national *yeshiva* that he created did indeed fulfill this mission, and the aspiration accompanied Lithuanian action and thought throughout its history. If Torah "*li-shmah*," for its own sake, means for the sake of the Torah and its development, and if man and his capacities are subjugated to the Torah, then the individual's personal strengths should be directed toward this task. Unlike in the past, when scholastic achievement and the desire to reach it were often suspected of being an expression of personal ambition, Rav Chayyim *Mi-Volozhin* assigned Torah creativity a most central place in the Torah world. From now on, insight, creation and achievement are the life potion of the Torah enterprise and not the death drug of the evil inclination.[3]

In other words, a *yeshiva* that sees itself as having been raised on this understanding is not only an educational institution but also an academic one, and the role of the *Rav* is not only to educate but also to gain new insights in the Torah. He is expected to be an expert on the Torah, and not just a gifted teacher for his students. What is expected of him is not only good interpersonal communication, but also impressive Torah capacities.[4]

---

3. The fear of personal ambition and the accompanying tension between Torah creativity and moral inspection are known to us throughout the generations, documented in the sources during every period of scholarly advancement, and is not unique to this period. The novelty of the modern *yeshiva* world was its readiness to approve of creativity in a declarative manner and to glorify scholastic achievement. For the sake of illustration, it is worth noting that the full title of Rav Soloveitchik's seminal work in praise of the world of Torah scholarship is: *Halakhic Man and his Creative Capacity*.

4. The rise of the *yeshiva* as a central Torah institution is connected to the changes that occurred in the early nineteenth century regarding the significance of Torah study and the place of Torah in the religious Jewish system. Rav Chayyim *Mi-*

Here we have reached the heart of the split in the essence of the *Yeshiva* Rabbinate. On the one hand, the educational work demands the most attention, and the day-to-day educational effort demands a great investment of time and energy, on the part of both the institution and its Rabbis. The creation of the desired educational activity requires personal attention, individual-existential conversations, and constant inquiring about the *talmid*'s well-being. All this takes a lot of time. On the other hand, the *Rav*'s intellectual Torah development also requires personal resources. In-depth examination of the issues studied, breaking through into new fields of study, and committing novel insights to writing cannot be done haphazardly or at times that are neither day nor night. All of these require full attention.

A partial solution to the situation that was created involved the diversion of the creative energy to the fields that were ordinarily studied in the *yeshivot* according to the standard *yeshiva* curriculum. One of the main characteristics of Rabbinic literature in the twentieth century was the split into *yeshiva* literature and non-*yeshiva* literature. In fact, a new literary genre was created in which the oral *shi'urim* were committed to

---

Volozhin maintained that Torah study is not a means to achieve the goal of observing the *mitzvot* and he negated the dominant view until that time that the Torah was intended to satisfy the needs of man and its role is to help him fulfill the will of the Creator, and therefore Torah study in itself is of no importance unless it is of help in practice. This view constituted the ideological foundation of the institution of the *yeshiva*. As long as the Torah was perceived as the source of halakhic guidance, most novel Torah insights came from *poskim* (halakhic arbiters) who served in the major cities, where most of the halakhic questions were raised. However, when the primary value of Torah study became the study itself, and the definition of the goal was the development and elaboration of the Torah itself, the focus of innovation shifted to the institution that had the tools to carry it out, that is to say, the *yeshiva*. The model of the *yeshiva* that Rav Chaim *Mi-Volozhin* instituted as a tool for realizing his vision was an institution detached from contact with the world of actual practice and halakhic decision-making. It was geographically located in a small village and it brought together the best young minds from all over the country and it dealt with all aspects of the Torah, and not just the more practical issues. All of these factors were ideal for the development of the abstract discipline of Torah *li-shmah*, but clearly inappropriate for the development of the halakhic aspect of the Torah.

writing and published as written Torah novellae.⁵ In this way the *Rav* could focus on his teaching role and also create a literary legacy.⁶

But this was a very partial solution since it subordinated the written work to other ends that did not necessarily accord with the needs of the written tract. Publication of the novellae of the *Rashei Yeshiva* was

---

5. In fact, this is a return to a model that was common to a certain extent among the Tosafists, and this is one of the points of contact between the Tosafists and the modern *yeshiva* world, but this is not the forum in which to expand upon this point.
6. The clearest example of this is the work of Rav Elchanan Wasserman, the head of the *yeshiva* in *Baranowitz* and one of the outstanding leaders of the *yeshiva* world between World Wars I and II. The title of his later work, *Koveitz Shi'urim* (Tel Aviv: 1963-1964) testifies to this phenomenon like a thousand witnesses. The title page of this book, which was published by the author's son after the Holocaust, attests to this explicitly: "*Sefer Koveitz Shi'urim, shi'urim* that were delivered in the *Yeshiva* by the great *Ga'on*, our master Rav Elchanan Bunim Wasserman, *Rosh Yeshiva* of Ohel Torah in *Baranowitz*." Any additional word to illustrate the phenomenon is unnecessary. His second book as well, *Koveitz He'arot* (Piotrkow, 1932), is an anthology of scholarly remarks, which were originally transmitted orally and then committed to writing, more or less in their original form, and in a manner that the lack of editing and literary consolidation is exceedingly prominent. This phenomenon is also prevalent among his colleagues, the *Rashei Yeshiva* and *Ramim* who served in the various *yeshivot*, but this is not the place to spell this out in detail. Nevertheless, it is worthwhile citing from the personal testimony of some of these authors. On the title page of the book *Imrei Moshe* (Tel Aviv 1923) of Rav Moshe Sakalowski, *Rosh Yeshiva* of the local *yeshiva* in *Brisk* at the beginning of the twentieth century, it says: "These are the words that Moshe spoke before the excellent young men in the *Yeshiva* of *Brisk*." And in the introduction to the book *Divrei Yechezkel* (Benei Berak 2007) of Rav Yechezkel Borstein, who was a *Ram* in the *Slobodka Yeshiva*, the author relates: "God greatly spread His grace over me when He brought me here to study and to teach before my colleagues who listen to my voice in our holy Yeshivat Or Yisrael in *Slobodka*, and granted me the privilege to comment upon and illuminate several profound matters in the *Gemara*, and I said I would record them in a book." Similarly, in the book *Even Ha-Ezel* (Jerusalem 1988) of Rav Isser Zalman Meltzer on Rambam's *Sefer Kinyan*, we find in the back of the volume, after the regular index, "a list of expanded matters most of which were said in *shi'urim* in the *Yeshiva*." This is a list of the issues that merited broader discussion because they were the subjects of general *shi'urim* delivered before the entire *yeshiva*. As time went on, this tendency grew in strength, to the point that most of the scholarly literature in the post World War II period came into the world in this manner, as is evident from the titles of the books: *Kunteres Shi'urim, Reshimat Shi'urim, Shi'urim Le-Zekher Abba Mari, Shi'urei Ha-Rav* […] as recorded by his *talmidim*, and the like.

essentially a casting of Oral Torah into a written form, rather than a conscious and planned writing of Torah from the outset. In this way, the selection of the material, its scope and the organization of the material are not dictated by an orderly literary program, but by the *talmidim*'s needs and the *Rav*'s commitment to meet them. Indeed, the more elaborate and complete works created in the twentieth century were not the work of *Rashei Yeshiva*.[7]

The modern university world consciously gave up the pretense of joining together these two aspirations; the humanistic vision of existential knowledge pulsating through the soul of the *talmid* does not exist in the teacher-student relationship in modern academia. The scholar devotes his time to research and hardly ever comes into personal contact with the students he teaches. The system is designed to allow him to delve into his research with maximum efficiency, at the expense of his connections with his students. The school year is short, the weekly reception hours are very few, and a considerable part of the contact with the student rests with the research assistant. If both of them, the professor and the student, are lucky, the scholastic material and its existential messages seep into their souls as a fertilizing force. But this is not a process that takes place together in a shared dialogue, but rather it passes over each separately. Each element stands apart. The ideal of "Your sons – these are the disciples" is not taken into account, and therefore the student is exposed only to the knowledge of his professor, and not to his soul, and this too only at fixed times.

In the *yeshiva*, on the other hand, Chazal's recommendations regarding joint study and their sharp condemnation of one who studies by himself – "May a sword fall upon the neck of the foes of scholar-disciples, that sit and engage in the study of Torah solitary and apart" (*Makkot* 10a) – are in full force.[8] What then should the *Rav* do? How should he spend his time

---

7. The literary implications of this phenomenon are not our concern in this article. In an article dealing with *yeshiva* Torah literature that I intend to publish, I hope to address this issue in detail.
8. In order to avoid any misunderstanding, it is important to note that this is, of course, a euphemism, for the Torah scholars themselves. The Talmudic statement continues: "And furthermore, such people wax foolish. It is written here: 'And they shall become fools' (*Yirmeyahu* 50:36); and it is written elsewhere: 'Wherein we have done foolishly' (*Bamidbar* 12:11). And, furthermore, they also become sinners, as it is added there: 'And wherein we have sinned.'" In other words, Chazal identify two problems with solipsistic study: 1) it is less effective; 2) existentially it is sinful.

and energy? Should he free himself up for another personal conversation with a troubled *talmid* or plunge to the depths of a problematic issue? Should he give more personal attention to one of the *talmidim* in his class, or should he attempt to crack a difficult Rambam? The *Ram* is torn between these two extremes and there does not appear to be a satisfactory solution to his dilemma.[9]

---

9. It seems to me that the demands on the part of the *talmidim*, at least in the Religious-Zionist world, have only worsened over the years. In the Lithuanian *yeshiva* world of the late nineteenth and early twentieth centuries – the period during which the institution of the *yeshiva* developed with great momentum and its modern character was shaped while strong conceptual and educational agitation accompanied what was happening within its walls – one of the central elements of these *yeshivot* was the sense of the cohesive group and the deep bond of friends. The struggle with the current and eternal issues that preoccupied Jewish society of that time was done as a group with discussions among the *talmidim*, and not only within each person's individual soul, and the sense of existential partnership of those who chose the path of the *yeshiva* in the face of the currents that were blowing on the outside was a cohesive and unifying factor. Under these circumstances, in which the existential encounter with the great questions of life took place primarily in the framework of collegial relationships, the group was the important framework. If we allow ourselves to borrow the formulations found in *Avot*, "Acquire for yourself a friend" was primary from an existential perspective, and "Make for yourself a Rabbi" was an educational and spiritual need, but less central on the personal level.

In fact, it should be added that in many cases the *Rav* himself was included in the group, considered one of them and established deep ties with his *talmidim*. However, for our purposes, it is important to note that the systematic and orderly personal treatment of the *talmidim*, the likes of which we find in contemporary *yeshivot*, did not fall upon him as one of his responsibilities. Anyone who reads the memoire literature of the period is impressed by the deep involvement of the *Rashei Yeshiva* in what was happening in their institutions and by their concern for the *talmidim*, but he also observes that there is almost no mention of significant personal conversations between them and the *talmidim*, and certainly there was no deliberate policy or desire to have such a conversation with each *talmid*. In the current reality, the sense of the group and the preoccupation with fateful questions have diminished, and the center of gravity has shifted from the group to the *Rav's* attitude toward the individual. When society is in a period of weakened ideological tension and individualism is quite strong, the existential tension no longer serves as such a cohesive factor as it was in the past, whereas the individualistic spirit that prevails in our time heightens the *talmid's* expectation that the *Rav* will take care of his personal needs.

III

At this point, I wish to turn to Rav Soloveitchik's philosophical teachings in order to characterize the Rabbi's situation. According to Rav Soloveitchik, man is faced with many challenges and various principles that he must fulfill. The problem is that this is not merely a matter of additional tasks, but in many cases we are dealing with conflicting values that clash with one another. The fulfillment of one comes at the cost of canceling the other, the two being unable to coexist. In heaven, under the wings of the *Shekhina* (Divine presence), peace can be made between the conflicting forces, but here on Earth one must live in a reality full of contradictions.

Chazal already attest in their discussion regarding arbitration versus strict law about the inherent contradiction between different values:

> Rabbi Yehoshu'a ben Korcha said: There is a mitzva to settle by arbitration, as it is stated: "Execute the judgment of truth and peace in your gates." Surely where there is strict justice there is no peace, and where there is peace, there is no strict justice! But what is that kind of justice with which peace abides? We must say: Arbitration. So it was in the case of David, as it is stated: "And David executed justice and righteousness [charity] towards all his people." Surely where there is strict justice there is no charity, and where there is charity, there is no justice! But what is the kind of justice with which abides charity? We must say: Arbitration. (*Sanhedrin* 6a)

The proper way for a person to deal with the existential state of life in a world full of contradictions is not to favor one principle over others, because in this way his world will be manifestly unbalanced. Rather, he must move between the two contradictory poles. This way no single principle is fully preserved, for each one exacts a price from the conflicting principle, but there is also no disregard of either principle. Thus, for example, a person cannot fully realize truth in his life, because such a realization would deliver a fatal blow to peace. On the other hand, peace too may not fully be realized, because in this way truth would disappear. One has no other choice, but to choose a middle path and a way to execute it, in the course of a to-and-fro between the various principles, sometimes emphasizing the one and sometimes the other, and each time paying the price of inconsistency and partial achievement.

What this means is that a person will never get to live one truth fully, but, on the other hand, he will merit to materialize many partial truths, and this partialness is the appropriate spiritual truth for the world of contradictions in which he lies. Metaphorically it may be argued that a person does not receive only one cup to drink and taste thereby the taste of life, but rather two cups rest before him. Were there only one cup before him, it would be possible to drink it fully and exhaust it, but when there are two, one cannot fully drink both of them, because the taste of the one will ruin the other, and vice versa. If he drinks from both of them, he can finish, for example, only about eighty percent of each. The dilemma faced by each individual is whether to drink a hundred percent of the one, or eighty percent of the two cups. Rav Soloveitchik's conclusion is that the correct thing to do is drink the two partially, and not the lone single one (for a hundred and sixty is a lot more than a hundred), and thus his life is richer. The price he pays is that the drinking of one full cup to the end and fulfilling one matter in full manner gives great satisfaction, whereas drinking two halves leaves a person with the sense of missing an opportunity and incompletion.

The work of a *Ram*, as we described it above as torn between the educational extreme and the scholarly ideal, accords well with this model. A *Ram* can choose to focus on one of the two principles – the training of his *talmidim* or Torah creativity – and realize it fully. Indeed, there are cases in which this choice is liable to be the most fitting and most correct one in light of personal or institutional circumstances. However, the choice of holding on to the one without letting go of the other is the fitting one in most cases, but it presents the Rabbi-educator with a greater and more complicated challenge, with the realization of which his life and role will be fuller and more meaningful, but the sense of the lack of satisfaction in each of the two realms and the gnawing uncertainty regarding finding the appropriate balance will accompany him at all times. A *Ram*, like any other person, is forced to recognize that only half of his desires is he able to realize.[10]

IV

Thus far we have related to the individual work of the *Ram* within the *yeshiva*, through an examination of the relationship between him and his *talmidim* and between him and himself. However, that same tension that is found between the walls of the *yeshiva* and that stems from the aspiration to reach two different goals is found also in the encounter between the *Yeshiva* Rabbinate and the world outside the *yeshiva*.

As noted above, the Lithuanian *yeshiva* world (which is the prototype of most contemporary *yeshivot*) was founded on secession from general society and entrenchment in small towns and communities with insignificant public weight, while drawing Rabbis and students from the large cities into the *yeshivot*. The establishment of *yeshivot* in small villages such as *Volozhin*, *Mir*, *Radin*, and the like was a highly logical move, stemming from the ideological concept that maximum resources should be dedicated to the development of the Torah. The location of these institutions in what can be called "academic towns," which provided a quiet environment far away from the hustle and bustle of life, did a good job of nurturing the *talmidim*, but there was also a considerable price that had to be paid, namely, the removal of some of the greatest Rabbis from the large cities.

This situation of severing the Rabbinical leadership in the *yeshivot* from the centers of public activity and general leadership could not be maintained for long because of the demand that those Rabbis of stature who stood at the head of the *yeshivot* should grapple with the needs of the public at large and shine upon it of their wisdom and their Torah. Indeed, these *Rashei Yeshiva* found themselves time after time being called to the flag, to participate in Rabbinic gatherings that discussed important issues of the day. However, the changes that took place over the years

---

10. This dilemma should also influence the considerations of the institution in selecting a Ram when it is necessary to balance the Rav's ability to provide personal treatment and be a father to his talmidim and his scholarly talents.

among the Jewish people brought about that the halakhic and community leadership gradually shifted from the Community Rabbinate to the *Yeshiva* Rabbinate, to the point that with the passage of time the *yeshivot* became a most important center of community leadership. Paradoxically, a process, the starting point of which involved leaving the large communities and entrenching themselves outside of them, eventually bestowed great communal power upon the *Rashei Yeshiva*.

It is important to emphasize that it is not only the personal greatness of today's *Rashei Yeshiva* that brings them to positions of public leadership, but also their institutional standing. We are dealing with a process of the transfer of institutional power centers, and not just personal charisma. If once someone like the Netziv was called upon to participate in such gatherings because he was one the great leaders of all generations, and not because he was a *Rosh Yeshiva*, but rather despite his position, today the very status of *Rosh Yeshiva* translates into a leadership position. An analysis of the causes that led to this situation goes beyond the framework of this article, but in the post-Holocaust religious world – in the State of Israel and across the world, in the Religious-Zionist world and in the Ultra-Orthodox world, the *Rashei Yeshiva* have become the community leaders.[11]

This situation is not without its problems. Ultimately, the inherent limitations imposed by *yeshiva* reality, namely, dealing with a sector comprised of a specific age and gender, the detachment from the community and from activity on its behalf, are significant. If we assume that most *Rashei Yeshiva* are internal appointments, that is, individuals who developed and advanced within the institution or others like it, we are dealing with people who spent most of their lives within a *yeshiva* framework, which does not necessarily expose them to the broader complex of the real world.

---

11. This phenomenon is more prominent in the Ultra-Orthodox world because of the greater importance of the Torah leadership vis-à-vis the political leadership, as opposed to the situation in the Religious-Zionist world (in which the political importance of the Rabbinic component is also significant), and because of the greater involvement of the Rabbis in the totality of practical life. However, regarding the issue of the relative weight of *Rashei Yeshiva* versus community Rabbis, I do not see a significant difference between the two worlds. In both cases, the *Rashei Yeshiva* of our time have the upper hand.

Needless to say, a person with a broad view and a deep understanding of life can serve as an impressive public leader, and examples of such people are not lacking. But there is no guarantee that such will necessarily be the case. When the office, and not just charisma, underlies the *Rosh Yeshiva*'s standing, there is potential for problems.

This point brings us to the heart of the problem regarding *yeshiva* leadership, which is that the skills that are highly regarded for the purpose of appointing *Rashei Yeshiva* are not necessarily the skills required for public leadership. Thus, we come back to the basic tension noted earlier between the role of a *yeshiva* as a center for magnifying and glorifying the Torah and caring for the Jewish people. The appointment takes into account the appointee's skills from the "professional" perspective, i.e. his ability to come up with new Torah insights and to deliver *shi'urim*, and not necessarily his capacity to serve as a public leader. In most cases, this is of little significance because most *Rashei Yeshiva* are not public leaders, but rather teachers who engage in the instruction of their flock. Moreover, some of them even recognize their limitations and make no claims on any crown of leadership. However, turning a person into a public leader by virtue of his intellectual abilities in the field of study and his position as *Rosh Yeshiva* often causes considerable problems, since there is no guarantee that one who excels in analyzing scholarly texts will succeed as a community leader, just as there is no need for a great leader to be a great scholar. Every man and his talents, every man and his own unique qualities.

Regarding this point there has been a certain split in recent years between the Ultra-Orthodox world and the Religious-Zionist world. The great prestige enjoyed by outstanding Torah scholars in a society that is centered around *yeshiva* life and is united and organized by the value of Torah study as the focus of religious life often bestows upon them positions of leadership and influence, without taking into account the personality of the appointee or his understanding of the world around him. In this context, note should also be taken of the decline in the status of the *Mashgichim* (spiritual supervisors) who were once central figures in the Lithuanian *yeshiva* world in Europe. These leaders drew their power from personal strengths and charisma rather than knowledge, and therefore had more impressive leadership skills and in many cases were more attentive to the pace of life. The *Rashei Yeshiva* assisted them as expert scholars but did not wield significant influence. However, in the *yeshiva* world after the Holocaust, the center of gravity shifted to the *Rashei Yeshiva* who were chosen on the basis of purely academic considerations.

In the Religious-Zionist world, on the other hand, we have of late[12] witnessed a growing phenomenon of the process taking place in the opposite direction. Individuals with charisma and a flair for spiritual leadership, but lacking the Torah scholarship skills that are necessitated by the perception of the *yeshiva* as an academic institution, are appointed to serve as *Rashei Yeshiva* thanks to the public stage and leadership position that the office gives them. If at first the modern-day *yeshiva* removed itself from society in order to magnify and glorify Torah *li-shmah*, and afterwards it developed into an important factor in the leadership of the religious community owing to its unique qualities, prestige and central place in the post-Holocaust religious world, this latest development that is taking place before our very eyes sees the *yeshiva* as a public stage and its scholarly enterprise as subordinate and secondary to its public dimension.[13] Thus, the circle has been closed, and the purpose of the *yeshiva* is once again perceived as a contribution to the community and a benefit to the people, and not as an institution aimed at magnifying the Torah.[14]

This process has advantages and disadvantages. On the one hand, it protects us from the danger that at the head of the camp there will stand

---

12. Fifteen to twenty years ago the process described here was very striking. In recent years the situation has somewhat moderated, but I believe that the basic pattern described here is still valid and the trends it points to are still strong in the contemporary Religious-Zionist world.
13. The absence of a significant Communal Rabbinate in Israel contributes significantly to the acceleration of this process, for it is convenient for someone who is seeking a public platform to be drawn to the institution of the *yeshiva* and take advantage of its status and prestige.
14. This is, of course, the declared objective of the pre-military preparatory programs, whose name suggests that they are committed to a goal outside of them and therefore do not pretend to be *yeshivot*. Our argument is that this process is taking place in a more concealed manner even in institutions that define themselves as *yeshivot*, and thus the essential difference.

Rashei Yeshiva with no leadership skills and no understanding of the complex reality of life, but on the other hand, it jeopardizes the status of the *yeshiva* as an institution of learning. If the scholarly development of the institution as a place where the Torah is magnified is not the primary concern of the *Rosh Yeshiva*, but rather this is perceived as a secondary goal, then the institution will not project Torah strength. This will undermine the central goal underlying the *yeshiva* world, our commitment to develop and perfect the Torah. In the end, if it follows in this path, the institution will find it difficult to maintain its public standing, and the benefits will be outweighed by the losses.[15]

V

The weakening of the Torah's strength through the dilution of the scholarly component in Religious-Zionist *yeshivot*, and the diminished involvement of the Modern Orthodox community in the *yeshiva* enterprise and in the Torah creativity that takes place within its walls, constitute a double danger, both to the Torah world, and to Religious-Zionist society.

Let us open with the first point. First, the very relinquishing of significant Torah forces that will necessarily result from the weakening of Torah study in these *yeshivot* is a loss to the Torah world. However, this is not the crux of the matter, since today's *yeshiva* world is large and wide-ranging, and many forces – young and old, new and long-standing – knock on the doors of the *Beit Midrash* and study Torah night and day with perseverance and dedication. Rather, the problem lies in the loss of the added value that the Religious-Zionist world of Torah has to offer.

---

15. The selection of *Ramim* in these *yeshivot* is also influenced by this, and the appointment to the position of *Ram* has become increasingly dependent on the candidate's educational abilities rather than on his Torah scholarship. As stated above, an appropriate balance should be sought between the two components of the position. However, if a reality is created in which charismatic individuals who are weak in their Torah scholarship are awarded the title of *Ram* (rather than *Mashgi'ach* or some other educational title), this would be an additional sign of the decline of the scholarly dimension, which, as stated, should be an integral aspect of the position.

The root of the matter lies in the fact that the Torah is a system of ideas that sets halakhic and legal principles on human reality. The world of man, in all of his situations, both private and public, is the platform upon which *halakha* operates. It follows from this that two skills are required for serious Torah study. On the one hand, it is necessary to acquire the internal logic of the *Gemara*, which operates according to the accepted methods of deduction in the Oral Torah and makes its arguments and reaches its conclusions by applying the methods of study developed over the generations. The study of the give-and-take of the Talmudic passage and the analysis of Rambam's rulings and the opinions of the various *rishonim* in light of the rules of Talmudic logic and the various methods of study provide the learner with scholarly tools that will enable him to critique that which already exists and also reach new insights. This process is based on the rules of Talmudic logic that are found within the system and that can be acquired by way of correct methodological direction. Providing the *talmid* with the proper scholarly training will give him these tools and thus he will reach the level of "*talmid chakham*" (Torah scholar). In *yeshiva* jargon, it may be said about such a person that "he knows how to learn" (*ken lernen*). This is by no means a trivial matter; it is the engine that leads the entire scholarly *yeshiva* project. As in any intellectual discipline, consistency, systemacity, drawing conclusions in one field and applying them in other areas, the use of deductive tools, and the like, provide the tools of control and analysis that are required for the advancement and development of the field.

However, *halakha* cannot suffice with pure and abstract legal logic, and its methods of study cannot be likened to geometric conclusions drawn from within themselves. If Torah scholarship is based only on internal logical development, we can reach the first stage of Torah creativity, from which it would be possible to extract from the texts that which logical analysis can deduce from them. However, Torah creativity also requires familiarity with the world and life, because of the encounter that is reached in the Torah between idea and reality. Only knowledge of the religious experience and the human psyche, social dynamics and the business world will allow a better understanding of the passages, since it is this world that is the subject of their discussions.[16] And it should be emphasized that for our purposes it makes no difference which approach we adopt regarding the tension between idea and reality in the Torah. Whether we emphasize its abstractness and the abstract Platonic element in it or adopt a more mystical approach that sees the Torah as rooted in lofty higher worlds, or we emphasize its connection to this world and see it as aimed at instructing Am Yisrael what to do, the object of the manifest discussion in the Talmudic passages is the human world familiar to us. Knowing this reality and understanding its principles and implications leads to a deeper understanding of the Torah itself, which requires the learner to integrate this perspective into his study.

Regarding this point, it seems that the Religious-Zionist or Modern Orthodox community can make a significant contribution. In general, it is possible to say that the worldview of this community, which requires leaving the *Beit Midrash* for various aspects of life, whether military service, business or academia, leads to greater contact and interaction with the variety of situations that reality sets before man. A richer experience of life, whether it is based on a person's personal experiences in his encounters with general society or it is based on literary exposure to the lives and insights of the finest intellectuals across the generations, among the Jewish people and among the nations, opens the door and allows for a better understanding of the Torah. Does not knowledge about human nature contribute to a deeper understanding of the laws of mourning and prayer? Is it possible to say that familiarity with the world of business does not allow for a better understanding of the question regarding "a *migo*[17] argument countering

---

16. What I say here in this section is not directed exclusively to the world of halakhic decision-making and the literature dealing with practical *halakha*, regarding which the assertion regarding the importance of familiarity with the real world is self-evident. Rather, my words apply even to the theoretical Torah scholarship of the *Beit Midrash*. Even abstract Torah *li-shmah* which is far from the world of actual practice requires familiarity with the real world, and not just halakhic decision-making that is directed at actual halakhic implementation.

17. The *Gemara* in *Bava Batra* 5b discusses the possibility of accepting a "weak" legal claim that stands in opposition to an accepted legal assumption from someone who could have presented a "stronger" argument that would certainly have been accepted.

the assumption that a person does not repay a loan before it becomes due?" This applies not only in clear areas of encounter between experience and *halakha*, like prayer or mourning, but in all parts of the Torah. Even the laws of marriage, torts, evidence and the like are enriched by the encounter between existential human experience and halakhic logic.

Thus, it is within the power of Religious-Zionist Torah scholars, who are firmly planted in a society that maintains closer and more meaningful contact with the surrounding world, to uniquely contribute to the deepening of the Torah, over and beyond their ordinary scholarly abilities. To a certain extent, this is evident in the world of Biblical exegesis of our generation (in which the contact with reality is much closer) if we compare Religious-Zionist Biblical commentary with that of the world of the Lithuanian *yeshivot*. Even considering the fundamental difference between the two spheres, it is easy to see the difference between the Religious-Zionist approach to the Written Torah and that of the Ultra-Orthodox, and that these gaps are not detached from the more general approach to the mundane world. It seems that in classical Torah scholarship as well, there is a similar valley that the Religious-Zionist community has the power to fence in and build up by way of scholarship that connects textual analysis to the existential world in which man lives and works.

What I have said here seems to be particularly applicable in our generation owing to the nature of the theoretical analysis that prevails in contemporary *yeshivot*. The scholarly breakthrough at the end of the nineteenth and beginning of the twentieth centuries, known as the method of "*iyyun*," at the heart of which stands the *Brisker* method that prevails in modern *yeshiva* Torah scholarship (and that includes additional approaches that developed in its wake), focuses primarily on the first stage described above. The method developed by Rav Chayyim of *Brisk* is fundamentally analytical, drawing on a precise logical analysis of the Talmudic passages. This process, which has continued for over a hundred years, greatly advanced the discipline of Torah scholarship and has had impressive achievements. However, the second stage described above is entirely missing, and therefore the next stage in the development of the world of Torah scholarship should be directed toward attaining this goal, if the generation is worthy.

As one who is devoted to Religious Zionism and Modern Orthodoxy, I must assert that the formation of a type of Torah scholar who is familiar with the analytical methods and is ready to connect them to existential reality is a present Torah need, and the matter is in our hands. Woe to us if we miss the opportunity by lowering the scholarly tension in our *yeshivot*.

The shifting of the *yeshiva*'s center of gravity from its scholarly enterprise to dealing with matters of public interest, which will be the necessary consequence of appointing *Rashei Yeshiva* and *Ramim* whose primary strength lies not in *Gemara*, Rashi, and *Tosafot*, will also undermine the attempt of the Religious-Zionist community to attain positions of community leadership. In the long run, a community and leadership that lacks a seal of Torah will fail in its attempts to establish religious leadership. It is possible that a model of leadership based on religious charisma that does not rest on halakhic authority or greatness in the Torah may exist for a time within the National-Religious community itself, but it is difficult to see this pattern as capable of breaking through the circle of the Religious-Zionist community. The problem is not with one particular leader or another but in the image of the community as a whole. If the community is perceived as religious but not Torah-centered, and its institutions do not stand with respect to the intensity of their study in the same line with parallel institutions, then the Religious-Zionist vision will be delegitimized and its ability to lead will be lost. The staffing of educational posts, the appointment of Rabbis, and the selection of *dayyanim* (judges) will not be passed into the hand of people and a community that lacks the necessary Torah scholarship. If the Religious-Zionist community fails to establish a learning system capable of producing Torah scholars, then its halakhic-Torah voice, which is nourished by its worldviews, will not be heard at all.[18]

---

18. Comparing and contrasting what is happening in the Religious-Zionist world in Israel to what is happening to Modern Orthodoxy in America and its flagship, Yeshiva University, can help us test the thesis proposed here and illuminate the matter under discussion in an interesting light. However, an analysis and discussion of the Torah reality overseas would take us beyond the framework of this article.

We find ourselves, therefore, between the hammer and the anvil. On the one hand, the appointment of *Rashei Yeshiva* as community leaders exclusively on the basis of their scholastic abilities is a recipe for chronic problems and constant friction. On the other hand, the priority status enjoyed by today's *yeshivot* in the religious world sets the *Rashei Yeshiva* in the forefront of the public arena and brings the Torah community in general, and their thousands of *talmidim* and *bogrim* in particular, to seek their every word. In this reality, the *Rashei Yeshiva* giving up their pretensions to religious and spiritual leadership and turning to other Rabbinic models, whether in the form of the Chief Rabbinate or in the form of community Rabbis, are not in sight. The public desires their leadership and they agree to it. An alternative model of leadership of a non-*Yeshiva* Rabbinate is certainly possible and existed in many communities in the past, as it exists today to a large extent in the Chassidic world and in many Sephardic communities. However, in the current Israeli reality it has not yet come of age as a solution for the general public, and it cannot solve today's needs.[19] Also, let us not forget that this will not resolve the need of the *yeshiva* itself to provide spiritual guidance to its *talmidim*, both those currently studying within its walls as well as those who see it as their spiritual home throughout their lives. Therefore, the *Rashei Yeshiva*, even those who lack the vision and imagination for spiritual leadership, will continue to be leaders in contemporary religious society. But the possibility of appointing spiritual leaders as *Rashei Yeshiva* based on their vision and religious charisma, but without the required scholarly background, will bring no good, for it is proven recipe for lowering the status of the Torah.

Therefore, it is clear that the ideal solution to the aforementioned dilemma should be to combine the two factors, that is, to appoint individuals with leadership skills and strong Torah scholarship as *Rashei Yeshiva* and choosing appropriate candidates who combine both qualities. If Torah and greatness gathered in one place, and a certain individual merited that these two qualities be merged in his soul – fortunate is he, and fortunate are his *talmidim*!

---

19. It seems to me that the first cracks in the public leadership model of the *Rosh Yeshiva* have begun to appear, but even if this is correct, we are still dealing with very preliminary cracks.

However, not every person and not every institution is that fortunate. Therefore, it may be necessary to consider other models as well. These may include joint leadership of a *yeshiva* by more than one *Rosh Yeshiva*, thereby enabling the relative strengths of each to contribute to the intellectual, educational and leadership roles, each with his respective and unique contribution,[20] the inclusion of communal Rabbis in public policy decisions, or some other paradigm that will bolster the *yeshiva*'s capacities to fulfil its roles while addressing the problems inherent in the current situation and thus allowing the *yeshiva* to confidently face the challenges which stand before it.

* Translated by David Strauss

---

20. To a certain extent, this is the model of the *Rosh Yeshiva* and *Menahel Ruchani* (spiritual leader) that was common in the not-too-distant past and whose utility has not yet expired. This paradigm, though, was rooted in a sharp distinction between the two roles: the *Mashgi'ach* provided spiritual guidance, educational supervision and public leadership, while the *Rosh Yeshiva* focused upon teaching Torah and developing its intellectual aspects as a learning discipline.

A Note on the Order of the Chapters and the *Mishnayot* in *Masekhet Gittin**

HaRav Yaakov Medan

I.

The heart of *Masekhet Gittin* is found, as we shall see, in the ninth and final chapter. The beginning of this chapter deals with the relationship between permitting a woman to remarry by way of giving her a *get* and detaching her from her husband because of the *get*; are we dealing with two separate matters, or one matter and its consequence? The chapter continues with the text of the *get* and its contents. It then moves on to discuss the essentiality of the witnesses in the *get* (and the time recorded therein). Afterwards it deals with the need to specify the wife and husband for that particular *get* and with the laws of writing the *get li-shmah* (for its sake). From there it moves on to the writing of the *get* and the signing of the *get* by witnesses, to the language in which the *get* is written, to a *get* written by the husband against his will, to the presumption that a woman is divorced, and it ends with the question of when is a man permitted (or commanded) to divorce his wife.

These are the central issues in the laws of divorce, and it is somewhat surprising that they were pushed aside until the last chapter of the *masekhet* and recorded only after secondary matters related to the *get* and the act of divorce, which fill up the previous eight chapters. We will suffice with several examples:

The *masekhet* opens (the first four *mishnayot*) with the testimony offered by a messenger who delivers a *get* from abroad, testimony that can stand in place of the testimony of two witnesses that is generally required in matters dealing with ritual prohibitions. The next *mishna* deals with the validity of a Kutite witness in a *get*, even though he is disqualified for other *shtarot*, and it continues with additional differences between a *get* and *shtarot* in general. At the beginning of chapter 2, there is another *mishna* (2) that, according to Rabbi Shimon, is more lenient regarding a *get* than regarding other *shtarot*, concerning a *get* or a *shtar* that was written during the day but signed only at night.

Chapter 2 continues with a *get* that was written with questionable ink or on questionable parchment, and deals in three *mishnayot* with the messenger mentioned above.

The first three *mishnayot* in chapter 3 address a fundamental and essential issue concerning a *get*, namely, writing the *get li-shmah*, that is, for the sake of the particular woman being divorced. Two additional *mishnayot* (5-6) return to the laws of a messenger delivering a *get*. Three other *mishnayot* deal with sundry matters, the connection between them and *Masekhet Gittin* being indirect or associative. We shall touch upon one of them, *mishna* 4. The *mishna* deals with the testimony of Rabbi Elazar ben Parta regarding cases in which a woman's husband was lost in some tragic event, and it is not known that he survived the disaster, but there is also no evidence of his death. In the cases discussed in the *mishna*, the woman is not permitted to remarry.

The first two *mishnayot* in chapter 4 continue with the laws governing a messenger who delivers a *get* and the enactment of Rabban Gamli'el the Elder for the protection of the woman being divorced. The rest of the *mishnayot* in this and the following chapter deal with various matters of *tikkun ha-olam*, "maintaining the social order," similar to the *tikkun ha-olam* in Rabban Gamli'el's enactment. By the way, reference is made to the enactment helping repentants, the enactment benefitting the altar, and enactments to advance peaceful relations.

The sixth chapter returns once again to the laws governing a messenger in the case of a *get*; it opens with an agent appointed by the woman to receive her *get*, and concludes with an agent appointed by the husband to deliver the *get*, the husband lying on his deathbed and wishing to exempt his wife from *chalitza*.

The beginning of the seventh chapter continues to deal with a person who is ill or on the verge of death and wishes to give his wife a *get* so that she not be an *aguna* or to exempt her from *yibbum*. The second part of the chapter deals with various laws connected to *tena'im* (conditions), the main ones being *tena'im* designed to prevent the woman from becoming an *aguna* should the husband not return home by a certain date, or should he disappear.

The eighth chapter opens with the laws governing a person who throws a *get* to his wife from a distance, and continues with various details in divorce laws and in various non-divorce laws.

II.

Let us return briefly to the first *mishnayot* in chapter 9. These *mishnayot* record a fundamental dispute between Rabbi Eli'ezer and Chakhamim concerning a man who divorced his wife, permitting her with a *get* to all other men in the world, with the exception of one, regarding whom the woman was to remain prohibited as a married woman.

It is difficult to assume that the *mishna* is dealing with a purely theoretical case. The simple understanding is that a man might divorce his wife in this manner when he suspects that his wife engaged in illicit relations with another man, and he does not want her to marry the man who destroyed his marriage. According to this understanding, the first *mishnayot* in the chapter connect with the last *mishna*, which deals with divorce resulting from the husband finding out about his wife's unseemly conduct. The divorce discussed in chapter 9 is divorce resulting from hatred ("spoiled his food"), or what is worse than that, divorce following adultery or something close to that. This is the divorce referred to in the Torah according to the plain sense of the verses (*Devarim* 24:1): "When a man takes a wife, and marries her, and then it comes to pass, if she finds no favor in his eyes, because he has found some unseemly thing in her;" or (ibid. 22:13-14): "If any man takes a wife, and goes in unto her, and hates her, and lays wanton charges against her, and brings up an evil name upon her, and says: 'I took this woman, and when I came nigh to her, I found not in her the tokens of virginity.'"

Chazal, however, wished to open up the *masekhet*, and deal at length, specifically with divorce that stems from love and concern for the woman, from a desire that she not fall before a *yavam* whom she does not want to marry, or that she not become an *aguna*, when her husband is abroad and he is in doubt whether he can return home in light of the circumstances and the traveling opportunities of that time. The *get* that most interested Chazal was a *get* that prevents a woman from becoming an *aguna*.

Perhaps it may be assumed that the *mishnayot* in *Gittin* were originally written after *Masekhet Yevamot* was studied in the *beit midrash*. (The final order of the *masekhtot* in most orders of the *mishna* is according to their length.) The end of *Yevamot* deals with a husband who went abroad, and with the question of when may the woman be permitted to remarry. Let us examine the last *mishna* in the *masekhet*:

> Rabbi Akiva said: When I went down to *Neharde'a* to intercalate the year, I met Nechemya of *Beit Deli* who said to me: 'I heard that in *Eretz Yisrael* no one with the exception of Rabbi Yehuda ben Bava permits a married woman to marry again on the evidence of one witness.' 'That is so,' I told him. 'Tell them,' he said to me, 'in my name: "You know that this country is in confusion by reason of raiders; I have this tradition from Rabban Gamli'el the Elder: A married woman may be allowed to marry again on the evidence of one witness."' And when I came and recounted the conversation in the presence of Rabban Gamli'el, he rejoiced at my information and exclaimed: 'We have found a colleague for Rabbi Yehuda ben Bava!' As a result of this talk, Rabban Gamli'el recollected that some men were once killed at *Tel Arza*, and that Rabban Gamli'el the Elder had allowed their wives to marry again on the evidence of one witness. And the law was established that a woman shall be allowed to marry again on the evidence of one witness who states that he has heard the report from another witness, from a slave, from a woman or from a bondwoman. Rabbi Eli'ezer and Rabbi Yehoshu'a ruled: A woman may not be allowed to marry again on

the evidence of one witness. Rabbi Akiva ruled: A woman is not allowed to marry again on the evidence of a woman, or that of a slave, or that of a bondwoman or on that of relative. They said to him: 'It once happened that a number of Levites went to *Tzo'ar*, the city of palms, and one of them who fell ill was taken by them into an inn. When they returned they asked the innkeeper: "Where is our friend?" And she replied: "He is dead and I buried him." And it was on this evidence that his wife was permitted to marry again. Should not then a priest's wife be believed at least as much as the innkeeper?' He answered them: 'When she will be giving such evidence as the innkeeper she will be believed; the innkeeper as a matter of fact had brought out to them his staff, his bag and the *Sefer Torah* that he had with him.' (*Mishna Yevamot* 16:7)

This *mishna*, as well as the ones that precede it, deals with a special enactment that allowed a single witness to be believed as if there were two witnesses, in order to rescue women from becoming *agunot*. As stated, this is also the subject matter of the first *mishnayot* in *Gittin* – believing the single messenger delivering the *get* and not requiring two witnesses. As stated earlier, Rabbi Elazar ben Parta deals with a similar matter, not connected to divorce. In the fourth chapter, mention is made of the enactment instituted by Rabban Gamli'el the Elder to maintain the social order that would prevent a woman from becoming an *aguna*, and this parallels the words of Rabban Gamli'el the Elder regarding those who were killed at *Tel Arza* and rescuing their wives from becoming *agunot*.

Starting in the middle of the sixth chapter, the *mishnayot* deal primarily with saving the woman from falling before the *yavam*, which in some cases is like becoming an *aguna*. This is followed by the laws of *tena'im*, which are attached to a *get* primarily in order to save a woman from becoming an *aguna*: "If I do not arrive from now until twelve months," and the like.

The law of throwing a *get* to one's wife in the eighth chapter might also be fundamentally connected to this issue. According to its simple reading, the *mishna* is dealing with the period during which the ruling government banned divorce, alluded to in *Gittin* 6:2 and mentioned explicitly in *Ketubbot* 9:9 and other places. Ran (*Gittin* 40b in the *Rif*) notes that it makes no halakhic sense that if a man threw a *get* some distance away from the woman, but it is closer to her than it is to him, that this should be regarded as proper delivery of a *get*, even outside of the woman's four cubits. Ran says that Chazal instituted an enactment for the benefit of the woman. This enactment is based on the authority granted to the Rabbis to annul marriages. But why would Chazal have done this? It would appear that it was their intention to save the woman from becoming an *aguna* in a time of persecution, when people were afraid to deliver a *get* directly to their wives. Once again, we are dealing with an enactment for the welfare of *agunot* in times of persecution.

Only after Chazal finished dealing with "good *gittin*," *gittin* given out of the husband's concern for his wife and by the authority of Rabbinic enactments for the benefit of the woman, did they begin to deal with the *get* arising from the plain meaning of the scriptural verses, the *get* stemming from hatred and adultery. Thus, the chapter dealing with the fundamental principles of divorce became the final chapter of *Masekhet Gittin*.

* Translated by David Strauss

A *Rebbe* as a Father: *Divrei Hesped* for HaRav Aharon Lichtenstein *zt"l*[1]

Rabbi Dr. Michael Rosensweig

Introduction

I appreciate the opportunity to share some thoughts and feelings about *Moreinu* HaRav Aharon Lichtenstein *zt"l*. Although we are in the aftermath of the *sheloshim*, the sense that our community has been significantly diminished by his passing remains palpable. This feeling transcends personal sentiment and nostalgia, although the pain of personal irrevocable loss for his family first, and, then his extended *banim-talmidim*, certainly remains raw, profound and intense as well.

What accounts for this feeling, elusive and almost inchoate as it is? The loss of one of the rare *chakhmei ha-mesora* of any generation necessarily engenders this instinctive, yet visceral reaction. In the normal course of life and human emotion, *bekhi* (weeping) precedes *hesped* (eulogy), but for the truly impactful and irreplaceable leaders (as with Sara *Immeinu*, *Bereishit* 23:2), reviewing and articulating their legacy – *hesped* – also adds a new layer of *bekhi*, as it reopens the wound, further accentuates the magnitude of the loss, and, worse, perpetuates and even engenders anew uncertainty, even existential crisis – how will we proceed in the vacuum? But, additionally, it highlights the mysterious sense of present instability and the sense of being diminished that is independent of future concerns and that we should try to identify.

The departure and absence of any great *talmid chakham* stimulates this cycle of *bekhi-hesped-bekhi*. Yet, by definition, each member of this

---

1. This *hesped* was delivered at the Jewish Center in Manhattan, June 2015.

rare club or cadre, and *Moreinu* HaRav Lichtenstein *zt"l* particularly exemplifies this, is singular in his accomplishments, persona and legacy. It behooves us – as individuals and as a community – to reflect upon and try to better articulate these characteristics, qualities and motifs, which themselves become part of the *mesora* of *Torat Yisrael* and Kelal Yisrael, so that we can facilitate and secure the continued impact – neutralizing the sense of diminution – through the vibrancy of the *demut* of our *Rebbe*, for generations to come.

These remarks do not constitute an effort to assess or even put into perspective Rav Lichtenstein's massive contribution in *talmud Torah*, *hashkafa*, or leadership, each a formidable task, requiring time and thoughtful analysis, best reserved for an appropriate time. His incredible range, breadth, mastery and nuanced positions militate against a cursory account. Instead, I speak unabashedly as an immensely appreciative *talmid*, whose course and aspirations were transformatively impacted by the substance of his learning and teaching, and, perhaps even more, by the enduring experience of *Rebbe-talmid*, and the ethos of his persona, *ishiyyut, gavra*.

I came to Yeshivat Har Etzion at a very young and impressionable age. I was immediately enthralled by Rav Lichtenstein's Torah – its sweep, depth, and the *kevod* and *chibbat ha-Torah* and *yirat Shamayim* implied by its content and style-mode of presentation. I was even more captivated – enchanted even – by his persona: his humanity, empathy, passion and integrity. These were not themes I could then articulate, but I recall vividly experiencing and processing them intuitively. It was self-evident from the outset that we were in the presence of a singular *gadol be-Yisrael*. Rav Lichtenstein was hardly a flashy or "charismatic" personality (in modern parlance, at least). Indeed, he was someone who *be-shitta* was wary of guru-esque influence. But, and partially because of that substantive posture, he was the most enduringly impactful and compelling role model.

It was self-evident to his *talmidim* that his staggering intellectual virtuosity and his mastery of the vast corpus of Torah and *Torah ve-chokhma*, western civilization, replete with complexity, subtlety, and nuances, was mobilized to facilitate an experiential and spiritual journey of "*lifnei Hashem*." It was equally clear that this objective-telos was rooted in, and driven by, the simple fundamental (though never simplistic) and compelling values of *yirat Shamayim, ahavat Hashem,* and *ahavat Yisrael*. Rav Lichtenstein's synthesis of classical learning and innovative terminology-vocabulary and his expansion of Torah's inner agenda – both narrowly and its application to values and broader life – was exhilarating. His persona-*gavra* of empathy, humanity, and humility, and his consistency and constancy, his balanced and seamlessly integrated approach to a broad Torah life, was compelling. It was immediately obvious to his *talmidim* that his achievement as a sophisticated thinker-*chakham*, and *oved Hashem*, a *Rebbe* par excellence, remained rooted in his continued identity as an idealistic *talmid* of his *Rebbe'im*, an exuberant *yosheiv beit ha-midrash*, even a perennial *bachur yeshiva*, who continued to be totally captivated by *devar Hashem*. His face would shine and his eyes would light up when he recounted his experiences or impressions as a devoted *talmid* to his *Rebbe'im* – the Rav, Rav Hutner and Rav Ahron Soloveichik.

The fact that a 16-year-old's impressions cohere with, and are deeply reinforced by, a decades-long relationship, speaks to Rav Lichtenstein's consistency, integrity, and special stature as a *Rebbe*. I feel strongly, as do all his *talmidim*, that this relationship was pivotal, defining in my life. For his *talmidim*, Rav Lichtenstein was the paradigm for understanding and integrating many challenging facets of Torah life. He certainly embodied for us the notion of "'*ve-shinnantam le-vanekha*' – *eilu talmidekha*" – that *talmidim* are to be nurtured as spiritual children – a role he executed with diligence, generosity, and kindness. I am grateful for the opportunity to express personal *hakkarat ha-tov* for all of the guidance, direction, and impact I was privileged to enjoy throughout the years.

I would like to briefly explore the reverse side of this concept of *ve-shinnantam le-vanekha* – the notion that a *Rebbe* is also perceived as a father – with Rav Lichtenstein's contribution and persona as a model to better comprehend and assimilate this concept, as well as to further accentuate his enduring impact.

Notion of Parental Relationship, and Link to the *Shekhina*

Rambam, based on *Bava Metzi'a* 33a, formulates the role of a *Rebbe muvhak* as a parallel to the parental model. He states as follows:

> Just like one is commanded to honor his father and fear him, so too one is obligated to honor and fear his Rabbi more than his father, as his father brings him into this world and his Rabbi brings him into the World to Come. If one sees his father's lost item and his Rabbis' lost item, his Rabbi's lost item takes precedence. If his father and Rabbi are carrying a load, he first assists his Rabbi and then his father. If his father and Rabbi are taken captive, first he redeems his Rabbi and then he redeems his father. (Rambam *Hilkhot Talmud Torah* 5:1)

It is significant that he does this in a substantive halakhic context that even assesses the normative consequences of a competition between the two "fathers." While we are familiar with the more fathomable direction of this paradigm, the *Rebbe*'s core obligation and posture toward his *talmidim* rooted in *ve-shinnantam le-vanekha*, that is invoked by Rambam at the very onset of *Hilkhot Talmud Torah* (1:2) as the foundation of national Torah education, the notion that a non-biological *Rebbe*, even an impactful one, is a "father" requires clarification, at least reflection! After all, many of the salient characteristics of the parental contribution that triggers an ambitious, demanding *kibbud av* appear to be blatantly absent: the biological DNA (and implications for impact of nature), the fact that parents partner with God in their child's creation – "*shelosha shuttafin ba-adam*" (*Kiddushin* 30b) etc. Even the nurture factor in the parental dynamic seems largely inapplicable to a spiritual-educational mentor, calling into question the competitive supremacy of the *Rebbe* over that of the biological father. How can one compare the impact of literal childrearing – the investment of quantitative time, the influence exerted in all the formative phases of childhood growth, the consistent and constant sharing of experiences and molding of values and persona that typifies that relationship – with the bond between a *talmid* and *Rebbe*? The *Rebbe* model in comparison seems much attenuated. Yet, the *halakha* is not given to hyperbole.

Moreover, Rambam seems to compound the problem by significantly expanding this already difficult *halakha*, integrating it with other unrelated *Gemarot* that equate a *Rebbe muvhak* with the *Shekhina* itself! He states:

> There is no greater honor than the honor of a Rabbi, and [no greater] fear than the fear of a Rabbi. Our Sages said, "[let] the fear of your Rabbi be like the fear of Heaven." Therefore, they said that one who disagrees with his Rabbi is like disagreeing with the *Shekhina*… and one who fights with his Rabbi is like fighting with the *Shekhina*… and one who gets angry at his Rabbi is like getting angry at God… and one who doubts his Rabbi is like doubting the *Shekhina*… (Rambam ibid.)

It is noteworthy that the link between the two sections in Rambam's ambitious formulation is introduced with the word "*lefikhakh* (therefore)" – a tacit admission of novelty, but with a claim of justified logic!

Rambam in *Sefer Ha-Mitzvot* (positive 209) extends and reinforces these themes by noting that independent *mitzvot* establishing *kevod* and *yirat rabbo* in the *minyan taryag* are redundant because of the compelling character of these equations and considerations! We are left to ponder the complex character of this model that integrates parenthood and Divinity. Moreover, how can the philosophically purist Rambam (see *Hilkhot Yesodei Ha-Torah* ch. 1, *Hilkhot Teshuva* ch. 3, *Hilkhot Avoda Zara* ch. 2) theologically justify the link between a human *Rebbe muvhak* and the Divine presence of the *Shekhina*?[2]

It is also extremely telling that this link to the *Shekhina* is limited to *rabbo ha-muvhak* and therefore evidently radiates from the relationship between *Rebbe* and *talmid*, rather than the status or stature per se of the *talmid chakham*!

---

2. See also *Perisha* (YD 242:1). He argues that *kevod rabbo* is inseparably linked with *kevod Shamayim*.

I believe, however, that the explanation of these phenomena is very basic. My understanding of these concepts has been immeasurably enhanced by my own experience as a *talmid* of *Moreinu* HaRav Lichtenstein *zt"l*.

Dimensions of the Parental and *Shekhina* Relationship

A special *Rebbe muvhak* is, indeed, one whose contribution and impact justifies the parental mold and paradigm, albeit paving a course for life in the World to Come. This is true on the most basic level, as he transmits the *mesora* – substantive and methodological – of *devar Hashem*, the foundation of quality of life – "*ki heim chayyeinu ve-orekh yameinu*." In this sense, he, too, is a *shuttaf*-creator who shapes personalities and destinies. Moreover, his approach is not limited to conveying information; his mode and approach to teaching and mentoring is designed to impact his *talmidim*'s fundamental values, commitment, and the charting of their own course in Torah life. He must not only teach the content of *devar Hashem*; he must also communicate, especially by unself-conscious example and personal posture, the axiological import and defining role of *devar Hashem* in life, often most effectively through osmosis. In this capacity, he also serves as a halakhic authority and hashkafic guide in navigating Torah life, especially in complex times, challenging circumstances, or innovative situations. *Moreinu* HaRav Lichtenstein *zt"l* magnificently embodied these functions.

We were blessed that our *Rebbe*'s Torah was unusually comprehensive and broad. Rav Lichtenstein taught all *sedarim* and all topics. He taught the big *kelalim* and arcane or pragmatic *peratim*. And he taught them all rigorously and suffused with *yira* and exuberance. His range was astonishing. It was not until I left Yeshivat Har Etzion that I realized this was not the norm. And he taught all topics as topics from a *Shas* perspective. I refer not only to the parallel *sugyot*, but to the themes and motifs his personal mastery and unique perspective linked them to, as well. The image of our *Rebbe* dragging his *Shas* to each *shi'ur*, and effortlessly integrating its presence into the themes, is indelibly etched in all our memories. We used to joke that it gave new meaning to "*ashrei ish she-ba le-khan ve-talmudo be-yado!*" Again, it was not until some years later that it dawned on me that this was not routine or typical for all *maggidei shi'ur*; not the mastery, and certainly not the capacity and will to integrate and provide unique perspective. Topics were analyzed comprehensively, and rigorously, as well. The range of *rishonim*, parallel *sugyot*, and even specialty or exotic *rishonim* – Ittur, Ra'avya, Manhig, ge'onim – was part of this comprehensive aspiration to master the entire Torah, to be immersed in *devar Hashem* and the values and spiritual connection to God that they provided.

This greater *hekef*, scope, was not primarily quantitative. The capacity to project a larger landscape for the topic, and to structure the issues, and their interrelationships, as well as to juxtapose positions to illuminate one another, turned quantitative, mastery *hekef* into qualitative depth. By changing the background and landscape you sometimes alter the substance! His recently reprinted articles on *hefker*, *li-shmah* and others exemplify this *hekef*, and its comprehensive-innovative contribution, as did typical *shi'urim*. I began my own tenure as a *talmid* experiencing a masterful assessment of the massive and complex theme of "*ein adam makneh davar she-lo ba la-olam*," but that unforgettable initial exposure could easily have been interchanged with almost any other beginning point. This comprehensive approach and mode of presentation, grounded in mastery and toil, produced *chiddush*-innovation and insight.

His comprehensiveness and rigor in Torah and *halakha* – classically and narrowly defined – was applied equally to his hashkafic *sichot*, and to his integration of Torah and western civilization, as well. Moreover, Rav Lichtenstein eschewed compartmentalization. His approach was seamlessly holistic in his Torah, and in his *Torah ve-chokhma*.[3] One could fathom from Rav Lichtenstein's *lomdut*, *hashkafa* and persona why the Torah was necessarily both "*chatuma nittena*," as well as "*megilla megilla nittena*" (see *Gittin* 60a). Our *Rebbe's* persona and approach illuminated why Rambam (based on *Yerushalmi Chagiga*) insisted that to render decisions in any specialty of *halakha*, one had to be comprehensibly knowledgeable in

---

3. I believe that the combination of these particular central characteristics has important implications for evaluating Rav Lichtenstein's contribution to *brisker lomdut* generally, and particularly for assessing his halakhic and intellectual portrait vis-à-vis that of his *Rebbe muvhak*, the Rav *zt"l*, but this is not the forum for that discussion.

all areas of Torah (*Hilkhot Sanhedrin* 4:8), a walking *Sefer Torah* who is defined by, but also transcends, the sum of its parts (based upon the image of *Makkot* 22b).

Rav Lichtenstein's methodological focus was also innovative. His approach was a priori-mapping out the topic and the likely interrelationships in anticipation of the actual material and diverse views. This had both a methodological purpose, and probably also reflected his intellectual orientation and style, but also his Torah comprehensiveness: to be attuned to all potential insights. His relentless analytical mode of examining possibilities, and stripping them down to isolated assumptions in an effort to more accurately pin down their essential character (*"ofyam ve-tivam ha-yesodi"*), and his openness to multiple tracks (*"maslulim"*) within in a single topic or theme, reflected comprehensiveness, exuberance and entailed, I believe, a hashkafic motif about the range of *"eilu ve-eilu divrei Elokim chayyim"* (*Eiruvin* 13b) and the breadth of halakhic themes that requires further elaboration.

His striking methodological focus, including the a priori component, certainly came, obviously intentionally, at the expense of a more dramatically appealing style of presentation. Typically, this might consist of a question-heavy or problem-identifying introduction, closely followed by an exploration and rejection of tantalizing solutions, climaxing with a punch-line *mehalekh* that solves initial queries and resolves a host of issues in one fell swoop. Certainly, Rav Lichtenstein's ambitious objective to present the full range of halakhic discourse on a topic, rather than merely to resolve particular difficulties or challenging positions, precluded this classical formula. But I presume that a fundamental educational orientation was particularly reflected in these issues of style and presentation. The heavy methodological concentration stemmed from our *Rebbe's Torat chesed*, as it facilitated and invested in the future growth of *talmidim* by providing them with mechanisms to progress independently. Moreover, it contributed to cultivating an additional dimension of independence, that of personal initiative and *chiddush*. Rav Lichtenstein believed passionately in *"ha'amidu talmidim harbeh* (raise many students)" (*Avot* 1:1) and in the theme of "she-tehei ha-shalhevet ola mei-eleha (the flame should rise on its own)" (Rashi *Bamidbar* 8:2), in the sense of providing the tools for students to find their own voice and niche. In any case, the structural and methodological component was a true hallmark of his *shi'urim* and lectures. It manifested itself in a certain style of presentation and analysis, but it particularly also cultivated a *derekh ha-chashiva*, a halakhic and hashkafic mode of thinking that had broader aspirational implications.

The *chibbat ha-Torah* was singular as well. The meticulous preparation and organization of each presentation – the *amal* and *yegi'a* that were inscribed on his very visage, the mental energy expended in the rigorous analysis [and of all possibilities] – left no doubt that *ki heim chayyeinu*, that nothing was more important or inspiring, a powerful lesson that never needed additional articulation. The expanded canon of the topic, including the singular use of exotic *rishonim* in the pre-computer database era, cited earlier, was ringing testimonial to "*shoteh be-tzama et divreihem*" (*Avot* 1:4), especially as understood by Rabbeinu Yona and Rav Chayyim Mi-Volozhin (*Ru'ach Ha-Chayyim*) (ibid.) as an unquenchable thirst that merely whets the appetite for more. It is surely no coincidence that *Moreinu HaRav Lichtenstein zt"l* often invoked and was strongly drawn to Rambam's (*Sefer Ha-Mitzvot* positive 3) compelling depiction of Avraham *Avinu* as the paradigm of an *oheiv Hashem*, one whose infectious enthusiasm and exuberance to share Torah with others derived from an overflow of his own intoxication with God and His Torah.

His singular capacity and willingness to engage broader themes and challenges – classical issues, and, of course, the interface between modernity and Torah – in an effort to expand the arena and impact of *avodat Hashem*, driven by the faith in Torah's relevance and "*hafokh bah de-khulah bah*," the conviction that one could, with *hatmada* and depth, adduce these perspectives in the classical canon, distinguished him in our generation even among other *chakhmei mesora*. His integrative and holistic approach to these topics was a model of sophistication that was animated and suffused by the basic values of *yira* and *emuna*. His moral clarity and ethical sensitivity manifested unequivocally in these complex subjects and set a standard for the Torah world.

But, as we experienced with our *Rebbe*, the parental model of *Rebbe muvhak* also presupposes transformative impact on religious sensibilities and the cultivation of a clear spiritual orientation that cannot be limited to specific content, methodology, *chibbat ha-Torah*, or even broader *hashkafa* alone. One must also transmit and convey the transcendence of *devar Hashem* – both as content, and as a framework for spiritual odyssey. It is crucial that learning Torah also engender a religious experience in its varied meanings – Ramban's notions of *devar Hashem* as "*Sheimot shel Ha-Kadosh Barukh Hu*."[4] It is in this respect that the *Rebbe-talmid* bond particularly forges a new identity and reality. The *Gemara*'s (*Kiddushin* 30b) rousing depiction of the emotional rollercoaster associated with the *milchamtah shel Torah* that is so central to that relationship – the stakes and emotional vacillations ("*oyevim... ohavim*") – captures this motif. "*Va-yeilekhu sheneihem yachdav*" of the *akeida* (*Bereishit* 22:6,8) refers also to the journey of *Rebbe* and *talmid*, the voyage through the peaks and valleys of *devar Hashem*. The moments of specific and broader breakthroughs in *talmud Torah* and *avodat Hashem*, insights, illuminations, and consequential interactions with the *Rebbe*, can and should be as formative and memorable as parental-child milestones. Shared vision and the conviction of common destiny redefine relationships in parental terms and forge personalities. I venture to speculate that every one of Rav Lichtenstein's *talmidim* has their own vivid memories, experiences, and milestones that fit this parental model and pattern.

Furthermore, like a biological parent, the trust and faith one has in a spiritual mentor, a *Rebbe muvhak*, is a cornerstone of stability and a foundation for basic values and beliefs. Rav Lichtenstein noted often that faith and other Torah values under pressure can be bolstered significantly by the trust we cultivate in those who have abundant faith and greater insight. The role of the *ilan gadol* in this issue cannot be overstated. In our community, in our generation, we looked to Rav Lichtenstein to bolster our confidence, to help fortify our own bedrock of faith and values. Our *Rebbe*, (perhaps without his awareness, because of his colossal integrity

---

4. See Ramban's introduction to his Commentary on the Torah, and in *Sefer Ha-Mitzvot shikhechat ha-asin* no. 15: *birkat ha-Torah*, based upon Berakhot 21a.

and intense "*yirato ha-kodemet le-chokhmato*,") notwithstanding and because of both his broadness and openness, has been an inspirational and influential force in this calculus. For this reason, among many others, his passing leaves not only a hole, but a sense of uncertainty, even instability.

There is a further, final dimension as well. The interaction of *Rebbe* and *talmid* provides a framework and relationship that facilitates a critical spiritual objective-telos: the feeling and link to transcendence. *Talmidim* of Rav Lichtenstein felt that they were in the presence of a *gadol be-Yisrael*. Despite and especially because of his *tzeni'ut*, modesty, and unself-consciousness, there radiated a certain special quality of greatness, inchoate, ineffable, numinous. But it was something more. You felt – intuited as a deep conviction – that you were in the presence of someone who himself was, with all of his humanity, empathy, and lack of pretension, and even disdain for special treatment, ubiquitously "*lifnei Hashem*" as a constant and consistent *oved Hashem*. By extension, being *lifnei* a "*lifnei Hashem*" conveys and concretizes spiritual greatness and even transcendence, and its accessibility.

This is the principle of "*Rebbe muvhak ka-Shekhina*." Indeed, it is the foundation of the mitzva of "*u-vo tidbak/u-ldovka vo*," especially as expanded by Rambam in *Sefer Ha-Mitzvot* (positive 6), beyond his formulation in *Hilkhot Dei'ot* (6:2).

There is nothing mystical about this touch of transcendence. Certainly, Judaism emphatically rejects vicarious spirituality. But the role of special *chakhmei mesora*, and particularly the institution of *Rebbe muvhak*, plays a vital role in Judaism. It is a cornerstone in *avodat Hashem*. It does not substitute for the individual attainment-aspiration of "*lifnei Hashem*," but concretizes it and inspires it and also allows for different manifestations of this elusive but crucial motif of *kedusha*.

This notion, and even the actual identification with "'*et Hashem Elokekha tira*' – *lerabbot talmidei chakhamim*,"[5] poses no challenge to theological purity, but is a recognition of the process that concretizes a powerful bond with the Divine, and allows for constructive transference in the subtle, elusive quest for transcendence and spirituality.

---

5. See, especially, *Perisha* on *Tur* (YD 242:1), cited earlier.

Let us return briefly to the difficulties in Rambam's formulation, cited previously, including the transitionary word "*lefikhakh*." If it is possible to engender a parental-type relationship through *talmud Torah* and *avodat Hashem* despite the formidable differences between spiritual and biological relationships, it is only due to the existential bond generated by *devar Hashem*, the experience of *talmud Torah* mediated by the profound multidimensional way that *Rebbe muvhak* impacts his *talmidim*. This linchpin perspective is predicated on, and the basis for, the link to the *Shekhina*. Thus, Rambam's precise portrayal that the *Rebbe*'s status as a 'father" presupposes and further reinforces his special stature as a link and paradigm to the *Shekhina*.

Indeed, in light of our analysis, "*mevi'o le-Olam Ha-ba*" here may have broader spiritual and transcendent meaning as well, as Rambam[6] seems to indicate. The reference is not merely to ultimate reward in the afterlife, but to an appreciation of transcendence itself, in this world! Indeed, our *Rebbe* gave us some glimpse of greatness and transcendence – *Olam Ha-ba* – in this world, especially as his personal style and halakhic orientation was one which sought to elevate this-worldly life. We were able to witness and participate, if only peripherally, in his journey of "*lifnei Hashem*." In the process, this enabled us, his *talmidim*, to begin to chart our own path.

The feeling of being diminished reflects precisely that beyond the ache of physical and even irrevocable loss, there is a palpable sense of being less connected with greatness and especially transcendence, modeled by and sometimes accessed through the *Rebbe muvhak*. There is, however, a dimension of *nechama*, comfort, as well. While the loss of a great man and mentor is most painful, his unforgettable persona, values and *hashkafat olam* are enduring.

Fortunate are we that we were blessed with a *Rebbe* "*she-hevi'anu le-Olam Ha-ba be-Olam Ha-zeh*," who brought us into the World to Come in this world, and whose continued impact – through his Torah, *hashkafa* and persona – will continue to flourish.

---

6. *Sefer Ha-Mitzvot*, cited earlier; also see *Ru'ach Ha-Chayyim* on *Avot*.

HaRav Aharon Lichtenstein *zt"l*: A *Talmid*'s Remembrance

Remarks of Terry Novetsky at Etzion Foundation/Yeshivat Har Etzion Dinner 6 Nisan 5776/April 14, 2016

The *Gemara* (*Berakhot* 42b-43a) describes a group of *amora'im* returning from Rav's funeral. A complex issue of *zimmun* arises for which they are uncertain of the *halakha*. Without clear resolution, Rav Adda bar Ahava tears *keriya* a second time and cries out: "Rav is gone, and we have not yet completed the *halakhot* of the Grace after Meals."

On one level, of course, Rav Adda bar Ahava's statement is dramatic hyperbole – the *zimmun* issue, while complex, was a relatively minor matter and undoubtedly, these *amora'im* knew how to *bentcsh*. Yet, on another level that reflects the true measure of this *Gemara*, Rav Adda bar Ahava's outburst reflects an emotional state that we here tonight all relate to – of a *talmid* distressed at the loss of his *Rebbe*. It was not this particular *halakha* that we don't know, it's that our foundation for understanding all *halakha* has been unmoored, our touchstone snatched from our grasp. Rav Aharon is gone, and we are so challenged, the wellspring of his Torah sealed off forever, our model for *middot* and *emuna* missing, our confidence that ignorance and intolerance will surely be vanquished by the overwhelming force of his *ahavat Yisrael* and intellectual rigor shaken – we are so lost, we are so forlorn, *ki-veyakhol*, we no longer know even how to *bentsch*.

When Yoel Weiss asked me to speak this evening, I quickly pointed out that I was not among Rav Lichtenstein's many notable and great *talmidim*, just one of literally thousands of loyal *talmidim*. Yet I reluctantly accepted this opportunity to express my deep, abiding and continuing sense of gratitude for my 35-year relationship with Rav Lichtenstein.

In his essay, "On the Teacher," Augustine writes:

> Those who are pupils consider within themselves whether what has been explained has been said truly; looking of course to that interior truth, according to the measure of which each of us is able. Thus they learn, and when the interior truth makes known to them that true things have been said, they applaud...

Let us consider this statement in its constituent parts:

First, Augustine's student is bound by an obligation to "consider within themselves." He is not a mere receptacle of information from the teacher.

We brash Americans, especially those of us who had already started university, were raised in an educational model that celebrated our brilliance and talents, extolled our privileges and took seriously the obligation of the institution to engage us. From our first day, Rav Lichtenstein set forth a profoundly different educational model. The opportunities for growth in Torah in *Yeshiva* were unparalleled, but the duties and obligations of development were squarely on our shoulders. Let there be no mistake: our success as students was dependent on accepting those responsibilities.

Secondly, Augustine argued that students must consider "whether what has been explained has been explained truly, looking to that interior truth."

Here too Rav Lichtenstein emphasized our duty and obligation to examine the possibilities of the material – to critically analyze and to not presume knowledge. Volume – while important – was something we could accomplish on our own time. Learning required rigor, in order to arrive at what Augustine termed the "interior truth."

But Rav Lichtenstein also made clear that we were not chemists being taught to cleverly mix and manipulate complex terms – we were *ovdei Hashem* searching for understanding in text laden with *kedusha*. We should rejoice – "applaud" in the words of Augustine – at the recognition of profundity, the identification of coherence and even the creation of *chiddush*, but the entire endeavor was bound by our eternal obligation to Torah itself, the fear of its misrepresentation, the admonition against its perversion, the revulsion to the simplistic – the trivialization of Torah, or even worse, learning laden with agenda.

I mention these three themes at the outset:
- Our duties and responsibilities to Torah and Am Yisrael
- Our recognition of the complexity of Torah and humanity itself
- Our duty to respect the *kedusha* of Torah in its full complexity and the concomitant rejection of simplistic, agenda-laden learning

because these lodestars for a religious life became relevant to us, for the most part, only as adults, as we first were confronted with the challenges of finding a spouse, raising children, building a career, continuing to engage in Torah and of course, dealing with our own, and others', inherent flaws and shortcomings as human beings.

This, perhaps, is the essential point in my remarks tonight. We have all encountered religious leaders who possessed great charisma; but as I grew older, they and their views became progressively less relevant – and, in many cases, quite troubling. Rav Lichtenstein was hardly charismatic, and certainly did not offer me any direct advice as to what I must do. But, as I grew older – perhaps only as I grew older – his nuanced human and religious outlook first came into focus, becoming only more relevant and more meaningful.

Dr. Tovah Lichtenstein noted in her presentation at the *sheloshim* that Rav Lichtenstein may have had more influence on Americans from Israel than were he to have stayed at YU. It is a fascinating thought, one that is certainly true when applied to me personally, but I wish to add one essential fact to that claim: it didn't happen by coincidence.

Here we are at the Dinner – and of course every *yeshiva* and *midrasha* has a *shabbaton* and Dinner – not so thirty-five years ago. Rav Lichtenstein came to America at least twice yearly, and in large part to meet with *talmidim*. When he was home, he told us to call – after 11:00 at night in

Israel, so we could reach him immediately. If he remained relevant, it was – as with almost everything in his life – the result of his conscientious and volitional effort.

This was particularly true for me with respect to the gracious access he afforded me in three arenas. The first was family matters – my parents, my children, my nephew – for which I will not detail here other than to note that many of us share an abiding appreciation for his compassion and empathy in this area specifically.

The second area involved women's *chinnukh*. Just over twenty years ago when a number of parents were not satisfied with high school options for their daughters, I was fortunate enough to arrange for Rav Lichtenstein to meet with a parent group on several occasions. Much of which he said is reflected in his iconic speech at the *chanukkat ha-bayit* of Ma'ayanot, but I wish to highlight one essential point.

Rav Lichtenstein's view was that we should not teach our daughters as a defensive measure; rather we should teach our daughters out of respect: for their religious standing, their intellect, their equal status as *ovdei Hashem*. Our curriculum should reflect that respect, and that meant serious *Gemara* learning. That sounds simple – the standard at Migdal Oz and generally in all high schools – but twenty years ago this was hardly a consensus view.

When I was president of a shul, I had the opportunity to hire Shayna Goldberg as the first *yo'etzet* in Teaneck. First, I called Rav Aharon. As a person who was defined by his measured response to nearly everything, he was positively effusive in his praise of Shayna, her intellect, mastery of material, and humility. When I asked about communal reticence, he assured me that bringing Shayna would result only in greater *shemirat ha-mitzvot*, and encouraged me without hesitation.

I had the privilege of handling a number of legal matters for the Lichtensteins. One day, my loyal and dedicated secretary, Flora Matarazzo, came into my office to tell me that my friend, that very nice man from Israel, Aaron, had called. I told Flora that he was not my friend and to please refer to him in the future as Rabbi Lichtenstein. Flora then asked why I always stood at my desk when he called? I had never noticed.

HaRav Aharon Lichtenstein zt"l: A *Talmid*'s Remembrance | 105

I stood because, like most *talmidim*, I loved and also feared Rav Lichtenstein. I've spent some time considering what it was about this kind man who never threatened a fly that inspired fear. Ultimately, I realize that it was not him I feared, but my own recognition of unmet personal expectations that Rav Aharon's very presence caused me to confront.

We were a brilliant group of students – truly brilliant minds – but each of us acknowledged the obvious: that we did not approach his almost other-worldly brilliance. Our intellect made us arrogant, he was humble; we used our gifts as an excuse for sloth, he knew everything and yet remained an incredible *masmid*; we claimed difficulty in davening, he, without recognizable sin, cried out to God with perfect faith.

He never asked of us anything more than to accept our duties and responsibilities as o*vdei Hashem* with integrity, and with Rav Aharon in the front of the *beit midrash*, our aspirations and objectives were clearly established, our unworthiness overt and laid bare.

The Torah informs us (*Bamidbar* 20:29): "And when all the Congregation saw that Aharon had perished, they mourned for Aharon thirty days, the entire House of Israel." Rashi comments (s.v. *va-yiru*):

> When they saw Moshe and Elazar descend, and Aharon did not descend, they inquired, "Where is Aharon?" He responded, "Deceased." They said: "Can it be that one who confronted the Angel [of Death] and stopped a plague has himself succumbed to the Angel of Death?"

Can it be? Can it truly be?

"*Lo Tevashel Gedi*": The Thrice-Banned Mixture

Rabbi Yitzchak Etshalom

The phrase "*lo tevashel gedi ba-chaleiv immo* (do not seethe/boil/cook a kid in its mother's milk)" appears in three of the Torah's law collections, as presented below. In each case, it is presented as the final law in a series, apparently operating as a culmination to the particular code. Over the millennia, exegetes since Philo have struggled with one or more of these issues relating to the prohibition:

1. Why is the prohibition repeated thrice?
2. Why is the prohibition – understood to encompass far more than cooking a young goat in its *own* mother's milk – worded in this unusual fashion?
3. What is the impetus behind the prohibition at all?

The first issue – repetition – was the focus of the *tanna'im*, and the *midreshei halakha* have various explanations for it, several of which will be presented below.

The second issue is a matter of *parshanut* and, as shown below, the medieval commentators (as well as modern) address the unusual wording. The third issue falls under the domain of what is known as *ta'amei ha-mitzvot*. The literature of *ta'amei ha-mitzvot*, which properly begins in pre-millennial Alexandria, evolved into a popular avenue of Rabbinic literature in the Middle Ages – and nearly everyone who engaged in the search for "meaning" in *mitzvot* addressed the prohibition of *basar be-chalav*, some of them also addressing the unusual wording. We will survey a number of these exegetes and their explanations.

The Texts

At the foot of Mount Sinai, we were given a law code which makes up the bulk of *Parashat Mishpatim* (*Shemot* 21-24). The final section of it (ibid. 22:24-23:19) may be summarized as follows:

> 24: The prohibition of lending with interest
> 25-26: The obligation to return a pledge to a borrower by sundown (each day)
> 27: The prohibition of cursing leaders
> 28-29: The obligation bringing first fruits and first-born in a timely fashion
> 30: The prohibition against eating a *tereifa*
> 1: The prohibition against enabling false testimony
> 2: The prohibition against following the "many" to do evil or to enable a perversion of justice
> 3: The prohibition against the judge favoring the poor man
> 4-5: The obligation to help a fellow's animal with its burden
> 6: The prohibition against perverting the case against the poor
> 7: Warning against falsehood in court and against executing innocent people
> 8: The prohibition against a judge taking a bribe
> 9: The prohibition against oppressing a stranger
> 10-11: *Shemitta* and the allowance for the poor to eat from one's field
> 12: *Shabbat* and the allowance for the disenfranchised to rest
> 13: The prohibition against using names of foreign gods
> 14-17: The thrice-yearly pilgrimage festivals
> 18: The prohibitions against slaughtering the Pesach offering while owning *chametz* and against leaving the offering overnight (*lina*)
> 19: The obligation to bring first fruits – and our prohibition: "*lo tevashel gedi ba-chaleiv immo*"

Note that the thrust of this passage is aimed at the courts and the judiciary. A sub-text of this passage, it may be argued, is fair treatment under the law. The section begins with a warning, accompanied by an imprecation, against charging interest to the "poor among you." The passage continues in this vein, warning against favoring one class over another in court and enforcing the "good Samaritan" law to help even those with whom our relationship is rocky. Although a number of the laws in this section focus on the agricultural cycle and the related pilgrimage festivals, even those are punctuated with an argument for social justice and class equity. The law of *shemitta* is intended so that "the poor among you may eat." *Shabbat* is presented as a day of rest so that "the son of your handmaid, and the stranger, may be refreshed." (This theme is picked up again in Moshe's re-presentation of the Decalogue in *Devarim*.) It is within the broader framework of societal concerns and equal treatment that the first instance of the prohibition of *basar be-chalav* is introduced.[1]

That covenant, however, was broken (and evidently rendered null) almost immediately as a result of the episode involving the *eigel ha-zahav*. As a result of that grievous sin, God wanted to destroy the people and reestablish a new nation with Moshe alone; Moshe's pleas on the behalf of the people minimized the punishment and led to the great moment of God's announcement of His compassionate attributes – the thirteen *middot ha-rachamim*. In the aftermath of that forgiveness, a new covenant had to be formed. This is the thrust of that passage (*Shemot* 34:10-26):

10-11: Introduction of the (new) covenant and the promise to drive out the pagan nations of *Kena'an*

12: The prohibition against making a covenant with the residents of the Land

13: The command to destroy their worship sites

14-17: Warning against intermarriage and the inevitable idolatry that would follow

---

1. Although the "law code" includes ritual laws as well, the overwhelming thrust of the laws leading up to our prohibition are societally-oriented. As developed in *Devarim*, even the pilgrimage festivals have a strong societal base, including the widow, orphan, stranger and Levi in the celebration.

18: The command to keep the festival of *matzot*

19-20: The requirement to bring the first-born to God

21: *Shabbat*

22-23: The pilgrimage festivals

24: God's promise that the Land will be secure when they make their pilgrimage

25: The prohibition against offering up the Pesach while owning *chametz* or leaving it over (*notar*)

26: The command to bring first fruits to God – and the prohibition of "*lo tevashel gedi ba-chaleiv immo*"

Unlike the original covenant, the focal point and underlying emphasis here seems to be on idolatry and all manner of avoiding it. This change is easily understood, considering that the event that necessitated a new covenant was the people's involvement with foreign worship.[2] In lieu of an inward focus regarding the treatment of the potentially disenfranchised of society, the setting of this presentation of the pilgrimage festivals and related laws is *avoda zara*:

> But you shall break down their altars, and dash their pillars into pieces, and you shall cut down their *asherim*. For you shall bow down to no other god… you shall make you no molten gods. **You shall keep the festival of** *matzot*… (*Shemot* 34:13-18)

It is within the context of idolatry that the law code culminates with our prohibition: *lo tevashel gedi ba-chaleiv immo*.

In Moshe's (re-)presentation of the law code, which comprises the bulk of *Sefer Devarim*, he introduces a new section with a heretofore unheard statement, "*banim atem la-Shem Elokeikhem* (you are the children of the Lord your God)," and follows this with another new(ish) phrase, albeit one that echoes a theme in *Vayikra* (and one that he had already introduced

---

2. Whether the *eigel ha-zahav* was an actual instance of idolatry or not is subject to much discussion; that dispute is moot here, as in any case the *eigel* was foreign and explicitly prohibited worship.

earlier in his speech) – "*am kadosh ata la-Shem Elokekha* (you are a holy nation unto the Lord your God)." This theme of "*am kadosh*" bookends a section relating to forbidden foods which culminates with our prohibition:

> You are the children of the Lord your God. You shall not cut yourselves, nor make any baldness between your eyes for the dead. **For you are a holy people unto the Lord your God**, and God has chosen you to be His own treasure out of all peoples that are upon the face of the earth… (vv. 3-20 detail the forbidden foods…) You shall not eat of anything that dies of itself; you may give it unto the stranger that is within your gates, that he may eat it; or you may sell it unto a foreigner; **for you are a holy people unto the Lord your God**; *lo tevashel gedi ba-chaleiv immo*. (*Devarim* 14:1-21)

This is the not the first time that we hear about specific **prohibitions** applying outside of the *mishkan* context framed as *kedusha*.[3] However, this passage takes the notion of "national sanctity" beyond even where *Vayikra* 19 went. In that case, there is an opening "anthemic" statement of "*kedoshim tihyu*," but that phrase isn't repeated throughout nor given as an explanation for any of the *mitzvot* or prohibitions. Here, national sanctity is presented as a *reason* for not cutting oneself etc. The abstention from certain idolatrous practices – such as cutting oneself as an act of mourning – and forbidden foods is an expression of being a "holy nation unto the Lord your God." This is the setting for the final mention of our prohibition – *lo tevashel gedi ba-chaleiv immo*.

---

3. The list of these prohibited foods (and others) in *Vayikra* 11 is set against the backdrop of the *mishkan* and the impurity that contact with these animals generates. The series of laws presented in *Vayikra* 19 with the heading (and repeated refrain) of "*kedoshim tihyu*" do not point to specific prohibitions as expressions of that sanctity; rather, they make up a societal and family code that reflects our mirroring God's *kedusha* – "*Kedoshim tihyu – ki kadosh Ani Hashem…*"

The *Midreshei Halakha*

As mentioned above, the focus of tannaitic literature, predictably, is on the three-fold mention, using the exact same words, of the prohibition. There are numerous suggestions made in the *midreshei halakha*, some quoted in the *Gemara*; we will cite a selection:

1) Rabbi Akiva (*Mishna Chullin* 8:4) interprets the three-fold mention as coming to *exclude* certain classes of animals from the prohibition – including poultry, non-kosher animals and undomesticated animals (*chayya*) e.g. venison.

2) Rabbi Shimon ben Elazar (*Mekhilta Mishpatim, Masekhta De-Kaspa parasha* 2) explains that the three mentions are intended to *include* the flock, the herd and – at odds with Rabbi Akiva (above) – the *chayya* in the classification of "meat" that may not be cooked with milk.

3) Rabbi Shimon bar Yochai (ibid.) maintains that the three-fold mention is intended to include a prohibition against cooking, a prohibition against eating and a further prohibition of any benefit. This is the most well-known interpretation and application, as it also appears in the *Talmud Bavli* (*Chullin* 115b) in the name of the school of Rabbi Yishma'el. (Note that the *mekhilta* on *Shemot* is assumed to be composed in that school.) This same *derasha* appears in the *Talmud Yerushalmi* (*Avoda Zara* 5:1) without attribution. In addition, Rashi quotes it in the first mention in *Shemot* (23:19) as well as in his commentary to *Devarim* (14:26). It is significant to note that while the prohibition of *hana'a* is assumed by the *mishna* (*Chullin* 8:4), the *Gemara* (ad loc. 114b-116a) suggests numerous sources for this extension (although the dissent of Rabbi Shimon as quoted by Rabbi Shimon ben Yehuda is noted in *Chullin* 116a)[4], only one of which is the repetition of our verse.

4) An unattributed statement in the *Sifrei* on *Devarim* (*Re'eh parasha* 104) gives yet another explanation – the three-fold mention of the

---

4. This is clearly at odds with the tradition in Rabbi Shimon bar Yochai's name, quoted above from the *mekhilta*, which identifies the *issur hana'a* as stemming from the three-fold mention of our verse.

issur corresponds to the three covenants signed by Am Yisrael – at *Chorev* (Sinai), at *Arvot Mo'av* and at *Gerizim/Eival*. This last one is most curious as it does not use the repetition for halakhic application; rather, it identifies each one as associated with a different occasion of historic covenanting with God.

The *Rishonim* and *Ta'amei Ha-Mitzvot*

Even though, as mentioned above, the earliest scholar to suggest a reason for the prohibition is Philo of Alexandria, we will focus our survey of this area on the era of the *rishonim*. Not surprisingly, Philo's explanation is echoed over a thousand years later. It is helpful to note that commentators who suggest explanations for the *issur* itself inevitably address the unusual phrasing as well.

There are three general approaches, with specific and diverse nuance to each, raised by the *rishonim*.

Approach 1: *Avoda Zara*

Rambam (*Moreh Ha-Nevukhim* 3:48) makes an unusual proposal. After having stated that his discovery of the book of the Sabeans which contained a description of their idolatrous practices and beliefs helped explain numerous laws in the Torah (including cross-dressing and *sha'atnez*), he cautiously suggests: "…it is not unthinkable that it has the 'scent' of idolatry; perhaps this [cooking a kid in its mother's milk] was what they would do as part of their worship or on one of their holidays." Rav Ovadya Seforno adopts this approach and presents it without hesitation in his commentary to *Shemot* 23:19: "Do not do these sorts of things in order to increase your yield, as is the belief of the practitioners of idolatry, rather 'bring the first fruit of your land…'" Seforno not only focuses on the specific ceremonial aspect of cooking a kid in its mother's milk – thus explaining the wording – but also addresses the associated affirmative practice of bringing *bikkurim* and why the two are presented together.

Parenthetic note: In 1929, a tablet was found at Ugarit, a well-known cultic center in the second millennium BCE. The tablet is called "the birth of the beautiful and pleasant gods." One of the lines was reconstructed as "seethe the goat in milk, the young lamb in cream" and this was hailed as material support for Rambam's explanation. Since then, the reconstruction of the text has been disputed.

Approach 2: Cruelty
By far the most common approach taken among the *rishonim* is that introduced by Ibn Ezra, echoing Philo's take (in *Virtues* 142-144). Ibn Ezra states:

> Perhaps it is because it is cruelty of the heart to cook a kid in its mother's milk – similar to [the prohibition of] "regarding an ox or lamb, you may not slaughter it and its young on the same day." (*Shemot* 23:19)

Again, each of the approaches has a number of variations, and, of course, completely innovative approaches that spread the tent of *parshanut* wider. For instance, Rav Yosef Bekhor Shor (*Shemot* 23:19) suggests that the *meaning* of the prohibition is that we should not allow the goat to be raised with its mother's milk, rather bring it to God immediately – similar to the first fruits – but then he concedes Ibn Ezra's point about compassion as "the truth." Rashbam, as well, adopts an approach of avoiding cruelty as being the root of the prohibition.

Approach 3: Sanctity
Ramban, before adopting a version of Ibn Ezra's reason, argues for a third approach, based on the "*am kadosh ata*" context in *Devarim* 14:

> For it is not a disgusting food (i.e. cooked mixture of milk and meat) but He forbade it as we are sanctified in our eating.

Although Ramban doesn't provide further insight into his associating the prohibition with sanctity, it seems that he sees abstaining from specific foods due to Divine fiat as an expression of our sanctity – which is in line with his broader portrait of the sanctified person in his mini-essay on "*kedoshim tihyu*" (*Vayikra* 19:2).

Although there are other approaches to explaining the prohibition, these three represent the "mainstream" schools of interpretation.

A Necessary Interlude Regarding *Ta'amei Ha-Mitzvot*

Halakhic discourse is distinct from other Rabbinic discussion in many ways; the idioms are different and, quite often, the personalities are different. Perhaps the most germane difference is in the end-goal of the discussion. Whereas halakhic dialogue recognizes that (*Eiruvin* 13b) "these and those are both the words of the living God," ultimately the second half of that epigram must be stated: "and the *halakha* follows Beit Hillel." No matter how much truth, reason and support we may recognize in both – or all – positions, ultimately, the *halakha* must be decided in favor of *chayyav* or *patur*, *tahor* or *tamei*. As such, the rules of *Midrash Halakha* are much more demanding and exacting than those of *Midrash Aggada*; whereas disputants in a halakhic discussion must first disprove their opposite number's arguments before advancing their own, in *Midrash Aggada* (and related literature) each suggestion, explanation or symbolic "take-away" can stand on its own and is neither threatened by – nor threatens – the acceptability of any of the other explanations proffered.

The field of inquiry into the meaning behind the Law – something made somewhat famous by Rabbi Shimon bar Yochai – although anchored in halakhic discussion (and, per Rabbi Shimon, having real halakhic application), generally falls under the rubric of aggadic commentary. As such, there is nothing to keep us from simultaneously accepting the validity – not just in potential – of multiple and varied explanations for the *mitzvot*. Instead of reading each position as independent and exclusive, we might view them all as making up a single, complex picture.

By way of example, the *Midrash Aggada* (*Bereishit Rabba* 22:8), commenting on the "missing words" between Kayin and Hevel,[5] offers

---

5. "Kayin said to Hevel his brother, and it was when they were in the field, Kayin arose over Hevel his brother and slayed him." (*Bereishit* 4:8)

three suggestions as to what was said. The first, unnamed opinion is that they had originally split up the world, Kayin taking the land (he was a farmer) and Hevel the chattel (he was a rancher). Kayin subsequently told Hevel to get off his land – and the fight ensued. Rabbi Yehoshu'a of Sikhnin quotes Rabbi Levi as associating their fight with a specific plot of land – in whose territory would the *mikdash* be built? Rav Huna suggests that they fought over the "extra" twin sister; Kayin and Hevel each married their own twins, but Hevel was a triplet and had two sisters. Hevel wanted to marry her as she was his sister; Kayin claimed her as his due, since he was the *bekhor*.

Unless someone thinks that these *ba'alei aggada* are trying to reconstruct an actual conversation (see Ibn Ezra ad loc. for the *peshat*-take on the "missing words"), we understand that they are using the textual lacuna in this, the story of the first murder, to make a statement and observation about violence and murder. There is no reason to think that they are at odds with each other. The first *darshan* points out that power and money are at the root of violence; the second points to the role of religion; and the third – to the "face that launched a thousand ships" and the impact of sexual desire as a root cause of belligerence. These *ba'alei aggada* are not disputing each other – witness, none of them challenges the other's take – but each is adding another perspective to a larger picture.

I'd like to suggest, by way of analogy, that this phenomenon may exist in the multi-millennial search for *ta'amei ha-mitzvot* – that multiple meanings and explanations may exist side-by-side and each reflect a unique perspective, lesson and purpose of the mitzva or, in our case, *issur*.

Back to the Repetition

As mentioned above, the *Sifrei* provides an alternate explanation for the repetition of the *issur* – that each mention corresponds with one of the three covenants which Am Yisrael made with God.

The *brit* at Sinai was prefaced with the invitation, that if we accept the covenant, we will become a "*mamlekhet kohanim ve-goy kadosh* (Shemot 19:6)." The experience at Sinai was intended to inaugurate us into a life of sanctity – indeed, the three-day waiting period is commanded in those terms: "*ve-kiddashtam ha-yom u-machar.*"

The *brit* at *Arvot Mo'av* was occasioned because of two things – neither of which gives us any bragging rights. The first was that it was an entirely new generation entering the Land, this due to the terrible reaction of the first generation to the report of the scouts and the mitigated Divine decree that that generation would have to die out in the desert and that their children would enter the Land. The second sin which may have occasioned the need for another covenant was the large-scale involvement of the people in *Pe'or*-worship while encamped in the plains of *Mo'av* – before that covenant was initiated by Moshe. This grievous sin is mentioned in Moshe's speech and seems to stand in the "dark background" of the stand at *Mo'av* – indeed, Pinchas does not hesitate to invoke it in his harsh words to the two and a half tribes that built a "breakaway" altar (*Yehoshu'a* 22). As such, the context and motivation of the *brit* at *Arvot Mo'av* is *avoda zara* and the insistence, at all costs, to avoid it.

The *brit* at *Gerizim* and *Eival*, commanded in *Devarim* 27 (but already mentioned in *Devarim* 11) is worthy of its own treatment. Chazal understand that the "new feature" of that *brit* was *arvut* – mutual responsibility. The fact that the tribes are divided, standing over the place that we associate with the sale of Yosef (even though he was sold in *Dotan*), and the stand of facing each other, committing to avoid "secret" sins, seems to speak of a new type of covenant – a commitment to the welfare of the community and to not abuse power or take advantage of the less fortunate.

If we take a look back at the context of each of the three mentions of our prohibition, we'll see that one to one, they match up with these three covenants. As pointed out above, the first mention comes in the context of caring for the less fortunate. This fits perfectly with the most common explanation of the *issur* – of compassion, extending not only to the stranger, the widow and the orphan, but even (in a sense) to the animal. This seems to be associated with the commitment that we make to each other, facing each other from *Har Gerizim* and *Har Eival*.

The second mention took place after a breach in the relationship with God and is anchored in the prohibitions relating to *avoda zara*. This matches well with Rambam and Seforno's "anthropological" explanation which grounds the *issur* in pagan practices that we are to avoid. This aspect fits nicely with the brit at *Arvot Mo'av*, a commitment to maintain our loyalty to God.

The final instance of the *issur* is framed in the declaration that we are a holy people to God, echoing the terms of the *brit* at Sinai – and echoed in Ramban's explanation of the prohibition.

Three Prohibitions

Indeed, the three distinct prohibitions of cooking, eating and benefit seem to also speak to this tripartite refractive understanding of the *issur*.

The prohibition of cooking, which is an unusual one and one we do not find relating to other forbidden foods per se, seems to speak to the issue of compassion (or lack thereof); the parallel which Ibn Ezra cites of "*oto ve-et beno*" is illustrative. Just as we are to avoid acts that speak of an internal dismissing of the animal's "feelings," so to speak, similarly we are to avoid this act of cooking an animal in its own mother's milk. As several of the *rishonim* suggest, such an act has the potential to inhere a cruel attitude in us towards God's creatures – if not reflecting an already ruthless mien.

The prohibition of eating, which categorizes *basar be-chalav* among a much larger group of prohibitions, seems to speak to our sanctity; as Ramban expresses it – we are sanctified in our foods. Indeed, Rambam included two sets of laws in his *Sefer Kedusha* – abstention from forbidden foods and from forbidden sexual liaisons.

The prohibition of *hana'a*, on the other hand, is not all that common among forbidden foods. It is, however, ubiquitous among prohibitions relating to *avoda zara*. Perhaps it is the "idolatrous aspect" of the prohibition, argued by Rambam and Seforno (and numerous modern commentators) that is underscored by this additional prohibition.

In summing up what we have discovered and proposed here, the Torah presents us with the *issur* of *lo tevashel gedi ba-chaleiv immo* in three different contexts, representing and addressing three different components to our covenantal relationships – with God, with each other and with ourselves. The three distinct prohibitions speak to these relationships and serve to further sanctify us as a people who eschew idolatrous notions, increase compassion and idealize sanctifying the mundane specifically in the areas of human pleasure.

Brit Mila: The Father's Obligation

Rabbi David Brofsky

In addition to the *Yeshiva*'s commitment to *talmud Torah* and its contribution to Torah learning throughout the world, HaRav Lichtenstein *zt"l* and HaRav Amital *zt"l* charged their *talmidim* with the task of deepening their commitment to the 'covenant' and sharing it with others.

Accordingly, this article deals with one aspect of the mitzva of *brit mila*: the father's unique obligation and the community's responsibility to ensure that a young Jewish male is circumcised and initiated into the *brit* of Avraham *Avinu*. A close examination of this mitzva reveals that it reflects different aspects of the parent's and community's obligation to take responsibility for the spiritual collective. These themes represent one example of the educational legacy of our *Rashei Yeshiva zt"l*, and a pillar of the *Yeshiva*'s educational and religious philosophy.

Introduction

"On the eighth day the flesh of
his foreskin shall be circumcised." (*Vayikra* 12:3)

The Torah teaches that a male child should be circumcised on the eighth day after birth. This commandment raises an interesting question: Who is obligated in this mitzva? In the context of a well-known discussion regarding those *mitzvot* which the father is obligated to fulfill vis-à-vis his son, the *Gemara* (*Kiddushin* 29a) concludes that there is a three-tiered obligation. First, the father is obligated; if the father cannot or does not circumcise him, the *Beit Din* is responsible;[1] and if the child becomes an adult (*Bar*

---

1. It would appear that the *Beit Din* represents the community and carries out their responsibility regarding the circumcision of the child; see, for example, Rosh (*Chullin* 8:8), *Devar Avraham* 2:1, and *Sefer Ha-Mikna* (*Kiddushin* 29a). Rav Akiva

Mitzva) without being circumcised, he assumes the responsibility for this mitzva. The *Gemara* excludes the mother from the obligation of *brit mila*.

In this article, we will focus on the father's obligation to circumcise his son and its conceptual, halakhic and hashkafic ramifications.

The Father's Obligation[2]

The *achronim*[3] raise the following question: Is the father commanded to circumcise his son, or is he responsible for ensuring that his son is circumcised?

One might suggest that this depends on the source for *brit mila*. The *Gemara* cites the verse, "And Avraham circumcised his son Yitzchak" (*Bereishit* 21:4), as the source for the father's obligation. This verse may imply a direct, paternal obligation to circumcise the child. By contrast, the *Yerushalmi* (*Kiddushin* 1:5) cites the verse, "On the eighth day the flesh of his foreskin shall be circumcised" (*Vayikra* 12:3), which may imply that the father is not actually obligated to perform the *brit mila*, but rather, as a member of the Jewish people, he is obligated to ensure that this child is circumcised.

The *rishonim*, in different contexts, also appear to relate to this issue. For example, Rambam[4] writes: "A father is commanded to circumcise his son; and a master, his slaves." Rambam appears to believe that the father himself is obligated to circumcise his son. If the father will not, or cannot fulfill his personal obligation, then *Beit Din* or the son assumes the responsibility.

Eiger (responsa 42), however, implies that the *Beit Din* alone bears the obligation.
2. While we are unable to relate to this question in its entirety, we must mention that the *rishonim* appear to debate whether a father may, or can, appoint a *shali'ach* (agent) to fulfill the obligation of *brit mila* for him. Some maintain that the father cannot appoint a *shali'ach* to fulfill his mitzva, either because he must personally fulfill the mitzva whenever possible, or because fundamentally it doesn't really matter who performs the circumcision. Others believe that the father can and must appoint a *shali'ach* if he does not wish to perform the *brit mila* himself. See Rosh (*Chullin* 6:8), *Shakh* (CM 382:4; see also *Or Zaru'a Hilkhot Mila* 106:5), *Darkhei Moshe* (YD 264:1), and *Shulchan Arukh* (YD 265:9; see also *Tevu'ot Shor*, cited by *Ketzot Ha-Choshen* (182:1)).
3. See, for example, Rav Me'ir Dan Plotsky's *Keli Chemda, Parashat Lekh Lekha*.
4. Rambam *Hilkhot Mila* 1:1.

A number of *rishonim* disagree and describe the father's relationship to this mitzva differently. Some reveal their approach to this issue while explaining the mother's exemption from *brit mila*. While the Gemara derives her exemption from a verse, many *rishonim* question why the mother is not exempt for the simple reason that *brit mila*, which can only be performed during the day, is a *mitzvat aseh sheha-zeman gerama* (time-bound commandment), from which women are generally exempt?

Some *rishonim*, such as Tosafot[5], explain that since the mitzva can be performed every day after the eighth day, it is not considered to be time-bound. Others, however, suggest that the nature of *brit mila* may be fundamentally different from other *mitzvot*. For example, Ramban[6] explains that women are exempt from time-bound commandments which one is personally, physically obligated to perform, such as *tefillin*. However, this exemption would not apply to a broader, general obligation to ensure that someone else performs their mitzva. Ramban thus implies that the mitzva of *brit mila* belongs to the child, and the father is merely entrusted with the responsibility of ensuring that the child's mitzva is fulfilled.

Tosafot Rid[7] offers a similar, yet slightly different explanation. He explains that the father is not personally obligated to circumcise his son; rather, he must ensure that the circumcision is performed. Although Tosafot Rid and Ramban offer slightly different answers, they both clearly believe that *brit mila* is not the father's personal obligation to perform.

Interestingly, Or Zaru'a's son, Rav Chayyim Eli'ezer,[8] asserts that the mitzva is to ensure that that the child is no longer an *"arel,"* i.e. that merely being circumcised is itself a mitzva. As a proof, he cites a passage from the *Gemara* (*Menachot* 43b), which relates how when "King David entered the bathhouse and saw himself naked, he exclaimed: 'Woe is me! I am no longer clothed with Your mitzvot.' When, however, he remembered that he was circumcised, he regained his calm." In other words, David *Ha-Melekh* believed that merely being *nimmol* (circumcised), or not being an *arel*, is itself a mitzva.

---

5. *Tosafot Kiddushin* 29a s.v. *oto*.
6. *Ramban Kiddushin* 29a; see also *Ritva* ibid.
7. *Tosafot Rid Kiddushin* 29a.
8. *Maharach Or Zaru'a* 11.

We have delineated four understandings of the father's relationship to the *brit mila*: The father is personally and physically obligated to circumcise his son (Rambam), he assumes the responsibility for the fulfillment of the child's mitzva (Ramban), he is obligated to ensure that someone else circumcises his son (Tosafot Rid), or the father must simply make sure that the child is no longer an "*arel*" (Maharach Or Zaru'a).

It is interesting to note that Chatam Sofer[9] asserts that there are actually two separate obligations: There is a special obligation upon the father to circumcise his son, and there is a separate mitzva, incumbent upon the entire Jewish people, to ensure that other Jews are properly circumcised.

Of course, it is not surprising that *brit mila* is perceived in these different ways, as they reflect the various, general layers of responsibility we have towards our children, community, and the Jewish people.

The *Berakhot*

This disagreement may find expression in a series of debates regarding the proper *berakhot* recited at the *brit mila*.

The *Gemara* (*Pesachim* 7b) mentions that a *birkat ha-mitzva* is recited before the circumcision. Rambam,[10] based upon a certain understanding of the *Gemara* (ibid.), writes that when a father circumcises his own son, he says "*la-mul et ha-ben*." If another person, however, performs the *brit mila*, the *mohel* instead says "*al ha-mila*." Elsewhere,[11] Rambam explains that when one performs a mitzva for another person, the proper formula is "*al*," while when performing a mitzva which one is personally obligated to perform, such as a father who must circumcise his son, the proper text is "*la-*." This formulation is consistent with Rambam's view that the father has a personal obligation to circumcise his son.[12]

---

9. *Chatam Sofer Chullin* 87a s.v. *ve-khatav*.
10. Hilkhot Mila 3:1; see also *Or Zaru'a Hilkhot Mila* 107.
11. Hilkhot Berakhot 11:11.
12. Me'iri (*Magen Avot Inyan Ha-Shemini*) records that despite local protests, the custom was in accordance with Rambam. Other *rishonim* (see Rashi *Pesachim* 7a s.v. *ve-hilkheta*, Ran *Pesachim* 3b s.v. *ve-kashya*, *Hagahot Maimoniyyot Hilkhot Mila* 3:2, *Sefer Ha-Yashar* 259), however, rule that the *nusach* "*al ha-mila*" is always recited. This is the custom of Ashkenazim (see *Rema* YD 265:2).

Brit Mila: The Father's Obligation | 125

This question may also impact upon the second *berakha* recited at the *brit mila*, "*le-hakhniso bi-vrito shel Avraham Avinu*" (see *Shabbat* 137b). The *Gemara* teaches that in addition to the standard *birkat ha-mitzva*, i.e. *al ha-mila*, "the father of the [circumcised] child recites: "Who has made us holy through His commandments, and commanded us to bring him into the covenant of Avraham, our father (*le-hakhniso bi-vrito shel Avraham Avinu*)." The *rishonim* offer different understandings as to the nature of this *berakha*, which may reflect differing understandings of the father's obligation to circumcise his son.

Most *rishonim* attempt to align this *berakha* with other *berakhot*. For example, Rashbam[13] maintains that this *berakha* is a *birkat ha-mitzva*. In accordance with the principle, mentioned above, that the *birkat ha-mitzva* always precedes the performance of the mitzva (*over la-asiyyatan*), Rashbam insists that the father recite the *berakha* of "*le-hakhniso*" before the *mohel* says the *berakha* of "*al ha-mila*." Furthermore, Rashbam emends the standard text of the *Gemara* and places this passage, which describes the father's *berakha*, before the *mohel's berakha*, which is recited immediately before the act of cutting. This is also the view of Rif.[14]

Aside from the textual difficulties, this approach raises a more fundamental question. Hagahot Maimoniyyot[15] cites Rabbeinu Simcha as having asked, "What is the nature of this '*le-hakhniso*' *berakha*? And why is it not sufficient that his agent, the *mohel*, say the '*al ha-mila*' *berakha*?"[16]

Rabbeinu Tam (ibid.) rejects the view of Rashbam, his older brother, restoring the original text of the *Gemara* as well as the custom of French communities. He asserts that the *berakha* should be said after the *mila*. Rabbeinu Tam apparently believes that *le-hakhniso* is a *birkat ha-shevach*, blessing of praise, recited by the father as his son enters the "covenant of

---

13. *Tosafot* ibid. s.v. *avi ha-ben*.
14. *Teshuvot Ha-Rif* 293.
15. *Hagahot Maimoniyyot Hilkhot Mila* 3:3.
16. Interestingly, Rema (YD 265:2) rules that if the father circumcises his own son, and only says the *le-hakhniso berakha*, he has fulfilled his obligation. The Gra (ibid. 14) explains that *le-hakhniso* is similar, yet broader than *al ha-mila*, and therefore if the father only said *le-hakhniso*, he does not need to say *al ha-mila*.

Avraham *Avinu*," and is therefore recited after the *mila*. Indeed, Rosh[17] explains that, according to Rabbeinu Tam, "this blessing is not for this specific *mila* which is being performed now, but rather he thanks and praises God who has commanded to perform this mitzva when he has the opportunity, and they instituted that this is the place to reveal and declare that the mitzva is performed for God, and not for murna (i.e., medicinal reasons)." Similarly, Ran[18] explains that "this blessing is praise and thanksgiving for being able to enter [the child] into the covenant of Avraham."[19]

Rambam's position regarding this matter is unclear. Kesef Mishneh[20] assumes that Rambam believes that *le-hakhniso* is said after the *mila*. Rambam himself, in two responsa[21], rules that one may say *le-hakhniso* before or after the *mila*, "as its text is not *ve-tzivvanu*." This is also the position of a number of ge'onim.[22] However, Rambam's son, Rav Avraham ben Ha-Rambam, testifies that his father ruled that the *berakha* should be recited before the *mila*.[23]

Shulchan Arukh[24] rules in accordance with Rosh that the father should say *le-hakhniso* after the *mila* and before the *peri'a* (peeling of the corona). Interestingly, Taz and Shakh both view this practice as a "compromise," but for different reasons. Shakh[25] explains that since some require that the *berakha* be said before the *mila*, and some say that it should be said after the *mila*, lest the *mohel* change his mind and not perform the *mila*, in which case the *berakha* would be in vain, it is best to say the *berakha* before the

---

17. Rosh *Shabbat* 19:10.
18. Ran *Shabbat* 55b s.v. *avi ha-ben*.
19. Rosh (*Shabbat* 19:10, *Kiddushin* 1:40, and *Teshuvot Ha-Rosh* 26:1) appears to disagree with Rabbeinu Tam, although he proposes that the *berakha* be recited immediately after the *mila*, i.e. the cutting of the foreskin, but before the *peri'a*, i.e. the removal of the thin membrane covering the glans. Assuming that *peri'a* is part of the mitzva, *le-hakhniso* is thus said before the completion of the mitzva.
20. *Hilkhot Mila* 3:1.
21. *Teshuvot Ha-Rambam* 331, 332.
22. *Sha'arei Tzedek* 3:5:4.
23. See, for example, *Maharam Alshakar* 18, who cites Rav Avraham ben Ha-Rambam.
24. *Shulchan Arukh* YD 265:1.
25. *Shakh* ibid. 1.

peri'a, which is still considered to be *over la-asiyyatan*, but after the *mila*, as the *mohel* can no longer change his mind. Alternatively, Taz[26] implies that this practice fulfills the views of both Rashbam and Rabbeinu Tam, i.e. it is still *over la-asiyyatan* yet after the *mila*. Taz adds that if the father himself performs the *mila*, he should say both *berakhot* before cutting, as he will be too preoccupied with performing the *mila* to say the *berakhot* properly. Rav Ovadya Yosef[27] claims that Sephardic practice is to say the *berakha* before the *mila*, in accordance with the aforementioned views of Rif and Rambam.

Rishonim disagree regarding another aspect of this *berakha*. Rambam[28] writes that this *berakha* is uniquely the father's and should not be recited by anyone else. Ra'avad (ibid.), however, agrees with the view rejected by Rambam, and insists that the *berakha* may be recited by the *Beit Din* or another person. He relates that, in practice, it is customary for the *sandak* to recite this *berakha*. How are we to understand this debate between Rambam and Ra'avad?

Some propose that this debate may relate to different understandings of the relationship between the father's obligation and that of the *Beit Din*. For example, we might suggest that the father's obligation differs from the community's, as he is actually obligated to circumcise his son, while the community is merely charged to ensure that the boy is circumcised, as we discussed previously. If so, we can understand why the *berakha* of *le-hakhniso* is only said by the father, whose obligation is indeed unique and distinct from the *Beit Din*'s. Rav Yosef Rosen, known as the "Rogatchover Ga'on" (1858 – 1936), in his commentary to Rambam, *Tzafenat Panei'ach* (ibid.), suggests that this disagreement reflects a broader debate regarding the obligation of *Beit Din* in *brit mila*: Rambam maintains that *Beit Din* is charged with the responsibility of ensuring that the Jewish people are not "*arelim*," and therefore the *berakha* which celebrates entering the covenant of Avraham is irrelevant. Ra'avad, however, believes that *Beit Din*'s obligation is to ensure that every Jewish male is circumcised, and therefore *le-hakhniso* is certainly appropriate.

---

26. *Taz* ibid. 1.
27. *Yabbi'a Omer* YD 7:21.
28. *Hilkhot Mila* 3:1.

Alternatively, some suggest that this debate hinges upon the different understandings of *le-hakhniso* as discussed above. Ra'avad may agree with Rabbeinu Tam, who views this *berakha* as a *birkat ha-shevach*, in which case anyone may recite it. Rambam, however, follows Rashbam in maintaining that *le-hakhniso* is a *birkat ha-mitzva*, and therefore may only be recited by the father.

Here too, we encounter the difficulty raised above: Why would the Rabbis institute two separate *birkhot ha-mitzva* for *brit mila*? It appears that in addition to the general mitzva of *brit mila*, the father fulfills an additional, unique mitzva when circumcising his son, related to the very essence of his role as a parent, as encapsulated in the words "*le-hakhniso bi-vrito shel Avraham Avinu*." Indeed, Ba'al Ha-Ittur writes:

> Since the father is commanded to circumcise, redeem, and to teach his son Torah, and to marry him off, he says the blessing, as from the child's birth the commandment to enter his son into the covenant, and [to teach him] Torah and *mitzvot*, and to marry him off, the father's blessing for his son includes all of this. (*Ittur Hilkhot Mila* 53a)

Ba'al Ha-Ittur explains that ultimately, the father is responsible for the religious welfare of his child, and therefore the *berakha* is both unique and distinctly his.

When the Child Becomes an Adult

Minchat Chinnukh[29] discusses whether the father's obligation to circumcise his son applies only when the child is a minor, or even after he becomes an adult (i.e. after his Bar Mitzva). He raises some practical ramifications stemming from this question, including whether the father, if he is a *mohel*, must be offered the opportunity to circumcise his adult son.

Interestingly, Semak counts this commandment as two separate *mitzvot*. He dedicates one mitzva (157) to the commandment "to circumcise his son," and another mitzva (289) to the child's obligation "to

---

29. *Minchat Chinnukh* 2:2.

circumcise himself." Seemingly, even if the child becomes an adult and is not yet circumcised, these two *mitzvot* overlap.

Some suggest that according to Rambam, when the child becomes obligated in *mitzvot*, the father's obligation is replaced by the child's. Indeed, Rambam rules (*Hilkhot Korban Pesach* 5:5) that only when one's young children (*milat ketannim*) are not circumcised may the father not participate in the *Korban Pesach*. Similarly, in his *Commentary to the Mishna* (*Shabbat* 19:6), he writes: If the child grows up and reaches the age of punishments, the obligation is removed from others and he becomes obligated to circumcise himself immediately.

However, Rivash[30] insists that Rambam believes that even after the child becomes an adult, the primary mitzva is still incumbent upon the father. Indeed, Rambam, as demonstrated above, believes that the mitzva of *brit mila* is the father's personal, even physical obligation. Tosafot (*Kiddushin* 29a s.v. *oto*) also explain that after the eighth day, the father's obligation continues uninterrupted, and therefore it cannot be considered a time-bound commandment. Seemingly, if the commandment fundamentally belongs to the child, or if the father was merely entrusted with the responsibility of ensuring that the son is circumcised, then once the son becomes obligated in *mitzvot*, the mitzva of *brit mila* would certainly fall upon him.

Is a Grandfather Responsible for the *Brit Mila* of his Grandson?

Rambam teaches that in addition to the father's obligation to teach his son Torah, a grandfather also enjoys a unique obligation:

> Just as a person is obligated to teach his son, so, too, is he obligated to teach his grandson, as it commands: "And you shall teach them to your sons and your grandsons." (*Hilkhot Talmud Torah* 1:2)

Kesef Mishneh[31] suggests that according to Rambam, the grandfather is obligated to hire a teacher for his grandson, just as a father must hire a teacher to teach his son Torah.

---

30. Rivash 131.
31. *Kesef Mishneh* ibid.; see also *Shakh* YD 245:1, who cites Maharshal.

Rav Akiva Eiger[32] suggests that his unique relationship between the grandfather and grandson finds expression regarding *brit mila* as well. In his opinion, if the father is not present, the grandfather recites *le-hakhniso*: just as he is obligated to teach his grandson Torah, so too he participates in the mitzva of bringing the child into the covenant through *brit mila*.

In addition to the explanations mentioned above, Abudraham suggests that the *berakha* of *le-hakhniso* relates to the various responsibilities of the father:

> This blessing was established because the father is commanded to circumcise his son, redeem him, to teach him Torah, and to afford him a wife to marry. [This blessing] hints that from this day onwards all these obligations are incumbent upon him. (*Abudraham sha'ar* 8 Hilkhot Berakhot)

This *berakha* relates to raising a Jewish child. If this is true, it makes sense that the grandfather certainly plays an important role in raising this child, and it is, therefore, appropriate that he should say the *berakha* of *le-hakhniso* if the father is not present.

The Special Role of the Father in *Brit Mila*

We demonstrated above that the father's obligation to circumcise his son may be part of his greater responsibility of *chinnukh* (i.e. educating his children), which may lead us to conclude that a grandfather may partially share this responsibility. We may add another layer to our understanding of the obligation of *brit mila* and suggest that it is the father, who himself was circumcised, and in his absence, the community, who initiates this child into the covenant of Avraham *Avinu*.

Interestingly, regarding the father's obligation of *mila*, Rambam[33] refers to a different verse than that which appears in the *Talmud Bavli* or *Yerushalmi*: "As for you, you and your offspring to come throughout the ages shall keep My covenant. Such shall be the covenant between Me and

---

32. Rav Akiva Eiger *Mahadura Kamma* 42.
33. *Sefer Ha-Mitzvot* positive 215.

Brit Mila: The Father's Obligation | 131

you and your offspring to follow which you shall keep: every male among you shall be circumcised" (ibid. 17:9-10). This verse may imply that the father is obligated to initiate his son into the covenant through *brit mila*.

A similar idea may be found regarding the *berakha* of *le-hakhniso*. We discussed above whether *le-hakhniso* is a *birkat ha-mitzva* or *birkat ha-shevach*. However, some *rishonim* suggest that this *berakha* does not align with the familiar categories of *birkat ha-mitzva* and *birkat ha-shevach*; rather, it is most similar to the *"she-hakkol bara li-khvodo"* *berakha* recited at a wedding. Accordingly, Rashi[34] explains that the *berakha* is meant to publicly welcome the child into the covenant of Avraham. He describes how as the child is brought into the room, the congregation says *"barukh ha-ba,"* and the father takes the child and recites the *le-hakhniso berakha*, like any other *birkat ha-mitzva* which is said before the mitzva is performed. After welcoming the child into the covenant, he is then circumcised.

Similarly, *Seder Rav Amram*[35] brings that when the father is not present, the entire congregation recites *le-hakhniso*. The *berakha* is not a *birkat ha-mitzva* or a *birkat ha-shevach*, but a public welcoming of the child into the *brito shel Avraham Avinu*.

As described above, the father's obligation and the community's responsibility to circumcise the newborn son, along with the other *mitzvot* incumbent upon the parent,[36] reflect a broader religious imperative of ensuring that our children, and the community's youth, are afforded the opportunity to become religiously functioning members of the Jewish people, initiated into the covenant and exposed to the depth of the religious experience. As Yeshivat Har Etzion reflects upon its fifty-year legacy, it can proudly look back upon its many achievements and accomplishments, including its commitment to educating Jews of all ages, throughout the world.

---

34. See *Machzor Vitri* 505.
35. *Seder Mila*.
36. See *Kiddushin* 29a.

The Prohibition of Withholding Wages

Rabbi Dr. Moti Novick

Biblical Sources and Two Perspectives
The prohibition against withholding a laborer's wages appears twice in the Torah:

> You shall not defraud your fellow. You shall not commit robbery (*lo tigzol*). The wages of a laborer shall not remain with you (*lo talin*) until morning. (*Vayikra* 19:13)

> You shall not abuse a needy and destitute laborer, whether a fellow countryman or a stranger… You must pay him his wages on the same day (*be-yomo titten sekharo*), before the sun sets, for he is needy and urgently depends on it; else he will cry to God against you and you will incur guilt. (*Devarim* 24:14-15)

These two sources provide very different perspectives on the prohibition under discussion. The first, as is clear from the context ("defraud," "robbery") relates to withholding wages as a form of theft, a monetary matter. The passive formulation ("shall not remain with you") suggests that the sin of the employer is purely one of neglecting to carry out a financial duty.

In contrast, the second source relates to the economic hardship of the laborer ("needy and destitute") and to the anguish he feels when he is not paid for his work ("he will cry to God"). Rashi on verse 15 quotes the *midrash* on the words "[he] urgently depends on it (*eilav hu nosei et nafsho*)" which describes how the worker is so desperate for his payment that he risks his life in the course of his labor. This *midrash* appears also as part of a *beraita* in *Bava Metzi'a* 112a,[1] which continues to learn from the same verse that withholding wages from a worker is comparable to taking his life ("*notel nafsho*"). This comparison indicates that we do not view the sin purely in monetary terms. The severity of withholding wages, according to the verses in *Devarim*, seems to lie not in the theft as much as in the emotional trauma caused to a less fortunate member of society.

According to the perspective in *Devarim*, one might think that these verses do not apply to a wealthy laborer who does not depend on his wages to survive. However, the commentators to *Chumash* are quick to point out that the prohibition applies to every worker (see, for example, Ramban and Rasag on *Devarim* 24:14). The woeful description of the worker's plight is meant to emphasize the severity of the employer's neglect in certain extreme cases, not to limit the *halakha*'s applicability.

Nonetheless, the two perspectives which emerge from the verses may indeed represent different general approaches to this sin. On the one hand, withholding payment from a laborer is a type of passive theft, comparable to refusing to repay a loan or return a deposit. On the other hand, it is a form of exploitation of a person at a disadvantage by someone in a loftier position. Even if a worker is not objectively poor (even, indeed, if he is wealthier than his employer), the relationship of employer to employee is inherently asymmetric. The employee depends on the employer for his income. He therefore feels a certain fear in confronting his employer over unpaid wages. The sin of the negligent employer lies in taking advantage of this discomfort to delay meeting his obligations toward his workers.[2]

---

1. Unless stated otherwise, every Talmudic reference quoted in this article is from *Bava Metzi'a*.
2. The personal and moral nature of this prohibition finds support in a comment of Maharsha at the end of the second chapter of *Sukka* (29b). The *Gemara* there claims (according to Maharsha's understanding) that wealthy landowners who delay payment of wages beyond the time prescribed by *halakha* are punished by losing their riches. In explaining why a seemingly minor violation leads to a severe punishment, Maharsha points out that it has roots in a major character flaw: "this sin comes because of their excessive pride (*ga'avatan*);" the wealthy landowner sees the worker as lowly, not worthy of being dealt with on an equal level, and easy to exploit.

The dual nature of the prohibition of withholding wages – the monetary and the interpersonal – seems to emerge from the conclusion of a discussion in *Bava Metziʿa* 61a. The *Gemara* there determines that the prohibition of *gezel*, stealing, in the verse from *Vayikra* quoted above ("*lo tigzol*"), forbids not "ordinary" theft (whose prohibition can be inferred from other sources) but rather withholding payment from a laborer. The *Gemara* then asks why this is necessary, when there is an explicit verse prohibiting withholding payment in *Devarim*.[3] It answers that *gezel* adds a second prohibition to the act of withholding payment (*laʿavor alav bi-shnei lavin*). Although *laʿavor alav bi-shnei lavin* might be purely quantitative – two warnings are stronger than one – the double prohibition may reflect a conceptual duality. In this case, the verse of "*lo tigzol*" forbids withholding wages as a form of theft, while the verse in *Devarim* addresses the interpersonal violation of exploiting the weak.

Rambam too, in codifying the prohibition of withholding wages, seems to emphasize the dual nature of this prohibition. In *Hilkhot Gezeila* 1:4 he lists it as one example of *oshek* (passive theft or cheating) along with refusal to repay a loan or return a deposit. In *Hilkhot Sekhirut* 11:1-2 he counts the prohibition as an independent mitzva (based on the verses in *Devarim*). There, he also quotes the *beraita* from 112a with the comparison to taking the worker's life, and only then makes reference to the additional violation of "*lo tigzol*." The dual codification of this prohibition among laws of theft and among laws relating specifically to hiring workers reflects the dual nature of the prohibition itself.

In the coming sections we examine specific details of the prohibition of withholding wages that distinguish it from other monetary sins by highlighting its interpersonal nature. We begin with the question of how (if at all) *Beit Din* can punish the intransigent employer, move from there to a discussion of how to categorize the prohibition, and then investigate why the *halakha* does not apply in some exceptional cases. We conclude by suggesting a hybrid approach blending the two perspectives we have formulated.

---

3. The verse of "*lo talin*" in *Vayikra* is not considered an explicit prohibition because of its passive formulation noted above.

Punishment

The injunction against withholding wages comes with a strict timeframe: A day worker must be paid by the end of the following night, and a night worker must be paid by the end of the following day (110b). Is an employer punished if he withholds wages beyond the allotted time? Rambam (*Hilkhot Sekhirut* ibid.) rules that the usual punishment of lashes (*malkot*) for violation of a negative commandment is inapplicable here. Since the employer is required to pay even after the halakhic deadline, this is an example of a case that is *nittan le-tashlumin*, i.e. where monetary compensation can negate the violation's effects, so that there are no lashes. In this regard, withholding wages is similar to robbery (*Hilkhot Geneiva* 1:1).[4]

However, Tosafot (s.v. *la'avor*) on the aforementioned *Gemara* in 61a seem to believe not only that the penalty of lashes applies here, but that the violating employer would receive double lashes because of the double prohibition,[5] as per the conclusion of the *Gemara*. Why do Tosafot assume that this penalty applies despite the fact that withholding wages is *nittan le-tashlumin*?

The answer may lie in a comment in *Minchat Chinnukh* (230: 5) who questions Rambam's conclusion by referencing the prohibition upon a lender to enter the borrower's house to seize a collateral as security for his loan (*Devarim* 24:10). Regarding the latter, Rambam rules that the violating lender is subject to lashes (*Hilkhot Malveh Ve-Loveh* 3:4).[6] In defending Rambam's position,[7] *Maggid Mishneh* (ibid.) explains that even though the

---

4. In the case of theft, *gezel*, this consideration is unnecessary as a more basic factor precludes lashes; an explicit commandment to return the stolen object (*Vayikra* 5:23) makes the prohibition a *lav ha-nittak le-aseh*, a prohibition attached to a compensatory positive commandment.
5. In this manner they explain why the *Gemara* doesn't simply answer that the extra verse of "*lo tigzol*" adds a second prohibition to ordinary theft (*gezel*); since there are no lashes for *gezel* because it is *nittak le-aseh*, a second prohibition would add nothing of substance.
6. The prohibition is in fact *nittak le-aseh* where the *aseh* is returning the seized item, so lashes would apply only when it is impossible to do so (e.g. if it was destroyed or lost).
7. Ra'avad (ad loc) rejects the opinion of Rambam precisely for this reason – the prohibition is *nittan le-tashlumin* because the collateral can be returned to the borrower.

The Prohibition of Withholding Wages | 137

collateral can be returned or otherwise compensated for, that has nothing to do with the prohibition against taking it. The problem with seizing a collateral from the borrower's home is not about limiting the rights of the lender to the borrower's property – on the contrary, those rights are fully recognized. The sin of the lender is in how he chose to exercise his rights. Rather than showing the borrower the respect of standing outside and waiting for a collateral to be brought to him, the lender barged inside and grabbed it on his own. This behavior is exploitative, as it takes advantage of the inherent inferiority the borrower feels toward the lender: "*eved loveh le-ish malveh*" (*Mishlei* 22:7). As such, it cannot be compensated for even if the collateral is returned, and hence the penalty of lashes.

Minchat Chinnukh states that the same argument should be applicable to the employer who withholds wages. Even if the wages are subsequently paid, this does not in any way compensate for the delayed payment. The entire prohibition is thus not at all *nittan le-tashlumin* and therefore the penalty of lashes should apply. This suggestion is clearly based upon an understanding of withholding payment which sees it not merely as a form of theft (for as such the delayed payment would indeed serve as compensation), but rather as exploitative behavior which takes advantage of the relative weakness of the worker, comparable to the lender who takes collateral by force.[8] Perhaps for this reason Tosafot apply the penalty of lashes.

In line with our suggestion above that the double prohibition of withholding a worker's payment reflects two aspects of the sin, the monetary and the interpersonal, we can suggest a third possibility, aside from that of Rambam (no lashes) and Tosafot (double lashes for the double prohibition). As a monetary violation, the sin is subject to compensation once the employer eventually pays, and hence there is no further penalty, as Rambam suggests. But the interpersonal violation can never be compensated for, as was suggested in *Minchat Chinnukh*, and therefore the employer would be subject to a single penalty of lashes.

---

8. It is interesting to note that the prohibition of seizing a collateral from the borrower's home appears immediately prior to the prohibition of withholding wages in *Devarim* (24: 10-13). While *Parashat Ki Teitzei* is essentially a list of commandments which jumps from one topic to another, there is often within that list a logical transition between adjacent *mitzvot*, and this may provide evidence for the common denominator suggested by *Minchat Chinnukh*.

This analysis, aligning compensation with a monetary approach to the prohibition and lashes with an interpersonal approach to the prohibition, leaves us with questions on Rambam and Tosafot, each of whom leans toward one approach more than the other. Why does Rambam, who requires only monetary compensation, mention this ruling in *Hilkhot Sekhirut*, which emphasizes the interpersonal, rather than in *Hilkhot Gezeila*, where the monetary aspect is addressed? And why do Tosafot require double lashes when this punishment is relevant only to the interpersonal aspect of the prohibition (and presumably they require monetary compensation as well)? We will return to these questions at the end of our discussion, where we suggest a more nuanced understanding of withholding wages that incorporates elements of both approaches.

Classification of the Prohibition
The two perspectives we have developed on the prohibition of withholding wages may affect how it should be classified. At first glance it would seem to belong to the category of monetary law, *dinei mamonot*, as it deals with the manner in which a type of debt must be paid. However, if we view the sin as one of exploiting the worker, especially if no compensation is possible for violating it, the appropriate classification may be simply as an *issur*, prohibition, comparable to *lashon ha-ra* and verbal harassment (*onaʾat devarim*). We mention here three opinions that seem to side with the latter view, or at least seem to consider the prohibition as having aspects of both *mamonot* and *issur* – both monetary and criminal law.

The *Gemara* (111a) records a debate between Rav and Shmuʾel regarding the deadline for paying a laborer who works part of the night. According to Rav, he must be paid by the end of the same night; according to Shmuʾel, the employer may pay until the end of the following day. Rosh (9:43) rules in accordance with Rav, with a dual explanation. First, he states that the *halakha* always follows Rav in matters of *issur*. He then gives a second reason: the *Gemara* later finds that the debate between Rav and Shmuʾel was earlier a debate between *tannaʾim*, with Rav ruling like Rabbi Yehuda and Shmuʾel like Rabbi Shimon, and in any debate between those *tanna'im* we always accept the view of Rabbi Yehuda (*Eiruvin* 46b). Rosh in his second explanation may retreat from the position that this is a matter of *issur*, in which case his two explanations regarding this seemingly small detail reflect divergent perspectives on the nature of the entire prohibition. Rosh may believe that both perspectives are correct, and he is unsure which is dominant when they conflict in a matter of *pesak*.

The classification of withholding wages as *issur* rather than *mamonot* may help explain a surprising comment of Rav Betzalel Zolty in his *Mishnat Ya'avetz* (CM 45). Relating to a suggestion in *Sefer Chasidim* that an employer is exempted from the prohibition of withholding wages if he stipulates in the employment contract that he be allowed to pay late, Rav Zolty contests the validity of such a stipulation (*tenai*). A stipulation is valid regarding monetary aspects of the employment agreement, e.g. how much food the employer will provide. However, claims Rav Zolty, withholding wages is an outright *issur* and therefore no stipulation can take effect at all (*ein matnim al ma she-katuv ba-Torah*). This is a difficult suggestion to accept, as a person can always waive his claim (*mechila*) to money owed to him; even if we view the prohibition as one of exploitation, the worker should have the right to decide that he does not feel exploited by receiving his wages late. Perhaps Rav Zolty views the stipulation as itself a form of exploitation, as the worker would feel pressured to accept it. However we explain the conclusion, it is clearly built on a perspective which views withholding wages as an *issur* not entirely rooted in monetary considerations.

A third indication that the prohibition may be disconnected from the usual principles which govern monetary law is found in two Provencal *rishonim*: Ra'avad and the Me'iri. The *Gemara* (111b) quotes the opinion of Rav Assi that the prohibition of withholding wages applies even to a worker who is hired to pick a single cluster of grapes. What new detail is added by this comment? Rashi explains this to mean that the worker is hired for a very short time, but others reject this explanation, since the *mishna* (110b) already makes clear that the *halakha* applies even to an hourly worker. Ra'avad (quoted in *Shitta Mekubbetzet*) and Me'iri both suggest that Rav Assi adds that it is forbidden to withhold wages even when they amount to a negligible sum of less than a *peruta*. In monetary law, such a small amount is functionally equivalent to zero (for example, regarding *kiddushei kesef*, redeeming *ma'aser sheni*, and returning a stolen object), but as Me'iri states explicitly, the prohibition of withholding wages is "not dependent on monetary value." This perspective fits well with the idea that the prohibition has a strong interpersonal component and is not only about finances.

Limitations in Scope

The *Gemara* (111a) records two cases in which the prohibition of withholding wages does not apply. Both may provide insight into its nature, depending on the different understandings of each case which appear in the *rishonim*.

In the first case, an employer asks a *shali'ach* (agent) to hire workers for him. The *halakha* in this case is that the *shali'ach* himself may be subject to the prohibition if he assumes personal responsibility for paying the workers he hires; however, if he clarifies to the workers that the employer assumes responsibility for payment, then the prohibition doesn't apply even to the employer. The explanation for this surprising ruling is: "he [the employer] did not hire them (*lefi she-lo sekharan*)." This explanation is difficult because of the well-known and universally accepted principle that a *shali'ach*'s actions have the same effect as if done by the one who sent him (*shelucho shel adam kemoto*). Is hiring workers not subject to the usual rules of *shelichut*?[9]

Tosafot Rid seems to suggest that the answer lies in the psychology of the worker. Only a worker who reaches an agreement with the employer himself expects to be paid on time. In reaching an agreement with the *shali'ach*, while the laborers certainly expect to be paid, they implicitly

---

9. The commentary attributed to Ritva, in a far-reaching attempt to answer this question, suggests that the principle of *shelucho shel adam kemoto* only applies to the extent that it benefits the sender. Thus, the workers, once they agree to work, would be legally hired (as this is a benefit) but not covered by the employer's obligation to pay in a timely manner (as this is a restriction, hence not a benefit).

waive any claim on timely payment.[10] Rav Yosef Sha'ul Nathanson (*Shut Sho'el U-Meishiv* 6th edition ch. 1) sees Rid's explanation in a different light altogether. He understands that this is not a psychological consideration but a purely halakhic one. Certain actions are simply not subject to *shelichut* – for example, one cannot hire a *shali'ach* to put on *tefillin* or pray in one's place. These actions are referred to as *davar shebe-gufo*, meaning they attach sufficiently to the physical presence of the one who performs them such that they cannot be delegated to a *shaliach*. Rid, according to *Shut Sho'el U-Meishiv*, maintains that hiring workers is a *davar shebe-gufo* as far as the prohibition of withholding wages is concerned.

This is a very surprising assertion. No one would deny that the hiring itself can be done through a *shali'ach*; why does the prohibition not get "carried along" as a detail of this monetary agreement? The only way to understand this is to conclude that the prohibition is not merely monetary in nature. It is not only about passively stealing from the worker his due but rather part of the personal relationship between employer and employee. Only when the two have met, face to face, is the stronger one subject to the prohibition of exploiting the weaker by delaying payment. This is by no means an obvious or necessary conclusion, but it is entirely plausible.

The second case recorded in the *Gemara* (111a) is that of the marketeers of *Sura*. These employers only have cash available on market days, and hence any worker they hire understands that he will only be paid then. Thus (again based on an implicit waiver of a right to timely payment) the employers are not subject to the prohibition of withholding wages beyond the usual time. The *Gemara* adds, though, that they are nonetheless subject to the milder, non-Biblical injunction of *"bal teshaheh"* which forbids needlessly making a worker wait for payment longer than necessary. In which case is the employer subject to this milder prohibition? And is the Biblical prohibition really suspended entirely?

---

10. The idea that the prohibition would not apply just because the workers waive their right to be paid on time is by no means obvious; see *Mishnat Ya'avetz* discussed in the previous section. For our purposes here we nonetheless accept this suggestion.

According to Rashi's reading, the Biblical prohibition is indeed suspended entirely, and only the minor prohibition of "*bal teshaheh*" applies once the market day has passed. Me'iri finds this reading very difficult. Delaying payment to the market day would seem to merely postpone the usual deadline imposed by the *halakha*. Once that deadline arrives, why should the Biblical prohibition not apply?[11]

One way to explain Rashi in light of Me'iri's difficulty is that he understands the prohibition of withholding wages in a very technical and limited sense – the prohibition is only "until morning" or "until evening," depending on the worker, and thus whenever these specific times lose their relevance, the entire prohibition cannot apply. We suggest, however, that the limitation of the prohibition to these specific times is based on the interpersonal element of the prohibition.

Perhaps delaying payment is only considered exploitative because the worker is assumed to need his wages immediately, since he lives from day to day and his labor represents his constant means of sustenance. If he can wait – and if this willingness to wait is built in to the employment agreement in the form of an implicit waiver – then the transaction is less one of "employer-employee" in the personal sense than a financial arrangement between two parties of equal standing, and withholding payment beyond the agreed time does not carry the same moral stain (even as it certainly violates the terms of the agreement).

We note that, unlike previous ramifications we have suggested regarding the interpersonal nature of withholding wages, the two in this section – Rid regarding *shelichut* and Rashi regarding implicit acceptance of delayed payment – are leniencies rather than stringencies. This raises a difficulty, as a leniency would seem only to apply if the simpler, monetary perspective with its attendant stringency is dropped altogether; yet it seems unlikely that anyone would reject entirely the monetary component of the prohibition. We return to this difficulty in the next and last section of this article.

---

11. In place of Rashi's reading, Me'iri suggests that after the market day the Biblical prohibition is in force, and "*bal teshaheh*" applies even before the market day, if the employer happens to have cash available but does not pay the worker even upon request.

Integration and Conclusion

We have developed here two perspectives on the prohibition of withholding wages: the first as a form of theft and essentially a monetary sin from the world of *dinei mamonot*, and the second as a form of exploitation of a weaker party in a relationship by the stronger one from the world of *issur*. The second perspective is the less obvious one, and we have focused on providing evidence for it in the opinions of several *rishonim* and *achronim*. These opinions need not reject the first approach entirely but presumably see it as only part of the story, supplemented by an interpersonal aspect with the attendant stringencies we have addressed – lashes, applicability to less than a *peruta*, ineffectiveness of *tenai*, etc. What about the occasional leniency associated with the second approach, like those of Rashi and Rid suggested in the preceding section? Is there any way to adopt them without rejecting the first approach entirely?

We conclude by suggesting a possible interplay between the two approaches which would explain these leniencies, and also answer two open questions we posed earlier. The *Gemara* in 61a, discussed above, concludes that the primary verse prohibiting withholding wages is the one in *Devarim*, while the seemingly extraneous verse of "*lo tigzol*" simply adds a layer of double prohibition ("*la'avor alav bi-shnei lavin*"). Our understanding of this conclusion was that the first verse addresses the interpersonal aspect of the sin and the second verse forbids it as a form of theft. In that case, though, what emerges may be that only after the act is prohibited as a form of intolerable exploitation can it also be viewed as a form of theft. Or, in other words, withholding wages is only problematic on a monetary level because the Torah *first* sees it as a serious moral and ethical breach. In circumstances when it cannot be characterized as such there would not even be a monetary violation, and hence Rashi and Rid can be justified in limiting the scope of the entire prohibition on this basis.

With this suggestion in mind we return to questions posed earlier regarding the punishment for withholding wages. Tosafot require a double penalty of lashes, seemingly based on the dual nature of the prohibition. But how can lashes address the monetary aspect, for which compensation should suffice? The answer may be that even on a monetary level, withholding wages is only problematic because it is morally repugnant. As such, the financial sin is really an ethical sin as well, and so another set of lashes may be called for along with restitution. Along similar lines, Rambam records his ruling that only monetary compensation is required in *Hilkhot Sekhirut*, where the interpersonal aspect is emphasized, rather than in *Hilkhot Gezeila*. Withholding wages is only a form of *gezel* because it is a serious breach in the way an employer is supposed to relate to his workers. Perhaps the compensation, aside from refunding lost wages to the worker, is also meant to help the employer atone for this moral breach.

There are instances in *halakha* where a certain moral and ethical outlook shapes the parameters of monetary law. One example of this may be the prohibition of *ribbit* (interest) which, though agreed to and handed over freely and willingly by one person to another, is referred to in many sources as a form of theft.[12] Another is the broad concept of "*lifnim mi-shurat ha-din*," going beyond the letter of the law, which by its very name is outside the strict parameters of *halakha* and yet seems to have ramifications very much within the confines of monetary jurisprudence.[13] Perhaps our topic is another example of this phenomenon. Unlike a deposit in the hands of a *shomer* (guardian), which belongs to the depositor, or a loan which has come due, there is no basis which is strictly monetary for requiring punctual payment of wages. It is a debt with no clear due date, as indeed in modern society we witness examples of employers (government offices very often among them) who delay payment by long stretches of time when they find it difficult to do otherwise. The Torah introduces the moral imperative to pay a worker in a timely fashion, providing a strict definition of "timely." Once this ethical mandate has been established, to violate it becomes a form of theft. *Halakha* sets a moral and ethical standard, and the contours of monetary law adjust accordingly.

---

12. See *Bava Metzi'a* 61a as well as, for example, Me'iri on *Kiddushin* 6b and Ramban in his *hasagot* to Rambam's *Sefer Ha-Mitzvot* (*shoresh* 6).
13. See *Bava Metzi'a* 24b and 83a, and Ra'avya quoted in *Hagahot Maimoniyyot* on *Hilkhot Gezeila* 11:7.

Kiddush on Wine: Welcoming the Challenge

Rabbi Yehoshua Grunstein

Introduction

Many *talmidim* of Yeshivat Har Etzion have fond memories of *Shabbat Zakhor*, the *Shabbat* before Purim, when we would attend the *tisch* of the *Rashei Yeshiva*. Inevitably, a *talmid* would pass HaRav Yehuda Amital *zt"l* a stiff drink, and he would quip: "You think this scares me? The Nazis didn't scare me…."

Still, somewhere during that night, he would also warn us against overindulging, declaring: "I know my limits! Your problem is that you don't know your limits when you drink!"

Indeed, Rav Amital recommended that we take everything in proportion, and a small, yet important, manifestation of this habit was not to be scared of a good glass of whiskey or wine, but to know when to say, "Enough."

With this anecdote in mind, I would like to explore how Chazal view the use of alcohol in our weekly *Shabbat* experience: the wine of *kiddush* and *havdala*. Our contemporary society constantly reminds us of the dangers of alcoholism, so much so that some Jewish institutions implement a "no alcohol" policy. What would Chazal say, and what can we learn from their approach to the halakhic and ethical implications of drinking? I hope that this article will follow our *Rebbe*'s example in finding the proper balance.

Source

"Remember the Sabbath day, to sanctify it" (*Shemot* 20:7) – remember it over the wine at its commencement. I know it only of the night: whence do we know it of the day? Because it is said, "Remember the Sabbath day, to sanctify it." (*Pesachim* 106a)

The core of the mitzva is to declare that the day is *Shabbat*.[1] This is facilitated by reciting the words of *kiddush* on Friday night (and if this is not possible, throughout *Shabbat* day[2]) over a cup of wine, at the place in which one is about to eat the *Shabbat* meal.[3]

According to the majority of authorities,[4] saying *kiddush* over a cup of wine is a Rabbinic obligation.[5] According to all authorities, the recitation of *kiddush* during the day of *Shabbat*[6] (assuming it has been said at night) is Rabbinic.[7]

Finally,[8] *Shabbat* ends with the recitation of *havdala*. This is accomplished in the *Amida* prayer of *arvit*,[9] as well as in a separate text over a cup of wine (together with a candle and spices).[10] In all the above cases, one is forbidden to eat until one recites *kiddush* or *havdala*.[11]

---

1. Rambam, *Sefer Ha-Mitzvot* positive 155; *Mishneh Torah Hilkhot Shabbat* 29:31.
2. *Shulchan Arukh* OC 271:8.
3. *Pesachim* 101a, *Shulchan Arukh* OC 273:1.
4. Tosafot (*Pesachim* 106a s.v. *zokhreihu*, *Nazir* 4a s.v. *mai*), Rambam (ibid. 29:6) and many others; with a small minority, such as Rashi (*Nazir* 4a s.v. *harei*), Ran (*Shabbat* 10a in *Rif* s.v. a*mar Rabba*) and Rabbeinu Yona (quoted by Rosh *Pesachim* 10:5), stating that *kiddush* over wine is part of the Biblical requirement.
5. Details of this obligation of Friday night *kiddush* can be found in *Shulchan Arukh* OC 271.
6. *Shulchan Arukh* ibid. 289:1-2.
7. *Mishna Berura* ad loc. 3.
8. Rambam (*Hilkhot Shabbat* 29:1) indeed says that *havdala* is the mirror image of *kiddush*. However, many feel that *havdala* is just Rabbinic; *Berakhot* 33a states that "the Men of the Great Assembly ordained the *berakhot* and *tefillot*, *kiddush* and *havdala*" (though one can argue that this is limited only to the text of *havdala*, and not to the obligation to say it, per se). This is the opinion of Rosh in the name of Rabbeinu Tam (*Shut Ha-Rosh* 11:3), Tosafot Rid (*Pesachim* 106a), *Maggid Mishneh* (on Rambam ibid.) and more.
9. *Shulchan Arukh* OC 294:1.
10. Ibid. OC 296:1. As for why Chazal ordain to say *havdala* both during *arvit* as well as on a cup of wine, see *Berakhot* 33a.
11. Regarding Friday night *kiddush*, see OC 271:4; regarding *Shabbat* morning, see ibid. 289:1; regarding *havdala*, see ibid. 299:1.

Exception to the Rule

We have a slew of Biblical commandments that involve verbal recitation:

- To recite *Shema* twice daily[12]
- To remember *Yetzi'at Mitzrayim* (the Exodus from Egypt)[13]
- To recite specific verses (*Devarim* 26:5-10) that accompany the bringing of *bikkurim* (first-fruits) to the *Beit Ha-Mikdash*[14]
- To remember the actions of the nation of Amalek against the Jews.[15]

However, none of the above Biblical obligations require a cup of wine, so why would *kiddush* (or *havdala*)?[16] The requirement seems to be unusual.[17]

The Uniqueness of Wine

I believe the answer lies in the special status wine has within *halakha*:

- Wine is unique in that, even though we say the *berakha* of *"borei peri ha-eitz"* on grapes, on wine (pressed out of these very same grapes), we say a more specific and special *berakha* of *"borei peri ha-gefen."*[18] This is in counter-distinction to the other fruit juices, upon which one usually says *"she-hakkol."*[19]
- Wine is a unique beverage at a meal. The *berakha* over bread exempts one from any subsequent *berakhot* over food or drink – except for wine.[20]

---

12. Rambam *Hilkhot Keri'at Shema* 1:1; *Shulchan Arukh* OC 58 and 235.
13. Rambam ibid. 1:3.
14. Rambam *Hilkhot Bikkurim* 2:1 and 3:10.
15. *Megilla* 18a, Rambam *Hilkhot Melakhim* 5:5, *Sefer Ha-Chinnukh* mitzva 603, *Shulchan Arukh* OC 685:7.
16. There are other situations in which there is a Rabbinical enactment to recite a text over a cup of wine, such as at a *brit mila* (YD 265:1), for the week after a wedding (EH 62:1), etc.
17. Indeed, according to Rambam quoted above, "remember the Sabbath day" includes *havdala* as well; though, as mentioned, not all *rishonim* agree (see supra fn. 8).
18. *Mishna Berakhot* 6:1, *Gemara Berakhot* 35a, *Shulchan Arukh* OC 174:1.
19. *Berakhot* 38a, *Shulchan Arukh* ibid. 202:8, with the exception of olive oil.
20. *Berakhot* 41b-42a, *Shulchan Arukh* OC 174:1, unlike other beverages (ibid. 7).

- Wine is unique even within the specific world of beverages; if one makes the *berakha* on wine, this *berakha* alleviates the need to recite *berakhot* on subsequent beverages at the same sitting.[21]
- Wine is part and parcel of every Jewish holiday on which we are commanded to be happy.[22]
- On a more somber note, wine is singled out to be the means by which to comfort the mournful and depressed,[23] as *Mishlei* 31:6 states: "Give strong drink to the one who is perishing, *and wine to those of bitter soul.*"

The wine of *kiddush* and *havdala* is transitional, moving us from one week to the next. It has the capacity to elevate one's consciousness and spirit.

> And therefore, we are obligated to do this action with wine, as the nature of the human being is greatly awakened by it when one eats and is happy, and I have already told you that whatever arouses and activates a person is what affects him. (*Sefer Ha-Chinnukh* mitzva 31)

Indeed, wine awakens a person to the beauty of living in God's world, and thus, gives one the motivation to make it better. Drinking a glass may inspire one to be thankful for the experiences of the previous week,[24] and inspire one, without excuses, to aim higher. In other words, a person will be happier with what one has and motivated to reach for what one does not yet have!

The Duality of Wine: Constructive and Destructive Power

While wine has great positive potential, it also has the ability to do the opposite – to destroy and harm – as explicitly described in the following famous Biblical episode:

---

21. *Shulchan Arukh* OC 154:2. See *Mishna Berura* ad loc. 3 for the details.
22. *Pesachim* 109a; see also Rambam *Hilkhot Yom Tov* 6:18, who adds meat.
23. *Eiruvin* 65a, *Sanhedrin* 71a.
24. In the words of Ben Zoma (*Avot* 4:1): "Who is rich? One who is happy with his lot."

No'ach, the man of the soil, planted a vineyard. And he drank of the wine and became drunk, and he uncovered himself within his tent. Cham, the father of Kena'an, saw his father's nakedness, and he told his two brothers outside. Shem and Yefet took the garment, placed it on both of their shoulders, walked backwards, and covered their father's nakedness, with their faces turned backwards, so that they did not see their father's nakedness. And No'ach awoke from his wine, and he knew what his small son had done to him. He said, "Cursed be Kena'an; he shall be a slave among slaves to his brethren." And he said, "Blessed be the Lord, the God of Shem, and may Kena'an be a slave to them. May God expand Yefet, and may He dwell in the tents of Shem, and may Kena'an be a slave to them." (*Bereishit* 9:20-27)

No'ach and his family are the survivors of a mass extinction event, the flood – and the first thing No'ach says to them in the new world is to curse Kena'an, his own grandson, creating tension and separation in this close-knit family. Ultimately, the Jews are commanded to eradicate the nation of Kena'an, all going back to this episode that transpires due to wine.

Throughout *Tanakh*, we find an ambivalent approach to wine. On the one hand, it is the most profound expression of thanksgiving and happiness, as Malki-Tzedek gives bread and wine to Avraham after his victory in war[25] and Yitzchak drinks wine as a prerequisite to giving a *berakha*.[26] Moreover, an essential part of the sacrificial service is the offering of libations (*nesakhim*).[27] On the other hand, wine is the catalyst for Lot's incest with his daughters[28] and for Avimelekh's corrupt seizure of the throne,[29] as well as the substance used to celebrate Haman's decree of genocide against the Jewish people, with Achashverosh's blessing and signature.[30]

---

25. Ibid. 14:18.
26. Ibid. 27:25-29.
27. *Bamidbar* 15:1-16, ibid. ch. 28-29.
28. *Bereishit* 19:31-28.
29. *Shoftim* 9:4.
30. *Esther* 3:15. For other examples of the danger of wine, see also *Yeshayahu* 23:7, *Mishlei* 23:20, amongst many other places.

Beyond the Biblical narrative, Chazal go out of their way to tell many stories in which wine represents a slippery slope to tragedy and sin,[31] to the extent that they can state: "*Every place* you find wine, you find failure" (*Midrash Tanchuma Yashan Bereishit* 8:21). In other words, "Don't get drunk and you won't sin" (*Berakhot* 29a).

Chazal also warn against using wine to deal with grief. An *onen* (one whose loved one has died but not yet been buried[32]) may not drink, as this may interfere with the proper mindset warranted at the moment or lead one to unwise actions or words.

Wine can build and enhance, yet it can also destroy and ruin.[33]

A Calculated Risk

It is precisely for this reason that, in my opinion, when we stand before God on *Shabbat*, at the very crossroads between the week that was and the week that will be, we declare clearly: *We are willing to take a chance!* We are willing to take wine, with its potential to destroy, and show how we will use it to bless, build, get closer to one another, enhance and appreciate all we have, and strive together for the better.

Thus, with regard to *kiddush* (OC 271:14), we find an opinion (though not unanimous) that if the person reciting *kiddush* doesn't drink the wine, the obligation has not been fulfilled. Moreover, *kiddush* must be recited wherever one is eating the meal.[34] A festive meal with friends and family is a challenging situation for drinking wine: does this facilitate felicitous conversation, or lead to uncomfortable or embarrassing interactions?

---

31. *Midrash Tanchuma* (*No'ach* 13, *Shemini* 7 s.v. *va-ydabber Hashem*, ibid. 8 s.v. *ve-khein atta*, ibid. 9 s.v. *ashrei adam*). See also *Midrash Vayikra Rabba* 12, *Bereishit Rabba* 36:4, *Bamidbar Rabba* 10:2 s.v. *ish*, *Berakhot* 29b, *Pesachim* 113b.
32. *Berakhot* 17b, *Shulchan Arukh* YD 341:1.
33. See, by example, Rambam (*Hilkhot Dei'ot* 5:3 and *Moreh Ha-Nevukhim* 3:88), Ramban (*Vayikra* 19:2), *Chovot Ha-Levavot* (*Sha'ar Ha-Perishut* 85), Shela (*Tetzaveh, Torah Or* 22) et al.
34. *Pesachim* 101a, *Shulchan Arukh* OC 273. As to the custom of some (*Shulchan Arukh* ibid. 269:1) to say *kiddush* at the end of services in the synagogue on Friday night, see ibid. that there were once many who actually ate in the synagogue, and thus arose the custom to say it there, in the place where they would shortly have their meal.

Chazal highlight how important a meal can be:

> Rabbi Yochanan, in the name of Rabbi Yosei ben Kisma, said: "A mouthful can be consequential, as it separated two families from Israel, as it says (*Devarim* 23:5): 'Because they didn't come to greet you with bread and water.'" Rabbi Yochanan himself said: "It can separate those close to you, and bring closer those that are far from you!"... "It can separate those close to you," as [said above] in the case of Ammon and Mo'av. "And bring closer those that are far from you," as in the case of Yitro, as Rabbi Yochanan said: "In the merit of (*Shemot* 2:20) 'Call [Moshe] and he shall eat bread,' his grandchildren were members of the Hight Court." (*Sanhedrin* 103b-104a)

Thus, Ammon and Mo'av come into existence due to wine, but because they do not invite their cousins Benei Yisrael to dine with them subsequently, their descendants are never allowed to intermarry with the Jewish people, even after conversion!

This idea is further sharpened by a rather cryptic statement of Chazal (*Eiruvin* 40b) that, when one that makes a *berakha* on a cup of wine, in conjunction with another mitzva, "The one who makes the *berakha* must drink from the cup."[35] Rashi explains (ad loc. s.v. *leitveih*): "It is a disgrace to the cup of blessing that no one benefit from it right away, as the *berakha* over the wine of "*borei peri ha-gefen*" would be unnecessary."

Indeed, it seems that part and parcel of blessing God over a cup of wine is to "enjoy it;" even in the *midst* of a meal, one must make the *berakha* over wine, indicating its unique status.[36] In the words of *Berakhot* 42a, "Wine is different, *as it causes a blessing to itself!*" Rashi explains (ad loc. s.v. *de-gorem*): "In several places it comes and we make a *berakha* on it, *even though we didn't need to drink it.*"

---

35. Indeed, the context of the *Gemara*'s exchange there is how to say the *berakha* of "*she-hecheyanu*" (see below) on Yom Kippur, when we can't drink the wine.

36. Indeed, if we are speaking of things that are not part of the actual meal, such as dessert, one does make a separate *berakha* on them, as they are separate from the meal (OC 177).

Indeed, we may not need to drink it to quench our thirst, but rather for a far bigger and greater reason.

Applications

1) *She-hecheyanu* over Wine

"*She-hecheyanu*" is the *berakha* that we recite on seasonal *mitzvot*,[37] thanking God for allowing us to be "alive…and reach this time." Does it have to be said over a cup of wine? *Eiruvin* 40b discusses this, and the ultimate conclusion is that one can say this *berakha* without a cup of wine.[38] Still, in accordance with the *Gemara*'s conclusion, if we have a cup of wine at these events, we follow the example of Rav Kahana (*Sukka* 46a) and postpone the *berakha*, in order for it to be said over the cup of wine. In fact, Rav Yosef Karo notes in OC 641:1 that although one may make the *berakha* of *she-hecheyanu* upon completing one's own *sukka*, it is better to wait and incorporate it into *kiddush*. Why wait? Why postpone the *berakha* until the wine is in hand? Rashbam explains (*Pesachim* 101a s.v. *af*) that once Chazal associate a specific mitzva with wine, it makes sense that it should be the wine imbibed during a meal, "for it is significant."

It is clear that one can praise God or the day without wine, but when one does take wine in hand, it becomes more significant; one can now thank God not just for arriving at a milestone, but for overcoming challenges along the way – such as the consumption of wine itself. It indicates hope for the future too.

2) Long Strides

This might explain a homiletic statement in the *Gemara* about *talmidei chakhamim* (Torah scholars):

> Some add that a *talmid chakham* should not take long strides, because a master has said: "Long strides diminish a man's eyesight

---

37. *Shulchan Arukh* OC 473:1, 494:1, 600:2, 619:1, 641:1, 668:1.
38. This is codified in *Shulchan Arukh*, e.g. on Yom Kippur when one may not drink (OC 619:1).

by one five-hundredth." What is the remedy? He can restore it with the *kiddush* wine of *Shabbat* eve. (*Berakhot* 43b)

Assuming (as Rashi does, ad loc.) that the reference is to drinking the wine rather than applying it to one's eyes,[39] what does this mean?

In my humble opinion, Chazal's message is that we shouldn't walk so fast, getting from place to place without being a *true part of where we are*.[40] Of course, the world is filled with many distractions,[41] and it is much easier to take long strides to avoid them. However, this is the wrong approach, and the best remedy is drinking the wine of *kiddush*. Just as the glass of wine has its dangers, so does engaging with the outside world, but a true *talmid chakham* must embrace the challenge.

3) Proportion in Drinking

Gittin 70a lists wine as one of the "eight things which in large quantities are harmful but in small quantities are beneficial." While overindulging is discouraged,[42] the right amount allows one to feel happy, satisfied and able to deal with far bigger challenges.

Thus, wine enhances one's current situation, and allows one to say that, despite the clear potential danger in drinking wine, when drinking responsibly, at the proper age and time, with the proper amount and limits, one shows a willingness to take chances, as the benefits emanating from it are great.

> When a person drinks one cup of wine, he acts like a lamb, humble and meek. When he drinks two, he becomes as mighty as a lion and

---

39. See *Shabbat* 108b and *Shulchan Arukh* OC 329:20.
40. In this regard, see the reaction of our *Rebbe*, Rav Amital, to those who remove their glasses so as not to see "forbidden sights," missing out on permissible and beautiful ones: https://www.kipa.co.il/-החינוכית-משנתו-בלעדיו-שנים-שבע/עדות/והמוסרית-של-הרב-עמיטל-זצל/.
41. *Bamidbar* 15:39 states: "And you shall not wander after your hearts and after your eyes after which you are going astray." See *Sifrei* (ibid.), *Yerushalmi Berakhot* 1:5, et al.
42. Rambam (*Hilkhot Dei'ot* 5:3) warns against extensive drinking by a *talmid chakham*.

proceeds to brag extravagantly, saying, "Who is like me?" When he drinks three or four cups, he becomes like a monkey, hopping about, dancing, giggling, and uttering obscenities in public, without realizing what he is doing. Finally, when he becomes blind drunk, he is like a pig; wallowing in mire and coming to rest among refuse. (*Midrash Tanchuma Parashat No'ach* 13)

4)   Friday Night *Kiddush* versus *Shabbat* Day *Kiddush*

Ramban explains why we need to make *kiddush* twice, once at night with a special *berakha* and then again the next morning with only the standard *berakha* over wine (and, depending upon custom, a few verses):

> "Remember the Sabbath day to sanctify it" – and in *Devarim* (5:11), it says, "Observe the Sabbath day to sanctify it." Our Sages have taught us (*Rosh Ha-Shana* 27a) that "remember (*zakhor*)" and "observe (*shamor*)" were said simultaneously. The Sages mean that "remember" refers to the positive laws of *Shabbat*, to remember the Sabbath day to sanctify it and not forget it, and "observe" to the negative laws of *Shabbat*… being careful to observe it in sanctity and not desecrate it…
>
> In the *Midrash* of Rabbi Nechunya ben Ha-Kaneh (*Sefer Ha-Bahir* 182), he mentions another great secret regarding "remember" and "observe" – the former is during [the *kiddush* of] the day, and the latter is during [the *kiddush* of] the night…
>
> This is indeed true, because "remember" connotes the positive commandments, which emanate from the trait of love [of God] and the trait of mercy, because one who performs the commands of his master is loved by him and his master has mercy on him. In parallel, "observe" connotes the negative commandments, representing the trait of strict judgment and emanating from the trait of fear [of God] because one who guards himself from doing what is wrong in the eyes of his master is fearful of him. Therefore, a positive commandment is greater than a negative commandment,

just as love is greater than fear, because one who fulfills the will of God with his body and money is greater than the one who merely guards himself from doing something wrong in His eyes. (Ramban *Shemot* 20:7)

Thus, we may say that using wine for *kiddush*, according to Ramban, encompasses both aspects: firstly, *kiddush* over wine at night connotes the vital need to guard oneself from over-drinking; secondly, during the day, *kiddush* over wine can be beautiful, when the above limitations from the night before are in place, as it can bring out the very best in the person.

This may help us understand the common custom concerning the end of the middle *berakha* of the *Shabbat Amida*.[43] The phrasing is as follows: "And Israel will rest on it, the sanctifiers of Your Name." Most prayer books have a different pronoun for each time of today: on Friday night, it is "*vah*" (feminine, singular); on *Shabbat* morning, it is "*vo*" (masculine, singular); in the afternoon, it is "*vam*" (plural). *Kenesset Ha-Gedola* explains:

> On Friday night, [*Shabbat*] is like a betrothed still in her father's house, and therefore we say "*vah*." At *shacharit*, the bride is in the home of her father-in-law, as the most central happiness is in the house of the groom, and thus we say "*vo*." Finally, at *mincha*, we say "*vam*," as both are vital! (*Kenesset Ha-Gedola* OC 268:2)

Indeed, when dealing with wine, we first have the limitations in place (like a betrothed couple), but then we actually enjoy it (like a husband and wife living together.) Still, both are vital (as we say it in the plural at *mincha*): living together, but with limitations.

The Reward for Using Wine

> Rabbi Yochanan says: One who recites a blessing over a full cup [of wine] will receive an inheritance without limitations… Rabbi

---

43. There are other customs: Rambam mandates to say "*vam*" throughout *Shabbat*; see *Shut Yechaveh Da'at* 5:30 for the variety of sources on the proper term to use.

Yosei bar Chanina says: He will receive the inheritance of both worlds: this world and the World to Come. (*Berakhot* 51a)

The *Gemara* above asserts, according to the interpretation of Maharsha,[44] that saying a *berakha* over wine will make one feel "eternal," unshackled, without barriers. When one drinks wine, one is saying that despite the challenges, one is willing to reach for the stars, and aspire for more: an inheritance without limits – in this world and the next.

A similar statement is made about *havdala*:

Rabbi Yochanan says: Three people are sure to inherit the World to Come: One who lives in *Eretz Yisrael*, one who raises his children to study Torah, and one who says *havdala* on wine at the end of *Shabbat*. What does this [latter] statement mean? It means one who leaves over enough wine from *kiddush* for *havdala*. (*Pesachim* 113a)

How can this statement be understood? Raising Jewish children is extremely difficult, and living in Israel is even more challenging! How can these two be on the same level as saying *havdala* on a cup of wine, and, more specifically, by merely ensuring that enough wine is left in the bottle? Based on what we have seen above, this is indeed defensible. Childrearing and living in Israel are certainly challenges, but indulging in wine to the appropriate degree and no more is no simple task. Thus, Chazal state:

A person who is diligently careful in saying *havdala* over wine when *Shabbat* ends will have fine children, as it says (*Vayikra* 10:10), "To make a distinction between the holy and mundane and between the impure and pure," and then it states (ibid. 12:1), "When a woman will get pregnant and have a child." (*Shevu'ot* 18b)

Wine can be dangerous, yet it can also be beneficial. It is all about observing the moderation required. *Shabbat* is a bubble in time, and as we enter and

---

44. *Maharsha Chiddushei Aggadot* ibid. s.v. *kol ha-mevareikh.*

leave it, we actively declare that we are willing to engage with the challenges of wine. If we demonstrate the appropriate behavior in this regard, we have good reason to be confident that our children will absorb the message and learn to balance a Torah outlook with a broader worldview.

Overindulging poses a danger both to the drinker and the family; metaphorically, there is nothing left in the bottle for *havdala*. However, if one maintains the proper balance, the leftover wine will initiate a productive week.

Summary

As we raise a glass of wine each Friday night, *Shabbat* morning and Saturday night, we declare that we are willing to push on despite the challenges (of wine-drinking and other "indulgences"). We hope to see the world become better and better, as the positive feeling after drinking will naturally allow us to be happy with what we have, but also to take a chance (despite all the excuses) to aspire for more, with proper limitations and safeguards in place. One can feel limitless, on a day that glimpses into the World of Eternity, where no limits will stand in our way.

Drinking wine holds great danger, yet great hope as well. At the beginning, midpoint and end of *Shabbat*, we take a full glass in our hands. This makes clear that we don't dodge the challenges, but rather we confront them, reaping the benefits therefrom.

The Dynamic Relationship Between *Kevod Ha-Av* and *Kevod Ha-Rav* in Rambam's View

Rabbi David Nachbar

I. Introduction

This essay will explore the qualitative relationship between *kibbud u-mora av va-eim* (honoring and revering one's parents) and *kibbud u-mora ha-Rav* (honoring and revering one's Rabbi) within Rambam's perspective. Broadly speaking, Rambam viewed the relationships between parents and a child, on the one hand, and a *Rebbe* and *talmid* (Rabbi and student), on the other, as roughly analogous to one another. As he puts it: "Just as an individual is obligated in his father's honor and reverence for him, so too is he obligated in his *Rebbe*'s honor and reverence for him to an even greater degree than his father."[1] Rambam's "just as... so too" formulation establishes a comparative relationship between the two institutions which, as will be demonstrated below, testifies to their symbiotic relationship and the fluid, two-directional transport of *halakhot* between the two contexts. At the same time, this essay will seek to demonstrate that Rambam's concluding comment, "to an even greater degree than his father (*yeter mei-aviv*),"[2] introduces not only a differentiation in extent and prioritization between the two respective obligations, but fundamentally and conceptually divergent qualities.

II. The Halakhic Symbiosis Between *Kevod Ha-Av* and *Kevod Ha-Rav*

The *beraita* which defines the primary expressions of *kibbud av va-eim* lists six defining activities of *kavod*: "feed and give to drink, clothe and

---

1. *Hilkhot Talmud Torah* 5:1.
2. Based on the *mishna* in *Bava Metzi'a* (33a).

cover, and transport in and out."[3] In Rambam's view, this list of activities is not exhaustive in nature. Rather, the six listed activities serve as representative examples of the types of service that fulfill *kibbud av va-eim*; they possess innumerable *toladot*, subsets, that exceed quantification – "*rabbim mi-lispor*."[4]

In the *Mishneh Torah*, Rambam adds two specific activities to the six listed expressions of *kavod*: methods through which a *shammash* assists his *Rav*, and standing before one's parents just as one stands before one's *Rav*.[5] Rambam's two additional illustrations both draw upon the comparison between the two relationships and are imported to *kibbud av va-eim* from the laws of *kevod ha-Rav*.

Adopting a wider angle on the comparison demonstrates that *kibbud av va-eim* not only imports *halakhot* from the context of *kevod ha-Rav* but exports *halakhot* to that context as well. In Rambam's view, the very feature of *mora ha-Rav* in a *Rebbe-talmid* relationship exists solely due to the influence of the parent-child relationship; moreover, many of the contours of *mora ha-Rav* are derived from and shaped by *mora av va-eim*.

As was highlighted above, Rambam opens the chapter dedicated toward *kevod u-mora ha-Rav* with a sweeping statement of comparison between the *Rebbe-talmid* relationship and the parent-child relationship. In his *Sefer Ha-Mitzvot*,[6] Rambam further clarifies that the relationship between *kevod u-mora ha-Rav* and *kevod u-mora ha-av* is not merely a comparative one; rather, it is derivative in nature. There is no direct source which teaches the concept of *mora ha-Rav*; instead, its existence is derived through a *kal va-chomer* (*a fortiori* argument) from *mora av va-eim*.

The *mishna* in Bava Metzi'a 33a records that a child should prioritize his *Rebbe* ahead of his parent for returning lost items, providing assistance unloading heavy burdens, and paying a captive's ransom. The *mishna's*

---

3. Kiddushin 31b, Yerushalmi Pei'a 1:1, Torat Kohanim Kedoshim parsheta 1:10. In the *Yerushalmi*'s list of six activities, the term "*u-manil* (put on their shoes)," replaces the term "*u-mkhasseh* (cover them)," presumably, due to its redundancy following "*u-malbish* (clothe them)."
4. *Peirush Ha-Mishna Kiddushin* 1:7.
5. *Hilkhot Mamrim* 6:3.
6. *Sefer Ha-Mitzvot* positive 209.

rationale is: "One's father has brought him into this world, whereas one's *Rebbe* brings him into the next world." On this basis, Rambam argues, if a parent-child relationship features not only a dimension of *kavod* but also one of *mora*, then a *Rebbe-talmid* relationship must necessarily possess a dimension of *mora* as well: "The law regarding one's *Rebbe* is stricter than the law regarding one's father, for Scripture has obligated him to honor him and revere him."

In addition to introducing the basic concept of *mora*, *mora av va-eim* plays a defining role in shaping the specific expressions of *mora* in the *Rebbe-talmid* relationship. The *beraita* which defines the expressions of *mora* in context of *mora av va-eim* lists four specific manifestations: "not to stand or sit in parents' designated spaces, not to contradict their words, and not to decide their debates."[7] Rambam defines the expressions of *mora ha-Rav* in strikingly similar fashion: "He should not sit in his *Rebbe*'s designated place, and should not decide his debates in front of him, and should not contradict him."[8] Kesef Mishneh provides the source for Rambam's definition by referencing the *beraita* in *Kiddushin* regarding *mora av va-eim*.

Similar to his mentality concerning the *beraita*'s six *kavod* activities, Rambam maintains that the *beraita*'s list of four *mora* manifestations are mere representative examples, and were never intended as an exhaustive list.[9] Two additional expressions of *mora* that Rambam adds to the *beraita*'s list include not referring to one's parents by their names and, additionally, even refraining from calling others by their given names without some

---

7. *Kiddushin* 31b. The *beraita* also appears in *Torat Kohanim* (*Parashat Kedoshim parsheta* 1:10) and in the *Yerushalmi* (*Pei'a* 1:1); however, in both of the other presentations of the *beraita*, the list only consists of three expressions. "Not to stand in their designated spaces" and "not to decide their debates" are omitted and are replaced with "not to speak in their place." Me'iri (*Beit Ha-Bechira Kiddushin* p. 184 s.v. *eizehu*) also presents a modified list of four expressions, replacing "not to stand in their designated spaces" with "not to stand before them," which he interprets to mean not to take leave without first receiving permission. Interestingly, this feature of *mora* finds parallel expression in the *Rebbe-talmid* relationship as well (Rambam *Hilkhot Talmud Torah* 5:6).
8. *Hilkhot Talmud Torah* 5:6.
9. *Peirush Ha-Mishna Kiddushin* 1:7.

modification if they share the same name as one's parents.[10] These two additional features find rough parallel expression in Rambam's presentation of *mora ha-Rav*, and Rambam explicitly cross-references and relies upon the institution of *mora av va-eim* in establishing the *halakha*: "the way he does with his father's name."[11]

In summary, Rambam views the institutions of *kevod u-mora av va-eim* and *kevod u-mora ha-Rav* as sharing a symbiotic relationship in which *kevod ha-Rav* fleshes out the multiple expressions of *kibbud av va-eim*, and *mora av va-eim* establishes and helps to define the features of *mora ha-Rav*. A sharpened understanding of the common, middle ground in the two relationships may help facilitate the two-directional transport of *halakhot*.

III. Shared Dimensions Between *Kevod Ha-Av* and *Kevod Ha-Rav*

One of the central and defining aspects of the parental relationship is the educational role that parents play in a child's life. The *Gemara* highlights this feature in explaining that the Torah prioritizes a mother in the verse regarding *mora* ("*ish immo ve-aviv tira'u*"), as a result of a child's instinctual *mora* felt for one's father due to his role of teaching him Torah.[12] Additionally, a child may exhibit *kavod* toward parents by referring to them as *abba mori* or *immi morati*, my father or mother, my instructor.[13] Furthermore, Bach[14] argues in favor of Rema's viewpoint, against Maharik, that a grandparent must certainly be included in the mitzva of *kavod*, on some level, due to the grandparent's obligation to teach Torah to their grandchild.[15] Although parents play a multifaceted role in their child's life, a principal role that they play is that of teacher and educator.

On the flipside, although the defining role of a *Rebbe* is as a teacher of Torah, the *Rebbe-talmid* relationship can be seen in more comprehensive terms. A *Rebbe*, in addition to teacher and instructor, plays a quasi-

---

10. *Hilkhot Mamrim* 6:3.
11. *Hilkhot Talmud Torah* 5:5.
12. "*mippenei she-melammedo Torah*," *Kiddushin* 31a.
13. *Kiddushin* 31b. Interestingly, Rashi there (s.v. *ve-amorei*) interprets the term "*mori*" as meaning my master rather than my educational instructor.
14. YD 240:24 s.v. *katav Maharik*.
15. *Devarim* 4:9-10, as interpreted by one opinion in *Kiddushin* 30a.

parental role in the life of his *talmidim*. When Eliyahu was taken from his *talmid*, Elisha, the latter exclaimed, "my father, my father, chariot of Israel and its horsemen!"[16] Similarly, the obligation to teach Torah to all *talmidim* irrespective of familial relationship is derived from the verse, "*ve-shinnantam le-vanekha* (you shall teach your children)" – they are your students.[17] In fact, Rambam is of the opinion that when a person's *Rebbe* passes away, both the manner and permanence of *keri'a*, the rending of his garments, parallel that performed for a parent – all layers to the heart and irreparably.[18] Rambam captures this parental role that *Rebbe'im* play in the lives of their *talmidim* in characterizing them as "the *chakhamim*, who are the fathers of everybody."[19] Fathers and mothers play a parental role vis-à-vis their children in a family setting, while *talmidei chakhamim* play a parental role in relation to the communities that they guide.

Against this backdrop, the mutually illuminating institutions of *kevod u-mora av va-eim* and *kevod u-mora ha-Rav* are better understood. A parent's comprehensive relationship with his or her child revolves around the central educational role that he or she plays in a child's upbringing, and, at the same time, a *Rebbe*'s educational focus is complemented by a multifaceted, quasi-parental role that he plays in his *talmid*'s growth and development.

IV. *Kibbud Av Va-Eim* – A Humanistic Approach

Despite the common ground that the parent-child and *Rebbe-talmid* relationships share, and the two-directional transport of *halakhot* that results therefrom, Rambam views the two as divergent relationships that qualitatively differ from one another.

Ramban[20] observes that the first five of the *Aseret Ha-Dibberot* (Ten Commandments) center around *kevod ha-Borei*, honor pertaining to the

---

16. "*Avi, avi, rekhev Yisrael u-farashav!*" *Melakhim Bet* 2:12.
17. *Devarim* 6:7, as explained in *Sifrei* (*Parashat Va'etchanan* no. 9) and cited in Rashi (s.v. *le-vanekha*).
18. *Hilkhot Talmud Torah* 5:9.
19. "*Ha-chakhamim, she-heim avot ha-kol.*" *Peirush Ha-Mishna*, *Pei'a* 1:1 s.v. *u-feiroteihem*.
20. Commentary on the Torah, *Shemot* 20:13 s.v. *lo tirtzach*.

Creator, while the concluding five *Dibberot* focus on *tovat ha-adam*, the benefit of humankind.[21] *Kibbud av va-eim*'s position as the fifth *Dibbera*, on the surface, casts it in an exceedingly theocentric light. The inclusion of *kibbud av va-eim* within a *kevod ha-Borei* framework is surprising, at first glance, and potentially theologically alarming upon further consideration. After all, the identification of any figure with God and the equation between that individual's deserved *kavod* and God's *kavod* seems inordinately imbalanced as no human being in physical form is synonymous with God.[22]

The basis for such a viewpoint rests on a *beraita*[23] that establishes an equation between a person's relationship with one's parents and with God. Pointing to parallel verses in the contexts of *av va-eim* and *Makom* (God), the *beraita* equates ("*hishva ha-katuv*")[24] between parents and God in the expressions of *kibbud*, *mora*, and *berakha* (a euphemism for cursing). The *beraita* concludes with an affirmation of the equation's logic – "this is logical since there are three parties, God, father, and mother, that have partnered in the child's creation."[25] Procreative partnership with God is responsible for the surprising equation between *kibbud av va-eim* and *kevod ha-Borei*.

Rambam's citation and reformulation of this *beraita* reflects a paradigm shift in his conceptualization of *kibbud av va-eim*'s basis: "*Kibbud av va-eim* is a great positive commandment, as is *mora av va-eim*: the Torah weighed them ("*shekalam ha-katuv*") [on par] with honor of Him [God]

---

21. The appearance of God's Name in each of the first five *Dibberot* alone, but not in the latter five, further underscores their focus on *kevod ha-Borei*. See *Chizkuni* (*Shemot* 20:11 s.v. *asher*), and, in particular, his second explanation of this point in which he argues that the first five *Dibberot* are "*eino ra ela la-shamayim* (are only bad towards Heaven)." Ramban also notes and analyzes the attachment of reward and punishment to the fulfillment and violation of the first five *Dibberot*, but not to the latter five.
22. In this spirit, see *Kiddushin* 57a and Rashi s.v. *peireish*.
23. *Kiddushin* 30b.
24. Notably, the term for comparison that appears in *Torat Kohanim* (*Kedoshim parsheta* 1:4-7) as well as in the *Yerushalmi* (*Pei'a* 1:1) is "*hikkish*" rather than "*hishva*," i.e. a comparison rather than equation. This language of comparison appears elsewhere in the *Bavli* (*Bava Metzi'a* 32a) and is used by Rashi (*Kiddushin* 30b s.v. *vaddai, ve-khein*). Comments by *Shitta Lo Noda Le-Mi* (*Kiddushin* 30b s.v. *ne'emar*) and *Perisha* (YD 240:1), which treat the mechanism as a mere "*gilluy milta*," rather than a "*hekesh*," further temper the comparison's strength.
25. "*Ve-khein be-din she-shloshtan shuttafim bo*."

and reverence of Him."[26] In paraphrasing the *beraita*, Rambam replaces the term "*hishva ha-katuv* (the Torah *equated*)" with the expression "*shekalam ha-katuv* (the Torah *weighed*)."[27] Rambam describes the *mitzvot* of *kibbud u-mora av va-eim* as great *mitzvot* that are balanced with and equally as weighty as *kevod u-mora ha-Makom*, honor and reverence of God; however, he avoids substantively identifying one with the other. Rambam's modification is starkly contrasted with his usage of the *beraita*'s expression of "*hishva ha-katuv*" in the immediately following *halakha* regarding the *Gemara*'s third comparison, the identical punishment of stoning for cursing one's parents and God: "*hinnei hishva otan be-onesh*."[28] An identification between *av va-eim* and *Makom* is reasonable when comparing an objective, mechanical action like stoning; however, it is inappropriate with respect to the substantive qualities of *kavod* and *mora*. *Kibbud av va-eim* and *kevod ha-Makom* are equally important, but conceptually distinct from one another.[29]

Rambam's organization and classification of the *halakhot* of *kibbud av va-eim* sheds light on his understanding of *kibbud av va-eim*'s conceptual nature if it is independent from *kevod ha-Borei*. Rambam presents the *halakhot* of *kibbud av va-eim* in the sixth chapter of *Hilkhot Mamrim*, a subsection of *Sefer Shoftim*. Surveying the surrounding landscape in *Sefer Shoftim* and *Hilkhot Mamrim* illuminates the appropriateness of *kibbud av va-eim*'s placement. Five sets of *halakhot* comprise *Sefer Shoftim*: Hilkhot Sanhedrin, Eidut, Mamrim, Eivel,[30] and Melakhim U-Milchamoteihem. The *halakhot* pertaining to *kibbud u-mora av va-eim* appear alongside the *halakhot* concerning the judges who serve on various *Batei Din*, the elders of the *Beit Din Ha-Gadol* who are tasked with interpreting the Oral Law, and the *halakhot* pertaining to a king of Israel. In fact, *Hilkhot Mamrim*,

---

26. Hilkhot Mamrim 6:1.
27. Kesef Mishneh notes that the *beraita*'s formulation is close, but not identical, to Rambam's language. Most likely, Rambam's formulation of "*shekalam ha-katuv*" draws upon Rabbi Yehuda Ha-Nasi's expression of the comparison (*Mekhilta Parashat Yitro parasha* 8 s.v. *kabbeid*): "*she-shakal kevodan u-mora'an li-khvodo ve-kilelatan le-kilelato*."
28. Hilkhot Mamrim 6:2.
29. Relatedly, see *Bach* (YD 240:1 s.v. *mitzvat assei*).
30. *Hilkhot Eivel* seems like an outlier in this grouping of *halakhot*, and Rambam addresses its surprising incorporation in his *koteret* (title) to that section.

specifically, opens with the *halakhot* governing a *zakein mamrei* (rebellious elder) who has rejected a legal ruling of the *Beit Din Ha-Gadol*, and concludes with the *halakhot* dealing with a *ben sorer u-moreh* (rebellious son) who has rebelled against his parents' moral and religious instruction.

The pairing of *av va-eim* alongside judges and kings in *Sefer Shoftim* indicates Rambam's conceptual orientation and embrace of a human authoritative model as the source for parents' honor. An analogy emerges based on Rambam's organization – the parents' role within the family unit parallels the elders' and king's roles vis-à-vis the nation. Religious, political, executive, legislative, and judicial authority must be respected in the familial domain just as it must be safeguarded on the national plane.

Against this backdrop, Rambam's surprising paradigm for *mora av va-eim* can be understood with greater depth. When Rambam in his *Sefer Ha-Mitzvot* (positive 211) searches for a model of comparison to help illustrate the concept and feeling of *mora av va-eim*, he overlooks the most accessible paradigm of *mora ha-Makom*, and instead likens *mora av va-eim* to two human models – a king who has the capacity to punish and a tormentor who has the capability to carry out repulsive consequences.[31] Rambam's first illustration of a king is a natural point of comparison in light of his organization in *Sefer Shoftim*.

Rambam's import of two additional expressions of *kavod* from the context of *kevod ha-Rav* – service and standing, as was highlighted earlier – is illuminated against this backdrop. The association between one's parents and *Rebbe* is particularly sensible, as an individual's *Rebbe* serves as an additional human authoritative figure in his life alongside the national figures of a king and judges. What is particularly striking, yet consistent, is Rambam's conspicuous modification of the *Gemara*'s treatment of the issue. The *Gemara*[32] cites the practice of Rav Yosef who used to stand whenever he heard his mother's footsteps, reasoning, "Let me stand before the Divine presence that has entered." Rambam records the *halakha* of standing in

---

31. Rambam's definition of "*mora*" is significant from a second perspective, since he defines the concept of "*mora*" as fear of consequence instead of inspiring reverential awe.
32. *Kiddushin* 31b.

one's parent's presence; however, the foundation for the *halakha* is shifted from the identification between one's parent and the Divine presence to a *human* authoritative model of *kevod ha-Rav*.[33] [34]

V. The Identification of *Kevod Ha-Rav* with *Kevod Ha-Shekhina*

Despite Rambam's careful circumnavigation to avoid any identification between *kibbud av va-eim* and *kevod ha-Makom*, he fully embraces just such an equation between *mora ha-Rav* and *mora ha-Shekhina* (reverence for the Divine presence). Both in his *Sefer Ha-Mitzvot* as well as in the *Mishneh Torah*, Rambam articulates the series of equations that appear in the *Gemara*: "One who disagrees with one's *Rebbe* is as if he has disagreed with the *Shekhina*, and one who quarrels with one's *Rebbe* is as if he has quarreled with the *Shekhina*, and one who complains against one's *Rebbe* is as if he has complained against the *Shekhina*, and one who thinks disparagingly of one's *Rebbe* is as if he has thought disparagingly of the *Shekhina*."[35] Furthermore, Rambam highlights in both places the *mishna*'s statement (*Avot* 4:13), "reverence for one's *Rebbe* is like reverence for Heaven."[36]

Rambam's embrace of the identification between *mora ha-Rav* and *mora ha-Shekhina* defines the *Rebbe-talmid* relationship in several practical ways. In addition to the expressions of *mora* that are transported from

---

33. See *Arukh Ha-Shulchan* YD 240:24.
34. Rambam's view that the obligation to honor one's older brother (*Hilkhot Mamrim* 6:15), and possibly even one's stepmother and stepfather (*Sefer Ha-Mitzvot, Shoresh Sheini*), is conceptually independent from the honor accorded to one's biological parents, as well as his unique portrayal and modification of the *Gemara*'s three derivations (*Shoresh Sheini* as compared to *Ketubbot* 103a), likely stems from this conceptual orientation. Each extension can be viewed as a quasi-parental figure who obtains authoritative status within the familial unit despite each one's absence from the procreative process. Ramban (in his *hasagot* to *Shoresh Sheini*), in contrast, views each of these cases as merely honoring one's biological parents indirectly – "it all goes back to the respect for one's parents (*ha-kol chozer el kevod ha-avot*)" – as only the biological parents partnered with God in procreation.
35. *Sefer Ha-Mitzvot* positive 209 and *Hilkhot Talmud Torah* 5:1 based on *Sanhedrin* 110a.
36. Tosafot (*Bekhorot* 6a s.v. *peireish*) similarly capture this fundamental distinction between *mora av va-eim* and *mora ha-Rav* and each relationship's identification with *mora Shamayim*.

mora av va-eim to *mora ha-Rav*, Rambam adds that a *talmid* should take leave of his *Rebbe* recoiling backward while still facing his *Rebbe*, instead of turning his back.[37] Kesef Mishneh[38] notes that this feature of *mora ha-Rav* is derived in the *Gemara*[39] from the manner in which *kohanim* would back away from their Temple service and *levi'im* would descend the *dukhan* (platform). Taking leave of one's *Rebbe*, then, is likened to taking leave of servicing the *Shekhina* in the *Beit Ha-Mikdash*.

Furthermore, Rambam, basing himself on the *Gemara*, cautions a *Rebbe* against preventing his *talmid* from serving him, as this would amount to impeding the *talmid*'s engagement in *chesed* and the unshackling of his *yirat Shamayim*. In the other direction, a *talmid* who belittles the *kavod* of his *Rebbe*, even one iota, causes the *Shekhina* to depart from the Jewish people.[40] Rambam's embrace of the equation between *mora ha-Rav* and *mora ha-Shekhina*, then, expresses itself in numerous ways throughout his treatment of the topic.

VI. *Kevod Ha-Av* and *Kevod Ha-Rav* – Conceptually Divergent Relationships

Rambam distinguishes between *kevod u-mora ha-Rav* and *kevod u-mora av va-eim* regarding the classification of the two components of *kavod* and *mora*. Rambam counts *kevod av va-eim* and *mora av va-eim* as two distinct *mitzvot* in *Sefer Ha-Mitzvot*;[41] however, Rambam integrates the two values of *kevod ha-Rav* and *mora ha-Rav* by incorporating the dimension of *mora* into the framework of the mitzva of *kavod* – "not that it [*mora ha-Rav*] is an independent mitzva."[42]

The two discrepancies concerning the degree of identification with *kevod ha-Shekhina* and the classification as distinct or integrated *mitzvot* likely stem from a common conceptual core. The *mishna* in *Bava Metzi'a* formulates the difference between a child's relationships with his father

---

37. *Hilkhot Talmud Torah* 5:6.
38. *Hilkhot Talmud Torah* 5:6 s.v. *u-m"sh*.
39. *Yoma* 53a.
40. *Hilkhot Talmud Torah* 5:8, based on *Ketubbot* 96a and *Berakhot* 26b.
41. *Sefer Ha-Mitzvot* positive 210-211.
42. *Sefer Ha-Mitzvot* positive 209.

as compared to his *Rebbe* in terms of: "One's father has brought him into this world, whereas one's *Rebbe* brings him into the next world." Rambam understood the *mishna*'s distinction as not simply prioritizing competing obligations of a similar nature, but issuing a fundamental distinction between the nature of the two relationships and their attendant obligations of *kavod u-mora*.

The *halakhot* of *kibbud av va-eim* are recorded in *Hilkhot Mamrim* in *Sefer Shoftim* because one's parents play an authoritative role within the familial unit similar to the role of the judge and the king on the national scale. They create, raise, nurture, sustain, guide, discipline, train and educate the child as he enters and traverses this world. The *halakhot* of *kevod ha-Rav*, though, are recorded in *Hilkhot Talmud Torah* in *Sefer Madda*, a book dedicated to the knowledge of, closeness with and return to God, and of fostering a godly personality in the Divine image. The *Rebbe-talmid* relationship is imbued with a sublime quality, as the *Rebbe* offers the *talmid* a glimpse and deepened understanding of the living God and helps carve a pathway for the *talmid*, stretching from this world into the metaphysical World to Come.

For this reason, Rambam adopts the judge and king as the most fitting associations for one's parents, but *mora ha-Shekhina* as an approximate model for *mora ha-Rav*. In addition, the *kavod* accorded to one's parents ought to be counterbalanced by an abiding sense of *mora*, the type of fear that accompanies one's relationship with a multiple. Multiple counterbalancing emotions are invoked in a parent-child relationship: a sense of love and fear, closeness and healthy distance, nurture and reverence. Consequently, *kavod* and *mora* are counted as independent *mitzvot*. The transcendental nature of a *Rebbe-talmid* relationship generates not a fear-driven *mora*, but a sense of reverential awe, *yirat ha-romemut*, that flows from the very same point as the dimension of wondrous *kavod*. In the context of this relationship, the dimension of *mora* is an outgrowth of the aspect of *kavod*; as a result, Rambam integrates both elements into a single mitzva whose fundamental base is the mitzva of *kavod*.

VII. Forgoing Honor – *Av Va-Eim*, *Rebbe*, and *Melekh*

The issue of *mechila*, the ability to forego due honor, offers an important window into the essential nature of *kibbud av va-eim* and its relationship to *kevod ha-Rav* and *eimat ha-melekh* (fear of the king). The *Gemara's* discussion[43] gives uneven attention to each of these figures and their ability to forgo their *kavod*. Rav Chisda opens the discussion with an axiomatic assertion that is never explained, challenged or debated: "a parent may forego his or her due honor (*ha-av she-machal al kevodo, kevodo machul*)."[44] [45]

The question of a *Rebbe's* ability to be forgo his *kavod* is far more contentious, and is the subject of dispute within the *Gemara*. Rav Chisda believes that a *Rebbe* may not forgo his *kavod*; however, Rav Yosef disputes this point and, instead, argues that a *Rebbe* may do so. Their debate revolves around the sentiment of "it is [the scholar's] Torah (*Torah di-lei hi*)," particularly whether this line should be read rhetorically, "is the Torah his to forgo?!," or as an emphatic affirmation, "the Torah is his own!," since human effort, personal insight, and depth of understanding transform the objective corpus of Torah into a personal acquisition.

An unstated assumption in the *Gemara's* analysis of a *Rebbe* who forgoes his *kavod* is that an individual has no right to forego *kavod* that is not attributable to him personally. In this light, the conceptual underpinnings of Rav Chisda's axiomatic position that is unanimously endorsed – "a parent may forego his or her due honor" – supports Rambam's conceptual orientation that a parent's source of *kavod* is based on his own human authoritative status, and, as such, is his to demand or to forego.

The *Gemara's* conclusion seems to equivalently grant a parent and *Rebbe* the ability to forgo his/her *kavod*; nonetheless, the relationship between the two requires investigation. In the context of *kevod ha-Rav*, the

---

43. *Kiddushin* 32a-b.
44. See *Shut Radbaz* (1:524), who argues that parents may forgo the obligation of *kavod*; however, a child who chooses to still honor them, fulfills the mitzva of *kibbud av va-eim*.
45. See Rambam (*Hilkhot Mamrim* 6:8 and *Hilkhot Talmud Torah* 7:13), who encourages an attitude of forgiving and overlooking, for parents and *talmidei chakhamim* alike. This not only safeguards others from violation, but also allows the figures of honor to elevate themselves above perceived or actual slights, thereby making them even more deserving of honor.

Gemara[46] states that despite the *Rebbe*'s *mechila*, the *talmid* is still required to show some measure of respect. For this reason, despite Rava and Rav Papa's presumed *mechila*, their *talmidim* are still rebuked for not having honored them with "*hiddur.*" Rashi[47] explains that "*hiddur*" requires some small movement as if one intends to stand.[48]

It is possible that the requirement for *hiddur* simply reflects appropriate behavior, but may also indicate that *kevod ha-Rav* possesses a dual nature. One aspect of *kevod ha-Rav* is personal to the *Rebbe* as an individual, and is subject to his *mechila*. *Kevod ha-Rav* may contain a second aspect, however, that is identifiable with *kevod ha-Torah* and *kevod ha-Shekhina* and is, hence, not subject to the *Rebbe*'s personal *mechila*. That second dimension expresses itself through a lingering obligation of *hiddur* despite the *Rebbe*'s *mechila* of the first aspect, his own personal honor.

Rambam records the requirement of *hiddur* in the context of *ha-Rav she-machal*, the *Rebbe* who forgoes his *kavod*,[49] but omits any mention of the requirement in the context of *kibbud av va-eim*.[50] Me'iri and Ritva[51] imply that the requirement for *hiddur* applies equally to both a *Rav* and an *av* despite each figure's *mechila*. The different indications as to whether the obligation of *hiddur* also extends to *kibbud av va-eim* is particularly intriguing in light of Rambam's analysis of *kibbud av va-eim*'s fundamental nature and relationship to *kevod ha-Rav*.

Regarding *kibbud av va-eim*, Rambam likely denies a second dimension of *kavod* that would be unforgivable due to its identification with *kevod ha-Makom*, and instead permits a parent to entirely negate the obligation of *kibbud av va-eim*, as the *kavod* is entirely his or her own. In contrast, *kevod ha-Rav* is identifiable with *kevod ha-Shekhina*, and possesses an aspect which the *Rav* is not entitled to forgo. This second dimension finds expression through the residual obligation of *hiddur*. Me'iri and Ritva might believe that *kibbud av va-eim*, too, contains a second dimension of

---

46. *Kiddushin* 32b.
47. *Kiddushin* 32b s.v. *hiddur*.
48. In contrast, see Me'iri, *Beit Ha-Bechira Kiddushin* p. 186 s.v. *ha-av*.
49. *Hilkhot Talmud Torah* 5:11.
50. *Hilkhot Mamrim* 6:8.
51. *Kiddushin* 32a s.v. *isi*.

kavod that is identified with *kevod ha-Makom* and is not subject to *mechila*. They, therefore, extend the requirement of *hiddur* from the context of *kevod ha-Rav* to *kibbud av va-eim*.

From a second angle, Rambam's identification of *kibbud u-mora av va-eim* with the human authoritative figure of a king seems highly problematic within the *Gemara*'s discussion of *mechila*. To the degree that *kibbud av va-eim* is indisputably subject to *mechila*, a king, in a parallel opposite manner, is unquestionably incapable of foregoing his honor. The *Gemara*[52] cites the uncontested viewpoint of Rav Ashi that "a king cannot forgo his due honor (*ha-melekh she-machal al kevodo, ein kevodo machul*)," based on the verse, "you shall surely place a king over yourselves,"[53] which establishes an absolute insistence on casting *eimat ha-melekh* over the nation. Despite Rambam's association between *mora av va-eim* and *mora ha-melekh*, the *Gemara* assesses parental and royal honor in a diametrically opposed fashion.

Derisha's son, in a note on his father's commentary,[54] addresses *halakha*'s uncompromising stance against negotiating *eimat ha-melekh*, and why it is distinct from a *Rebbe* and parent's ability to forego their respective honor.[55] The fundamental question on which the distinction hinges is the conceptual relationship between the dimensions of *kavod* and *mora*. A king is incapable of foregoing his *kavod* because the defining quality of his relationship with the nation is *mora* and *eima*. For this reason, a king cannot forgo his *kavod* because that will necessarily compromise the dominant quality of *mora*. In contrast, the dominant or equally as prominent dimension of a parent's relationship with his or her child is the quality of *kavod*; hence, if a parent wants to forego his or her deserved honor, they are entitled to do so irrespective of what impact that *mechila* might have on the quality of *mora* which is secondary or parallel to the aspect of *kavod*.

What emerges, then, are three related, yet conceptually distinct models of human authority according to Rambam. The primary dimension in a

---

52. *Kiddushin* 32b.
53. *Devarim* 17:15 and based on Sifrei's derivation (*Parashat Shoftim* no. 14).
54. YD 240:4.
55. See *Tosafot* (*Sanhedrin* 19a s.v. *Yannai*) and *Perisha* (YD 242:31), which address the discrepancy between a king, *Rebbe* and parents from different angles.

Rebbe-talmid relationship is *kavod* with the aspect of *mora*, reverential awe, emerging as a natural outgrowth from the transcendental spirit of *kavod*. A king's relationship to the nation fundamentally differs, with a base fear of punishment and consequence serving as the core of the relationship. Any expression of tepid *kavod* merely mirrors one's base *mora*. The parental relationship lies between the two poles of *kevod ha-Rav* and *eimat ha-melekh*, and draws from both with its counterbalancing values of both *kavod* and *mora*.

Halakhic Dilemmas of the "Knife Intifada"

Rabbi Dr. Shlomo Brody

Introduction
During the "knife intifada" between 2015-2016, Israeli society grappled with many issues relating to neutralized terrorists who were considered "lone wolf" attackers because they were individuals not sent by organizations such as Hamas or Islamic Jihad. This led to larger questions of how to address cases of violent adversaries who were not members of a foreign army or terrorist organization. Israelis have no ethical or halakhic compunctions in doing what it takes to stop these threats during the acts of terror, or by preventing them through preemptive security measures. This follows the halakhic mandates of necessity and self-defense, exemplified in the Talmudic principle, "If one is coming to kill you, arise and kill him first (*im ba lehorgekha, hashkem lehorgo*)."[1]

Once the threat has been neutralized and the terrorist captured or wounded, however, those rationales no longer seem relevant. Let's take, for example, an all-too-common scenario during the "knife intifada," in which a terrorist was shot and wounded by a soldier or citizen, leaving him incapacitated on the ground. At that moment, may one shoot him dead? Should emergency personnel treat him, or should they attend to victims first? If he dies, should Israel bury him? If, alternatively, he is arrested and tried in court, may Israel execute him for his heinous acts?[2] All these painful dilemmas played out in the court of public opinion. In this brief essay, we will try to sketch some of the major halakhic considerations in creating an ethical framework for addressing these complex moral questions.

---
1. *Sanhedrin* 72a.
2. On the question of capital punishment for terrorists, see my "Should Israel Execute Convicted Terrorists?," *The Jerusalem Post*, July 14, 2016.

May One Kill a Subdued Terrorist?

Halakha prohibits the intentional killing of innocent human life.[3] There are times, however, when a person may kill someone else, as in cases of mandated warfare or in acts of self-defense. The right to self-defense is exemplified within *halakha* by the law of "*rodef*" (the pursuer). Chazal contend that the verse "You shall not stand idly by the blood of your neighbor" (*Vayikra* 19:16) not only demands saving a friend from drowning or from a hungry lion, but further dictates stopping an assailant from committing murder.[4]

Yet this does not mean that there are no guidelines for trying to stop the assailant. The *Gemara* (*Sanhedrin* 74a) records the position of Rabbi Yonatan ben Sha'ul that if the assailant could be neutralized by injuring one of his limbs, and a person instead kills the *rodef*, the former is liable to be prosecuted for homicide ("*neharag alav*"). Some *rishonim* indicate that other *chakhamim* disagreed, maintaining that the rescuer may kill under all circumstances because the attempted murderer has, as it were, abdicated his right to life by making himself subject to the laws of *rodef*.[5] Yet the normative ruling asserts that when possible, one must use a less lethal method, such as cutting off a hand or debilitating the legs.[6]

Some figures, including Rabbeinu Ya'akov ben Asher, believe that a person is even liable for murder for using excessive force in stopping the pursuant, following the plain meaning of the *Gemara*.[7] Rambam, however, deems it a serious sin worthy of "heavenly punishment" but not warranting penalty from a judicial court. Some explain that Rambam interprets the *Gemara* this way because he believes it unfair to punish someone rushing to stop a murder. As such, had the individual been warned on the spot that he

---

3. On this prohibition, see Rav Ya'akov Ari'el, *Halakha Be-Yameinu*, pp. 397-398, and Rav Ari'el Finkelstein, *Derekh Ha-Melekh*, pp. 19-47.
4. *Sanhedrin* 73a, citing *Vayikra* 19:16.
5. See Rashi *Sanhedrin* 57b s.v. neharag. See also Rav Yisrael Rosen, "*Hitgonenut Atzmit Be-Mechir Chayyei Ha-Rodef*," *Techumin* 10.
6. See Rambam *Hilkhot Rotzei'ach* 1:13 and *Hilkhot Melakhim* 9:4. There are those who proposed an intermediate position that would permit the intended victim alone (as opposed to bystanders) to always use lethal force. See, for example, the commentary of Rav Eliyahu Mizrachi to *Bereishit* 32:8. This position, however, did not gain widespread currency.
7. *Tur* CM 425.

was using excessive force, but killed the assailant anyway, he would indeed be liable for murder.[8] Others assert that while the rescuer erred, Rambam believes that we should not punish someone for killing an assailant who ultimately brought his death upon himself.[9]

Of course, no one expects a citizen or even a security officer who has seconds to act to calculate exactly how much force might be necessary to stop an assailant. This would be utterly unreasonable and would prevent people from acting to save the victim.[10] Moreover, it is not always easy to know when a threat has been fully neutralized,[11] especially when a wounded terrorist continues to struggle. Nonetheless, once the assailant is clearly incapacitated, we do not allow one to kill him, whether out of a sense of vengeance or vigilante justice. Thus, to take a simple example, an attempted murderer who has been significantly wounded and handcuffed to an ambulance gurney may not be shot.

During the height of this intifada, however, Rav Shmu'el Eliyahu and Rav Moshe Tzuri'el contended that these terrorists should be treated not as regular criminal assailants but rather as enemy soldiers.[12] This is in line with the sentiment, found in *Masekhet Soferim*, that "the best of gentiles may be killed [in war]," which was regularly interpreted to apply to enemy combatants during wartime.[13] Accordingly, they assert, a terrorist should be killed, even once the threat has been neutralized.

Against this view, one could argue that so-called lone wolf attackers should be seen no differently than civilian murderers. Yet given their

---

8. *Even Ha-Ezel Hilkhot Rotzei'ach* 1:13.
9. Radbaz to *Hilkhot Melakhim* 9:4.
10. For similar reasons, Chazal decreed that a rescuer does not pay for property damages that he/she causes during his/her act of heroism. See *Bava Kamma* 117b.
11. To exemplify this point, it should be noted that many police officers have been killed while in the process of handcuffing a suspect, i.e. when the threat seems to have been neutralized. For a recent example, see "Police: Texas Deputy Shot by Handcuffed Suspect," *The Houston Chronicle*, Feb 1, 2018.
12. Some news outlets reported that Rav Ben-Tziyon Mutzafi went so far as to assert that we should punish those who keep them alive.
13. *Masekhet Soferim* 15:7. See also *Tosafot Avoda Zara* 26b s.v. *ve-lo moridin*. For the history of this expression (including the inclusion of the term "in war") and its polemical use against Jews, see Rav Menachem Kasher, *Torah Sheleima* to *Shemot* 9:20 and Excursus 19 in that volume. See also Jacob Katz, *Exclusiveness and Tolerance*, pp. 107-108.

nationalistic motivations and the wider culture of terror, it is reasonable to argue that they should be categorized as enemy soldiers and not regular assailants.[14] That said, another objection to this militaristic reading is that it's unclear why combatants retain that status once they've been captured or debilitated. As Rabbeinu Bachya argues, the logic of the expression in *Masekhet Soferim* is that during wartime when gentiles are coming to kill us, we should rise and kill them first. Yet once the threat has ended, peace, not violence, should be the goal.[15]

We may ask further: according to the militaristic logic, why not wipe out the jail cells of all convicted terrorists? Indeed, Rav Eliyahu argues that if kept alive and ultimately tried and convicted, these assailants might ultimately go free in a prisoner swap and return to terror. Yet the proper response to that problem is to stiffen jail terms and not engage in lopsided prisoner swaps that free murderers.[16] Alternatively, for those who believe in the wisdom of such prisoner swaps, then keeping terrorists alive as trading cards is a prudent move.

Similarly, according to this line of thought, it's not clear why the IDF should not kill enemy soldiers who drop their guns and wave a white flag on the battlefield. Admittedly, that was indeed the way of warfare for most

---

14. This is the reasonable claim of Rav Henkin, *Shut Benei Banim* vol. 3 p. 193. See also Rav Re'eim Ha-Kohen, "*Nitrul Mechabbel*," *Shabbat Be-Shabbato* 1597 (25 Marcheshvan 5776), who argues that there is no need to aim to only wound when in the midst of a terrorist attack, and therefore one may shoot to kill. Rabbi Ya'akov Ari'el argued that when possible, one should aim to only wound the terrorist, but he recognizes that this too is frequently not possible given the circumstances. See his statements in *Ye'erav Sichi: Sichot im HaRav Ya'akov Ari'el*, ed. Arale Harel, p. 135. It should be noted that among contemporary philosophers, there is also a debate regarding whether there is a legal or moral obligation to neutralize an enemy combatant during conflict through the least harmful means. For references to the literature on this topic, see the articles of Ryan Goodman and Michael N. Schmitt in the *European Journal of International Law* 24:3 (1 August 2013), and the replies of Geoffrey S. Corn, Laurie R. Blank, Chris Jenks and Eric Talbot Jensen, "Belligerent Targeting and the Invalidity of a Least Harmful Means Rule," *International Law Studies* 89 (2013), pp. 536-626.
15. Rabbeinu Bachya to *Shemot* 14:7.
16. Regarding the halakhic propriety of swapping enemy prisoners to release captives (dead or alive), see my book, *A Guide to the Complex: Contemporary Halakhic Debates* (Maggid Books, 2014), pp. 262-265.

of history.[17] Yet military conventions of the twentieth century, in 1929 and especially the Third Geneva Convention of 1949, have attempted to end this vengeful phenomenon, and for good reason.[18] As Rav Eli'ezer Waldenberg wrote in the early 1950s, *halakha* recognizes the wisdom of swapping prisoners of war at the end of hostilities.[19] This, in part, is for the practical goal of securing the release of one's own POWs, but also because the *Tanakh* itself offers examples and reasons for being merciful to foreign prisoners who are no longer combatants.[20] Indeed, in an article published many years ago, Rav Yehuda Henkin (whose son and daughter-in-law were tragically killed in this wave of terror) argued that even if there were no technical legal requirement to keep a neutralized terrorist alive, it would still constitute a *chillul ha-Shem*, desecration of God's Name, given the widespread international belief in the prohibition of killing captured enemies.[21] This consideration was further raised by Rav Yuval Cherlow, who faulted many *poskim* for not citing this consideration.[22]

Moreover, as Rav Ya'akov Ari'el noted, the inevitable recording of such executions might further enrage our bloodthirsty and vengeful enemies and add to the threats against us, as opposed to serving as a deterrent. He

---

17. For statistics during the two World Wars of the 20th century, see Niall Ferguson, "Prisoner Taking and Prisoner Killing in the Age of Total War: Towards a Political Economy of Military Defeat," *War in History* 11:2 (2004), pp. 148-192.
18. The sentiment is well-summarized by Corn, et al, p. 537: "There is virtually no disagreement in the contemporary international discourse on the law of armed conflict (LOAC) with the rule that once an enemy belligerent becomes *hors de combat* – what a soldier would recognize as "combat ineffective" – the authority to employ deadly force terminates."
19. *Hilkhot Medina* vol. 2, *sha'ar* 5, *perek* 9, pp. 192-194.
20. In this spirit, he favorably cites the position of Rav Me'ir Simcha of *Dvinsk* (*Meshekh Chokhma*) that the laws of *eishet yefat to'ar* are not relevant when the military convention is to return prisoners after war. See also Rav Eli'ezer Melamed, *Peninei Halakha: Ha-Am Veha-Aretz – Likkutim* pp. 128-129, who argues that contemporary military mores have nullified the dispensations of *eishet yefat to'ar*. Regarding the *halakha* of *eishet yefat to'ar*, see my "Enemy Captives and Rape," *The Jerusalem Post*, October 27, 2016.
21. *Shut Benei Banim* vol. 3, *ma'amar* 4 (pp. 193-194). See also 40-41.
22. On this consideration in halakhic literature, see Prof. Avi'ad Ha-Kohen, "*Lama Yomeru Ha-Goyim*," in *Am Le-Vadad*, ed. Rav Binyamin Lau, pp. 88-123. See also Yitzchak Henska, "*Darkhei Ha-Goyim Ke-Basis Le-Shikkul Hilkhati*," *Tzohar* 34 (5769).

further argued that while military assassinations are sometimes necessary, those decisions must be made by military experts, not vigilantes. Indeed, the danger of citizens taking the law into their own hands has been tragically displayed by brutal attacks on innocent bystanders who were mistaken for terrorists.[23]

Rav Ari'el adds a more integral argument: even in the midst of war, one must still remember that we are fighting against human beings. Once the threat has been neutralized, we should not desire to kill anyone.[24] Another type of moral argument, this time relating to virtue ethics, was also invoked by Rav David Stav, who beseeched us not to descend to the moral depravities of our enemies by killing unnecessarily.[25] The terrorists deserve to die. Yet our own ethical development requires that we only kill when absolutely necessary. The goal of our nation is to execute justice, not captured prisoners.

Should Terrorist Victims Receive Medical Priority over their Attackers?
For the reasons mentioned above, it becomes a strategic and moral imperative to keep enemy combatants alive once the threat has been neutralized. Yet this raises a separate but related question: should medics or hospitals prioritize treating severely wounded terrorists over more moderately wounded victims? In the midst of this wave of terror, the heads of the Israeli Medical Association (IMA) and the *Magen David Adom* (MDA) ambulance service announced that professional protocol mandates treating the wounded exclusively on the basis of their medical condition, independent of their national origins or moral liability. Medical professionals should treat patients without judgment, leaving questions of moral and legal liability for other authorities at a later time. Just as we treat

---

23. During a terrorist attack in the *Be'er Sheva* Bus Station on October 18th, 2015, Haftom Zarhum, an Eritrean, was shot several times by police officers who mistook him for the terrorist. While lying on the ground, he was repeatedly kicked by Israeli bystanders. While a coroner's report concluded that he died from the gun shot wounds, the case highlighted the danger of bystanders taking the law into their own hands, as emphasized at the time by Prime Minister Netanyahu.
24. *Ye'erav Sichi: Sichot im HaRav Ya'akov Ari'el*, ed. Arale Harel, p. 135.
25. https://news.walla.co.il/item/2897134.

car accident victims equally without asking who caused the accident, so too we should act neutrally at the site of a terrorist attack.

This sentiment, in fact, seems to have basis in international law, as stated in the First Geneva Convention: "Members of the armed forces who are wounded or sick shall be treated humanely and cared for without any adverse distinction founded on sex, race, nationality, religion, political opinions, or any other similar criteria... Only urgent medical reasons will authorize priority in the order of treatment to be administered." In the commentary to this law, further clarity is provided: "Each belligerent must treat his fallen adversaries as he would the wounded of his own army."[26]

Yet as sophisticated ethicists have noted, matters are not so simple, both in theory and certainly in practice, as military doctors (or, for that matter, civilian health care providers assisting the army) have dual loyalties as both physicians and soldiers. The latter identity compels them to do what is best for military and security readiness, thereby dictating favoritism for one's own brothers-in-arms. Indeed, many studies and anecdotal evidence indicate that medical soldiers give precedence to their own comrades during times of conflict.[27] Indeed, during the "knife intifada," the pronouncements of the IMA and MDA drew sharp rebuke from the heads of the *Hatzola* ambulance service and the *Zaka* rescue organization, who announced that they would give priority to victims when they were sufficiently wounded to require immediate care, even if the terrorist was more severely wounded.

This passionate debate rests, in part, on questions of triage in which societies must prioritize how to allocate scarce medical resources, in this case, utilizing emergency medical personnel for a third-party rescue by a public servant.[28] Who should get priority in this situation? Some

---

26. Protocol Additional to the Geneva Conventions of 12 August 1949, and Relating to the Protection of Victims of International Armed Conflicts, art. 41, June 8, 1977, 1125 U.N.T.S. 3.
27. Michael L. Gross, "Teaching Military Medical Ethics: Another Look at Dual Loyalty and Triage," *Cambridge Quarterly of Healthcare Ethics* 19 (2010), pp. 458–464.
28. Triage dilemmas, of course, can also emerge when those in need are in possession of the life-saving resource itself. The *Gemara* addresses one such case in a well-known debate regarding two thirsty desert travelers of which only one possesses a bottle of water, sufficient to save himself alone (*Bava Metzi'a* 62a). For

poskim, including Rav Avraham Karelitz, point to a passage in the *Gemara* (*Horayot* 13a) as a potential resource for this dilemma. The *mishna* states that a man receives preference over a woman when it comes to sustenance and restoring lost objects, but a woman takes precedence when it comes to provisions of clothing and being redeemed from captivity. It similarly asserts that a *kohen* takes precedence over a *levi*, and that a *talmid chakham*, even if born a *mamzer*, takes precedence over an *am ha-aretz* (ignoramus), even if he is a *kohen gadol*. We thus have a series of criteria that prioritizes based on a variety of factors including genealogical sanctity, social utility, merit, and the level of threat.

Does this *mishna* serve as a source for life-saving triage in the contemporary era? Perhaps, as seen in the sixteenth century ruling of Rav Moshe Isserles that one should save a drowning man before a woman, seemingly because men are obligated in more *mitzvot* than women.[29] Yet as Prof. Avraham Steinberg has noted, many twentieth century scholars have questioned this ruling's feasibility or relevance in the contemporary era.[30] First, already in the eighteenth century, some *poskim* claimed that we cannot give priority to *kohanim* or *levi'im* since we are no longer sure of accurate genealogical lineage. More fundamentally, contemporary *poskim* including Rav Eli'ezer Waldenberg have noted that some *rishonim*, including Me'iri, asserted that the *mishna* was only establishing priorities in food handouts, as indicated in the parallel passage in the *Talmud Yerushalmi*.[31] Rav Waldenberg further argues that even if this *mishna* was referring to priorities in saving life, the rule giving preference to men over women was not codified in the major codes – *Mishneh Torah, Arba'a Turim,* and *Shulchan Arukh* – because the *mishna* ultimately cares more about the merit earned by the piety of the men and women (i.e. how many

---

a good overview of various Jewish positions on triage, including those that apply to contemporary medical systems, see Alan Jotkowitz, "A Man Takes Precedence Over a Woman When it Comes to Saving a Life": The Modern Dilemma of Triage from a Halakhic and Ethical Perspective," *Tradition* 47:1 (2014), pp. 48-68.
29. See *Rema* YD 252:8 and *Taz* ibid. 252:6.
30. Rav Dr. Avraham Steinberg, "*Pe'ilut Ba-Chazit Ha-Oref,*" *Assia* 21:1-2 (2008), pp. 5-39.
31. *Tzitz Eli'ezer* 18:1, based on Me'iri to *Horayot* 13a and *Yerushalmi Horayot* 3:4.

mitzvot and good deeds they actually perform), not the number of *mitzvot* they could theoretically perform. Such determinations, of course, cannot be easily made, particularly in the context of emergency care.

Other *poskim* have marginalized the *mishna* by asserting that these priorities would only apply when all other factors are equal. Yet if one patient begins treatment earlier, he should not be abandoned for someone else. Alternatively, if one patient's health situation is significantly worse than another's, that patient gains preference, irrespective of social position. Accordingly, Rav Moshe Feinstein and Rav Shlomo Zalman Auerbach contend that the *mishna* is of limited relevance in contemporary triage circumstances, in which we correctly tend to treat people equally based on medical criterion.[32]

That said, it remains problematic to apply such egalitarian notions when one patient is a citizen and another is an enemy or a terrorist. It's precisely in times of national emergency when giving priority based on social worth may be more easily justified. Support for such social distinctions may been seen within the *Gemara*'s ruling that a *kohen gadol* appointed specifically to lead the troops in war (*kohen meshu'ach milchama*) receives priority over a regular vice *kohen gadol*, even though the latter may be seen as of a higher spiritual level. Nonetheless, since the former was necessary for public needs, his treatment is given priority.[33] Indeed, many ethicists have wrangled with questions of the justness of giving priority to certain soldiers over others in different contexts based on their utility in warfare.[34] In the case in which we are deciding between treating a wounded civilian victim and an enemy terrorist, the claim to prioritize the former is particularly strong since the gap between the social merits of the two patients (one an innocent civilian victim, the other a ruthless terrorist) is so wide. This is particularly true given the demoralizing effect that civilian deaths can have on the nation's

---

32. *Igrot Moshe* 2:73-74; *Minchat Shlomo* 2:82:2.
33. See *Nazir* 47b, Rashi *Horayot* 13a s.v. *lehachayoto*, and the discussion of Rav Yitzchak Zilberstein in his *Nes Lehitnoses*, siman 67 pp. 207-215.
34. Some discuss the ethics of "reverse triage," in which lightly-wounded soldiers may be treated first so that they can return quickly to the battlefield and replenish troops. Another interesting question involves treating members of one's own army as opposed to allied soldiers from a different country.

fortitude to fight. It would thus appear that we should save the lives of neutralized terrorists, but we must first prioritize our national interests and fulfill our ethical duties to our own brethren.[35] At the end of the day, it remains difficult during wartime to justify prioritizing national medical resources for an enemy over the immediate health needs of a citizen.[36]

May Israel Withhold Burying the Corpses of Terrorists?
In the wake of repeated terror attacks, the Israeli government has debated whether to withhold returning the corpses of killed terrorists to their Palestinian families. Some claim this would deter future terrorists from seeking to become martyrs, especially given the heroic funerals they regularly receive. Others retort that such measures only further inflame the tense situation, and instead suggest demanding agreements from the terrorist's family to hold a modest funeral before returning the corpse.

Many countries, including Israel, create cemeteries for enemy soldiers in times of warfare, with the understanding that there will be a reciprocal return of bodies with the signing of an armistice. When dealing with terrorists, however, no such understanding can be assumed. Some thus further argue that Israel must retain these corpses as bargaining chips in future deals for the return of our dead soldiers, including Hadar Goldin and Oron Shaul, who were killed during Operation Protective Edge in 2014.

The Torah explicitly mandates burying executed criminals. "If a man is guilty of a capital offense and is put to death, and you impale him on a

---

35. On the role of "associative obligations" in wartime medicine, see Michael L. Gross, "Saving Life, Limb, and Eyesight: Assessing the Medical Rules of Eligibility During Armed Conflict," *The American Journal of Bioethics*, 17:10 (2017), pp. 40-52.
36. There is, however, one interesting counterargument made by the medical association. They've argued that terrorist attacks on Israeli streets are responded to by civilian (i.e. non-military) medics. Telling them to prioritize Jewish victims will introduce social distinctions into Israeli healthcare and lead to a dangerous slippery slope within hospitals which amazingly succeed in keeping politics out of healthcare decisions, with Jews and Arabs treated alike. This is a significant consideration, but should be combated with the following clarification: the distinction here is between terrorists and victims, not Jews and Arabs. Therefore, if there should be a case of a Jew who randomly attacks innocent Arab civilians (and alas, there are a few examples of such behavior), then the Arab victims in this case would take priority.

stake, you must not let his corpse remain on the stake overnight, but must bury him the same day. For an impaled body is an affront to God – you shall not defile the Land that the Lord your God is giving you to possess" (*Devarim* 21:22-23). The rationale offered by the Torah is very telling. It is an affront to God to leave a body unburied since, as the *Gemara* explains, all humans were created in the image of God. No actions, however horrific, can remove that fundamental element of a person's humanity.

This point was exemplified by Yehoshu'a, who at the beginning of Am Yisrael's military conquests – when symbolic actions of brutality might have instilled fear in enemies – punctiliously buried the kings of *Kena'an* (*Yehoshu'a* 10:27). Josephus, in his *Antiquities*, attests that ancient Jewish practice was to "let our enemies that fall in battle also be buried." Even the enemies in the apocalyptic war of Gog and *Magog* will be buried, leading the nations of the world to proclaim the greatness of the Jewish nation for burying their enemies (Rashi *Yechezkel* 39:13).

Yet the right to burial does not mean that every person is entitled to equal burial rites. The *Gemara* declares that an executed convict is not buried in his family's gravesite because "we do not bury a wicked person next to a righteous one."[37] Instead, the community must create a separate cemetery to bury these executed criminals, with many *poskim* further asserting that these criminals should be denied any honorary mourning rites. These *halakhot* signify society's eternal condemnation of that criminal's actions. Apostates or excommunicated community members were given similar treatments, and at times buried outside the cemetery walls.

While *halakha* mandates that Jews actively help to bury deceased gentile neighbors – in accordance with the Divine image found in all humans – it also maintains that only Jews be buried within Jewish cemeteries. (Indeed, in many societies, burial grounds convey cultural affinities, including familial, professional, religious, and national ties.) This has caused tensions[38] in Israel where, after years of debate, intermarried Jewish Israelis may be buried with their gentile spouses in state cemeteries reserved for non-Jews. It has caused particularly acrimonious debates over

---

37. *Sanhedrin* 47a.
38. https://www.jpost.com/Jewish-World/Judaism/Ask-The-Rabbi-185303.

separate military cemeteries since many Israelis, including a few *talmidei chakhamim*, believe that comrades-in-arms should be buried together, no matter what their religious affiliation.[39] These controversies highlight the powerful symbolism created by burial rites.

In the case of terrorists killed, there should be no debate: their corpses should ideally be interred in their own non-glorified area. To achieve this goal, could Israel even refuse to bury these terrorists entirely? Admittedly, some have contended that in extreme circumstances, we may suspend the mandate of burial for some broader societal purposes.[40] This might explain, for example, why David *Ha-Melekh* did not try to immediately bury the children of Sha'ul after they were executed by hanging (*Shmu'el Bet* 21). Similarly, according to a few traditions, the Jews allowed the bodies of Haman and his sons to be left unburied for several days in order to instill fear in their enemies.

Such an extreme approach would be a grave mistake. First, while one might believe that such treatment will discourage future lone wolf attacks, it is more likely that radical fundamentalists will find a theological explanation to assure their holy war soldiers that they have a place in Heaven, whether they are buried or not. Second, one must weigh the consequences of how fundamentalists will react to such a symbolic action, especially when they have their hands on an Israeli corpse. Most fundamentally, while in the midst of a campaign against terror, one must never forget that every human being was created in God's image. Burying terrorists sends an important message to ourselves: even as we fight a just war against our enemies, we should not lose sensitivity to the human tragedy of this wickedness.

Taking responsibility to bury these corpses, however, does not mean that Israel must return them to their families for burial.[41] The strategic

---

39. See *Gittin* 61a, the commentaries of Rashba and Rabbeinu Nissim, and my *A Guide to the Complex: Contemporary Halakhic Debates* (Maggid, 2014), pp. 330-332.
40. See the discussion in Rav Aharon Walkin, *Shut Zekan Aharon* 2:80. Yet ultimately, one is hard-pressed to find a notion that we would leave someone unburied, as emphasized by Aharon Kirschenbaum, *Beit Din Makkin Ve-Onshin*, pp. 696-697 and note 184.
41. This, in fact, was precisely the point of creating separate burial locations for criminals, as dictated by *Mishna Sanhedrin* 6:5-6. In 2013, when American

calculation of whether such an action helps or harms Israeli interests remains a decision of the political and military echelon. Spiritual leaders must continue to urge that we prioritize our safety without ever forgetting that all humans were created in the image of God. This balance, of course, is not always easy to make, but it is my belief that the halakhic sources cited in this article provide us with a good framework for grappling with the significant ethical dilemmas faced in our time.

---

officials couldn't find a burial spot for one of the Boston Marathon terrorists, I argued that he must be buried, but suggested that the following text be written on his gravestone: "Buried here is a terrorist who was born in the image of God with unlimited potential to do good but who desecrated that virtue with his violent actions. May his victims rest in peace, and may the society that buried him continue to emulate the ways of God and merit to live in a world of peace." See my "Even Criminals Rest in Peace," *Tablet Magazine*, May 9, 2013. (The title, alas, was not chosen by me and is somewhat misleading regarding its content.)

The Interplay of the Interpersonal and Divine Commandments

Rabbi Joel Finkelstein[1]

The distinction between interpersonal *mitzvot*, "*bein adam la-chaveiro*," and *mitzvot* relating to God, "*bein adam la-Makom*," is as old as the Ten Commandments, divided between the interpersonal and man-God *mitzvot*. The terms *bein adam la-chaveiro* and *bein adam la-Makom* emerge in the *mishna*, mostly in connection to the difference in methods of *teshuva* for the two types of *mitzvot* (*Yoma* 8:9).

But as much as there are distinctions between man-God and man-man *mitzvot*, what we would like to explore is the relationship of the two to each other and the ways in which they are actually the same, overlapping, or related. Of course, the two types of *mitzvot* are related in numerous ways. It is not our purpose to discuss ways in which they simply are similar, i.e. how in both realms love of the other, both of God and man, is a central part of the underlying motivation to act. It is not our purpose to discuss which is more important or how one realm can affect or lead to the other, i.e. how being good to others can affect being good to God or vice versa.

Rather, our purpose here is to find ways in which the relationship between man and man is also, at the same time, a relationship with God. We would like to show ways in which one can be relating to a person but also relating to God simultaneously. How can one mitzva be both relevant to our relationship with God and our fellow man at the same time?

---

1. Much thanks to my son, Natan Finkelstein (Gush 2017-19), for his help with this article.

The Good and the Right

One way to look at the relationship of the interpersonal and the God-related *mitzvot* is that when we relate well to others, we conform to the ideals that God holds dear. This is summed up nowhere better than the verse in *Devarim* (6:18), "You shall do that which is good and right in the eyes of God." Whatever we do as far as *mitzvot* are concerned, whether interpersonal or not, could be said to be simply doing what is right in God's eyes. As Ramban puts it:

> And the intention of this is that from the beginning God said to keep God's commandments, testimonies, and laws as God has commanded them. And now, it says: Even regarding what God did not command, pay attention to do what is good and right in God's eyes, because God loves goodness and righteousness. And it is important because it is impossible to mention in the Torah [what should be] everyone's conduct, with their neighbors and friends, in any business matter, and regarding ordinances of any town or country, because the Torah already mentions many of these laws, such as: "Do not gossip" (*Vayikra* 19:16); "You shall not take vengeance or bear a grudge" (*Vayikra* 19:18); "You shall not stand idly by the blood of your neighbor" (*Vayikra* 19:16); "You shall not insult the deaf" (*Vayikra* 19:14); "You shall rise before the aged" (*Vayikra* 19:32), etc. Once more for emphasis, generally one should do what is good and right regarding everything, including compromise, acting beyond the strict demands of the law.... until one reads about all matters of honesty and integrity. (Ramban *Devarim* 6:18)

For Ramban (and the *Netziv*), this verse is a catch-all for all ethical and honest behavior toward our fellow, but based on context one could suggest (and perhaps Bekhor Shor concurs) that it refers to all the commandments mentioned in the previous verse: "Surely guard all the *mitzvot* of the Lord your God and His testimonies and laws (*chukkim*) that He has commanded." Moshe goes on to say that we should do what is right in God's eyes, presumably referring to doing those very commandments. The relationship between the ethical and the Divine *mitzvot* is that they are all in accordance with God's goodness and will. As we act kindly to our neighbor, we are simultaneously acting in accordance with that which is good and right in the eyes of God.

Walk in His Ways

The *Gemara* in *Sota* indicates that our relationship to others is driven by our relationship with God, and our desire to emulate Him and be close to Him in deed:

> And Rabbi Chama bar Rabbi Chanina says: What is [the meaning of that] which is written (*Devarim* 13:5): "After the Lord your God shall you walk, [and Him shall you fear, and His commandments shall you keep, and unto His voice shall you hearken, and Him shall you serve, and unto Him shall you cleave]?" Is it [actually] possible for a person to follow the Divine Presence? But hasn't it already been stated (*Devarim* 4:24): "For the Lord your God is a devouring fire [a zealous God]," [and one cannot approach fire? He explains:] Rather, [the meaning is] that one should follow the attributes of the Holy One, blessed be He. Just as He clothes the naked, as it is written (*Bereishit* 3:21): "And the Lord God made for Adam and for his wife garments of skin, and clothed them," so too, should you clothe the naked. Just as the Holy One, blessed be He, visits the sick, as it is written [with regard to God's appearing to Avraham following his circumcision] (*Bereishit* 18:1): "And the Lord appeared unto him by the terebinths of *Mamrei*," so too, should you visit the sick. Just as the Holy One, blessed be He, consoles mourners, as it is written (*Bereishit* 25:11): "And it came to pass after the death of Avraham, that God blessed Yitzchak his son," so too, should you console mourners. Just as the Holy One, blessed be He, buried the dead, as it is written (*Devarim* 34:6):

"And he was buried in the valley [in the Land of Mo'av]," so too, should you bury the dead. (*Sota* 14a)

Clearly, our interpersonal interactions are driven, at least in part, by a desire to relate to God inasmuch as we emulate Him. As we help our fellow, we also emulate God.

God within Man?
Another possible relationship of the interpersonal and the God-related *mitzvot* regards the controversial question as to whether God is within us or without. Some (Ibn Gabirol and others) take the position that God is inside us based partially on the verse in *Iyov* (19:26), "*umi-besari echezeh Elokah* (and from my flesh I see God)." One can find such a concept in Chassidic and non-Chassidic literature alike. According to this, when we relate to our fellow, we are also relating to the aspect of God that is within him or her; when relating to others, we relate to God as we do when we relate to God Himself.

In fact, Rabbeinu Bachya in his *Chovot Ha-Levavot* (*sha'ar ahavat Hashem* ch. 1) says that one's soul longs for God precisely because of its similarity, its affinity for something spiritual, of a nature similar to itself. But even if one maintains that the soul is not a part of God but is a created being (Rav Sa'adya Ga'on and Rambam), one's soul longs for its fellow created soul in others (see *Mesorat Ha-Rav Siddur* pp. 6-9).

Perhaps this was Ben Azzai's point in the *Sifra*, that "this is the book of the generations of man... in the image of God He made them" (*Bereishit* 5:1) means that it is the image of God that is the major principle in Torah, and as we relate to our fellow, we relate to the image of God within him.

This comes out in the following discussion, even without the mystical notion of God being within. The Torah states:

You must not let his corpse remain on the stake overnight, but must bury him the same day. For an impaled body is an affront to God; you shall not defile the land that the Lord your God is giving you to possess. (*Devarim* 21:23)

Rashi comments (s.v. *kelalat Elokim*, based on *Sanhedrin* 46b): "An affront to God — i.e. a degradation of the Divine King, for man is made in His image and the Israelites are His children. A parable: It may be compared to the case of two twin brothers who very closely resembled each other. One became king and the other was arrested for robbery and was hanged. Whoever saw him on the gallows thought that the king was hanged."

Our obligations to this hung soul's body are related to and intertwined with our respect for God whose image is bound with ours. As it says in *Bereishit* (9:6): "Whoever sheds the blood of man, by man shall his blood be shed; for in His image did God make man." Rashi explains (ibid., from *Bereishit Rabba* 34:14), "By man shall his blood be shed — if there are witnesses you kill him. Why? Because in the image of God [God made man] and he has destroyed the Divine image." People have many of the characteristics of the *sefirot* that God possesses, albeit in a less perfect form. People, like God, have kindness, kingship, splendor, etc.

On a similar note, the *mishna* in *Sanhedrin* (46a) states: "Rabbi Me'ir said: When man suffers, what expression does the Divine Presence (*Shekhina*) use? 'My head is too heavy for Me, My arm is too heavy for Me.'"

Moreover, the *Gemara* in *Sanhedrin* (58b) writes: "Rabbi Chanina said: He who smites an Israelite on the jaw, is as though he had thus assaulted the Divine Presence; for it is written, 'one who smites man [i.e. an Israelite] attacks the Holy One.'" There is an identification of God with man that runs deep.

God as Friend

Perhaps the most famous attempt to summarize all of Judaism in one statement is made by Hillel who said, "What you hate, do not do to your friend (*de-alakh senei, le-chavrakh la ta'aveid*)." Rashi on this passage says:

> What you hate, do not do to your friend – "Your friend and the friend of your father do not abandon" (*Mishlei* 27): this is the Holy One, blessed be He.[2] Do not violate His words for it is hated by you

---

2. The notion of God as friend is found in *Midrash Rabba Yitro* (27:1), where the *midrash* links this verse in *Mishlei* with the verse in *Tehillim* 122:8, "*lema'an achai*

that your friend should violate your words. Alternatively: 'your friend' is literal, such as robbery, theft, adultery, and the majority of the *mitzvot*. (Rashi *Shabbat* 31a)

Let's unpack this comment of Rashi. Rashi is addressing how this sentence, which seems to cover only the interpersonal *mitzvot*, can subsume the man-God *mitzvot*. One way to read his first version is that he redefines "friend" as both earthly or heavenly friend. Don't do to your earthly or heavenly friend as you would not want done to you. How do we define something that God does not want done? One might have answered that all the *mitzvot* are God's will and to violate it is doing something that your friend hates, but that would not entail "doing it" (*la ta'aveid*) to the friend. One cannot "do" anything to God. Perhaps that is why Rashi chose to say that what your friend doesn't like is to be violated, or to be ignored. We want others to follow what we say, and we hate it when others disregard or disobey what we demand. Both our friend, God, and our earthly friends in a sense feel the same way about this.

Off hand, this indicates a similarity between the interpersonal and the Divine commands but not a simultaneity of the two. When we go against God it is as much of an affront to God as it is when we go against someone's will. However, now we have come to a second kind of deep interconnectedness between the two types of *mitzvot*. Instead of viewing the interpersonal as a moral obligation to our fellow and the laws with God as matters of obedience, we have another concept: doing God's will as a friend causes the laws relating to God and people to be part of the same system. We act nicely to all our friends, God included, so to speak. There aren't two systems, one toward other people and one toward God: there is one system. We must relate to all our fellows as we wish to be treated, both our earthly and our Divine "friends."

---

ve-rei'ai (because of my brothers and friends)," which they take as God calling us His friends, and with *Yeshayahu* 41 in which Avraham is referred to as "My beloved." *Midrash Tehillim* (8:3) links the verse in *Mishlei* with the verse in *Shir Hashirim* (5:16) "zeh dodi ve-zeh rei'i (this is my beloved and this is my friend)." Rashi in *Chagiga* (7a) also explains the *Gemara*'s reference to God as friend in *Mishlei* 25:17, but Rashi brings a support verse from *Tehillim* 122 for God's friendship rather than from *Mishlei* 27:10.

The Interplay of the Interpersonal and Divine Commandments | 195

This recalls an idea Rav Joseph B. Soloveitchik expressed in *The Lonely Man of Faith* (p. 43), "The covenantal faith community manifests itself in a threefold personal union: I, thou and He." He based himself on a comment of Rashi (*Vayikra* 26:12) who in turn borrowed from the *Sifrei*, that "I will walk among you" means "I will stroll with you in *Gan Eden* like one of you without [your] trembling [before Me]. Lest you think that you will not fear Me – scripture says, "and I will be to you God." I.e., with all due deference, God can be part of the faith community not only as feared leader but as a member of the community.

"Ani Hashem"

The notion of interconnectedness of the two types of *mitzvot* is even embedded in the verse that is the paradigm for interpersonal *mitzvot*: "Love your neighbor as yourself" (*Vayikra* 19:18). It has been suggested (for instance, *Yalkut Lekach Tov Vayikra* p. 202,) that the reason the verse ends with "*Ani Hashem*" is to say that the love of one's neighbor stems from the love of God. "Since everyone possesses *Tzelem Elokim* (the image of God), therefore when you love him you love the Holy One, blessed be He" (*Yalkut* ibid. See also *Mei-Otzareinu Ha-Yashan Vayikra* pp. 340-41, who cites numerous authorities to this effect). *Pardes Yosef* says that if you love God, you should love His children (Israel) too. Similarly, *Semag* (positive 9) and others, who insist on *achikha be-Torah u-mitzvot*, namely that the one we love must be one who is our brother in Torah and observance, are essentially insisting that our link to others is connected to our being part of a covenant with God.

A Cautionary Note from Seforno

Seforno, in his newly published commentary called *Amar Ha-Ga'on*, claims that the reason the Torah writes, "You should love your neighbor as yourself, I am God," is that the Torah is warning us: "Do not be too close to Me to consider Me one of your friends." In other words, Seforno agrees with Rashi that among our friends in our moral universe is God, but don't treat God like a passing friend.[3] We need to treat Him better than a friend. Perhaps we can suggest that this is the reason Rashi retreats from his first interpretation; applying the same value to relating to God and to our friends is perhaps a diminution of our respect for, and our relationship to, God.

Our Responsibility toward our Ancestors

When we declare our fealty and subservience to God in the *Shema*, we are also saying that we have a moral obligation to Ya'akov *Avinu*. As it says in the *Gemara*:

> As Rabbi Shimon ben Lakish said that it is written (*Bereishit* 49:1): "And Ya'akov called his sons and said, 'Gather around and I will tell you what will occur to you in the end of days.'" Ya'akov wanted to reveal to his sons when the complete redemption would arrive at the end of days (see *Daniel* 12:13), but the Divine Presence abandoned him [rendering him unable to prophesy]. He said: Perhaps [the Divine Presence has abandoned me because], Heaven forfend, one of my descendants is unfit, as was the case with [my grandfather] Avraham, from whom Yishma'el emerged, and like my father Yitzchak, from whom Eisav emerged. His sons said to him, 'Hear Yisrael, our father, the Lord is our God, the Lord is One (*Shema Yisrael, Hashem Elokeinu Hashem Echad*).' They said, 'Just as there is only one God in your heart, so too, there is only one in our hearts. At that moment, Ya'akov *Avinu* said in praise,

---

3. As to the *Gemara*'s statement, "Can there be friendship regarding the Heavens (*chavruta kelappei Shemaya*)?!" (*Berakhot* 34a), Rashi sees it as an affront to God to repeat your remarks as if you are not concentrating on what you are saying to God. The statement implies that one cannot talk to God as one does to a friend. But see *Maharsha* there who reads it as "Does God have any friends?!" i.e. are there two gods that you address such that you need to repeat yourself? According to *Maharsha*, this statement is unrelated to whether God can be treated like a friend. *Tosafot*, brought in *Shitta Mekubbetzet Bava Kamma* 62b, ask how the *Gemara* excludes *hekdesh* from the word "*rei'akha*," your friend, when God is a friend, as it says in *Mishlei* (27:10).

'Blessed be the Name of His glorious kingdom for ever and ever (*Barukh Sheim kevod malkhuto le-olam va-ed*)' [as all his children were righteous]. (*Pesachim* 56a)

By reciting *Shema Yisrael* each day, we are affirming not only to God, but perhaps to our ancestor, Ya'akov, Yisrael, that we are still "fit" – that there is no blemish among his children. In other words, we have a moral obligation toward Ya'akov (and perhaps to all our ancestors who clung to the Torah) to follow their tradition. Whether it is an interpersonal mitzva or a mitzva relating to God, its performance honors the tradition of our father, Ya'akov (and all who came in his footsteps). Similarly, one can refer to the verse at the end of the Torah (*Devarim* 33:4), "Moshe commanded us the Torah, an inheritance to the congregation of Ya'akov" or to *Mishlei* (1:8), "Heed, my son, the discipline of your father, and do not forsake the instruction of your mother." Heeding Torah shows respect to the congregation and to our parents. In this sense, all *mitzvot* to God are also in response to my moral obligation to my fellow human beings, my parents and those before them. Before, we said that interpersonal *mitzvot* are also *mitzvot* with God. Now we are saying that *mitzvot* with God are also interpersonal *mitzvot*.

Love of God and Man
In the commentary attributed to Ramban on the 613 *mitzvot* it is written that even the mitzva to love our fellow is subsumed under the mitzva to love God.[4] I assume that this means that just as we love God, we love His creations and therefore love man as well. Here, again, love of man is a fulfillment of the love of God.

Maharal in *Netivot Olam* (*Ahavat Ha-Rei'a* ch. 1) writes that if one likes a person, one likes the things he makes, and if one likes what he makes, one usually likes him, showing the interconnectedness of loving God and man alike. We love man because God made him/her.

---

4. Thanks to my son, Asher, for this reference.

Conclusion

At Yeshivat Har Etzion, I experienced firsthand the interconnectedness of the interpersonal *mitzvot* and the *mitzvot* relating to God. A man once boasted to Rav Amital *zt"l*, that the first thing he did when he came into an army base was to check the kitchen, to which Rav Amital responded, "Have you forgotten about *eid echad ne'eman be-issurin*, that one witness is believed for matters of *teruma*, *shechita*, and removal of forbidden fats and sinews (Rashi *Gittin* 2b)?" The man was trying to show how careful he was with God's laws and Rav Amital reminded him of the equal importance of respecting each Jew. Rav Amital taught us that in the desert at *Mara*, the Jews received the laws of *Shabbat* and *para aduma*, relating to God, as well as the law to honor one's parents, because Judaism is also about the interpersonal. It's all part of our worship of God.

And of all the passionate *sichot* that Rav Aharon Lichtenstein *zt"l* gave, perhaps the most impassioned I heard was about the taking of undeserved privileges in *Yeshiva* because you were an upperclassman. This injustice disturbed the *Rosh Yeshiva* as much as he was perturbed by issues of *bittul Torah* (laxity in Torah study). The *Rashei Yeshiva* lived and modeled the link between the laws relating to people and the laws relating to God. They truly understood not only the intrinsic link and interplay with one another but that the interpersonal was part and parcel of a wholesome *avodat Hashem*. Perhaps we can say that although there are two types of *mitzvot*, interpersonal and with God, the interpersonal are also God-related and the God-related are also interpersonal. In some ways, there is only one kind of mitzva: *mitzvot* in relation to the other/Other (*lehavdil*).

Decision-Making on Matters of Halakhic Public Policy or Meta-Halakhic Issues: Some Tentative Thoughts

Rabbi Nathaniel Helfgot

A. Dedication

The Torah commands us that in the jubilee year each person shall return to their inheritance and each person shall return to their family: "*Bi-shnat ha-chamishim tashuvu ish el achuzato ve-ish el mishpachto tashuvu.*"

This verse, of course, refers to the specific *mitzvot* relating to returning to one's ancestral portion of land in *Eretz Yisrael* or the emancipation of an *eved ivri* allowing that individual to taste the sweet feeling of freedom regained and the ability to start "life" again with new opportunities for success in full liberty.

In homiletical terms, though, I am sure that I share the feeling, with all Yeshivat Har Etzion alumni, that the verse in *Vayikra* has a special meaning for us as the *Yeshiva* reaches the milestone of fifty years to its founding in December 1968. This year we reflect back with longing and nostalgia on the formative and transformative experience of learning and living at Yeshivat Har Etzion, the *beit midrash* that shaped who we became and continue to be as human beings, committed Jews and as *benei Torah*. We come back to our "place", our *achuza* – where we established a *kinyan* in Torah in profound ways and where we felt at home – amongst our *mishpacha* with a sense of belonging as we became part of a special unique *mishpacha ha-lomedet*. The unique education that we merited to experience at the Gush fills us with *hakkarat ha-tov* to our parents who encouraged us and let us be away from home for a year or two (or even three), to our *Rebbe'im* and to our beloved and sorely missed founding *Rashei Yeshiva zt"l*, as well as to all the support staff who gave of themselves so that we could grow in our *ahavat Torah* and *yirat Shamayim*, connection to *Am Yisrael* and experience first-hand the grand historical drama of *Shivat Tziyon* in the modern day State of Israel.

B. Introduction

This essay contains reflections on central elements that, I believe, should be central to decision-making on issues of halakhic public policy. On many occasions both Rav Amital *zt"l* and Rav Lichtenstein *zt"l* spoke and wrote on the interface between strict *halakha* and public policy and meta-halakhic issues. In numerous instances over their storied careers, they modeled for us how those elements impacted on real world issues. Thus, I believe it is fitting to explore aspects of the broader issues at hand in the context of this volume dedicated to educational messages of Yeshivat Har Etzion.

Before examination of some substantive issues, I would like to offer two disclaimers and two introductory comments.

1. While this short essay makes use of the writings and oral comments of both Rav Lichtenstein and Rav Amital, it in no way should be construed as to imply that they would necessarily concur with any specific formulation, claim or conclusion that I make here. These are my reflections alone, and I bear responsibility for them.
2. This essay is far from exhaustive, primarily, for two reasons:
   a. The limitations of the author
   b. The scope and vastness of the topic.
3. The essay below should be seen as containing initial thoughts to be examined and expanded in future analysis and debate. It is far from exhaustive.
4. In using the term of "issues of halakhic public policy or meta-*halakha*" we refer to:
   a. Matters of moral and Jewish significance that go beyond the more narrow confines of the life of the specific individual and his or her *she'eila*.

b. Issues which are not (or not primarily) strictly halakhic in nature as there are no clear substantive halakhic sources that are controlling. or

c. Issues which have substantial halakhic elements to them with legitimate halakhic perspectives on each side of the debate that ultimately require decision-making in one or another direction and have broad public policy implications.

C. Public Policy/Meta-*Halakha* and *Pesak Halakha*

All halakhically committed Rabbis and scholars study the same textual sources and examine previous precedents and the writings of the great *poskim* from past and present. But as Chazal teach us, human beings and their perspectives are diverse: "*Ke-shem she-partzufeihem shonim kakh dei'oteihem shonot.*"

Thus, *halakha* is rich with endless debates and different points of view emerge in every area of Jewish law whether in the complex areas of the laws of *eiruvin* through the intricate details of the laws of *ribbit* and business ethics. The *posek* is not a human computer that is simply fed information yielding an exact result without deviation nor is it a chemistry experiment that can be replicated in the exact same fashion in each and every situation. Differing readings of the sources and weight given to this factor or this position are run of the mill in all areas of halakhic discussion and practice. In these areas the ideological component is barely present. Thus, the debate as to whether one can move a fan on *Shabbat* (is it *muktzeh* or not?) does not generally break down along ideological lines (nor should it). (Indeed, in a counter-intuitive fashion, Modern Orthodox *poskim* are on a few occasions actually more stringent than Charedi ones in areas of *Shabbat* observance or marital issues, e.g. the Rav's rejection of the use of *shtar mekhira* to allow Jewish owned businesses to operate on *Shabbat* or his refusal to sign on to or encourage the use of *Heter Mei'a Rabbanim* on ethical grounds, Religious-Zionist *pesak* on the wearing of *tekheilet* on *tzitzit*, even at great cost, and other such examples.)

When one comes to other, more sensitive areas such as the appropriate role for women in ritual and leadership, attitudes to non-Jews in general, and those in the State of Israel in particular, attitudes towards the secular world, approaches to Zionism, *shemitta*, organ donations, and many other of these more meta-halakhic issues one finds that ideological, moral, sociological and philosophical components play a crucial role in the interpretation of sources, choice of emphasis of precedents, and the type of *posek* a community will adopt as their mentor. In this context, I would argue that a healthy and robust approach to "*pesak*" in areas of halakhic public policy, in our community, would include (at least) the following components that play, and **should play**, a critical role in evaluating the issue at hand and coming to a legitimate model of guidance and advice:

1. **Recognition That Some Fundamental issues are Not Ones of Pure *Halakha***

In some circles, the entire notion of "halakhic public policy" or "meta-*halakha*" is viewed with a jaundiced eye. In some formulations, there only exists pure "*halakha*" and every issue has a source that can be found or read to address the issue at hand. Both Rav Lichtenstein and Rav Amital clearly believed that not every issue of contention in our religious world was a purely halakhic one and often was one that involved values, meta-*halakha*, ethical concerns, and ideological perspectives that were in clash.

In his famous lecture, "*Lo Ha-Kol Halakha*" (and in many other public addresses), Rav Amital emphasized that not every religious and moral issue can be resolved by looking to formal halakhic sources and the dangers in such an approach:

> We live in an era in which educated religious circles like to emphasize the certainty of *halakha*, and commitment to it, in Judaism. I can say that in my youth in pre-Holocaust Hungary, I didn't hear people talking all the time about "*halakha*." People conducted themselves in the tradition of their forefathers, and where a halakhic problem arose, they consulted a Rabbi. Reliance on *halakha* and unconditional commitment to it mean, for many people, a stable anchor whose purpose is to maintain the purity of

Judaism, even within the modern world. To my mind, this excessive emphasis of *halakha* has exacted a high cost. The impression created is that there is nothing in Torah but that which exists in *halakha*, and that in any confrontation with the new problems that arise in modern society, answers should be sought exclusively in books of halakha. Many of the fundamental values of the Torah which are based on the general commandments of "You shall be holy" (*Vayikra* 19:2) and "You shall do what is upright and good in the eyes of God" (*Devarim* 6:18), which were not given formal, operative formulation, have not only lost some of their status, but they have also lost their validity in the eyes of a public that regards itself as committed to *halakha*. This phenomenon makes dealing with the issues I discussed above [e.g. territorial compromise, the Jewish nature of the State of Israel, etc. – NH] such as the relationship to democracy difficult. Topics, such as these, due to their inherent novelty, cannot be resolved by only looking to halakhic precedents.[1]

2. The Role of Ethics, Natural Morality, *Derekh Eretz*, Respect for *Tzelem Elokim* and Other Values in Addressing Meta-Halakhic Issues

In the halakhic calculus of weighing various texts and positions the role of ethical and moral intuitions should also be a critical factor. Halakhic decisors are not simply people who dispassionately evaluate written texts and sources but people who are, and should be, animated by the highest ethical and moral values that emerge from the study of Torah such as "*derakheha darkhei no'am*," "*ve-asita ha-yashar ve-hatov*," *kevod ha-beriyot* and every human being was created *be-tzelem Elokim*. In addition, the deep-rooted ethical values that are reflected here are complemented by our own inherent moral values that God has implanted in us, what Rav

---

[1]. "*Lo Ha-Kol Halakha*," *Alon Shvut Bogrim* 13, p. 96. For an example of Rav Lichtenstein comments on such phenomena see the Hebrew collection of eulogies for Rav Lichtenstein *"Ashrei Adam Oz Lo Bakh"* (Yeshivat Har Etzion, 2018) pp. 224-225.

Kook often termed *ha-mussar ha-tivi*, natural morality, as well as broader categories such as those Rav Yuval Cherlow has often written about as inherent in the concept of *derekh eretz kadema la-Torah*.[2]

These are, of course, points that Rav Amital often brought to bear in his discussion on public issues of great importance and are fully fleshed out in his small but seminal volume "*Ve-Ha'aretz Natan Li-Vnei Adam*." These are the moral intuitions that reason, philosophy, human intuition, societal progress and history have helped flesh out into the open. As Rav Lichtenstein wrote over thirty years ago:

> The parameters of ethics and its truths have an important role to play in understanding *halakha* and defining its boundaries. Of course, a Jew must be ready to answer the call "I am here" if the command to "offer him up as an offering" is thrust upon him. However, prior to unsheathing the sword, he is permitted, and even obligated to clarify, to the best of his ability, if indeed this is what he actually has been commanded…to the extent that there is a need and room for halakhic exegesis, and this must be clarified -- **a sensitive and insightful conscience is one of the factors that shape the decision-making process**. (my emphases – NH)
>
> Just as Maimonides in his day, consciously, was assisted by a particular metaphysical approach to the world in order to plumb the depths of the meaning of Biblical verses, so too one can make use of an ethical perspective in order to understand the content of *halakha* and, at times, to outline its parameters. (In the volume *Arakhim Be-Mivchan Milchama*, my translation)

The relationship between *halakha* and broad ethical and moral categories both explicitly found in Biblical and Rabbinic sources and those rooted in general human intuitions are, of course, central topics that engaged Rav Lichtenstein in many of his essays from the 1960's through the 2000's, such as: "*Ma Enosh*": *Reflections on the Relation between Judaism and Humanism* (1960's); *Does Judaism Recognize An Ethic Independent of*

---

2. See for example: https://www.ypt.co.il/beit-hamidrash/view.asp?id=7065.

Halakha (1970's); *Halakha Ve-Halikhim – The Sources of Ethics* (Hebrew, 1980's); *The Human and Social Factor in Halakha* (late 1990's); *Formulating Responses in An Egalitarian Age*.

His most robust presentation of his views on how they impact on concrete halakhic *pesak* and guidance is found in the essay "The Human and Social Factor in *Halakha*." In that essay he makes the forceful case for the measured use of all of the factors mentioned above by responsible *poskim* in their application of halakhic norms. As he puts it in a passage that is representative:

> The notion that "where there is a Rabbinic will there is a halakhic way" both insults *gedolei Torah*, collectively, and, in its insouciant view of the totality of *halakha*, verges on the blasphemous. What we do expect of a *posek* is that he walk the extra mile – wherever, for him, it may be – harnessing knowledge and imagination, in an attempt to abide by his responsibility to both the Torah with which he has been entrusted and to his anguished fellow, whose pangs he has internalized. For insensitive *pesika* is not only lamentable apathy or poor public policy. It is bad *halakha*. To the extent that *kevod ha-beriyot*, for instance, permits a "violation," be it of a *de-rabbanan* injunction, actively, or of a *de-oraita*, passively, failure to act on that principle undercuts a spiritual ideal. The Rav was fond of quoting the Chafetz Chayyim to the effect that interruption of *Keri'at Shema*, where enabled, *mi-penei ha-kavod*, was not permissible but mandatory. Human dignity – the Rav would have preferred the term, "human sanctity" – is hardly a neutral matter.

This can lead to far reaching leniencies in individual cases where *halakha* is stretched to engage differentially to cases of extreme need – *she'at ha-dechak* and the like. In some instances, when these challenges move to the larger plane of communal challenges they may even engender even greater leniencies.

At the same time, the thoughtful, sensitive, and responsible Orthodox decisor may find himself or herself in a position of the need to pull back when we move from the individual to the public plane. As Rav Lichtenstein notes later in that essay:

> Reference to the public sector serves to introduce a second comment. I have spoken throughout of sensitivity to the human or social factor as a basis for leniency. With regard to decisions a *posek* is called upon to render vis-à-vis an individual, this is indeed ordinarily, although not invariably, the case. In the communal arena, however, concern over the human factor may rather stimulate *chumra*. Decisions made at this plane, even of the nature of *pesika*, are less ad hoc in character and take a more panoramic view of public policy. Part of that policy surely involves sustaining the human aspect of a society and enhancing its moral fiber; and that may militate stringency as well as leniency.

This comment of Rav Lichtenstein, of course, points to the importance on the public level that the factor of communal cohesiveness, respect for tradition, and the integrity of the halakhic system must play in weighing proper decision-making and advice on divisive public policy issues. Revolutionary change, while possibly desirous from some perspectives, may come with too high a cost to the overall values of the halakhic system and tear the Orthodox community apart in a way that undermines the overarching goals of *avodat Hashem* and continuity. Recognizing that halakhic change is often a gradual evolutionary process that preserves the integrity of the system, expresses respect for custom and precedent and the ability of various parts of the community to come together as one, with all their differences, is a critical factor.

3. **Calibrating the Proper Use of the "Slippery Slope" Argument**

Many legal and ethical systems throughout history clearly recognize the validity of what is popularly known as the "slippery slope" argument. In its most basic form, the argument is built on the claim that the validity or permissibility of an action to be undertaken by an individual before you right now, should not be evaluated solely on its halakhic or ethical merits per se, but on its ramifications, even if these are only potential ramifications. Concern for potential negative consequences, by the person himself or even by other actors, is enough to justify limiting the action of the individual in the here and now. As many have noted this argument rests on a number of moral claims:

a) The individual himself, "other people," or society in the present or the future may fall into physical or ethical or spiritual danger. In light of that we withhold permission from the individual to engage in a morally permissible act to head off that possibility. The individual is asked to pay the ethical price in his or her autonomy and action for the potential mistakes, errors and corruption of others or the individual in the future, that society may not be able to stop from happening.

b) This price that the individual before you currently has to pay in pain, suffering, alienation or frustration is considered legitimate and worth the cost for the "greater" good of the individual in some potential future time, or for others and society in general.

c) There is a significant chance that indeed the future action viewed as a negative one will in fact occur.

d) The future potential ramification that may arise is indeed viewed as negative and unwanted.

All of these assumptions can be subject to moral, ethical and practical critique. For example, the first assumption posits that the real and immediate legitimate needs of the individual should be sacrificed on the altar of some potential good to the theoretical self, to "others" or to society, even at the price of great pain to the individual, in the here and now.

How does one measure the level of suffering or alienation that is morally acceptable to avoid some potential problem down the road? How does one realistically judge the potential risk? What percentage is significant to deploy the slippery slope argument and on what basis? How and who will determine these elements? Some have even pointed to an internally contradictory logical fallacy: The excessive use of the slippery slope argument may itself lead to a slippery slope where the individual who legitimately should be allowed to act in some way in this instance is thwarted because of the improper evaluation of the future threat or chance of deterioration. If the slippery slope argument is a legitimate concern then it may not be used because it can lead to a slippery slope of excessive use of itself. If it is not a legitimate concern then it cannot be used in the first place.

Despite these strong philosophical and practical challenges almost all systems adopted some form of the slippery slope argument as part of their legal and ethical jurisprudence.

Normative *halakha* also clearly adopted use of the slippery slope argument in many instances.[3] The entire notion of "*asu seyag la-Torah*" gives voice to the underlying notion that, sometimes, permissible actions must be limited in order to ensure the stability and integrity of the core of Torah values and practice. The entire notion of *gezeirot Chazal* is often based on the principle that allowing permissible actions in this or that instance may lead to violations of the law and thus the Rabbis used the full force of their authority to widen the scope of the normatively prohibited. At the same time, it is clear that the system itself did not see this move and halakhic tool as one that is unfettered and without constraints. For example, the notion that "*ein gozerin gezeira le-gezeira*" or that a *gezeira* must have widespread acceptance in the community reflects the tensions that Chazal felt in applying the slippery slope argument cavalierly. To cite Rav Yuval Cherlow in his wonderful Hebrew essay on this topic:

> Therefore, *halakha* gives validity to the slippery slope argument, and often makes use of it. However, the Sages, throughout the ages, were sensitive to the unbridled use of the slippery slope argument for two reasons. One was the harm to *halakha* itself. This is the danger that excessive stringency would become impossible to keep in practice so that it would lead to what the Rabbis term "stringency that leads to (inappropriate) leniency." In our terms,

---

3. See on this entire section, the important essay by Rav Yuval Cherlow, "*Halakha U-Madron Chalaklak*," *Tzohar* 23.

excessive use of the slippery slope argument could specifically lead to greater deterioration in [the world of *shemirat mitzvot* – NH] as a result of the lack of willingness to live up to these conditions [of stringency].

The sages also related to what we called the "price" that arises from use of the slippery slope argument. Excessive use of the slippery slope argument can bring intense harm to the rights of the individual, and potentially make life unlivable.[4]

In short, then, the careful *posek* will extrapolate and call for limited use of the slippery slope arguments, based upon serious and careful evaluation of the three elements of the chance that deterioration will indeed stem from this leniency, the real threat to the integrity of *halakha* if this scenario does occur – i.e. is it really so terrible? And at what cost is one asking the individual or group to lie with to ensure the potential avoidance of some problematic future? In some instances, the relative weight given to these elements is what distinguishes various and divergent approaches amongst Orthodox *poskim* and halakhic communities on important contemporary issues. It is interesting to note that Rav Lichtenstein would on occasion question the excessive use of the slippery slope argument in the heated discussion around charged issues in the Orthodox community as for example here:

---

4. In this context, Rav Cherlow cites a wonderful selection from Rav Kook's "*Ein Aya*" on *Shabbat* (9a), reproduced below in my translation with my additions for clearer comprehension:

> Everything that the Rabbis did in order to "make a fence around the Torah" was exactly and precisely weighed so that [these additional restrictions – NH] should not be added to or subtracted from. Just as the Divine wisdom [as manifested in Torah law – NH] evaluated how to establish all aspects of life properly in order not to efface the sublime moral project by diminishing their impact on action, and so as not to overly burden physical life, as Maimonides explains in the third portion of the Guide of the Perplexed, so too did the Sages assess the content of the fences they built around the Torah. When they found that [imposing] a small restriction was sufficient, they did not add to the burden even a hairsbreadth, in order to [excessively] burden the human will and prevent it from fulfilling its desire.

> Yet in evaluating the principle two factors will need to be weighed. We shall have to evaluate, first, the likely course of events. How truly slippery is the slope? What innovation is likely and how likely to generate what kind of pressure. Second, we shall need to examine at what cost – whether in the form of possible alienation of certain constituencies or in the dilution of the quality of spiritual life of an ultra-conservative stance.
>
> This last factor will itself require dual consideration, as we strive to both perceive the prospects of various alternative scenarios on the ground and to determine how much weight to assign this particular concern.[5]

This type of sensitive and nuanced approach to the use of evaluation of the cogency of slippery slope arguments is one that should be the hallmark of Orthodox *pesak* in halakhic and meta-halakhic discussions.[6]

4. Taking into Account Impact of Decision on Furtherance of *Avodat Hashem*

The third element that is crucial for these discussions, especially in dealing with issues relating to other human beings, is how does this affect the entire calculus of *avodat Hashem*, service of God, and are we bringing people closer to God or distancing them away. This is particularly critical in the loaded area of *pesak halakha* relating to women's role in ritual and participation in the public sphere of Judaism. A few years back, Beit Hillel, the more progressive Orthodox Rabbinical organization in Israel, issued a response permitting women in mourning who so desired to say *kaddish*

---

5. "Formulating Responses in An Egalitarian Age: An Overview" in the Orthodox Forum Volume *Formulating responses in An Egalitarian Age* (NY, 2005) p. 44. Later in that section, Rav Lichtenstein added in a personal vein: "As for myself, I presume that, with respect to both the women's issues, specifically, and the fear of the slippery slope, generally, I find myself somewhere in the middle – enthusiastically supportive of some changes, resistant to others, and ambivalent about many."

6. For a good example of a thoughtful discussion of the slippery slope argument in the context of the contemporary debate around Partnership *Minyanim* see the essay by Rav Aryeh Klapper: https://moderntoraleadership.wordpress.com/2014/11/04/are-partnership-minyanim-orthodox/.

in the synagogue during services. This *pesak*, in American terms, is not extremely radical, as this practice has taken root for many decades in many Modern Orthodox synagogues under the influence of the permissive *pesak* of Rav Soloveitchik *zt"l*. In Israel this ruling was more daring and received some vocal critique. In response, Rav Zev Weitman, a significant *talmid chakham*, the Rabbi of the *Tnuva* cooperative, and current Rabbi of Alon Shvut in Gush Etzion, (then serving as the head of the *Beit Hillel – Beit Midrash Hilkhati*,) published an essay in response in *Makor Rishon*. A number of lines in that essay perfectly sum up what I believe should be the Modern Orthodox approach to *pesak* in these areas:

> One who decides Jewish law solely based on the words of the *poskim* and books, while totally ignoring and misunderstanding the reality of the community he is relating to and the changing circumstances of the reality, is not a *posek halakha* in my eyes. And it is in this context that the words of the Seridei Eish (Rav Yechi'el Ya'akov Weinberg) regarding the *bat mitzva* ceremony were cited. He states that there is great significance in our day and age not to create discrimination between boys and girls and not to state positions that embarrass and hurt women, nor to issue *pesakim* that will cause women to distance themselves from Judaism, and these factors are in the eyes of a great and authoritative *posek* like the Seredei Eish legitimate and important factors in deciding Jewish law… We therefore should strive to achieve to the greatest extent possible, within the parameters of Jewish law and the Torah, equality between men and women. There are areas that are difficult for us [to understand and live with]; however, we are forbidden from changing clear cut *halakhot* [that have no alternative]. However, in every area that there is a halakhic opening to bring to greater equality in the world of *avodat Hashem*, we should choose this option, even if there are those who disagree with that approach, and even if there are those who are stringent and insist not to deviate from what was the traditional practice. In our day a

stringency in this area leads to much greater laxity, which leads to estrangement from Torah and *mitzvot* and Judaism. The recitation of *kaddish* by a woman is not forbidden and not one of those areas where we have no option and no wiggle room before the [binding] words of the Lord. Just the opposite: it appears that there is no problem and thus it should be no problem to tell that to women who request to recite *kaddish*.[7]

Summarizing Rav Weitman's words and significantly changing the thrust of the famous *bon mot* referenced to caustically by Rav Lichtenstein in the previous section above: We need to be animated in *pesak halakha* in these sensitive areas with the feeling that "when indeed there is a legitimate halakhic way, there should be a fully supportive Rabbinic will!"

5. Promoting *Kiddush Ha-Shem* and Minimizing *Chillul Ha-Shem*

The goal of enhancing *kevod Shamayim* and avoiding the desecration of God's Name in the world is one which all religiously committed Jews share in principle. It is a central theme of many of our sources and has played a significant role in responsa in past generations. In our contemporary era though, this element has sometimes been jaded amongst some religious communities for diverse reasons. In some more insular Charedi communities, the tremendous demographic growth, creation of a vast and self-sustaining infrastructure, political power and influence have sometimes led to a weakening of the perception that specific halakhic and meta-halakhic choices have the potential to lead to *chillul ha-Shem* in the eyes of the larger public, both Jewish and gentile. Similarly, in some more insular parts of the Religious-Zionist community in Israel, the impact of Jewish independence, military might of the IDF and disdain for western values has sometimes led to the factors of *kiddush* and *chillul ha-Shem* not playing a major role in the decision-making process. Rav Amital, in his life and *derekh ha-pesak*, fought vigorously against those trends. He constantly reminded us that, especially in our contemporary era, the factors of enhancing *kiddush ha-Shem* and minimizing *chillul ha-Shem*

---

7. *Makor Rishon, Mussaf Shabbat*, #831.

must be front and center. In his writings and life choices he laid out a vision of Orthodox *pesak* on meta-halakhic issues that brought those elements to bear as critical and central ones that must shape halakhic public policy. This is a model that should animate us all.

Disdain, Fear and Harmony: Themes in the Relationships Between Jews and Non-Jews

Rabbi Dr. Yossef Slotnik[1]

Introduction

From the inception of Am Yisrael, the relationship with non-Jews has been at the forefront of issues that needed to be resolved. On the one hand, there exists in our literature a great fear that such an interaction will lead Am Yisrael astray, a fear culminating in the Biblical demand to eradicate the seven nations of *Kena'an*. On the other hand, we hear of a different type of relationship between Moshe *Rabbeinu* and Yitro, or Shlomo *Ha-Melekh* and Chiram the king of *Tzor*, which appears to have been much more amicable. It is well beyond the scope of this short article to fully map out the different directions this discussion took, in the millennia from entering *Eretz Yisrael* until today, and even limiting ourselves to the *sugyot* in the *mishna* and *Gemara*, in an attempt to show the multiple approaches, would be a formidable task. We will limit our discussion to a few sources in the *mishna* and a few discussions in the *Gemara*. Although only a few sources will be engaged, I believe that the dominant voices and halakhic approaches are represented and that other directions will not vary so widely.

1) Cooperation or Avoidance: *Machloket Tanna'im*
When one wishes to examine the directives of Chazal regarding how one should conduct relations with their non-Jewish neighbors, there are two pivotal discussions in the *mishna* which pull us in different directions. The first is a foundational *mishna* which appears in *Shevi'it*:

---

[1]. I would like to thank my *talmid* and friend Elliot Cohen, who succeeded in making my Israeli English almost eloquent.

> And we encourage the work of non-Jews in the *shemitta* year, but not that of Jews. And we enquire after their wellbeing, for the sake of peace.[2] (*Mishna Shevi'it* 4:3)

The context of the first ruling of this *mishna* is the prohibition for Jews to work the land in the *shemitta* year, hence Chazal prohibit us from encouraging and supporting Jews who are violating this prohibition. Since there is no similar restriction on non-Jews, we are permitted to encourage their activities. The *mishna* further explains that we do not need to limit this encouragement to our encounters with non-Jews at work, rather we may enquire after their general wellbeing and are seemingly allowed to engage in conversation with them. The *mishna* explains this ruling by saying that this is so "for the sake of peace (*mippenei darkhei shalom*)." It is beyond the scope of this short article to fully flesh out the usage of this concept in the tannaitic and amoraitic works, but it will suffice to say that its application ranges between negatively limiting the cases of internal communal fighting, and positively achieving peace and harmony within the Jewish community.[3] The fact that the command to act generously towards non-Jews appears in a similar fashion to those rules regarding internal Jewish dynamics is very telling. The *mishna*'s formulation of the permissibility to ask after the wellbeing of non-Jews, "for the sake of peace," suggests that Chazal view both Jews and non-Jews as living in one community, and that we should aim to establish good relationships, peace and harmony within this shared community.

There are a few other tannaitic sources that seem to follow this particular model of relations between Jews and non-Jews. The abovementioned *mishna* is cited verbatim again in *Shevi'it* (5:9) and in *Gittin* (5:9). The triple appearance of the same *halakha* can perhaps be construed as a strong

---

2. Throughout this article, the English translations will be based on those found on the *Sefaria* website.
3. In the fifth chapter of *Gittin* there is a list of ten *halakhot* that were instituted in order to keep the peace, wherein all but one are limited to the internal dynamics of the Jewish community, and fall completely within the parameters mentioned. Numerous commentaries and articles have been written about this topic. For a brief overview, see the entry entitled "*Darkhei Shalom*" in the *Encyclopedia Talmudit*.

endorsement of this position. Moreover, the *tosefta* in *Gittin* takes this notion one step further:

> A city that has within it Israelites and gentiles: The community leaders collect from Israelites and gentiles **for the sake of peace**; the poor of among the gentiles are supported with the poor of Israel **for the sake of peace**; the dead of the gentiles are eulogized and buried **for the sake of peace**; the mourners of the gentiles are consoled **for the sake of peace**. (*Tosefta Gittin* 3:13-14)

While the *mishna* in *Shevi'it* limited interaction between Jews and non-Jews to a verbal exchange, the *tosefta* is clearly laying the foundations for a multicultural, cooperative community, where all individuals, regardless of religious affiliation, dedicate themselves to many social responsibilities including supporting the poor and caring for the dead and mourners. This expectation is not simply to care for the needs of the non-Jew, but to invite them into this welfare community by ensuring that they too share in the financial burden of this joint social group. Another example of this relatively harmonious coexistence may be found in a *beraita* that cites Rabbi Me'ir's *derasha* on the verse in *Devarim*, which states:

> You shall not eat any unslaughtered animal carcass; give it to the stranger (*ger*) in your community to eat, or you may sell it to a foreigner (*nokhri*). For you are a people consecrated to the Lord your God. You shall not boil a kid in its mother's milk. (*Devarim* 14:21)

Rabbi Me'ir interprets this verse and says:

> I have derived [from this verse] only that it is permitted to a resident alien through giving and to a gentile through selling. From where do I derive that it is permitted to transfer an unslaughtered animal carcass to a resident alien through selling? The verse states: "You

may give it…or you may sell it," meaning that one has the option to do either of these. From where is it derived that it is permitted to a gentile through giving and one is not required to sell it to him? The verse states: "You may give it…that he may eat it; or you may sell it to a foreigner." Therefore, you may say that he may transfer it to both a resident alien and a gentile, both through giving and through selling. This is the statement of Rabbi Me'ir. (*Pesachim* 21b)[4]

Rabbi Me'ir recognizes two types of non-Jews: those who are resident aliens (*ger toshav*), who have accepted the seven Noachide commandments, and other non-Jews who have not even accepted those commandments (*nokhrim*). Rabbi Me'ir's conclusion is that the Jew may bestow gifts to both groups regardless of their religious affiliation. Although the *beraita* does not connect Rabbi Me'ir's inclusive ruling with the *mishna* and *tosefta* mentioned above, it does recognize Rabbi Me'ir as one who allows giving an unwarranted gift to non-Jews, an act that creates bonds and brings two people together.

Nevertheless, although these voices are explicit in calling for a semblance of coexistence, this is by no means the only position. The *beraita* which presents Rabbi Me'ir's view, allowing giving an unwarranted gift to non-Jews, also presents Rabbi Yehuda's opposing opinion:

Rabbi Yehuda says: These matters are to be understood as they are written; one may transfer an unslaughtered animal carcass to a resident alien only through giving, and to a gentile only through selling. (Ibid.)

Rabbi Yehuda allows unwarranted gifts to be given only to those who share a set of basic religious assumptions with us. Although they are not committed to a full life of halakhic observance, the fact that they are committed to keeping the seven Noachide laws constitutes enough common ground to allow for an exchange of gifts. With non-Jews who do not share even a semblance of common religious commitments we may

---

4. This *beraita* appears in a few other places in the *Gemara*, including *Avoda Zara* 20a and *Chullin* 114b.

have commercial relations, and buy from them or sell to them, but closer or warmer relationships are forbidden. This approach conveys a fear of intercommunal interaction, perhaps motivated by the risk that Jews could be negatively influenced by their foreign religious outlook.

An extreme expression of this position may be found in *Mishna Avoda Zara*:

> One should not leave cattle in the inns of non-Jews, for they are suspect regarding bestiality. A woman should not be alone with them for they are suspect regarding fornication. A man should not be alone with them, for they are suspect regarding the spilling of blood. A Jewish woman should not be a midwife to a non-Jewish woman, for she is birthing one for [a life of] idolatry. But a non-Jewish woman may be a midwife to a Jewish woman. A Jewish woman may not nurse the child of a non-Jewish woman, but a non-Jewish woman may nurse the child of a Jewish woman, within her domain.
>
> One may accept their [non-Jews'] healing for one's property, but not healing for people. And one should not have one's hair cut by them under any circumstances, according to Rabbi Me'ir. And the Chakhamim say: It is permitted [to have a non-Jew cut a Jew's hair] in public domains, but not amongst the two of them [alone]. (*Mishna Avoda Zara* 2:1-2)

These *mishnayot* portray non-Jews in a very dim and suspicious light. Their moral conduct is so repugnant that we not only fear leaving our animals in their care, but we worry for our very lives. Even Rabbi Me'ir, who we earlier saw trying to promote a state of coexistence, is fearful and therefore does not allow them even to cut our hair.[5]

---

5. We can note that there exists a surprising contradiction between Rabbi Me'ir's two opinions. One explanation could be that *ideally* Rabbi Me'ir wishes to create closer relations with non-Jews, but *in reality* he is fearful of non-Jewish violence, and therefore acts with more suspicion. Nevertheless, this inconsistency requires further study. A similar ambiguity will be seen in Abbayei's two differing approaches in *Berakhot* and *Avoda Zara*.

While reacting to fear is a natural instinct, the *mishna* institutes another *halakha* that concerns more than merely fear: "A Jewish woman should not be a midwife to a non-Jewish woman, for she is birthing one for [a life of] idolatry." This *mishna* explicitly states its reasoning – we are not interested in aiding or facilitating the birth of an idol worshipper. Although not explicitly written, it seems that this is the reason for the next *halakha*: "A Jewish woman may not nurse the child of a non-Jewish woman." It is clear that these *halakhot* do not aim for a shared society based on principles of coexistence, but rather attempt to build strong partitions between the communities where even the most simple and basic action of caring for each other's infants is viewed as an endorsement of their way of life. I believe it is self-evident that this *mishna* in *Avoda Zara* would not endorse supporting adults, even if poor, granting them gifts, eulogizing and burying their dead, or comforting their mourners.

2) Greetings and Gentiles: *Machloket Amora'im*
The formative discussions between the *tanna'im* seem to continue into the period of the early *amora'im*. As an example of this ongoing conversation, let us examine a *sugya* in the *Bavli* in *Berakhot*:

> Abbayei would regularly say: "One should always be deliberate in fear of God, 'A gentle answer turns away wrath' (*Mishlei* 15:1), increase peace with his brothers and with his relatives and with all humans, and even with the non-Jew in the market, in order that he will be loved above and pleasant below, and he will be accepted by all creatures." They said about Rabban Yochanan ben Zakkai that no one ever preceded him in greeting, not even a non-Jew in the market. (*Berakhot* 17a)

When Abbayei calls for the proliferation of peace, he describes the different social circles that a person is situated within, starting from his immediate circle, his family, to the outer circle of all humankind. Abbayei stresses that this includes even the non-Jew. It seems clear that Abbayei's call for peace is an elaboration of the *mishna* in *Shevi'it* and *Gittin* cited earlier which says that one may actively greet the non-Jew as part of the Torah's ways of peace. When the *Gemara* states that Rabban Yochanan ben Zakkai was always the first to greet people in the market, even if they were non-Jews, there is little doubt that Chazal interpret this action in the same vein as Abbayei's statement: both Rabbis aim to establish a semblance of harmony in the mixed community of Jews and non-Jews.

While this is the conclusion in the *sugya* in *Berakhot*, a seemingly contradictory conclusion should be drawn from the *sugya* in *Gittin*. Regarding the *mishna* that encourages us to greet non-Jews, Rav Dimi in the name of Rav states:

> Rav Dimi bar Shishna said in the name of Rav: We should not hoe with the idol worshipper in the *shemitta* year, and we should not greet idol worshippers with "*shalom*" twice. (*Gittin* 62a)

We can clearly see that Rav seems to explicitly counteract the two statements of the *mishna* in *Shevi'it* cited earlier:

> And we **encourage** the work of non-Jews (*nokhrim*) in the *shemitta* year, but not that of Jews. And we **enquire** after their wellbeing, for the sake of peace. (*Mishna Shevi'it* 4:3)

Even before we focus on the content of Rav's statements, we can identify three differences that change the tone of the conversation. First, while the *mishna* outlines permissible discourse with non-Jews, Rav limits such discourse. Similarly, the *mishna*'s motivation seems to be "for the sake of peace," which does not appear to be an incentive shared by Rav. Finally, the *mishna* uses the neutral term "*nokhrim*," foreigners, while Rav speaks more pejoratively of "idol worshippers."[6] While one cannot claim that Rav's ruling is combative towards the non-Jew, it is nevertheless a far cry from the

---

6. For an analysis of the different uses of these terms, see *Menachem Kahana*, "Yachas Le-Nokhrim Bi-Tkufat Ha-Tanna'im Veha-Amora'im," *Eit Ha-Da'at: Chiddushim, Tagliyyot Be-Madda'ei Ha-Yahadut* 21, 2000.

mishna, tosefta and Abbayei's statement, which were trying to implement a more holistic community of Jews and non-Jews.

More specifically, Rav minimizes the *halakha* in the *mishna* that one may greet the non-Jew, and instead says that one should limit this conversation to a single greeting and not a double one. Immediately following the statement of Rav, the *Gemara* adds a description of the practices of two *amora'im*:

> We should not greet idol worshippers with "*shalom*" twice. Rav Chisda would be first to greet them with "*shalom*." Rav Kahana would say to them: "Greetings to *mar* (the master)." (*Gittin* 62a)

If one were to read these practices alongside the *mishna* in *Shevi'it* or *Gittin* we would conclude that these *amora'im* are enhancing and enacting the decree of the *mishna*. The normative expectation was to enquire after the wellbeing of the non-Jew, but Rav Chisda would go out of his way to be the one that starts the conversation, and Rav Kahana added titles of respect to the non-Jew, naming him 'sage' or 'master!' This reading would be in a similar vein to what we saw above in *Berakhot* regarding Abbayei and Rabban Yochanan ben Zakkai.

Although this reading is plausible, it is very surprising that the *Gemara* does not appear to deal with the clear contradiction between these practices and the words of Rav – after all, Rav is minimizing the ruling of the *mishna* while these *amora'im* are expanding it! It seems that the redactor placed these descriptions of Rav Chisda and Rav Kahana immediately following the statement of Rav in order to induce a reading of these two *amora'im* as promoting a more hostile relationship with non-Jews. This explains why many commentators, including Rashi, suggested that these *amora'im* are in fact following Rav's ruling and actually minimizing the conversation. For example, Rav Chisda is explained to have initiated the conversation in order not to have to state the greeting "*shalom*" twice, and Rav Kahana added the honorific title but in his heart did not accord it to the non-Jew.[7]

---

7. See, for example, Rashi's commentary wherein he explains that a Jew would not be thinking about a non-Jew when using the term "*mar*," and therefore

While these interpretations could be acceptable for the *sugya* in *Gittin*, we are not able to draw out such an alienating and distrustful position from the *sugya* in *Berakhot*, where Abbayei situates the greeting of the non-Jew as part and parcel of a discussion regarding greeting one's family members.

It is therefore quite plausible that the debate about the proper relationship with non-Jews in the community continued to be discussed unresolved from the tannaitic times into the amoraitic debates. Rather than attempting to offer a clear ruling for how to act, the *Bavli* retains a certain level of ambiguity regarding relations with non-Jews. It is thus worth turning to one further aspect that emerged in amoraitic times, namely the concept of "*mishum eiva* – due to enmity."

2a) An Additional Consideration: Enmity and Fear

Moving beyond the binary *machloket* of cooperation or avoidance, some *amora'im* raised the possibility of a third option. This stance permitted limited participation and involvement with non-Jews, but specifically out of fear rather than generosity. As mentioned above, the *mishna* in *Avoda Zara* contains a series of restrictions limiting the interface between Jews and non-Jews. Some of the restrictions were based on a fear that the non-Jew would harm the Jew, but the specific prohibitions for a female Jew to be a midwife or wet-nurse for a non-Jewish baby were based on the fact that Chazal did not want to aid in bringing another idol worshipper into the world or raising them. Regarding these restrictions, the *Gemara* in *Avoda Zara* features the following conversation between Abbayei and Rav Yosef:

> Rav Yosef thought to say: Delivering [the child of] a gentile woman on *Shabbat* for payment is permitted **due to enmity**.
>
> Abbayei said to him: She can say to her: For our own [women], who keep *Shabbat*, we desecrate [*Shabbat*] for them; For your own [women], who do not keep *Shabbat*, we do not desecrate [*Shabbat*].

---

must be referring to someone else. Although many *rishonim* challenged Rashi's interpretation, they did not change the general framework in which Rav Chisda and Rav Kahana enact Rav's restrictions. See, for example, Me'iri's interpretation of this *sugya* (*Gittin* 62a).

> Rav Yosef thought to say: Nursing [the child of a gentile woman] for payment is permitted **due to enmity**.
>
> Abbayei said to him: She can say, if she is unmarried: I wish to get married. If she is a married woman, [she may say]: I do not wish to become repulsive to my husband.
>
> Rav Yosef thought to say, as that which is taught [in a *beraita*]: Gentiles and shepherds of small domesticated animals, one may not raise [them out of a pit] and one may not lower [them into a pit]. It is permitted to raise them for payment, **due to enmity**.
>
> Abbayei said to him: One can say [an excuse] to him: My son is standing on the roof. Alternatively: A time has been appointed for me to [appear in the] courthouse. (*Avoda Zara* 26a)

Rav Yosef repeatedly tries to limit the *mishna*'s prohibition by claiming that it will cause hostility and animosity between Jews and non-Jews, repeatedly using the phrase "*mishum eiva* (due to enmity)." On the basis of this fear, Rav Yosef wants to allow a midwife to deliver a baby, even on *Shabbat*, or a wet-nurse to nurse the non-Jewish infant, both provided that she receives payment. It seems that Rav Yosef assumes that while one can easily avoid a demand for a free service, it would be fairly difficult to avoid an offer of payment without the Jew's motivation for this refusal being exposed. Abbayei fundamentally agrees with Rav Yosef that if indeed the Jew's refusal will expose their real motivation and lead to animosity, one should yield to the demand and aid the non-Jew, but he qualifies this claim by stating that in the examples mentioned by Rav Yosef that is not the case.[8] Since one could convincingly justify the refusal, even in the cases where the non-Jew is willing to pay for the service, the Jew is entitled to spurn the offer.

At first glance, Rav Yosef's innovation accepts the premise of the *mishna* in *Avoda Zara* that we should not have any contact with the non-

---

8. Although Abbayei never explicitly permits the engagement with non-Jews in our *sugya*, we can deduce his stance from the fact that he doesn't negate the concept of "*mishum eiva*," but rather offers excuses for cases where Rav Yosef's approach may not be relevant. Were these excuses not to be applicable, we can assume that Abbayei would concede to Rav Yosef.

Jew, thus rejecting the ideal set by the *mishna* in *Shevi'it* and *Gittin*. In practice, however, the results of Rav Yosef's approach end up similar to those of the *mishna* in *Gittin*, in that in actual fact he will aid and care for the non-Jew due to fear of repercussions, "*mishum eiva.*"

An interesting debate involving *amora'im* in both *Eretz Yisrael* and *Bavel* can show how this conflict was tested in reality. The *Gemara* in *Bava Batra* cites the following story:

> Ifra Hurmiz, the mother of King Shapur [of Persia], sent four hundred dinars to Rabbi Ami [to give out to poor Jews], but he did not accept them. She sent them to Rava, and he accepted them for the sake of peace with the kingdom. Rabbi Ami heard and was angry. He said: "Does [Rava] not accept [the lesson of the verse]: 'When the boughs are withered, they shall be broken off; the women shall come and set them on fire' (*Yeshayahu* 27:11)?" And [why did] Rava [accept the money]? For the sake of peace with the kingdom. But [why did] Rabbi Ami [not] also [support Rava's decision as it was done] for the sake of peace with the kingdom? [As Rava] should have distributed [the money] to the gentile poor [so as not to give Ifra Hurmiz the reward of supporting Jews]. [In actuality,] Rava also gave [the money] to the gentile poor. And [the reason] Rabbi Ami got angry – [because those who reported the story to him] did not conclude it before him. (*Bava Batra* 10b)

Rabbi Ami refused to accept the donation from Ifra Hurmiz strictly because she was a non-Jew. He explains his reluctance in the fact that giving charity will postpone the destruction of the non-Jew and encourage the proliferation of seemingly righteous deeds. Rava, on the other hand, accepted the donation. The *Gemara* explains Rava's logic with the justification of "*shelom malkhut*," peace with the kingdom, which appears to override Rabbi Ami's consideration. The term "*shelom malkhut*" is known to us from other contexts[9] and it seems to have a similar meaning to the term "*mishum eiva*," namely that we reluctantly act in certain ways in order

---

9. See, for example, *Gittin* 56a, ibid. 80a.

to gain favor in the eyes of the non-Jewish king or leadership. In other words, while Rabbi Ami is firmly opposed to any joint ventures with the non-Jew, Rava accepts the gift, because of the problematic consequences of not accepting it. It should be noted that in Rava's time, the infrastructure to distribute the gifted money amongst the non-Jewish poor must have already existed, indicating that he accepted the communal requirement to support the non-Jewish poor, although not embracing the harmonious tone in which this positive command was given in *Tosefta Gittin*.[10]

Therefore, we can see that the two contested positions of friendship and avoidance when considering relations between Jews and non-Jews remained open as viable options in the amoraitic period. There also existed in this literature an additional valence which emphasized acting in certain conciliatory ways, in order to prevent enmity or fear of negative fallout from not engaging with the non-Jewish population.

The picture painted thus far shows two or three very distinct directions:

1. A call for coexistence and perhaps harmonious coexistence in the communities of Jews and non-Jews. The clear sources for this direction are the *mishna*yot in *Shevi'it* and *Gittin*, and the supporting enhancements of those statements in the *tosefta* calling for the support of the non-Jewish poor and healing their sick, and some of the amoraitic statements.
2. A call for total separation may be seen in *Mishna Avoda Zara*, especially in the ban for feeding a non-Jewish infant since we are raising a child

---

10. I interpreted the section as it appears before us, but there is ample room to suggest that Rava himself did indeed embrace the communal responsibility in the positive, idealistic sense that the *tosefta* spoke of, as "*mippenei darkhei shalom*." By contrast, the redactor of the *Gemara* in our *sugya* accepted the more minimalistic position of avoidance, and thus reinterpreted both Rava's agreement and Rabbi Ami's rejection as accepting the idea of "*shelom malkhut*," and only accepting the charity in line with that placatory concept. Perhaps the strongest proof for this suggestion is the fact that in *Bava Batra* 8a there is a story of Rav Yosef accepting a similar gift from the same queen mother, Ifra Hurmiz, and the *Gemara* does not stipulate there that Rav Yosef accepted it because of the concept of "*darkhei shalom*." It is indeed surprising that the redactor in this earlier *sugya* did not seem to reframe the discussion in the same manner that it did in 10b.

Themes in the Relationships Between Jews and Non-Jews | 227

for idol worship. This direction is enhanced by the *sugya* in *Gittin* which minimizes the social interaction between Jews and non-Jews.

3. Rav Yosef and Abbayei in the *sugya* in *Avoda Zara* aim to permit certain activities, such as healing and aiding the birth of a non-Jew, in cases where not doing these actions would lead to animosity. It seems to me that Rav Yosef is planted in the second camp, although in actual fact he permits multiple actions that we would not have permitted otherwise.

Although I have portrayed these sources as being in tension with one another, the *Gemara* itself never contrasts the different opinions. Theoretically this could be for one of three reasons:

1. There truly is no contradiction, since the different *sugyot* are dealing with different *halakhot*. One must on the one hand aid and heal the non-Jew but draw the line at breastfeeding the babe of the non-Jew. Greet the non-Jew while he is working yet not help him out of the pit unless it will cause animosity. While this is technically a possibility, it really does seem very farfetched that all these *halakhot* live side by side without any tension.

2. The second option is to somehow "make peace" between the *sugyot*, and bring them to some common ground that appears to fit all of them. I believe that Ramban went in this direction in his monograph *Torat Ha-Adam*:

   > From the statement "one visits the sick of non-Jews as the sick of the Jews," and that visiting the sick has great healing powers for the sick as we said earlier in this work, it follows that one may heal the sick of non-Jews just as one does the sick of Jews because of *darkhei shalom*, the ways of peace, even though there (*Avoda Zara* 26a) it says that "non-Jews and shepherds of small cattle: one is not obliged to bring them up [from a pit] though one must not cast them in"[11] and it states there that Rav Yosef claimed that one should raise the non-Jew for

---

11. See *Avoda Zara* 13b.

payment lest there be animosity, and Abbayei said to him that one could claim that he is called away by his son who is on the roof, or that he was summoned to the authorities. Therefore, surely saving them from death is prohibited even if one would be paid??

[The answer is] that in *Avoda Zara* there was an excuse, but without one it is of course permissible. Abbayei is willing to even uses flimsy excuses, but in a case where there will be animosity of course it is permissible, as it is stated in the *mishna*: "a jewess may aid a non-Jewess in labor only if she is paid, but for free it is prohibited." And there is no greater saving of a life than a midwife aiding the newborn and the new mother, and even so it is permissible, but for free it is prohibited since there would be no animosity, as we cannot force a person to work for nothing; but for pay, since there would be animosity since she is a midwife, it is permissible, even though she is birthing a child for idol worship.

In medicine too this is the criteria: without payment it is prohibited, but for pay it is permissible. And indeed Rashi *z"l* wrote, in Chapter *Ein Ma'amidin* (*Avoda Zara* 26a), that one should not heal a non-Jew for free, as it says that we do not ascend nor do we lower, and hence, since the permission is granted because of animosity, both for free or for pay: where there is an excuse one should use it where he can; and where there is no excuse, like a doctor that heals the Jewish sick, and the non-Jew knows him, there could be great animosity, so he should of course heal Jews and non-Jews alike, whether for a fee or for free, because of the ways of peace. A proof for this is what it says in the end, "we support the poor of the non-Jews with the poor of Israel, and support is a way of giving life, hence we may give him livelihood and save him because of the ways of peace." And in Chapter *Mi She-achazo* (*Gittin* 70a), it is taught that Rav Shimi bar Ashi healed a non-Jew, and in the *tosefta* it is taught: "a city that has Jews and non-Jews, the collectors collect from Jews and non-Jews, and support the non-Jewish poor with the Jewish poor, because of the ways of peace." (Ramban *Torat Ha-Adam*)

Ramban, in essence, suggests that the *sugya* in *Gittin* allows for caring for the non-Jew from the fear that if we would not care for him there would be growing animosity between the Jews and non-Jews, which would be a source of danger, while the *mishna* in *Avoda Zara* which prohibits such activities speaks when there is an excuse not to care for the non-Jew, hence there would be no animosity. In essence, Rav Yosef, although not framing the question, is answering the contradiction between the two *sugyot*. If we were to accept Ramban's interpretations, the tension between the *sugyot* would be resolved, with all the *sugyot* working with two axioms: one should refrain from aiding or even having social contact with non-Jews, unless this could cause animosity.

Far be it for me to question Ramban's reading, but I find this a hard answer to swallow. First of all, the term "*mishum eiva*" is not synonymous to the term "*mippenei darkhei shalom*," despite their similar form. The latter is the will to achieve harmony within the community. Its foundation is the acceptance that at some level we should cooperate with, and even care for, all parts of our community regardless of their religious affiliation. As such, this concept promotes an idea and vision, not a tactic. The term "*mishum eiva*," on the other hand, is indeed a plan or a survival strategy. Had we been free to decide, we would neither care for, nor support, the non-Jew. Nevertheless, for now we recognize the perils of this approach and thus, when acting in such a distancing manner becomes too dangerous, we make a concession and care for the non-Jew, out of necessity rather than will. Secondly, it is not just a question of language; Ramban himself quotes the *tosefta* which calls for a communal joining which is not only limited to caring for the non-Jews but joining forces to work together – is all that only for fear?

3. Embracing the contradiction, the third direction recognizes that the tension between the *sugyot* exists, and yet does not aim to resolve it. The different *mishna*yot disagree, the different *amora'im* have different world views on this question, and both approaches are coded in the *Gemara*. Truly, there are some *sugyot*, as we have seen above, that attempt to "choose sides" and trough the techniques of redaction, showing us that they accept the stance of *Mishna Avoda Zara*, whereas other *sugyot*, by letting both sides have their say without conflict, leave us with a complex message where both values are part of our halakhic heritage. I realize this direction seems almost impossible where the *Gemara* leaves us with an unresolved contradiction (at times with the same person, like Abbayei or Rabbi Me'ir stating both sides of the dispute), but I see no other solution to this issue.

Not only do I not see another way of resolving the tension between the *sugyot* in the *mishna* and *Gemara*, I believe that this inert contradiction continues into the halakhic writings of Rambam.

3) Rambam's All-Encompassing Codification

I would like to spend the last part of this article focusing on the way Rambam understood and codified this discussion in his *Mishneh Torah*. In *Hilkhot Avoda Zara*, Rambam states:

> From here you are taught that it is forbidden to give medical help to an idol worshipper even for payment. But if [the Jew] feared them, or if he was fearful of their enmity, he may give them help for payment, but for free it is forbidden. A resident alien among idol worshippers, since it is mandatory for him to earn a living, [the Jew] may give free treatment…
>
> And it is forbidden to give them an unwarranted gift, but [it is permitted] to give to a resident alien, as it is said: "Give [any unslaughtered animal carcass] to the stranger in your community to eat, or you may sell it to a foreigner" (*Devarim* 14:21) – by sale, and not as a gift.

We support the poor of idol worshippers with the poor of Israel for the sake of peace. And we do not object to the poor of idol worshippers when gathering the gleanings, or a forgotten sheaf from the corners of the field, for the sake of peace. And we ask after their well-being, even on their holiday, for the sake of peace. And the greetings should never be repeated twice, nor should we enter the house of an idol worshipper on his holiday to greet him. When meeting him in the market, we give greetings to him softly and seriously.

All of these matters are spoken of only when Israelites are exiled among idol worshippers or when the idol worshippers have overpowered Israel, but if Israel has overpowered them, it is forbidden to allow idol worshippers to dwell amongst us, and even if one of them dwells temporarily or passes from place to place with merchandise, we do not let them pass through our land unless he accepts the seven Noachide commandments, as it is said: "They shall not dwell in your land" (*Shemot* 23:33) – not even temporarily. And if he accepts upon himself the seven Noachide commandments, he is a resident alien… (Rambam *Hilkhot Avoda Zara* 10:2-6)

In his opening statement, Rambam accepts the *mishna* in *Avoda Zara* that prohibits aiding and assisting the non-Jew even in medical issues, with the stipulation added by Rav Yosef that if a Jew is fearful that this action will cause animosity then it is acceptable to aid non-Jews. Rambam continues in that vein when he prohibits giving the non-Jew any free gifts, and only allows commercial relations. It is in this context that Rambam quotes the *mishna* and *tosefta* from *Gittin* that demands the Jews support the non-Jewish poor together with their own. Clearly, as this *halakha* is brought in the context of suspicion and avoidance, we must interpret "*mippenei darkhei shalom*" in a similar vein as "*mishum eiva*," namely, not a call for the creation of coexistence and a harmonious society, but rather a burdensome consideration we must bear in fear of repercussions. This is also evident from the following discussion where Rambam codifies Rav's ruling that one should minimize his enquiries of the non-Jew. The clearest proof that these gestures are done under duress is the fact that Rambam specifies that these *halakhot* are only applicable when Am Yisrael is subdued by the other nations, but that once the Jews have the upper hand there should be no interaction with the non-Jews, unless they accept the Noachide commandments.

These *halakhot* in Rambam reflect well the *mishnayot* and *Gemara*'s discussions in *Avoda Zara*, which called for a harsher approach to non-Jews, shying away from interaction as much as possible, except in cases of threat to Jewish life. This seemingly clear position that Rambam takes, however, is challenged when we consider the other *halakhot* that Rambam codifies, wherein a different picture emerges:

> Any "stranger (*ger*)" that is mentioned regarding gifts to the poor refers only to a convert, for it is spoken regarding *ma'aser sheini*, "Then the *levi* shall come…and the stranger" (*Devarim* 14:29). Just as the *levi* is a member of the covenant, so too the stranger is a member of the covenant. Nevertheless, we do not prevent the poor of idol worshippers from these gifts, rather they come together with the poor of Israel and take them, for the sake of peace. (Rambam *Hilkhot Mattenot Aniyyim* 1:9)

> We provide sustenance and clothe the poor of idol worshippers with the poor of Israel, for the sake of peace. And a poor person who goes from door to door, we are not required to give him a large gift, but rather we give him a small gift. And it is forbidden to turn away a poor person who asks emptyhanded, and even if you give him one dry fig, as it is said: "Let not the downtrodden turn away disappointed" (*Tehillim* 74:21). (Rambam ibid. 7:7)

> We bury the dead of idol worshippers, we comfort their mourners, and we visit their sick, for the sake of peace. (Rambam *Hilkhot Eivel* 14:12)

These *halakhot* codify the other harmonious statements found in the *mishna* and *tosefta* in *Gittin*. The simple reading of these *halakhot* does not indicate in any way that they apply only when Jews are under the subjugation of non-Jews. There is nothing to suggest that "*darkhei shalom*" should not indeed be taken at face value, as a call for peace and harmony within a diverse community. In other words, while Rambam in *Hilkhot Avoda Zara* embraces the position that aims to reduce the aid and interaction between Jews and non-Jews, in these *halakhot* it seems that Rambam embraces the other position that calls for cooperation and generosity.

Although not the most obvious reading of the *halakhot*, some interpreters of Rambam claimed that he identified his position and outlined his reasoning in *Hilkhot Avoda Zara*, and that all subsequent *halakhot* should therefore be read in light of this stance.[12] While Rambam does not explicitly reiterate in other places that the injunctions to accept charity, give charity, visit the sick and bury the dead only apply under duress, the commentators argue that this is clearly the case since he already stipulated such a condition in *Hilkhot Avoda Zara* regarding healing non-Jews and giving them gifts.

This answer is far from the simple understanding of Rambam's composition of *Mishneh Torah*, which was meticulous and consistent. Furthermore, one could still have accepted this solution had it not been for another statement made by Rambam, albeit as a tangent to another *halakha*. In the context of the rights of a non-Jew who accepted the seven Noachide laws, the *ger toshav*, Rambam says:

> And it appears to me that we act towards a resident alien with respect and lovingkindness as we would with a Jew, as we are commanded to keep them alive, as it is said, "Give it to the stranger in your community to eat" (*Devarim* 14:21). And that which the Sages said that we do not double our greetings applies to idol worshippers, not to a resident alien. And the Sages commanded us regarding even idol worshippers to visit their sick and bury their dead along with the Jewish dead, and to sustain their poor along

---

12. See, for example, Ri Kurkous to *Hilkhot Mattenot Aniyyim* 7:7.

with the poor of Israel, for the sake of peace, as it is said, "The Lord is good to all, and His mercy is upon all His works" (*Tehillim* 145:9), and it is said, "Her ways are pleasant ways, and all her paths are peace" (*Mishlei* 3:17). (Rambam *Hilkhot Melakhim* 10:12)

Rambam rules that the obligation to support a non-Jew who accepted the seven Noachide laws is identical to the *halakhot* regarding supporting a Jew. He continues to explain that there are no restrictions regarding enquiring twice as to their wellbeing, since those restrictions are limited to idol worshipers. Rambam concludes by saying that we are commanded to visit the sick, bury the dead and support the poor even of idol worshipers in order to enhance peace, since the path of the entire Torah is of peace. In my opinion, it is virtually impossible to read this *halakha* as sitting comfortably with what Rambam previously stated in *Hilkhot Avoda Zara*. For in this *halakha*, situated within a section regarding what occurs in a more utopian period of time when there is Jewish sovereignty, Rambam places peace on a pedestal and promotes considerate and generous relationships with non-Jews, regardless of their religious affiliation. In this ideal description, aiding non-Jews is nothing short of a quest for peace, which is understood as the very foundation of the Torah.

This contradiction between the two codified positions of Rambam lies at the core of a fascinating dispute between the former Chief Rabbi of Israel, Rav Isser Unterman,[13] and former Chief Rabbi of Tel Aviv, Rav Chayyim David HaLevi.[14] Rav Unterman based his response on Rambam's position specifically in *Hilkhot Melakhim* and thus concludes that even the terminology of "*mishum eiva*" is one and the same with the quest for peace and harmony:

> In order to foster feelings of peace and friendship among people, our Sages found it necessary to enact regulations to prevent feelings of envy and hatred. These regulations were called "*mishum eiva*," meaning that the aim is that there would be no anger and resentment which could lead to hatred.[15]

---

13. Rav Isser Yehuda Unterman, *Shut Shevet Mi-Yehuda* 3:70.
14. Rav Chayyim David HaLevi, *Shut Aseh Lekha Rav* 9:33.
15. Unterman, p. 296.

Rav HaLevi disagrees and claims that all *halakhot* regarding non-Jews are subject to the application of the phrase *"mippenei darkhei shalom"* specifically as it is found in Rambam's *Hilkhot Avoda Zara*. All assistance offered to non-Jews is given under duress and fear of repercussions, and so once the Jews are in a more secure and powerful position there is no longer any justification for interaction. Rabbi HaLevi emphasizes that even in *Hilkhot Melakhim* Rambam still stated that these *halakhot* are "for the sake of peace," the very same term he used in *Hilkhot Avoda Zara* to indicate the duress.

Respectfully, it seems to me that both positions are necessarily partial and are not good readings of Rambam's all-consuming codification. Rav HaLevi's reading is spot-on when applied to *Hilkhot Avoda Zara*, and Rav Unterman's reading is exact when applied to *Hilkhot Melakhim*. The first views interaction with non-Jews as an act of fear and self-preservation, while the second commends such interaction as part of fulfilling the ideal of peace embedded in Torah.

I am not aware of an easy solution to this contradiction. One could suggest that Rambam changed his mind over the span of time it took to write the entire *Mishneh Torah*, although this sort of speculative historicizing is a last-resort answer which we should do all we can to avoid. Alternatively, perhaps Rambam wished to codify all possible positions and thus simultaneously promote as well as limit relations with non-Jews.[16] It seems that our question remains an open one.

Conclusion

We have seen that two distinct positions regarding Jewish relations with non-Jews pervade the literature of the *tanna'im* and the *amora'im*. One model involves engaging harmoniously with non-Jews, asking after their welfare and generously giving gifts, perhaps in the pursuit of a peaceful, shared community. The second model consists of limiting interaction with non-Jews, exhibiting a fear and suspicion of non-Jews, and recommends

---

16. See, for example, *Tzafenat Panei'ach*, who suggests that Rambam is referring to different types of non-Jews: idol worshipers and those who simply did not officially accept the Noachide laws.

the path of avoidance. It was also noted that a third approach emerged in the time of the *amora'im* permitting interaction, although out of fear for repercussions and hatred, rather than out of respect and consideration. In the *Mishneh Torah*, Rambam seems to accept both positions, mentioning each one in a different section, which left us with an unclear resolution.

Perhaps Rambam's codification of two different approaches offers different parallel themes that may, or should, be used in different contexts. On a historical, albeit not textual, note, the modern era in general and the twenty-first century in particular have brought with them a desire for a different type of relationship between Jews and non-Jews, namely a relationship based upon common goals and social responsibility. It is a hard sell for the modern ear to hear the constant call for alienation. We can ask whether Rambam left an opening in his codex of *halakha* for a different way of approaching relationships to non-Jews.

I firmly believe that this is not mere wishful thinking, but that there is indeed room in our halakhic tradition to call for a different type of multicultural community. Not, God forbid, one that requires us to give up on any of our religious beliefs, but a community where Jews and non-Jews live together side by side in social support and harmony. It is time, in many communities, to abandon the negative relationship based on the *mishna* in *Avoda Zara*, the ruling of Rav in *Gittin*, Rav Yosef in *Avoda Zara*, and the *halakhot* presented in Rambam's *Hilkhot Avoda Zara*. Instead, the alternative, cooperative position should be embraced, as championed by *mishnayot* in *Shevi'it* and *Gittin*, Abbayei in *Berakhot*, and as codified in Rambam's *Hilkhot Melakhim*.

Although I do not remember learning these sources with my teachers and mentors HaRav Lichtenstein *zt"l* and HaRav Amital *zt"l*, it is clear to me that the seeds for this reading were planted by them, both in terms of the textual analysis and the moral overtone. For this, and for much of my spiritual development, I am eternally in their debt.

The Meaning of Prayer: Three Themes in Rav Soloveitchik's Writings

Rabbi Reuven Ziegler

Mystics and philosophers alike have wondered what effect our prayers can have on an infinite and omniscient God, and many thinkers have sought to understand why God accepts some prayers and not others. Yet, in his very rich and multifaceted discussions of prayer, Rav Soloveitchik eschews these questions. Instead, he focuses, as always, on the human side of the equation and not on the Divine side. What, he asks, is the precise nature of the activity we call prayer? What are the inner states that it requires? What effect does it produce on the praying individual? In other words, what is the meaning and function of prayer *for humanity*?

The Rav offers several answers to this question, each of which constitutes the focus of a different essay:

a) prayer is an encounter with God (*The Lonely Man of Faith*);
b) it is a means for man to find and shape himself ("Redemption, Prayer, Talmud Torah");
c) it is a form of self-sacrifice to God ("Reflections on the *Amidah*").

Let us briefly examine each of these themes, as well as the relationships between them.

Prayer as Encounter

Chazal debate the following question: must one have *kavana* (conscious intention) when performing a given mitzva act in order to be credited with having fulfilled one's obligation? Or is it sufficient merely to perform the mitzva action even without intending thereby to fulfill a Divine command? In the case of prayer, says the Rav, there is no dispute; everyone agrees that *kavana* is indispensable. The reason is that "*Kavana*, related to prayer, is, unlike the *kavana* concerning other mitzva performances, not an extraneous addendum but the very core of prayer" (*The Lonely Man of Faith* p. 74). Specifically, whereas the *kavana* pertaining to other *mitzvot* is merely "the normative intention on the part of the mitzva-doer to act in accordance with the will of God" (ibid.; this intention is called "*kavana latzeit*"), the *kavana* that defines prayer is of an entirely different order:

> What is to be understood by *kavana* [in prayer]? One should free his mind from all extraneous thoughts and see himself as if he is standing before the Divine presence. (Rambam *Hilkhot Tefilla* 4:16)

Echoing Rambam's description, the Rav writes that prayer is essentially an encounter with God:

> Prayer is basically an awareness of man finding himself in the presence of and addressing himself to his Maker, and to pray has one connotation only: to stand before God. (*The Lonely Man of Faith* p. 56)

As such, *tefilla* differs from the recitation of *Shema*, for the latter is not a personal encounter but rather a declaration of commitment to *kabbalat ol malkhut Shamayim*, accepting the yoke of Heavenly dominion. In the *Shema*, one speaks *of* God in the third person; in *tefilla*, one speaks *to* God in the second person.

The Rav develops this distinction between *Shema* and *tefilla* by analyzing not only their respective texts and the aggadic material concerning them, but also, characteristically, the *halakhot* governing them. For example, the *Amida* must be recited while standing, facing Jerusalem, assuming the physical posture of a slave, wearing appropriate clothes, standing in a proper location (e.g., not on top of a wall), sober, and without interruptions and long pauses. However, none of these requirements applies to the *Shema*. These *halakhot* reveal a clear pattern: the *Shema* is a declaration or dedication, directed at oneself or perhaps at other people, while in *tefilla*, one stands in God's presence and speaks to Him directly.

The central and longest part of the *Amida* is *bakkasha*, petition: the first three blessings of the *Amida* praise God, the last three offer thanks to Him, and the middle thirteen are requests, petitions. Nevertheless, the primary function of the *tefilla* encounter is not procuring God's favorable answers to our entreaties. Rather, it is forming a fellowship, or community, between human beings and God:

> Acceptance of prayer is a hope, a vision, a wish, a petition, but not a principle or a premise. The foundation of prayer is not the conviction of its effectiveness but the belief that through it we approach God intimately and the miraculous community embracing finite man and his Creator is born. The basic function of prayer is not its practical consequences but the metaphysical formation of a fellowship consisting of God and man. (*Worship of the Heart* p. 35)

The discussion of prayer in *The Lonely Man of Faith* focuses on prayer's role in forming a covenantal community – a central goal of Adam II, who is plagued by loneliness. First, the prayer encounter creates a community between man and God, and, as such, it is a counterpart to and continuation of the God-man community engendered by the prophetic encounter. The only difference between the prophetic and prayer communities is that in the former, God initiates communication, and in the latter, man initiates it.

Second, prayer creates a community between people. This is indicated by the halakhic emphasis on praying with the *tzibbur* (community), as well as by the fact that all requests in the *Amida* are formulated in the plural – "Grant us," "Return us," "Forgive us," etc. – even though the *Amida* is initially recited quietly by each individual. The Rav explains:

> When disaster strikes, one must not be immersed completely in his own passional destiny, thinking exclusively of himself, being concerned only with himself, and petitioning God merely for himself. The foundation of efficacious and noble prayer is human solidarity and sympathy or the covenantal awareness of existential togetherness, of sharing and experiencing the travail and suffering of [others]. (*The Lonely Man of Faith* p. 59)

Thus, the community of man and God formed in prayer must include one's fellow human being as well, instead of remaining focused selfishly on one's own personal requests or personal religious experience.

Yet, the prayer encounter is incomplete and not of optimal worth unless it is accompanied, or preceded, by a commitment to a godly way of life. (Within the prayer service, this is indicated by the halakhic requirement of *semikhat ge'ula li-tfilla*.) Indeed, says the Rav, "Any encounter with God, if it is to redeem man, must be crystallized and objectified in a normative ethico-moral message" (*The Lonely Man of Faith* p. 61). The Rav explains this idea in a powerful passage:

> Who is qualified to engage God in the prayer colloquy? Clearly, the person who is ready to cleanse himself of imperfection and evil. Any kind of injustice, corruption, cruelty, or the like desecrates the very essence of the prayer adventure, since it encases man in an ugly little world into which God is unwilling to enter. If man craves to meet God in prayer, then he must purge himself of all that separates him from God. The *halakha* has never looked upon prayer as a separate magical gesture in which man may engage without integrating it into the total pattern of his life… Prayer is always the harbinger of moral reformation. (*The Lonely Man of Faith* p. 65)

While the concept elucidated in this passage may not seem surprising at first, its consequence is indeed unexpected:

This is the reason why prayer *per se* does not occupy as prominent a place in the halakhic community as it does in other faith communities, and why prayer is not the great religious activity claiming, if not exclusiveness, at least centrality. Prayer must always be related to a prayerful life which is consecrated to the realization of the divine imperative, and as such it is not a separate entity, but the sublime prologue to halakhic action. (Ibid. pp. 65-66)

This demotion of prayer from the central position it holds in other religions – or, rather, the integration of prayer into a broader framework of religious activities – is a recurring theme in the Rav's writings. The Rav's book-length treatment of prayer, *Worship of the Heart*, opens by pointing out that, for Judaism, prayer is not the only means of reaching out to God. Judaism recognizes four separate media of religious experience – the intellectual (Torah study), the emotional, the volitional (mitzva observance) and the dialogical (prayer) – and therefore prayer must be understood within its proper context. Furthermore, following the *Sifrei* (*Eikev* 41) and Rambam (*Sefer Ha-Mitzvot* positive 5), the Rav points out that the term "*avoda sheba-lev*," worship or service of the heart, refers not only to prayer, but to Torah study as well. The heart serves God through both of these activities, and perhaps by means of integrating them. Let us now turn our attention to the second answer to the question posed earlier – what is the meaning of prayer for the human being? – and examine an essay that links the two forms of worship of the heart.

Prayer as Self-Acquisition

An interesting relationship prevails between the three terms appearing in the title of the essay, "Redemption, Prayer, Talmud Torah": redemption of the individual comes about not through Divine intervention, but rather through the other two activities mentioned there. In other words, instead of a two-step process, in which one engages in prayer and *talmud Torah* so that God, in turn, will bring redemption, the Rav portrays a one-step process: a person redeems himself by praying and studying Torah. How so? Like the Rav's essay itself, we shall focus on the issue of prayer.

Although prayer is addressed to God and stems from recognition of one's dependence upon Him, it is a process that starts within the self: one must consider and weigh one's needs, and then present them before God. A person can know what he truly needs only if he knows who he truly is and what are his goals. The prayer process, then, entails discovering and refining one's genuine need-awareness, and it is therefore a self-educational and self-transformative activity.

Thus conceived, prayer emerges as an important part of man's broader project of self-creation: "God wills man to be creator – his first job is to create himself as a complete being" ("Redemption, Prayer, Talmud Torah," p. 64). This view of prayer helps us understand the logic of presenting our requests before One who knows all our needs. Through prayer, man clarifies his need-awareness and thereby changes himself; and by transforming himself, he becomes more worthy of God granting his requests.

How is this process redemptive? Based on a passage in the *Zohar*, the Rav distinguishes between three stages in the progress from slavery to redemption. The Jews enslaved in Egypt were at first mute, feeling the pain of the lash but not the indignity of the servitude. The slave has no sense of self, no concept of his goals or his destiny. Therefore, he can feel *pain*, which is an instinctive reaction man shares with the animal, but he cannot *suffer*, for suffering is an existential experience resulting from a threat to one's sense of self. Because they lacked direction and knowledge of their genuine needs, because they could not yet conceive of another kind of existence, the Jews did not protest. Only when Moshe defended the helpless Jew against the Egyptian taskmaster did they realize the injustice of their situation. This led them, for the first time, to cry out to God (*Shemot* 2:23), marking their emergence from muteness to sound.

Yet, though they now had the *awareness* of need, they still lacked the *understanding* of need. They sensed that their existence was defective, that they were being treated unjustly, but they did not yet know how to fill their lives with positive content. Upon arriving at *Sinai*, they gained an understanding of their deeper needs based upon their covenantal destiny spelled out in the Torah. This marked the third stage of their redemption, namely, the emergence from sound to speech. Redemption from slavery "is identical with communing… i.e., the emergence of speech" (p. 56), for only one fully in possession of himself has a meaningful message to convey.

Slavery is not just a political institution, but a state of being. Man is a slave whenever he lacks a sense of self and an accompanying awareness of his needs. Although man may think he knows his needs, an accurate assessment can stem only from a proper understanding of his destiny.

> Man is surely aware of many needs, but the needs he is aware of are not always his own. At the very root of this failure to recognize one's truly worthwhile needs lies man's ability to misunderstand and misidentify himself, i.e., to lose himself. Quite often man loses himself by identifying himself with the wrong image. Because of this misidentification, man adopts the wrong table of needs which he feels he must gratify. Man responds quickly to the pressure of certain needs, not knowing *whose* needs he is out to gratify. At this juncture, sin is born. What is the cause of sin, if not the diabolical habit of man to be mistaken about his own self? (p. 62)

The antidote to this appears in prayer:

> Prayer is the doctrine of human needs. Prayer tells the individual, as well as the community, what his, or its, genuine needs are, what he should, or should not, petition God about. Of the nineteen benedictions of our *Amida*, thirteen are concerned with basic human needs, individual as well as social-national. Even two of the last three benedictions (*Retzeh* and *Sim Shalom*) are of a petitional nature… [Prayer] tells man the story of his hidden hopes and expectations. It teaches him how to behold the vision and how to strive in order to realize this vision, when to be satisfied with what one possesses, when to reach out for more. In a word, man finds his need-awareness, himself, in prayer. Of course, the very instant he finds himself, he becomes a redeemed being. (pp. 65-66)

In personal redemption, as in the Jews' liberation from Egypt, two stages succeed the mute unawareness of needs. The first of these is designated *tze'aka*, outcry, indicating the inchoate burgeoning of need-awareness – "sound" without "speech," in the *Zohar*'s terms. The next stage is *tefilla*, which derives from the Hebrew root *pl"l*, denoting "thinking, judging, discrimination" – in other words, to filter one's need-awareness through one's intellect, or "to ask intelligently" (p. 67). In *tefilla*, one defines goals, evaluates desires and establishes a hierarchy of needs.

Though *tefilla* is of a higher order than *tze'aka*, both coexist in our liturgy, with *tze'aka* represented by *selichot* and *tefilla* by the *Amida*.

> Prayer as *tze'aka* lacks the gradual development of theme, the structural formalism, and the etiquette-like orderliness which *halakha* required of the *mitpallel*, the prayerful person. While *tefilla* is a meditative-reflective act, *tze'aka* is immediate and compulsive. (p. 68)

Man has need of both heartfelt outcry and measured request.

The Rav then turns briefly to the redemptive role of Torah study in the process of self-acquisition. The *Gemara* teaches that a baby studies the entire Torah in utero (*Nidda* 30b). This means that Torah is part of one's very being, and when one studies Torah, one is, in effect, uncovering one's own self. Prayer and Torah study share the same structural pattern of discovery of the self, leading the Rav to note the aforementioned *Sifrei* that defines both prayer and Torah study as *avoda sheba-lev*.

The introduction of the term *avoda* allows the Rav to execute a sharp turn-about at the very end of the essay. In Rabbinic Hebrew, "*avoda*" generally refers to the sacrificial service in the *Beit Ha-Mikdash*, and the Rav suddenly introduces a new, seemingly contradictory, theme regarding the *avoda sheba-lev* of *tefilla*: prayer as self-sacrifice. The Rav himself notes the contradiction, or dialectic, between the presentation of prayer as self-acquisition earlier in the essay and the presentation of prayer as self-sacrifice toward its end:

Judaic dialectic plays "mischievously" with two opposites, two irreconcilable aspects of prayer. It announces prayer as self-acquisition, self-discovery, self-objectification and self-redemption… Yet there is another aspect to prayer: prayer is an act of giving away. Prayer means sacrifice, unrestricted offering of the whole self, the returning to God of body and soul, everything one possesses and cherishes. (p. 70)

These two aspects of prayer stand in a sequential relationship:

Initially, prayer helps man discover himself, through understanding and affirmation of his need-awareness. Once the task of self-discovery is fulfilled, man is summoned to ascend the altar and return everything he has just acquired to God. (pp. 71-2)

Although the idea of prayer as self-sacrifice comes as a surprise at the conclusion of "Redemption, Prayer, Talmud Torah," it stands at the heart of the next essay we shall examine, "Reflections on the *Amidah*."

Crisis and Prayer
While prayer redeems man, the Rav opens "Reflections on the *Amidah*" with the claim that prayer itself was redeemed by a man, namely, Rambam. He accomplished this redemption, continues the Rav, on both the halakhic and the philosophical planes. First, while most authorities ruled that daily prayer is mandated only by a Rabbinic enactment, Rambam (*Hilkhot Tefilla* 1:1) ruled that it is a commandment ordained by the Torah itself. The majority position could lead one to regard prayer as a kind of afterthought to the halakhic system, while Rambam's position clearly situates prayer in a more central halakhic position. Second, Rambam elaborated a conception of *avoda sheba-lev* as an all-pervasive attachment to God (*Moreh Ha-Nevukhim* 3:51), and, as we have seen, prayer is one form of *avoda sheba-lev*.

These two claims on the part of Rambam amount to a recognition that prayer is "the expression of the soul that yearns for God via the medium of the word, through which the human being gives expression to the storminess of his soul and spirit" (*Worship of the Heart* p. 146). Everyone acknowledges that Judaism commands "love and fear of God, total commitment to Him and cleaving unto Him" (ibid.) – yet these religious experiences would have remained mute and internalized were it not for the verbal expression given to them in prayer. Prayer thus functions as "the mirror of the lovesick religious soul" (*Worship of the Heart* p. 86). Therefore, even Ramban, in defending those who regard daily prayer as a Rabbinic command, admits that "the substance of prayer and its essence are derived from the Torah" (*Worship of the Heart* p. 146); in other words, the Torah recognizes the institution of prayer, but does not demand it on a daily basis.

In a different essay (*Worship of the Heart* pp. 29-33), the Rav offers an intriguing explanation of the dispute between Rambam and Ramban. Both, he says, acknowledge that the Torah mandates prayer when an individual or a community encounters an *eit tzara*, a time of distress. Jewish prayer stems from the twin feelings of crisis and of man's total dependence on God: "Out of the straits, *min ha-meitzar*, I have called upon the Lord" (*Tehillim* 118:5); "Out of the depths, *mi-ma'amakim*, I have called to You, O Lord" (ibid. 130:1); "Behold, as the eyes of servants unto the hand of their master, as the eyes of a maidservant unto the hand of her mistress, so our eyes look unto the Lord our God until He be gracious unto us" (ibid. 123:2). Yet these two authorities differ on the question of what kind of *tzara* engenders prayer. Ramban believes that "*eit tzara*" refers to external, obvious, surface crises, such as war, famine or disease. These occur only occasionally, and therefore the Torah does not require daily prayer. Rambam, however, believes that man is perpetually in crisis, for "*eit tzara*" refers to the inner, existential, depth crisis that stems from an awareness of man's constantly looming defeat due to his human limitations, frailties and finitude.

As the *midrash* states, "One does not leave the world with even half his desires fulfilled" (*Kohelet Rabba* 1:13).

The awareness of one's utter dependence on God comes to expression mainly in *bakkasha*: we realize that we are lacking and incomplete, and that only God can fill our needs. One could even say that the Rav describes a circular relationship between prayer and crisis. *Bakkasha* not only serves as a *response* to the crisis awareness, but it is also meant to *engender* the crisis awareness, by bringing to our attention the magnitude of our insufficiency; this, in turn, leads one to beseech God even more fervently.

Permission to Pray

Positing the centrality of crisis and *bakkasha* raises what the Rav considers a crucial question: how dare man bring his paltry requests before the Almighty God? This question is not philosophical, but religious: given the Rav's lofty conception of a transcendent God, and the *yirat Shamayim* (fear of Heaven) proceeding from it, is it not presumptuous for finite man to approach the infinite God, before Whom all recedes into insignificance, with his personal needs? In halakhic terms, the Rav is searching for a "*mattir*," something that will permit man to engage in the audacious enterprise of prayer.

Before we turn to the *mattir* for the whole enterprise of prayer, let me add that the Rav also sees the need to procure a *mattir* every time we pray. This is, in fact, a cornerstone of many of his *shi'urim* on prayer. The *Gemara* establishes that before one makes requests of God, one must first offer praise to Him:

> Rabbi Simlai expounded: One should always recount the praises of the Omnipresent and then offer one's supplications. Whence do we learn it? From [the prayer of] our teacher Moshe, which is recorded thus (*Devarim* 3:24-25): "O Lord God, You have begun to show Your servant Your greatness, etc.," and only thereafter [Moshe requests], "Let me go over, I pray, and see the good Land." (*Avoda Zara* 7b)

The Rav sees this not just as a matter of etiquette, but as permission to supplicate. Hence, he concludes that the praise contained in *Pesukei De-Zimra* and in the blessings of *Keri'at Shema* allow us to recite the *Amida*, and the praise contained in the first three blessings of the *Amida* permit us to continue with the requests in the next thirteen blessings. In halakhic terms, *shevach* is a *mattir* for *bakkasha*. Thus, the need for a *mattir* is not merely a philosophical question, but part of the very structure and experience of prayer itself.

It is not only *bakkasha* that requires a *mattir*; in his early *shi'urim* on *tefilla*, the Rav adduced two *mattirim* for the very possibility of prayer itself, and he cites them in "Reflections on the *Amidah*" as well:

> The Talmudic dictum, "The prayers were established by the Patriarchs," does not contradict a second statement of the Sages, "The prayers were established to correspond to the fixed daily sacrificial offerings, the *temidim*" (*Berakhot* 26b). Rambam quoted both opinions, for they are mutually complementary. Prayer is justified by both factors, historical precedent and the ceremonial law of the Temple cult. (*Worship of the Heart* p. 151)

The Rav's focus on the need for a *mattir* presents a powerful religious message: our ability to stand before God is a privilege that should not be taken for granted. A pervasive sense of *yirat Shamayim* must lead one to be cautious and circumspect in one's approach to God. However, in "Reflections on the *Amidah*," he adds an additional *mattir* of a very different tenor:

> [P]rayer is a vital necessity for the religious individual. He cannot conceal his thoughts and his feelings, his vacillations and his struggles, his yearnings and his wishes, his despair and his bitterness – in a word, the great wealth stored away in his religious consciousness – in the depths of his soul. Suppressing liturgical expression is simply impossible: prayer is a necessity. Vital, vibrant religiosity cannot sustain itself without prayer. In sum, prayer is justified because it is impossible to exist without it. (*Worship of the Heart* p. 150)

This is a significant departure from the Rav's earlier conception of prayer, since it is a *mattir* that essentially does away with the need for *mattirim*. Prayer is now seen as inevitable, for it is a basic human need. Is it not natural to speak to God, as did the great Biblical figures and, indeed, Jews throughout the generations? Is God not *Shomei'a tefilla*, the Hearer of prayers?

Rav Lichtenstein has observed that, because of these questions, the Rav grew troubled over time by the focus on the *mattir*, leading him to de-emphasize it in his subsequent thought. Rav Lichtenstein attributes this change to three factors. First, the Rav always rethought matters. Second, in many areas his thought moved over the years in a more humanizing direction, from the epistemological to the existential, engaged with and sensitive to human needs, agonies and hopes. Third, in Wordsworth's phrase, "a deep distress hath humanized my soul" (*Elegiac Stanzas* I.36); his wife's illness led him to soften and ameliorate his position on the availability of prayer to man.

Prayer as Self-Sacrifice

Yet Rav Soloveitchik's decreasing emphasis on the need for a *mattir* in prayer does not mean that he moved away from a view of God's transcendence towards one of God's immanence. Rather, in "Reflections on the *Amidah*," the Rav presents the daily *Shemoneh Esrei* as maintaining both of these conceptions in dialectical tension. This tension makes the *Shemoneh Esrei*, in the Rav's reading, into an emotional roller-coaster that takes one through a crisis experience thrice daily. The reason for the volatility of prayer is rooted in man's complex soul:

> Prayer, which is like a mirror reflecting the image of the person who worships God with heart and soul, is shot through with perplexity, for worship itself is rooted in the human dialectical consciousness. Hence prayer is not marked by monotonous uniformity. It is multi-colored: it contains contradictory themes, expresses a variety of moods, conflicting experiences, and desires oscillating in opposing directions. Religious experience is a multi-directional movement,

metaphysically infused. Prayer too does not proceed slowly along one straight path, but leaps and cascades from wondrous heights to terrifying depths, and back. (*Worship of the Heart* p. 148)

According to the Rav, the *Amida* has a chiastic structure of a-b-c-b-a. This structure can be perceived most easily in the following diagram, portraying a descent into the depths and an ascent therefrom:

1. Avot	*19. Sim Shalom*	love, grace	*Gadol*
2. Gevurot	*18. Modim*	fear, dependence	*Gibbor*
3. Kedusha 4-16. Bakkasha 17. Retzeh		paradox, sacrifice	*Nora*

The first blessing, *Avot*, opens the *Amida* with a joyous sense of Divine *chesed* and human adequacy. These are replaced in the next blessing, *Gevurot*, by a dread-filled sense of Divine strength and human weakness. The following blessing, *Kedushat Ha-Shem*, presents the paradox of Divine transcendence and human worship: "You are holy and Your Name is holy, and holy ones praise You daily." How can man approach the Infinite? Only by means of self-sacrifice, which is accomplished in the next thirteen petitional blessings. While, in its most straightforward sense, *bakkasha* means pleading with God for the fulfillment of our needs, it also entails a sacrificial admission of our dependence and incompleteness:

> The very gesture of falling before God and acknowledging His unlimited sovereignty and man's utter impotence, constitutes an act of sacrifice. Service of the heart is expressed in the middle benedictions. (*Worship of the Heart* p. 175)

The capstone of the middle blessings is *Shema Koleinu*, in which we ask God to "accept our prayer" – i.e., the previous twelve petitional blessings – "in mercy and favor." This is a general request to accept our requests.

The next blessing, *Retzeh*, ostensibly seems similar to *Shema Koleinu*, yet the Rav sharply distinguishes between them. *Retzeh* connects prayer to the sacrificial service (pp. 176-79), and, according to the Rav, constitutes the culmination of the theme of self-sacrifice, to which one has been building up throughout the previous fourteen blessings (*Kedushat Ha-Shem* and *bakkasha*). This is why he claims that "*Retzeh* is perhaps the central benediction in the text of *avoda sheba-lev*" (*Worship of the Heart* p. 177), understanding *avoda* specifically in the sense of sacrifice.

In other words, the thirteen middle blessings contain a dual theme: petitioning God for one's needs, and sacrificially admitting one's inadequacy. The first theme is highlighted by *Shema Koleinu*, the second by *Retzeh*. In *Retzeh*, one asks God not to accept one's supplications, but rather to accept one's offering:

> When a Jew says *Retzeh* he does not refer to the satisfaction of needs and the fulfillment of the desires about which he poured out his heart in the middle, petitionary section. For this he has already prayed in the previous benediction, *Shema Koleinu* ("Hear our voice"). When he reaches *Retzeh* these "petty" matters no longer concern him. His soul is bound up in a great, profound, world-embracing request. He asks God to accept the great sacrifice he has just offered, to accept his being that is returned to God, cleaving unto the Infinite and connecting itself to the Divine throne. (*Worship of the Heart* pp. 178-79)

This sacrificial element in this prayer can be understood in light of a passage in *Out of the Whirlwind*:

> Prayer flowing from a heart filled with the inner misery and despair of this contradictory experience [i.e., the self-assertion and self-negation that express one's depth crisis, which flows from the awareness of an incomplete existence and an unfulfilled destiny] is not intercessory petition, which is intended to relieve

one of his trouble, but rather has more of a subjective character. It does not ask for help, nor does it try to resolve the crisis. The prayer consecrates the defeat, redeems the misery and elevates it to the level of sacrifice. Prayer flowing *mi-ma'amakim*, from the depths, is a sacrificial service. The supplication imparts meaning and directedness to the crisis experience. The majestic personality of a while ago (at the hour of triumph) acquires dignity, and, of course, greatness through prayer, during which the free surrender is brought about or the defeat accepted. What this prayer accomplishes is remarkable. (*Out of the Whirlwind* p. 167)

In the Rav's various discussions of the structure of prayer, we discover differing, yet perhaps complementary, conceptions. "Redemption, Prayer, Talmud Torah" presents the *bakkasha* section of the *Amida* as a journey of self-acquisition, followed by a concluding note of self-sacrifice in *Retzeh*. By contrast, "Reflections on the *Amidah*" portrays *bakkasha* as a form of self-sacrifice, capped by *Retzeh*; yet in "Reflections on the *Amidah*," self-sacrifice is then *followed by* self-acquisition:

God is "satisfied" with this offering. He receives it and restores it to the one who has offered it. The praying individual annuls himself in order to acquire himself. From his prayer man emerges firm, elevated and sublime, having found his redemption in self-loss and self-recovery. (*Worship of the Heart* p. 179)

This contrast between "Redemption, Prayer, Talmud Torah" and "Reflections on the *Amidah*" raises an important question: Is the focus of prayer self-acquisition or self-sacrifice? Is self-sacrifice the terminus, or is it followed by reacquisition of the self? The answer is, of course, that both are true. When we consider the Rav's various works as a whole, we see that he constantly maintains a balance between affirmation and denial, majesty and humility. In the two essays just mentioned, the Rav finds this dichotomy within the *Amida* itself, while in *The Lonely Man of Faith* he discovers it in the contrast between the *Shema* and the *Amida*:

During the recital of *Shema*, man ideally feels totally committed to God and his awareness is related to a normative end, assigning to man ontological legitimacy and worth as an ethical being whom God charged with a great mission … In contrast to the *Shema* awareness, the *Tefilla* awareness negates the legitimacy and worth of human existence. Man, as a slave of God, is completely dependent upon Him… When the Talmud (*Berakhot* 14b and 15a) speaks of *kabbalat ol malkhut Shamayim shelemah*, the unitary acceptance of the Kingdom of God [attained by reciting *Shema* and *Tefilla* together], it refers to the two awarenesses which, notwithstanding their antithetic character, merge into one comprehensive awareness of man who is at the same time the free messenger of God and His captive as well. (*The Lonely Man of Faith* p. 75)

In "Reflections on the *Amidah*," *tefilla* presents not just two approaches to man, but a movement from affirmation to negation and then back to affirmation. "The order of the last three benedictions is the reverse of the opening three" (*Worship of the Heart* p. 179), climbing out of the depths back into the sunlight, and ending on a note of grace:

[A]fter all the transformations and oscillations from love and mercy to the experience of dread and human helplessness, after man comes crashing down from the heights of yearning and aspiration to the depths of confusion and terror, after self-negation and self-recovery, after the sacrifice, the binding and the offering on the altar, and after the return to existence – comes again the delightful, joyous and confident experience: God appears as a safe haven and secure abode… Man does not flee from God, but rather races towards Him and resides in the bosom of the *Shekhina*. All is blanketed in the serenity of peace and quiet. Over all, there flows the blessing of the Infinite; the *chesed* of God descends "like the dew on Mount Hermon" (*Tehillim* 133:3). The world is illuminated with the precious light that flows from the Infinite. (*Worship of the Heart* p. 181)

Conclusion: Why a Fixed Text?

If prayer is indeed the verbal expression of the stormy religious soul, why do we pray from a standardized text? Why not just express whatever is in one's heart? The Rav offers three different answers to this question, and these neatly reflect the three functions of prayer we have identified in his writings.

a) In *The Lonely Man of Faith*, where the Rav presents the essence of prayer as an experience of encounter with God (meant to overcome loneliness), the need for standardization is not specific to prayer. Rather, it reflects the general tendency of *halakha* to attempt to transcend the fleeting subjectivity of experience and to give it an objective dimension (p. 56).

b) According to "Redemption, Prayer, Talmud Torah," where prayer is seen as a medium for self-creation, Chazal penned a standardized text in order to teach man the hierarchy of needs (p. 67), as well as to provide him with a framework for personal meditation and supplication.

c) In "Reflections on the *Amidah*," with its stress on self-sacrifice and its focus on the paradox of how finite man can approach the infinite God, a set text is necessary because, otherwise, it would be impossible to pray; the endeavor of prayer would have been too bold to consider (p. 151).

Thus, Rav Soloveitchik's complex view of prayer presents a dialectic between sacrifice and acquisition, between Divine distance and nearness, between self-nullification and self-assertion. The reason for this dialectic is his dialectical view of man, which is evident in all his writings, nowhere more than in his teachings on prayer.

Understanding Rambam's "Necessary Belief" in God's Emotions

Rabbi Mark Smilowitz

In Book 3, chapter 28 of his *Moreh Ha-Nevukhim*, Rambam distinguishes between two types of belief we are instructed by the Torah to believe. The first he calls "true opinions," and it includes such examples as belief that God exists, that He is one, and that He has no body. The second he calls "necessary beliefs," and they include the belief that God gets angry at those who violate His laws and the belief that God responds immediately to the prayers of the oppressed. The reason the Torah calls us to believe the true opinions is that, as Rambam had just explained in chapter 27, true knowledge about God and His world is what allows people to attain eternity of the soul, i.e. the World to Come. The reason the Torah calls us to believe necessary beliefs is to ensure good social and political relationships in this world, by encouraging the acquisition of noble qualities and discouraging wrongdoing.

Classical commentators Ephodi and Shem Tov both understand the necessary beliefs to be beliefs that are not actually true, but are nonetheless necessary for the masses to believe for the good of society. Their interpretation of necessary beliefs as false beliefs comes from two sources. The first is that Rambam contrasts necessary beliefs with the "true opinions," implying that the latter are true, but the former are not. The second is that Rambam states clearly in a number of places that God doesn't really get angry, or have any passions at all, and that verses in *Tanakh* indicating that He does get angry are to be understood metaphorically.[1]

---

1. See *Mishneh Torah, Hilkhot Yesodei Ha-Torah* 1:11; *Moreh Ha-Nevukhim* 1:35,36,54.

Some modern scholars associate the necessary beliefs referred to by Rambam in this chapter with the "noble lie" discussed by Plato in his *Republic*.[2] There, Socrates suggests that it would be good for maintaining the stratified structure of society if people believed the myth that when God created men from the earth, He mingled gold into the composition of the nobles, silver in the composition of the servant class, and iron and brass in the composition of the farmers and craftsmen.[3] These scholars consider Rambam's view on belief in an angry God to be that it is a similar kind of myth invented for the masses in order to encourage just and moral behavior. The sophisticates of society need no such artificial motivation because they understand that being just and moral is its own reward.

However, there is a serious problem with understanding the necessary beliefs as a fiction to be taught to the masses. This interpretation stands in stark contradiction with Rambam's own teaching earlier in the *Moreh*. In chapter 34 of Book 1, Rambam explains why metaphysics should not be taught to the masses. He gives five reasons, but the main idea is that metaphysical knowledge about God and creation requires the kind of rigorous training and preparation that are possessed only by the select few and not the masses. Then Rambam devotes chapter 35 there to teach that the esoteric knowledge we hide from the masses does not include God's incorporeality and God's lack of emotion, sometimes called His impassibility. He says:

> Do not think that all we discussed in these previous chapters, regarding the greatness of the issue and its hiddenness, and the difficulty of grasping it, and keeping it away from the masses, that denial of corporeality by Him and denial of the affections are included. (*Moreh Ha-Nevukhim* 1:35)[4]

---

2. See, for example, Hannah Kasher, "*Mitos Ha-El Ha-Ko'es Be-Moreh Nevukhim*," *Eshel Be'er Sheva* 4 (1996), p. 98; Moshe Halbertal, *Ha-Rambam* (Jerusalem, 2009), p. 239.
3. Plato, *The Republic*, Book 3, 414e–15c.
4. All English translations of the *Moreh* are from the Pines edition, *The Guide of the Perplexed* (Chicago, 1978), 2 vols. Unless stated otherwise, all references in this article are to *Moreh Ha-Nevukhim*.

Understanding Rambam's "Necessary Belief" in God's Emotions | 257

Rambam's position here is that the masses must be taught that God has no body and no affections, meaning emotions – *"hipaʿaluyot"* in the Hebrew translation. As he says:

> The negation of the doctrine of the corporeality of God and the denial of His having a likeness to created things and of His being subject to affections are matters that ought to be made clear and explained to everyone according to his capacity and ought to be inculcated in virtue of traditional authority upon children, women, stupid ones, and those of a defective natural disposition. (Ibid.)

There is no doubt that one of the affections that we are instructed here to negate when teaching the masses is God's anger. Therefore, it is puzzling that Rambam instructs us here to teach the masses that God never gets angry, while in 3:28 he indicates that the preservation of a just and peaceful society depends on convincing the masses of the "necessary belief" in the apparent falsehood that God does get angry.

But the problem becomes even more vexing when one proceeds to read chapter 36 of Book 1. There, Rambam makes clear what is at stake were we to allow the masses to maintain their erroneous impression that God is subject to passions and emotions. On an ideological plane, believing God is subject to affections is worse than idol worship. That is because idol worship, while erroneous in its belief that there are other gods who deserve to be worshipped alongside God, at least leaves room for a correct understanding of God Himself, whereas attributing passions and bodily functions to God is a direct affront against God's very essence. Rambam lists believing God has emotions among such fundamental transgressions as believing God doesn't exist, believing there are two Gods, believing He has a body, or attributing to Him any imperfection, all of which he says makes one "more blameworthy than a worshipper of idols."

In light of this characterization of the belief that God is subject to passions as blasphemous, the notion described in 3:28 that the Torah requires that the masses believe that God gets angry at those who disobey

Him becomes incomprehensible. Not only does Rambam contradict himself regarding the question, what are we to teach the masses about God's anger? He also seems to suggest an absurdity, that the Torah requires us to teach the masses beliefs that are harmful for the eternity of their souls, while at the same time asserting that the main purpose of the Torah is to teach true beliefs about God in order to assist people in attaining immortality of their souls (see 3:27).

It is difficult to find in Rambam scholarship any mention of this blatant contradiction. How are we to interpret it? In his introduction to the *Moreh*, Rambam prepares us for the fact that there are contradictions in the book. He offers seven reasons why contradictions generally appear in books. The seventh cause for contradiction may be useful in our case, but it is subject to a fundamental dispute in interpretation. Rambam says there that for obscure matters it is necessary to conceal certain parts. He adds that contradiction is also necessitated. According to Leo Strauss, the purpose of the contradiction is in order to conceal. Strauss notes that great luminaries have to hide their more revolutionary ideas from the masses for political reasons while teaching them to the sophisticated, and contradiction is the tool which does the concealment. The masses will be confused by the contradiction, if they even notice it, and conclude that the more traditional side of the contradiction must be what the luminary meant. The sophisticated readers will understand that between the two contradictory versions they are to choose the more revolutionary one and ignore the more traditional one. This is called esoteric writing.[5]

This interpretation of the seventh cause of contradiction is challenged by Yair Lorberbaum, who argues that the contradiction referred to here is for epistemological, not political purposes. That is to say, the purpose of the contradiction is not to conceal but to reveal. When dealing with more obscure topics, sometimes it becomes impossible due to the limitations of language to directly communicate the idea. The idea must be concealed not to save the reputation of the luminary, but because the idea by its nature is too difficult to be taught explicitly. One way of conveying such

---

5. Leo Strauss, "The Literary Character of the Guide for the Perplexed" in *Persecution and the Art of Writing* (Chicago, 1988), pp. 38–94.

an obscure idea is to approach it from two opposite ends, encouraging the student to consider opposite views about the idea until the student grasps it intuitively. This is called dialectical teaching.[6]

Strauss' view involves certain difficulties, primarily that it makes it hard to trust the text one is reading. Furthermore, it is problematic to attribute esoteric writing to a contradiction regarding what to teach the masses, since the masses will discover the hidden opinion when it is taught to them. We therefore aim to explain this contradiction using Lorberbaum's approach to the seventh cause for contradiction, and to show that it involves a dialectical teaching. Let us consider the text in 3:28 carefully. Rambam says:

> [T]he Law also makes a call to adopt certain beliefs, belief in which is necessary for the sake of political welfare. Such, for instance, is our belief that He, may He be exalted, is violently angry with those who disobey Him and that it is therefore necessary to fear Him and to dread Him and to take care not to disobey. (3:28)

Significantly, despite the claims of the commentators, Rambam never says here or anywhere in this chapter that the necessary beliefs are only for the masses. To the contrary, he refers to belief in God's anger as "our belief." Furthermore, Rambam never says that the necessary beliefs are false. The main distinction between the necessary beliefs and the true opinions indicated in this chapter is that the true opinions are capable of having their truth demonstrated through logical argument. The necessary beliefs cannot be proven through argument, but are accepted through tradition. That Rambam believed there exist truths which cannot be demonstrated rationally is clear from his discussion in 1:31 and from his treatment of the creation of the world (see 2:25).

Consequently, the contradiction is greater than originally thought. In 3:28, Rambam treats God's anger not merely as a metaphor but as something true that the Torah expects us all to believe, in stark conflict

---
6. Yair Lorberbaum, "*Ha-Sibba Ha-Shevi'it:*' Al Ha-Setirot Be-'Moreh Ha-Nevukhim' – Iyyun Mechuddash," *Tarbiz* 69:1, pp. 211–237.

with his assertion in 1:35-36 that God is impassible, not subject to emotion. His equivocation about what the leaders are to teach the people is not only about what to teach the ignorant masses, but what to teach everyone, the layman and scholar alike, and reflects his equivocation about the truth of God's anger.

The dialectic approach suggests that in light of this contradiction, there is an obscure truth in the notion that God gets angry. Some have suggested, without noting this contradiction, that there is truth in the idea of God's anger, based on 1:54.[7] There Rambam explains that all descriptions of God involving moral qualities, that He is merciful and gracious, do not actually describe God Himself, but only His actions. They are called "attributes of action," and are true only in the sense of a metaphor, that were a human being to perform such actions, he would do so only upon feeling the affection of mercy or graciousness. Similarly, God is called "wrathful" because He brings calamities upon men who deserve punishment in such a way that were a human to wreak such destruction, he would only do so because of violent hatred or anger. God, on the other hand, deals out destruction only according to the measure of what is deserved. The "truth," then, in God's anger, as well as in His mercy and kindness, involves only the nature of actions He performs, not the character of His essence.

However, it is not a satisfying answer to our problem to say that when Rambam says the Torah prescribes the necessary belief that God gets angry at those who disobey Him, he means it only metaphorically. Considering his scathing condemnation in 1:36 of those who believe in the reality of God's emotions, it would be irresponsible of Rambam to preach the heretical belief he seeks to uproot and remain silent about a metaphorical meaning, hoping the reader not take it literally. If Rambam wanted to say that the necessary belief is only that God punishes the wicked, he should have said only that, and left God's emotions out of it. He references God's anger because he thinks it is necessary to believe in the anger itself. We

---

7. See the commentary of Shem Tov on the *Moreh* 3:28. Also see Arthur Hyman, "Spinoza's Dogmas of Universal Faith in the Light of Their Medieval Jewish Background," *Biblical and Other Studies*, ed. Alexander Altmann (Cambridge, 1963), pp. 183-195. Hyman's dialectical approach to the necessary beliefs differs from mine. See footnote 15 below.

Understanding Rambam's "Necessary Belief" in God's Emotions | 261

are back to our dialectical situation. The reality of God's anger can be understood only by considering it both a falsehood tantamount to heresy, as well as a truth prescribed by the Torah as a necessary belief.

A more promising pathway to grasping this dialectical teaching appears when we notice that Rambam commits a very similar contradiction regarding emotion in human beings. In 1:54, Rambam teaches that political leaders should imitate God's attributes, carrying out justice based on what is deserved and not out of passion, and not, for example, out of anger or mercy, "for all passions [*hippa'aluyot*] are evil." One would be surprised if Rambam, after condemning all passions, would teach that the whole purpose of the Torah is to develop certain passions. Yet that is exactly what he does in 3:52 when he says regarding fear of God that "the purpose of all the actions prescribed by the Torah is to bring about this passion [*hippa'alut*]."

How could the purpose of the Torah be to bring about something deemed "evil?" Fortunately, Rambam left enough clues to resolve this contradiction. Rambam works with two types of emotions. When instructing political leaders to rule without passions in 1:54, Rambam says that "he should not let loose the reins of anger nor let passion gain mastery over him." Clearly, what is undesirable here is allowing emotions to take control, causing the person to act not in accordance with justice and wisdom. When someone gets so angry that they lose control and let loose destructive forces that are unwise or undeserved, that is the evil of the passions Rambam refers to here. To a certain degree, the same is true of one moved by pity or compassion to waive the punishment of the evildoer, although here Rambam indicates that even wisdom dictates a certain leaning towards compassion in judgment. The point is that the motivation of the leader's actions must be wisdom and not passion. As Rambam says, the leader's actions should "proceed from him according to a determined measure and according to the deserts of the people who are affected by them and not merely because of his following a passion." The kind of emotion condemned by Rambam, thus, is emotion that causes actions not according to wisdom. It is rooted in physical urges that are part of the nature of all beings composed of physical matter (3:8).

The emotion of fear that is the goal of the Torah's commandments according to 3:52 is of a different type. Rambam's point in that chapter is that regular performance of the Torah's commandments leads to fear of God. "For it is by all the particulars of the actions and through their repetition that some excellent men obtain such training that they achieve human perfection, so that they fear, and are in dread and awe of God." We notice that whereas in 1:54, where all passions are condemned, the emotion *precedes* the action, here in 3:52, where a particular passion is praised, the emotion *follows* the action. What is important, however, is not the temporal order of action and emotion, but that the source out of which the emotion arises is wisdom. Fear that comes from wisdom can lead to further proper action, as Rambam continues in the *Moreh* to say that people "as a result [of this fear] act subsequently as they ought to." Emotions of this second type do not cause a person to lose control and act against wisdom, as those of the first type do. To the contrary, they guide a person to continue on the path of wisdom in which the emotion is rooted.

In light of this discovery that Rambam operates with two types of emotion, we notice that in his discussions of negation of God's emotions he emphasizes the first type. He writes:

> [A]ll affections likewise ought of necessity to be negated in reference to Him. For all affections entail change, and[8] the agent who effects those affections is undoubtedly not identical with him who is acted upon [or affected]. Accordingly, if He, may He be exalted, were subject to affection in any respect whatever, someone other than He would act upon Him and effect change in Him. (1:55)

Therefore, the problem with belief that God has emotions is not the emotions themselves, but the implications of those emotions that God is not in charge, that He loses control to some higher force that pushes Him to

---

8. I removed the word "moreover" from the Pines translation, because it undermines reading this passage as one continuous thought. The reading here presented is consistent with all the other English and Hebrew translations available to me.

act not in accordance with His essence. One indeed understands why such a belief is considered by Rambam to be worse than idolatry, for idolaters, while believing in multiple deities, may still believe that there is one God mightier than them all, while the believer in God's emotions – emotions of the first type – believes that God is weaker than some higher force. When explaining how to read the verses of God's anger in 1:54, Rambam's formulation again invokes the first type of emotions:

> He is called "jealous and avenging and keeping anger and wrathful," meaning that actions similar to those that *proceed from us from* a certain aptitude of the soul – namely jealousy, holding fast to vengeance, hatred, or anger – proceed from Him, may He be exalted, *because of* the deserts of those who are punished, and not *because of* any passion whatever, may He be exalted above every deficiency. (1:54; emphasis mine)

The error Rambam wishes to prevent in interpreting these verses is to think that God punishes *because of* His anger. Humans might do that, but not God. The imperfection Rambam associates with emotions is that God is "subject to affections" (1:35), meaning subordinate to them. Even the term introduced by Ibn Tibbon's Hebrew translation and followed by modern Hebrew translators, "*hippa'aluyot*," implies emotions of the first type. This word, like the Arabic original, is "a noun deriving from the passive form of the verb 'to act.'"[9] It refers to a state of being acted upon, being a receiver of an action originating elsewhere. The various English translations of this term, affections and passions, also connote this first type of emotion, "passions" indicating passively receiving something, and "affections" implying being affected by something. It is the notion of God being acted upon, manipulated, and controlled by outside forces that Rambam wages war against in his negation of God's emotions.

What would Rambam say about the attribution to God of the second type of emotion, which does not originate in some force outside God's essence, but instead originates in acts of wisdom that conform with God's

---

9. Pines, *Guide of the Perplexed*, vol. 1, p. 79, footnote 1.

essence? It is our contention that Rambam remains open to attributing this kind of emotion to God. Emotions of the second type, because they arise from wisdom, can be viewed as a kind of knowledge. Presumably that is why Rambam refers to emotional dispositions as "*dei'ot*," which literally means thoughts or opinions.[10] We consider someone who is unable to feel compassion for someone suffering who deserves assistance or to feel anger at evil committed against the innocent to be deficient, to lack a certain kind of understanding.[11] To say that God is incapable of feeling anger or compassion in such circumstances is tantamount to saying He lacks care or concern, that He acts only in an algorithmic fashion, mechanically following dictates of wisdom but essentially indifferent to good and evil. The Rav, discussing the issue of God's love in his essay *And From There You Shall Seek*, insists that Rambam never held the view that completely purifies God of the emotion of love. He points out that Rambam in his *Mishneh Torah* refers to God's love for Avraham *Avinu*, for converts to Judaism, and for the penitent soul, and the Rav considers it a fundamental tenet of Judaism that Man's love for God is reciprocated by God.[12]

We can thus resolve the contradiction between the passages in the *Moreh* that condemn belief in the reality of God's anger and the passages that maintain the "necessary belief" in God's anger by suggesting that, in a parallel way that he refers to two types of human emotion, Rambam refers to two types of God's anger. We negate the notion that anger causes God to lose control and act against His wisdom, but we maintain belief in an anger that is in conformity with God's wisdom and His essence. What is "necessary" to encourage moral behavior and the cultivation of good

---

10. See *Mishneh Torah, Hilkhot Dei'ot* 1:1.
11. The passage in *Hilkhot Dei'ot* 2:3, where Rambam prescribes complete negation of anger, needs to be examined in light of his recommendation in the previous chapter, 1:4, that one should maintain anger in moderation. That contradiction might be resolved in a similar manner as discussed here, but much has been written about this issue and it deserves its own treatment.
12. Rav Joseph B. Soloveitchik, *And From There You Shall Seek* (Jersey City, 2008), pp. 153-157, n. 2. To be clear, the Rav does connect Rambam's view of God's love with the attributes of action of 1:54, but his formulation, "the Creator's behavior toward His world reflects the pure lights of infinite love," seems to treat those attributes as more than mere metaphor.

character traits in people is not the false belief that God loses control with those who disobey, but the true belief that He cares about people being good. It may be more appropriate to attribute to God "feeling" instead of "emotion," because the word feeling does not carry with it an implication of being a cause or a setting into motion.[13] He punishes *with* anger, but not *out of* anger.

If this contradiction is resolved through a simple divide between different types of emotion, why refer to it as dialectical, and why invoke Rambam's seventh type of contradiction as interpreted by Lorberbaum?

The reason is that even this second kind of emotion involves certain difficulties. Whereas attributing the first type of anger to God is intolerable because even by popular standards it involves a deficiency, the second type of anger is appropriate to attribute to God, although it also hints at a kind of deficiency, but one noticeable primarily by philosophers, and one that is theoretically solvable. Again, it is helpful to consider this kind of emotion as a type of knowledge. Rambam was aware that God's knowledge involves at least two metaphysical problems. The first is that it implies a duality, splitting God between His essence and His knowledge, upsetting the notion that God is One. The second is that it puts God in a cause-effect chain as knowing things because the things have an impact upon Him, upsetting the notion that God is All-Powerful. Rambam resolves these problems by declaring that God's knowledge is different from human knowledge. Whereas human knowledge is caused by the things they know, God's knowledge comes from His essence. He knows everything because He knows His essence, not because those things impact Him, and His knowledge and His essence are one. Rambam says about this idea, "This matter is beyond the ability of our mouths to relate, [or our] ears to hear, nor is there [the capacity] within the heart of man to grasp it in its entirety."[14]

The same problems and the same solution regarding God's knowledge apply to God's emotions, as long as we are talking about the second type.

---

13. Zev Harvey makes this distinction in the thought of Rav Chasdai Kreskas. See Z. Harvey, "*Al Ha-Tehiyot Be-Torat Ha-Te'arim Shel Rav Chasdai Kreskas*" in *Divrei Ha-Akademi'a Ha-Yisraelit Le-Madda'im* (2000), pp. 133-144.

14. Rambam *Mishneh Torah, Hilkhot Yesodei Ha-Torah* 2:10. Translation from https://www.chabad.org/library/article_cdo/aid/682956/jewish/Mishneh-Torah.htm, accessed 26 August 2018.

This approach to God's emotion is hinted to by Rashi, who says on the verse "I am the Lord, I have not changed" (*Malakhi* 3:6) that God means, "I have not changed My opinion from the beginning to [now] love evil and hate good." That is to say, God's emotional states to love good and hate evil are in eternal unity with His essence, and not subject to change through a cause-effect chain. But because this resolution to the problem of God's emotions is not "within the heart of man to grasp it in its entirety," Rambam considered this issue of the type he describes in his explanation of the seventh cause of contradiction, where he says that "in speaking of obscure matters it is necessary to conceal some parts" and to teach the idea through a contradiction. Following Lorberbaum's view of that type of contradiction, in our case Rambam takes the view that we should teach people both that God does not get angry and that He does, because both are true, and it should be left up to the student to intuitively grasp how both can be true, since a full explanation is "beyond the ability of our mouths to relate [or our] ears to hear."[15]

In sum, we have been working with two contradictions. One is regarding God Himself, if it is true or false that He experiences emotion. The other is regarding what to teach people, if they should be taught to negate all emotions in God, or taught that God gets angry at those who disobey. Our answer to the first is that it depends on the kind of emotion. Our answer to the second is that people should be taught both in a dialectical fashion, and not be taught simply that He experiences one kind and not the other, because the full resolution of the metaphysical problems with God's emotion is too deep to understand through mere explanation.

One last point deserves mention. Our *Rosh Yeshiva*, Rav Aharon Lichtenstein *zt"l*, wrote an article about the experience of human suffering, in which he cites a *Gemara* which says that God grieves over the suffering of the righteous. He notes, "Awareness of that Divine anguish serves to

---

15. Note that this approach to the dialectical nature of the necessary beliefs, which says that the truth is too obscure to be fully captured in language, differs from that taken by Marc Shapiro, whose analysis indicates that the necessary beliefs are dialectical in the sense that they are true about *a* and false about *b*, where both *a* and *b* are fully explainable. See Marc Shapiro, *The Limits of Orthodox Theology: Maimonides' Thirteen Principles Reappraised* (Oxford, 2006), pp. 119-120.

ameliorate the human".[16] After citing a number of *midrashim* that further discuss God's grief, he adds, "I write these lines with anxious trepidation." One reason for his trepidation is, as he says, "I ask myself timorously: how would Rambam have responded to these speculations? I'm afraid the answer to this rhetorical question is clear. And it is, I repeat, troubling." Still, he insists that in this dilemma, one must choose, and "Knesset Yisrael has chosen: for *Midrash* against the *Moreh*." He concludes that "the grief Chazal daringly attributed to Him is both real, *per se*, and related to an objective correlative." In light of the study we have presented here, perhaps Rambam's response to our *Rosh Yeshiva*'s question is not in fact so clearly in the negative. It could be that Rav Lichtenstein's trepidation in affirming a kind Divine emotion, as opposed to wholesale negation, is precisely the educational goal Rambam had in mind when taking the dialectical approach to teaching God's anger.

---

16. Rav Aharon Lichtenstein, "The Duties of the Heart and Response to Suffering," *Jewish Perspectives on the Experience of Suffering*, ed. Shalom Carmy (Northvale, NJ, 1999), p. 49 ff.

Planning and Engaging Life: Globalization, Egalitarianism, Agency, and *Chesed*

Rabbi Dr. Shlomo Dov Rosen

1.

Moreinu HaRav Aharon Lichtenstein *zt"l* had a knack for delivering remarkable *chiddush* (innovation) as if it were indisputably commonplace. At one of our annual visits to his *sukka*, in response to a since-forgotten question, Rav Lichtenstein explained the following: The *Gemara* in *Mo'ed Katan* 9a-b, which rules that one should interrupt one's *talmud Torah* (Torah study) to do other *mitzvot* only when they cannot be done by others, does not mean to describe the extent of a person's involvement in *mitzvot*. A person must plan his or her life, allocating time to values such as *chesed*, while considering a variety of factors that do not feature in this context. The *Gemara* merely relates to how one should behave when a mitzva crops up during time already allocated for *talmud Torah*. In other words, the question of under what circumstances one should interrupt *talmud Torah* has nothing to do with the question of the proper comparative allocation of time and resources between learning and other Torah values.

This reading might strike some as unremarkable, just as how it was delivered to us – huddled together in our *Rebbe*'s *sukka* – as if it were what anyone might say. But, it is sufficient to reflect only scantily upon the vast expanses of Jewish thought, and complexities of our intellectual and social history, to realize that this is neither a naïve textual reading nor a non-polemical statement. When, so commonly, *talmud Torah* is viewed as an almost singular virtue, as an invariably preferable occupation, our *Rebbe* here taught us that its place in relation to other values is the proper subject of reflective consideration and planning. According to his interpretation, this *Gemara* does not aim to define the contours of Torah action, but rather the limits of *talmud Torah* when it potentially conflicts with action.

I do not recall that our *Rebbe* provided a source-based backing for his reading of the *Gemara*. He often would not. Perhaps much of the grandeur of Torah greatness is this ability to deliver innovation based on overarching scholarship by the wave of a hand. It might even seem hard for the *talmid chakham* (Torah scholar) to see how others naturally assume otherwise. The aim of this article is to provide a source-based foundation for this idea, and to analyze both its assumptions and its alternatives. If I do not do justice to the original idea, I hope to at least develop the *sugya* (topic) further.

2.

We can begin with an alternative interpretation of this *Gemara*, one which similarly struggles with its ethical ramifications, and grew out of the same *Beit Ha-Midrash*. Our *Rebbe* Rav Elyakim Krumbein *ybd"l*, a *talmid muvhak* (distinguished student) of Rav Lichtenstein *zt"l*, responded to the ethical dilemma that comes to expression in this *Gemara* in a totally different manner. In an article published by the Yeshiva,[1] Rav Krumbein focused upon another *Gemara*, which deals with the potency of *talmud Torah* and *chesed* in fending off a curse. The *Gemara* in *Rosh Ha-Shana* 18a states that both Abbayei and Rava (or perhaps Rabba) were descended from Eli, and hence destined to die by the age of twenty. Rava studied Torah, and consequently had twenty more years added to his life. However, Abbayei not only studied but also did *chesed*, and thus merited forty additional years. Rav Krumbein quoted Chafetz Chayyim who asked how this distinction between them could be possible if both were abiding by the *Gemara*'s criterion of interrupting *talmud Torah* only for a mitzva that cannot be fulfilled by others.

Chafetz Chayyim could obviously have answered with Rav Lichtenstein's reading of the *Gemara*, and explained that Abbayei planned his non-learning time differently. Instead, he argued that Abbayei's social status allowed his involvement in *chesed* to have a greater impact than that of others, so he instigated and not only responded, while Rava was of the opinion that one is not obligated to act unless faced with an actual

---

1. www.etzion.gush.net/vbm/archive/5-halak/04mitzva.php. Rav Krumbein builds off Chafetz Chayyim, *Ahavat Chesed*, note on 3:8 (the final chapter of the work).

ethical predicament. Rav Krumbein developed Chafetz Chayyim's idea: Abbayei considered even potential intervention and effects to be a basis for obligation. Thus, he actively searched to reveal hidden ultimate needs. When he "heard the cry of existence" he understood that "it depended upon him," and discovered *mitzvot* "that were hidden from others." He was thus legitimately under an obligation to interrupt his *talmud Torah*, and afford preference to action, on the basis of his own understanding, or perhaps, his own subjective perspective.

These two empathetic approaches, of Rav Lichtenstein and Rav Krumbein, to the comparative allocation of time and effort to *mitzvot* and *talmud Torah*, stand at stark counterpoise. They have their equivalent philosophical counterparts, which we shall note in conclusion. But I would like to first discuss a possible basis for each in a parallel *sugya*.

Questions concerning the allocation of *tzedaka* raise similar issues to those of time allocation between *talmud Torah* and action. The *Sifrei* famously teaches us that there are orders of preference for the giving of charity. The needs of close of kin are given first preference, and then those of the needy who are in geographical proximity, which themselves come before those of total strangers.[2] This layered approach to social obligation (which rather misleadingly goes by the Hebrew appellation "*aniyei irekha*") seems to have held well until the eighteenth and nineteenth centuries. But both Chatam Sofer (following his *Rebbe*, the author of *Sefer Hafla'a*) and Arukh Ha-Shulchan after him found it insufficient. I would suggest that the industrial revolution, with its urbanization and new possibilities of communication, what may be called the first stages of globalization, were the catalysts for a conceptual shift concerning responsibility to the distant impoverished. The problems that the *sugya* of *tzedaka* bring out are comparable to those of the *sugya* of *talmud Torah* verses action. Both exhibit a clash between values, which requires a normative resolution. Indeed, diverse needs of different groups of people in *tzedaka* calculations are not merely questions of allocation. They represent conflicting values, such as responsibility to close of kin, or communal responsibility, versus fair and equal division of wealth. And on occasion these quandaries invite other questions of comparative ascendancy of values, such as the place of *talmud*

---

2. *Sifrei Devarim* 116.

Torah.[3] I will suggest that the different solutions of Arukh Ha-Shulchan and Chatam Sofer concerning clashes of values in *tzedaka* are insightful in casting light upon the two options of interpretation presented by Rav Lichtenstein and Rav Krumbein concerning *talmud Torah* versus action.

3.

Arukh Ha-Shulchan explicitly queried: if everyone is expected to give precedence to the impoverished of their family, who will take responsibility for the poor who have no relatives? He answered that we are not told to give exclusively to close of kin, but rather to give them more than others. In other words, the *halakha* of giving precedence to those of proximity relates only to part of the charity that one gives. Some other part should be allocated freely.[4] This idea is similar to that of Rav Lichtenstein concerning the relationship between *talmud Torah* and action. Different values vie with each other for ascendancy concerning allocation of resources (money and time are resources; *talmud Torah*, action, and concern for both relatives and the poor at large reflect values). In both cases the *Gemara* seems to teach us that, until proven otherwise, some specific value overrides, either *talmud Torah* or responsibility to close of kin. In both cases we are told to reread the *Gemara* as relating to only part of the pool of resources. Some other consideration is supposed to already guide us, which, among other things, estimates the projected allocation of resources. This consideration underlies the situation discussed in the *Gemara*, and likely precedes it. Thus, in both cases the halakhic criterion for giving preference to a specific value is interpreted as relating to only part of one's total resources. And additionally, an assumption is made that before the situation to which the *halakha* relates was arrived at, some previous plan of action, based on other Torah values, had already been provided for. It is interesting that Arukh Ha-Shulchan, like Rav Lichtenstein after him, provided neither earlier sources to back up his innovation, nor explicit criteria for its application.

But relevant sources are not hard to come by. Or Zaru'a, seven hundred years prior, provided basis for Arukh Ha-Shulchan's later *chiddush*, even

---

3. See *Shut Mahari Weil siman* 26.
4. *Arukh Ha-Shulchan* YD 251:4 and 6.

though he himself ruled contrary to it. Or Zaru'a believed that obligation to close of kin is so tangible that it actually constitutes a *kinyan* (transaction) of sorts, so that the *tzedaka* already belongs to the relative even before it has been actually given[5] (Machaneh Efrayim took this idea to an extreme, suggesting a legitimization of quasi Robin Hood cases[6]). In a similar vein, he ruled that the entirety of a person's charity belongs to their impoverished close of kin.[7] However, in the course of explaining his position, Or Zaru'a exposed an alternative. The *mishna* in *Pei'a* says that a person may save up to half of his *ma'aser ani* (tithe for the poor) for his poor relatives, even when other impoverished people actually come and ask for it.[8] The *Yerushalmi* explains that halving *ma'aser ani* is allowed only after the poor who have come, and are not related, have already received the officially sanctioned amount defined by the *mishna* (half a *kav* of wheat).[9] Or Zaru'a read the *Yerushalmi*'s interpretation of the *mishna* into the *tosefta* of *Pei'a*, which says that one must allocate *pei'a* (the corner of one's field) only at the end, so that the farmer cannot take advantage of a moment when no poor are present, and invite a needy relative to take it all.[10] Or Zaru'a argued that the *tosefta* had no problem with giving half to relatives (or perhaps two thirds[11]), even in the case of *pei'a*. The *tosefta* was only averse to appropriating it in its entirety.

Or Zaru'a brought the *mishna* and *tosefta* to show that even *ma'aser ani* and *pei'a* can be allocated in part to relatives. Similarly, after a person has already set aside *ma'aser kesafim* (tithe of one's money), or *tzedaka* for poor people of the town or world, he can still give half of it to relatives. However, argued Or Zaru'a, if one allocated money to *tzedaka* without any specification at all, it can be given in its entirety to poor relatives. Since in the case of *tzedaka* we have an actual obligation to give precedence to relatives, Or Zaru'a understood that it is permissible and proper to give the entirety of one's *tzedaka* to them.

---

5. *Or Zaru'a, Tzedaka* 9 and 23.
6. *Machaneh Efrayim Hilkhot Tzedaka* 1.
7. *Or Zaru'a, Tzedaka* 22.
8. *Pei'a* 8:6.
9. *Yerushalmi Pei'a* 8:5.
10. *Tosefta Pei'a* 1:7.
11. *Tosefta Pei'a* 4:2.

4.

Working off Or Zaru'a's understanding of the *mishna* and *tosefta*, but following in Arukh Ha-Shulchan's footsteps, we can argue for an affinity between *tzedaka* and *ma'aser ani* (and *pei'a*). In all cases, some division must be made between familial or communal responsibilities and concern for society as a whole. The difference between *tzedaka* and *ma'aser ani* (and *pei'a*) is in their emphasis. *Ma'aser ani* and *pei'a* are in the first instance forms of general social responsibility, such that reserving them in their entirety for family would constitute a typical form of social corruption. However, general *tzedaka* explicitly incorporates the other value. In giving charity we are supposed to express communal responsibility. Now, in light of Arukh Ha-Shulchan's *chiddush*, there need not be any clash between these values (even if they typically express two different themes within charity). Whenever giving to the poor, two values present themselves, vie for ascendancy, and find proportional expression: (a) a responsibility towards poor people generally, considering the needs of society as a whole, and (b) a personal responsibility towards close of kin, or of geographical proximity.

In my humble opinion, both Arukh Ha-Shulchan in *Hilkhot Tzedaka*, and by association our *Rebbe* Rav Lichtenstein zt"l in analysis of the relationship between *talmud Torah* and action, draw support from this interpretation of the *mishna* and *tosefta*, whether or not they had these sources in mind. Perhaps nineteenth century developments made Or Zaru'a's conception (that the entirety of one's charity should be given to relatives) seem insufficient. Arukh Ha-Shulchan drew (perhaps unconsciously) upon the discussion in the *mishna* and *Yerushalmi* to find basis for a division within *tzedaka* for two different values of social responsibility. I suggest that Rav Lichtenstein's innovative conception about time allocation between *talmud Torah* and *chesed* is based on the same principles, and thus draws support from Or Zaru'a's analysis of the *mishna*, *tosefta*, and *Yerushalmi*. Rav Lichtenstein solved the problem of a clash of values by positing a preceding intentional allocation of time. Schedules are divided like pockets, to reflect different aims, and allow for one to invest in different values.

5.

Chatam Sofer and his *Rebbe* Hafla'a seem to have been disturbed by Arukh Ha-Shulchan's problem (although about a century prior). In his commentary on *Chumash*,[12] Hafla'a offered an innovative reading of the *Sifrei*. He argued that precedence based upon geographical proximity is limited to cases where levels of need are equal (or, at least, not of categorical difference). But when the distant poor lack basic necessities, which the nearby poor have, then preference should go to those whose needs are greater. Nevertheless, argues Hafla'a, a distinction should be drawn between different kinds of closeness. Poor people who are members of one's household may be supported generously, even if another's need is greater. He learned the rule of precedence by need from a previous *derasha* of the *Sifrei*: "*ha-ta'ev ta'ev kodem*," those who are desirous precede. He learned the rule of precedence for one's household from another *derasha*, "*bekha [evyon], ve-lo ba-acherim*," that first concern is to oneself. This innovative interpretation of the *Sifrei* is adopted as a legal ruling by Chatam Sofer, in his halakhic responsa.[13]

It is crucial to realize that Hafla'a made a double innovation, so that he moved simultaneously in two opposite directions. First, he responded to the egalitarian challenge concerning the moral basis for precedence of some over others. By arguing that one first caters to those of greater need, Hafla'a made the rule of precedence about choosing between beneficiaries of equal claims. So, the rule of precedence is really about decision-making in allocating resources, rather than preferring some at the expense of others. Second, Hafla'a formulated a new category for charity: oneself, and applied this category to a person's household. By so doing, Hafla'a responded to one major challenge within egalitarianism, the problem of giving preference to those with whom we build relationships of caring.[14] Hafla'a understood that the needs of people who are really close to you should be seen as your

---

12. *Sefer Hafla'a, Panim Yafot, Re'eh* (paragraph starting "*ki yihyeh*").
13. *Shut Chatam Sofer* YD 231.
14. See Ronald Dworkin, *Law's Empire* (Cambridge MS: Harvard University Press, 1986), pp. 196-202; Michael J. Sandel, *Liberalism and the Limits of Justice*, (Cambridge: Cambridge University Press, 1998), pp. 178-83; Samuel Scheffler, "Families, Nations, and Strangers," in *Boundaries and Allegiances* (Oxford: Oxford University Press, 2001), pp. 48-65.

own needs. In responding to these needs we are exempt from adopting a global egalitarian perspective.[15]

At this point, a distinction emerges between what Hafla'a wrote, and how Chatam Sofer quoted him. Hafla'a clarified explicitly that by members of one's household he meant a person's children that are dependent upon him. But Chatam Sofer wrote "the poor of his household and such (*aniyei benei beito ve-khadomeh*)." This formulation allows for wider interpretation. The *mishna* in *Avot* teaches that one should adopt poor people as members of one's household.[16] So, Chatam Sofer's formulation seems to suggest that the exemption from a singularly egalitarian distribution, afforded in relation to members of one's household, applies to all dependents, and not only one's children. In effect, when one takes responsibility over someone else, by inviting them to become a member of one's household, one makes that person become (from an ethical perspective) part of oneself. Caring for that person need no longer follow general universal guidelines of equality. Taking responsibility to care for someone else creates both obligations and rights.[17] Part of what a moral person does in the world is the creation of new categories of social responsibility which formulate new obligations.

6.

In negotiating the challenges of the earliest intimations of globalization, of growing awareness about what is happening elsewhere, and a greater ability to influence from afar, Chatam Sofer and Arukh Ha-Shulchan took different paths. Arukh Ha-Shulchan taught that we should divide our resources, so as to give proportional expression to our different values. One part of our charity should focus upon those people towards whom we have responsibilities due to familial ties or geographical proximity, while another part should be invested in concern for the poor generally. Chatam Sofer adopted a different approach. He followed Hafla'a in rendering the rules of precedence in *tzedaka*, practically speaking, as meaningless in a global

---

15. Rav Yisrael *Mi-Salant* is described as having the opposite approach. See the account by Rav Yitzchak Blazer in *Netivot Or* 118.
16. *Avot* 1:5.
17. See Rav Shlomo Kluger, *Chokhmat Shlomo* (printed on the page of the *Vilna* edition of *Shulchan Arukh*) EH 1, concerning adoption.

society. One's responsibility is always to the most needy. But he formulated an exception. Part of an ethical existence involves taking responsibility for particular people individually. The *mishna*'s teaching, codified in *Shulchan Arukh*, that one should adopt poor people as members of one's household, encourages a proactive approach towards one's surroundings. Ethics is not only about responding to the external world by allocating resources, but also about interacting, forming and reforming the conditions of the external world. Adopting another person as a dependent (actually, even, and particularly, giving birth[18]) is about changing the ethical conditions, categories, and contours of one's surroundings.

If Rav Lichtenstein's approach to *chesed* draws support from Arukh Ha-Shulchan's ideas about *tzedaka*, Rav Krumbein's conception may be fruitfully associated with Chatam Sofer's position. According to Rav Krumbein's interpretation, Abbayei merited an additional twenty years of life because he was not content with merely responding to his surroundings when they objectively and indisputably forced him into action. That is, by some objective criterion, which is acknowledged and appreciated equally by others. Rather, he felt that the world would be different if he would act upon it, and therefore concluded that he had an obligation to make his mark. Our ethical universe is not always amenable to preplanned calculation of ethically relevant resources. As one plots one's way along life, opportunities arise that redefine moral contours. Division of resources between various values is often a question of meeting the evolving challenges of life by changing them and creating unforeseen and new personal responsibilities as a result. All this cannot be planned in advance, as it is neither about investment in a set currency (time or money), nor about responding to foreseen and static challenges.

Now, from the perspective of the teaching of our *Rebbe*, Rav Lichtenstein *zt"l*, generally, he would certainly agree whole-heartedly with the imperative to be proactive, and to remold our ethical surroundings (the tendency to think this way may be associated with him specifically). Thus, Chatam Sofer's analysis is equally relevant to Rav Lichtenstein's *hashkafa* generally. But in the limited context of interpreting this particular *Gemara*,

---

18. See my article [forthcoming].

this approach is exemplified by Rav Krumbein's interpretation, while Rav Lichtenstein's interpretation is comparable to the approach of Arukh Ha-Shulchan. The central point of comparison between these concerns – that of action versus *talmud Torah*, and that of *tzedaka* globally versus locally – lies in that both allow the juggling of two values by either the proportional allocation of resources, or by interaction with, and remolding of, one's ethical surroundings. The first approach binds the position of Rav Lichtenstein to that of Arukh Ha-Shulchan, and the second binds that of Rav Krumbein to that of Chatam Sofer.

Of course, there is no contradiction between the ideas expressed by Rav Lichtenstein and Rav Krumbein. There is no reason not to adopt both approaches at different stages of engaging and navigating a moral dilemma. Yet, conceptually, there is an important difference of emphasis between them; and they typically represent conflicting mindsets and personalities. In meeting the challenges of a multifarious world of vying values, two approaches typically present themselves. The one is to acknowledge a clash and to allocate resources proportionally to some criterion. The other is to take advantage of the opportunities that randomly occur in the living of one's life to continuously recalibrate one's moral universe. The former lays the moral weight upon foresight, planning and organization, while the latter upon how one lives life and engages with particular cases personally.

7.

In this final section I would like to take note of the wider philosophical contours and associations of these two approaches. The idea that a life well lived is one lived according to a plan has been argued by some contemporary philosophers, and is associated particularly with John Rawls.[19] Although Rawls claimed that he was drawing upon supposedly metaphysically neutral arenas, such as psychology, he actually referenced the philosopher

---

19. John Rawls, *A Theory of Justice* (Cambridge MS: Harvard University Press, 1999), p. 358.

Josiah Royce, whose argument betrays theological motifs.[20] We don't have to get into the question of whether this approach is necessarily Protestant. It is sufficient to note that Western European and North American culture internalized a certain tendency to the rational organization of life, whatever its source. Preplanned allocation of time and resources is a typical (although certainly not exclusively) contemporary North American ethical perspective. These might indeed represent cultural influences behind Rav Lichtenstein's approach, even if its roots are ultimately in the tannaitic sources discussed above. For it is interesting to ponder the fact that we would be hard-pressed to come up with an aggadic piece that develops his theme explicitly. Similarly, at the other extreme, Rav Krumbein's alternative reading exhibits a comparable trail in the history of ideas. This is so in two ways. The obvious one is simply by being the opposite of its alternative. The idea that an ethical life can and should be lived according to a plan has naturally drawn much fire. Some philosophers think that the whole concept of ethics is fundamentally indeterminate and requires a person to continually plot new courses throughout life.[21]

There is a deeper sense in which Rav Krumbein's idea represents a crucial ethical alternative and is deeply contemporary. It is based upon the conviction that subjective perception concerning the value of one's own agency transforms certain interventions into obligations for some people, those who perhaps hear the call,[22] or feel the weight of the moment. This conception suggests a radical sense of human autonomy in ethics and underwrites a partially subjective ethical imperative. According to this conception, ethical obligation is not objectively constructed by external commands that are configured within a clear-cut context. Rather, the ethical agent's own interpretation of his or her situation fulfills an active role

---

20. Josiah Royce, *The Philosophy of Loyalty* (New York: Macmillan Company, 1908), pp. 168-72. I am indebted to David Heyd for pointing this out to me. See my article, "Rawls's Structural Response to Arbitrariness: An Echo of Calvin," *Philosophy and Theology* 30:1 (2018), p. 142.
21. Bernard Williams, "Ethical Consistency," in *Problems of the Self: Philosophical Papers 1956-1972* (Cambridge University Press, 1973); Bernard Williams, "Moral Luck," in *Moral Luck: Philosophical Papers 1973-1980* (Cambridge University Press, 1981).
22. *Sefat Emet Lekh Lekha* 1872.

in formulating obligations. Secular ethical conceptions can consider ethics itself subjective. To be sure, a Torah conception traces ethical command to God; thus, the basis of ethics is indisputably objective.[23] But there is still a lot of space for a person's own will or nature to enter into the construction of particular obligations, in a manner transformative of his or her own life, along the lines that Rav Krumbein suggested. The subjective perspective upon reality, which is an outcome of individual human autonomy and freewill, can be a pivotal ingredient in the formulation of ethical obligation. In this manner, a person actively molds his or her own ethical personality and creates an authentically personalized ethical path.[24]

Ari z"l formulated a similar idea, that of rising above the source of one's soul.[25] He furthermore taught that one way to facilitate this is through association with others.[26] Ari z"l's idea is couched in a mystical system, starkly different to the rationalist and halakhic analysis that we have been employing here. Nevertheless, it similarly reflects a deeply modern conception of individualistic human autonomy and navigates an approach for combining it with the ethical value of human interdependence. For meeting the challenges of conflicting values, particularly in an increasingly global context, requires the combining of opposite constructs and drives. It requires both individuality and interdependence. And it requires emphasis upon both the rationalization of life, directing proportional investment to disparate values, and also a proactive mode of human agency, continually engaging and reengaging the world from a personal subjective perspective.

---

23. Nevertheless, see my article, "Rabbinic Subjectivity: Innovation, Dispute, and Pluralism in a Revealed Religion," *Common Knowledge* 23 (1): (2017), pp. 120-142.
24. See my article, "A Theory of Providence for Distributive Justice," *Journal of Religious Ethics* 46:1 (2018), pp. 124-155.
25. Rav Chayyim Vital, *Eitz Chayyim* vol. 2 70d-71a.
26. Rav Chayyim Vital, *Sha'ar Ha-Gilgulim* ch. 2, 3, 10; Rav Chayyim Vital, *Sefer Ha-Gilgulim* ch. 11.

The *Shofar* and the Jewish Future

Rabbi Rafi Eis

According to Ba'al Ha-Ma'or (10b-11a in *Rif*), *shofar*-blowing did not have a standard "*birkat ha-mitzva*," blessing recited over a mitzva, with its formulation of "who sanctified us with His commandments and commanded us (*asher kiddeshanu be-mitzvotav ve-tzivvanu*);" rather, the three *berakhot* of *Malkhuyot*, *Zikhronot*, and *Shofarot* in the *Amida* prayer served as the *berakhot* for the mitzva of *shofar*.[1] While our practice has us say the *berakha* of "who sanctified us with His commands and commanded us to hear the sound of the *shofar* (*lishmo'a kol shofar*)," and one can fulfill the mitzva of *shofar* without the recitation of *Malkhuyot*, *Zikhronot*, and *Shofarot*,[2] the intricate connection between the blowing of the *shofar* and the *berakhot* of *Malkhuyot*, *Zikhronot*, and *Shofarot* remains.

The *mishna* in *Rosh Ha-Shana* 32a records a debate between Rabbi Yochanan ben Nuri and Rabbi Akiva about the ordering of the *berakhot* in the *mussaf Amida* on Rosh Ha-Shana. The background to their debate is the *Gemara* in *Berakhot* 29a which states that the *mussaf*[3] of Rosh Ha-Shana should have nine *berakhot*. A standard *Amida* on a *Shabbat* and *Yom Tov* has seven *berakhot* containing: the standard first three of *Avot* (Forefathers), *Gevurot* (God's Strength), and *Kedushat Ha-Shem* (Sanctity

---

1. This history can explain the reason we have variant customs for the proper *berakha* on the *shofar*. See *Shut Ha-Rambam* (*siman* 142) and *Rosh* (*Rosh Ha-Shana* 4:10).
2. See *Rema* OC 693:2.
3. The *Gemara* actually says that the "*Amida*" of Rosh Ha-Shana should have nine *berakhot*, leading Ba'al Ha-Ma'or (12a in *Rif*) to suggest that *all* the *amidot* of Rosh Ha-Shana should have nine *berakhot*.

of God's Name); the standard last three of *Avoda* (Service), *Hoda'a* (Thanks), and *Shalom* (Peace); and a special *berakha* of *Kedushat Ha-Yom* (Sanctity of the Day) as the middle, fourth *berakha*. When we add the three *berakhot* of *Malkhuyot, Zikhronot,* and *Shofarot* to the seven normally said on a *Shabbat* or *Yom Tov*, we now have ten *berakhot* that need recitation instead of the nine mandated by the *Gemara*.

Rabbi Yochanan ben Nuri and Rabbi Akiva advocate combining two *berakhot* but argue as to which of the *berakhot* should be combined. Rabbi Yochanan ben Nuri merges the *berakha* of *Malkhuyot* with the third *berakha* of *Kedushat Ha-Shem*, while Rabbi Akiva joins the *berakha* of *Malkhuyot* with *Kedushat Ha-Yom* in the fourth *berakha*. Both Rabbi Yochanan ben Nuri and Rabbi Akiva blow the *shofar* after the fourth, fifth, and sixth *berakhot*, and both have the *berakha* of *Kedushat Ha-Yom* as the fourth *berakha*. Rabbi Yochanan ben Nuri's fourth *berakha*, however, is just *Kedushat Ha-Yom*, and the *shofar* is not sounded for *Malkhuyot*. In objecting to Rabbi Yochanan ben Nuri's opinion, Rabbi Akiva states, "If one does not sound the *shofar* for the *berakha* of *Malkhuyot*, why does he mention it?" Rabbi Akiva believes that there is little point to saying *Malkhuyot* without the accompanying blowing of the *shofar*.

To appreciate the opinion of Rabbi Akiva, we will need to understand both the *berakha* of *Malkhuyot* and the mitzva of *shofar*.

Malkhuyot

Rav Soloveitchik (*Machzor Mesorat Ha-Rav, Rosh Ha-Shana* pp. 466-467) notes that this debate about the placement of *Malkhuyot* reflects differing visions of how God's kingship will be achieved in the future. The Rav notes that our elongated third *berakha* of *Kedushat Ha-Shem* is part of the text of Rabbi Yochanan ben Nuri's combination of *Kedushat Ha-Shem* and *Malkhuyot*. The Rav emphasizes that aside from the argument as to where to place *Malkhuyot*, Rabbi Yochanan ben Nuri and Rabbi Akiva disagree on the substance and tone of how God's kingship is brought about. According to Rabbi Yochanan ben Nuri, *Malkhuyot* will be realized through God powerfully imposing His will on humanity.

> And so, grant that Your awe, O Lord, our God, be upon all Your works, and Your dread upon all You have created; and [then] all [Your] works will fear You, and prostrated before You will be all [Your] created beings. And may they all form a single band to do Your will with a perfect heart. For we know, O Lord, our God, that rulership is Yours, strength is in Your hand, might is in Your right hand and Your Name is awesome over all You have created. (*Birkat Kedushat Ha-Shem*)

The motifs are God's power and humanity's fear of Him.

According to Rabbi Akiva's *Malkhuyot*, in contrast, God's power is mentioned in passing and in the passive voice, with the emphasis being on the change in humanity.

> We therefore put our hope in You, O Lord, our God, to soon behold the glory of Your might in banishing idolatry from the Earth; and the false gods will be utterly exterminated to perfect the world as the kingdom of God. And all mankind will invoke Your Name, to turn back to You, all the wicked of the Earth. They will realize, and know, all the inhabitants of the world, that to You every knee must bend, every tongue must swear allegiance to You. Before You, O Lord, our God, they will bow and prostrate themselves, and to the glory of Your Name give honor. And they will accept upon themselves the yoke of Your kingdom… (*Birkat Kedushat Ha-Yom*)

This difference becomes accentuated in how each responds to evildoers. For Rabbi Yochanan ben Nuri, "all the wickedness will vanish like smoke, when You remove the rule of evil from the Earth." Rabbi Akiva, however, aims for "to turn back to You, all the wicked of the Earth." Rabbi Yochanan ben Nuri wants the physical removal of evildoers while Rabbi Akiva wants their repentance.

The differences between the two run deeper still. In relating to the righteous and to Am Yisrael, Rabbi Yochanan ben Nuri wants God to:

> Grant honor, O Lord, to Your people, praise to those who fear You, good hope to those who seek You, confident speech to those who yearn for You, joy to Your land, gladness to Your city, flourishing of pride to David, Your servant, and an array of light to the son of Yishai, Your anointed, speedily in our days. (*Birkat Kedushat Ha-Shem*)

The virtuous, Am Yisrael and their land are currently denigrated, and their honor and dignity should be restored.

For Rabbi Akiva, the vision of the future is more universal, and Am Yisrael do not receive a special mention. The injustice of the present is not alluded to, nor is the desolation of the land. The only reference to present realities is that Am Yisrael are the few who currently recognize God as creator of the world. The aspiration wants universal recognition of God, without emphasizing an elevated status for Am Yisrael. They could have an elevated status, but it is not mentioned in the *tefilla* and definitely does not play the central role that it does in Rabbi Yochanan ben Nuri's portrayal.

Here we come to the essence of the matter. Rabbi Yochanan ben Nuri and Rabbi Akiva argue about how God's kingship is achieved and the role of Am Yisrael in it because they disagree about the essence of God's rule. Rabbi Yochanan ben Nuri emphasizes righteousness and justice. In Rabbi Yochanan ben Nuri's future, oppressors will be removed by a greater might and justice will be imposed by a higher authority. His *Malkhuyot* concludes with the verse: "And the Lord of hosts is exalted by judgment, and The Holy God proved holy by retribution" (*Yeshayahu* 5:16). Justice can be imposed, and the newly honored state of God's people vindicates their Divine imperative.

In contrast, the *Malkhuyot* of Rabbi Akiva, which is combined with *Kedushat Ha-Yom*, places the emphasis on the removal of false gods. Here, Rav Soloveitchik (*Machzor Mesorat Ha-Rav, Rosh Ha-Shana* p. 535) adds a critical explanation. God's creation of the world contains two sets of rules: natural law and moral law. Natural law is ever-present and cannot be violated. We can harness nature, shape it and tap it, hopefully for a more dignified life. Humans can never go against it or violate it. Similarly, God also created moral law. Unlike natural law which cannot ever be violated, man can violate moral law, due to God granting man free will, but with consequences.

This violation of moral law leads to human decay. It takes longer to see than attempted violations of natural law. Bertrand Russell writes about this demise of civilization:

> What had happened in the great age of Greece happened again in Renaissance Italy: traditional moral restraints disappeared, because they were seen to be associated with superstition; the liberation from fetters made individuals energetic and creative, producing a rare fluorescence of genius; but the anarchy and treachery which inevitably resulted from the decay of morals made Italians collectively impotent, and they fell, like the Greeks, under the domination of nations less civilised than themselves but not so destitute of social cohesion. (*A History of Western Philosophy*, Introduction)

In Rabbi Akiva's understanding of the human failings, humans too easily put their faith in false gods for salvation. They misunderstand what leads to human flourishing. Throughout history, humans have relied too much on polytheism, spirits and magic, science, reason, liberty and other humanistic causes to ease the human condition. Some of these have raised the status of humanity, but do not alone enable a thriving society or prevent the fall of civilization. Justice and fairness play a role, but they do not encompass all of morality. Rabbi Akiva's *Malkhuyot* includes God's moral laws, including boundaries and sanctity. Only through humanity putting its faith in the Torah's moral law will we have true human flourishing and God's kingship. This cannot be imposed; it must be chosen.

Malkhuyot is not a normal *berakha*; it is one recited only on Rosh Ha-Shana, the anniversary of the creation of man, and on Yom Kippur of the jubilee year. Highlighting its singularity is the fact that it comes along with the blowing of the *shofar*.

Shofar

Rabbi Akiva's challenge to Rabbi Yochanan ben Nuri is based on two premises. First, as articulated above, the *berakha* of *Malkhuyot* aspires for all human beings to choose Divinely articulated morality and God's kingship. Second, the *shofar* plays a critical role in this *berakha*. *Rosh Ha-Shana* 16a helps us appreciate Rabbi Akiva's stance. Rabbi Yehuda cites Rabbi Akiva who explains the deeper religious significance of the rituals of the yearly *chaggim*, like the *Omer*, barley sacrifice on Pesach, and the water libation on Sukkot. Regarding Rosh Ha-Shana, Rabbi Akiva explains the reason for our reciting *Malkhuyot* and *Zikhronot*. Instead of then proceeding to explain the reason we recite *Shofarot*, Rabbi Akiva says that the *shofar* acts as a conduit to bring our *tefillot* of *Malkhuyot* and *Zikhronot* to God. *Malkhuyot*, as a unique *berakha* for Rosh Ha-Shana, needs to be recited along with the *shofar* which channels the *berakha* to God.

While our *tefillot* normally reach God through our speech alone, on Rosh Ha-Shana, *shofar* acts as a direct pipeline to God. The *tanna kamma* in the *mishna* in *Rosh Ha-Shana* 26a states that any animal horn may be used as a *shofar*, except for that of a cow. In one of its explanations for the invalidity of a cow horn, the *Gemara* states the principles of "not having a prosecutor acting as a defense attorney." Since the *shofar* pleads on our behalf for a positive judgement from God, using a cow's horn conjures up the sin of the Golden Calf. This principle is used to initially explain the *kohen gadol*'s (high priest's) wearing his white garments, instead of his regular eight gold garments, when he enters the Holy of Holies on Yom Kippur, since gold reminds of the sin of the Golden Calf. Our *Gemara* extends this principle to invalidate a cow's horn on Rosh Ha-Shana. The *Gemara* continues by asking why the *kohen gadol* is allowed to wear his gold garments at other points in the Yom Kippur service. The *Gemara* answers that the prohibition of not having the prosecutor act as a defense attorney only applies inside the Holy of Holies, but not in other areas of the *Beit Ha-Mikdash*. The *Gemara* then points out that the *shofar* is not blown in the Holy of Holies and therefore surely any horn can be used. The *Gemara* responds that, since the *shofar* is meant to cause a remembrance of us for God, it is as if it is blown inside the Holy of Holies.

Now we understand the power of the *shofar*! The three unique *berakhot* of Rosh Ha-Shana, of *Malkhuyot*, *Zikhronot*, and *Shofarot*, are supposed to be direct and intimate *tefillot* to God, and that can only occur with the *shofar*. But what is the reminder within the *shofar*? The very next *Gemara* on 16a focuses on the *Akeidat Yitzchak* (Binding of Yitzchak). By blowing a ram's horn, it is as if we have offered ourselves to God.

We are now in a position to put together all of the above. After humanity fails several times, as described in *Bereishit* ch. 2-11, God chooses Avraham to be the founder of Benei Yisrael, whose descendants will become God's "kingdom of priests and a holy nation" (*Shemot* 19:6), and in the words of Yeshayahu, to be a "light for the nations" (*Yeshayahu* 42:6). We are supposed to embody the ideal society to influence all of humanity. They are supposed to see our good and choose the moral-monotheistic approach. The *berakha* of *Malkhuyot* takes us back to our original mission and we pray for its fulfillment. We hope that this year we can do good and that our better lifestyle influences the peoples of the world.

This *tefilla* should come with a *shofar*, because part of our covenant with God states that God needs us to bring about humanity's recognition of Him. Yes, we have a special relationship with God and have particular obligations and expectations. But we are also saying that God is dependent on Am Yisrael to shine His light. We are now, therefore, in a two-way relationship with God. We demonstrate our commitment to this covenantal relationship by blowing the *shofar* and harking back to our ultimate commitment of the *Akeida*. Now that we have demonstrated to God of our full commitment that we want to shine His light to all of humanity, so that they choose His kingship and that we are willing to make the ultimate sacrifice, we can now continue in our deep, impassioned, and intimate *tefilla* to Him.

Our relationship with God is where there is space for *tefilla*, and Rosh Ha-Shana, where we go back to the covenant's fundamental principles, allows for a more direct and closer *tefilla*, as if it were inside the Holy of Holies. *Berakhot* 29a states that the nine *berakhot* in the *mussaf* of Rosh Ha-Shana pattern *tefillat Channa*. Channa's prayer was in fact answered on

Rosh Ha-Shana, as she begins to carry the embryo of Shmu'el. Her *tefilla* with God is so intimate that *Berakhot* 31b remarks that she comes up with a new way for addressing God and desires a different type of relationship than God previously had with mankind.

Tefillat Channa also highlights her ultimate commitment. She takes an oath that if she were granted a child then that child would be dedicated to the service of God. That would be her *Akeida* and ultimate dedication. God, as we see, needs that child. At the beginning of Shmu'el's life, Benei Yisrael are in a deplorable state. We are in the aftermath of the civil wars stemming from the incident of the *pilegesh be-giva* (see *Shoftim* ch. 19-21), the sons of Eli have corrupted the service in the *Mishkan*, and, in a few years, the Pelishtim will have destroyed the Land and the *Mishkan*, while capturing the holy *aron*. By the end of Shmu'el's life, however, the Jewish polity has grown stronger under Sha'ul's leadership and David has already been anointed as Sha'ul's successor, ushering in one of the greatest periods of Jewish history. Shmu'el is God's agent for change.

We can now fully appreciate Rabbi Akiva's opinion. *Malkhuyot* combines with the *berakha* of *Kedushat Ha-Yom*, since it is the essence of the day. We proclaim our fundamental desire that while most of the nations do not recognize God's dominion and moral law, we want to partner with God to be agents for change for all of humanity to choose their better reality. We blow the *shofar* to highlight the totality of our commitment. Once we are in this spiritual domain, we can then engage God in the most intimate conversations about our lives.

The Ethics of Testimony

Rabbi Dr. Yaakov Jaffe

Witnesses rejected from testimony because of personal conduct is a narrow and self-contained topic in Jewish law, discussed in but a few short pages in *Sanhedrin* (24b-27b), one chapter of Rambam's *Mishneh Torah* (*Hilkhot Eidut* ch. 10), and one section of *Shulchan Arukh* (CM 34).[1] The conclusion, even if not clear at the onset,[2] is that a series of major religious violations

---

1. Moreover, it is based on one verse of the Torah (as per *Sanhedrin* 27a), and exists as one of the 613 commandments (Rambam, negative 286). It is unclear how this verse, which seems to focus on witnesses who *lie*, is used as the source for witnesses who have engaged in *unethical* conduct. Rambam argues (*Hilkhot Eidut* 10:1) that a tradition establishes the meaning of the verse against its simple sense – contrast *Semag* (negative 214) and *Yerei'im* (193). Rambam also argues that the prohibition against an invalid witness is actually directed first towards the co-witness, as is indicated by the verse, and only expanded later to include judges accepting the testimony.

Henceforth, all unspecified citations to the *Gemara* are to *Sanhedrin*, to Rambam are *Hilkhot Eidut*, and to *Shulchan Arukh* are *Choshen Mishpat*. Much of the Mechaber in this chapter of *Shulchan Arukh* is directly copied from Rambam, which creates some difficulty in disentangling the positions of the Mechaber from the positions of Rambam.

2. At the end of the lengthy Talmudic discussion, the *Gemara* posits that this very proposition is the subject of a debate between Abbayei and Rava. For Rava, a witness is invalidated only if he commits a crime related to financial benefit; according to Abbayei, anyone who violates any commandment is considered a *rasha* and deprived of the opportunity to testify. Though virtually always the law follows Rava – this is one of six cases when Abbayei is followed.

Rashi's commentary on the *Gemara* consistently offers Rava's rejected reason that the only reason for exclusion is being a *rasha de-chamas*, a wicked person in relation to theft: see Rashi at 24b (*ve-sochrei*), 25a (*loveh*), 25b (*sof sof*), 26b (*ochlei*, *u-paslinu*), even in cases when Abbayei might have invalidated the perpetrator on

– Biblical sins that merit lashes or the death penalty as punishment,[3] all render a Jew a *rasha* and unable to testify by dint of that status.[4]

The focus of this essay is the smaller, although more conceptually interesting, aspect of the discussion: witnesses excluded not because of the religious, ritual gravity of their crimes, but because their actions constitute a major ethical or moral breach. In these cases, the individual may have violated a minor sin, an *aveira* not bearing lashes, or perhaps no formal prohibition at all, but is still excluded from testimony because of a moral breach. A dozen such cases are discussed in the *Gemara*, and this essay focuses on these cases (Rambam 10:4, *Shulchan Arukh* 34:1-3).

Each case can be analyzed on two planes. First, each violation can be analyzed within the context of its own internal logic: what is the ethical violation, and which Jews might be invalidated as a result. Second, each case can be analyzed for what it teaches more generally about the types

---

the basis of the reasoning of violating a Torah command alone. This may be one of the best examples of Rashi reading a lengthy Talmudic discussion in accordance with a rejected view, so as not to presume the conclusion of the *Gemara* earlier in the discussion. It is hard to imagine that Rashi indeed accepts Rava's view, given his comments elsewhere that Rava is rejected, and the *Gemara*'s explicit conclusion that the *halakha* follows Abbayei.

3. The paradigmatic case of a *rasha* is someone who eats non-Kosher meat, which led Rambam (in the *Mishna* Commentary, and in *Hilkhot Eidut* 10:1-4) to conclude that any violation of a crime that merits Biblical lashes (like non-Kosher), and surely the death penalty, renders one a *rasha*. The *Gemara* never formulates this requirement explicitly, but it is reasonable within the context. The Tosafists (25a) raise the possibility that the violation of any negative commandment, even one without lashes, renders one invalid; this raises a whole host of problems including but not limited to how to consider the violation of negative commandments that involve merely speech or thought.

The end of the *Gemara*'s discussion (27a-27b) raises still other possible criteria such as severity of the crime or number of victims, but these are not accepted in *Shulchan Arukh*. Ran (27a) suggests that anyone *suspected* of eating Rabbinic non-kosher could become invalid if a court proclaimed they were invalid, which would radically expand the group of people who cannot testify.

4. Somewhat surprisingly, the status of being a *rasha* can be removed through receiving punishment, while being suspected of taking bribes and lying for money requires a greater *teshuva* to be reinstated (Rambam 12:4). This is somewhat based on the language of the *Gemara*, which provides a rigorous depiction of the required repentance for ethical violations (25b) but does not do so for those who are deemed a *rasha* for violating the Torah and not any ethical crime.

of cases and scenarios in which Jews can lose their privilege to testify. A recurring question is whether an ethical violation also brands the individual as a *rasha*, much like the Jew who eats non-Kosher, or whether the ethical violation merely invalidates a non-*rasha* because of the increased statistically likelihood that the individual will engage in a further ethical breach through accepting a bribe to lie in testimony.[5]

Of the dozen or so cases, some – shepherds,[6] sellers of non-Kosher meat,[7] those that steal objects found by children,[8] perpetrators of extortion,[9] conducting commerce with *shemitta* produce,[10] or using bird-

---

5. In Hebrew, often called the distinction between *sheim rasha* and *cheshash sheker*.
6. *Sanhedrin* 25b, Rambam 10:4, *Shulchan Arukh* 34:13, because the animals' grazing on private lands constitutes theft, see Rashi *Bereishit* 13:7 and *Shemot* 3:1. There is a discussion of the permissibility of being a rancher on private lands in the *Gemara* in *Sanhedrin* ibid. and *Bava Kamma* 79b, although that discussion is outside the scope of this essay.
7. *Sanhedrin* 25a, *Shulchan Arukh* 34:6.
8. 25b, for these individuals violate a Rabbinic law in order to receive money and are suspected of accepting bribes (Rashi). This case does not appear in Rambam *Hilkhot Eidut* (10:4), ostensibly because the case is obvious, though a gloss does add it to *Shulchan Arukh* (34:13).
9. In the *Gemara*'s case, someone who uses force to compel the seller to sell a good or property (*Sanhedrin* 25b, Rambam 10:4, *Shulchan Arukh* 34:13). Since in the end money is paid for the goods, the individual is not a thief and so the exclusion is only on a Rabbinic level. *Rishonim* discuss why such an individual is not excluded on account of his violation of the 10th commandment of *Lo Tachmod*; some reply that *Lo Tachmod* is not violated in this case; Tosafot *Bava Kamma* 62a seem to argue that the criminal erroneously believes that he has not violated the 10th commandment, and consequently does not have a self-concept of being an unethical person, though indeed they are in violation of Jewish Law for the purpose of achieving financial gain. We will discuss the self-concept justification further on in this essay.
10. Here, the primary violation is not towards another human being, but towards the Creator Who legislated *shemitta* in the first place. Still, these individuals are invalidated because a desire for financial profit encourages them to violate a law (*Sanhedrin* 26a, Rambam 10:4, *Shulchan Arukh* 34:16), and they also deprive the poor from a benefit that is rightfully theirs. This exclusion only applies to the farmer and not the purchaser, and one imagines that if the farmer relied upon the sale of land during the *shemitta* year, that this should suffice as a justification to maintain their testimonial validity. Small-scale farmers, who do not engage in large-scale industrial harvest or commerce may not be excluded. Ramban (positive 3) counts *shemitta* commerce as a violation of a Biblical positive commandment, because it runs counter to the imperative to eat the produce; clearly then a homeowner who

calls to steal birds[11] – are rare today, and we leave those topics largely in the background. We will evaluate a number of cases that exist commonly today and will discuss whether individuals engaged in those practices and their more modern applications should lose their privilege to testify today. The application of many of these categories might result in wholesale disqualification of large groups of people, and so we tread lightly when evaluating these cases, and raise these questions as a thought experiment, and not to disqualify a large range of individuals.

Collecting Food Stamps or Welfare

Perhaps the most surprising ethical violation which deprives the violator of the ability to testify is the taking of gentile charity (26b, euphemistically referred to as "those who eat the other thing;" see Tosafot, *Shulchan Arukh* 34:18). This exclusion is shocking, for it seems to deprive the poor of an ability to participation in jurisprudential society out of no fault to their own.

Rashi explains that it is not the receiving of gentile charity, per se, that is the source of the exclusion; it is instead the *public* consumption or taking of gentile charity which desecrates the Name of God, as people will say that the Jewish people do not take care of their own, and instead leave them destitute, hoping upon the beneficence of the other nations to take care of them.[12] Even so, this principle is astounding, but it is accepted by Rosh (12), Rambam (11:5)[13], and in *Shulchan Arukh* (34:18). Still, this exclusion does not apply if the only way to collect the needed charity was in public.

---

purchases to eat has not violated this law. See also *Tosafot* and *Tosafot Ha-Rosh* to *Sanhedrin* 26a, and Rambam *Hilkhot Shemitta* ch. 6, and Ramban's Torah Commentary to *Vayikra* chapter 25.

11. The *mishna*'s fourth category of an excluded individual is the dove flyer. Some interpret this scenario to be analogous to the gambler (Or Zaru'a), although the *Gemara* (25a) and commentaries (Ran, Rashash, Rav Akiva Eiger) note that there are numerous problems with this reading. Others argue the violation involves Rabbinic theft of semi-owned birds (*Shulchan Arukh* 34:16). Rambam's view on this question is complex - see his *Mishna* Commentary and his *Hilkhot Eidut* (10:4), where he seems to adopt an amalgamation of the two views.

12. It is also the way Rabbeinu Yehonatan and Or Zaru'a read the *Gemara*.

13. Rambam refuses to count this exclusion as a *rasha*, and instead includes it in the 11th chapter, which deals instead with those who don't conform with societal expectations more generally. Yet, its placement in the *Gemara* suggests that it shares a nature with the other exclusions in our discussion. Ramah's interpretation of the *Gemara* seems to concur with Rambam's.

Today, few Jews collect gentile charity in public, but many take governmental assistance. Though not public per se, food-stamp recipient data is widely available by zip code,[14] as is the population of Hebrew and Yiddish speakers by zip code,[15] and so one must ask whether a Jew taking government assistance in these zip codes runs afoul of desecrating the Name of God by implying that Jews cannot take care of each other, and instead must rely on a gentile government.[16] Rav Menasheh Klein (*Mishneh Halakhot* 16:72) indicates that in his view, the modern situation should be defined as the public acceptance of gentile charity, and then would potentially jeopardize the ability for someone in this category to provide testimony.

One could distinguish on several bases: even if the religion of the recipient is publicly known, the exact identity is not. Also, taking food-stamps or other governmental support programs might be different from taking handouts, as they are considered entitlements of citizenship in a modern democracy are not charity per se. Moreover, since Jews pay taxes into the American system of taxation, the "charity" paid out in entitlements might not be characterized as *gentile* charity even if it were public charity. Lastly, a Jew is not excluded if there was no way to take charity in private, and this case may qualify for this distinction since there is no way to collect government benefits without becoming part of the government's data set.

This case highlights some of the critical questions regarding the ethics of testimony. Are we prepared to exclude people even for the most minor considerations? Should we tend towards stringency, excluding everyone who may or may not be valid, or do we tend towards leniency, and give arguments to include more people.

The Recreational Gambler and Casino Owner

The *Gemara* concludes that two adults may make a conditional agreement that is contingent on a future performance or chance event, whereby

---

14. https://statisticalatlas.com/zip/#####/Food-Stamps
15. https://statisticalatlas.com/zip/#####/Languages
16. Ironically, this concern would not apply to a Jew residing in a zip code that is majority gentile, since no one can see whether the Jew or the gentiles of the community are the ones receiving charity assistance.

one party will become the winner of funds and the other the loser.[17] Consequently, a recreational gambler is not guilty of theft and has committed no ethical breach, and any earnings achieved are the result of a legitimate business transaction. Thus, Jews who gamble on occasion may testify, and they are not considered thieves or unethical individuals. [See also *Shulchan Arukh* CM 370.][18]

The only scenario in which a gambler might be considered a thief is if the loser in a gambling transaction was unaware of the likelihood of loss; by entering the transaction with the deck stacked against the unknowing loser – the winner engages in theft. This is not typical for the average recreational gambler, who knows fully well the likelihood of winning and losing. Casino owners do participate in gambling where the odds favor the house,[19] regular visitors think they are entering a fair game of chance and skill when their chances of winning are inferior. Thankfully, few Jews seeking to testify are casino owners, but this type of individual might be invalidated for engaging in fraudulent gambling.

The Unemployed

Though a recreational gambler may testify, a professional gambler cannot, because "they do not participate in the settlement of the world;" the exclusion comes from not having a profession. This limitation has been

---

17. This is a topic in debate in both the *mishna* (24b), and the *Gemara* (25a). The Rabbis of the *Gemara* continue to debate this same issue, as some believe both opinions of the *mishna* only invalidated a professional gambler, while others believe that the issue was indeed a debate in the *mishna*, and thus they invalidate even a recreational gambler, following the stringent opinion of the *mishna*.

18. See though *Yabbi'a Omer* CM 7:6. The exact details of when gambling is permissible are more complex (depending on when the moneys are paid, whether the gambler is judged to be only exaggerating, and whether the bet is entirely, somewhat, or not at all within the gambler's hands), see *Shulchan Arukh* CM 207. Most cases of recreational gambling can be constructed in a way that do not violate this prohibition. Rambam's view on the question is complex, as his treatment in *Hilkhot Eidut* seems to conform to neither of the two opinions in the *Gemara*.

19. This might depend, however, on whether the slight benefit to the house is a sign of unfairness, or merely the cut the casino takes for providing the staffing and space for the game. Sometimes, losers at casinos expect to lose, but consider those losses the cost of participating in the enjoyable games.

understood in many different ways, which speak both to the importance of working in Judaism, and also to the ethical standards that must be met for a Jew to serve as a witness.

Both Rashi and Rambam read this exclusion ambivalently: at times as being based on technical/practical principles, and at times as being based on wider, ethical considerations. Rashi's language (24b s.v. *she-ein*) speaks to both the practical lack of sensitivity to appreciate the nuance of business transactions,[20] and the more fundamental idea that such an individual "does not fear sin." In *Hilkhot Eidut* (10:4), Rambam surprisingly argues that though a recreational gambler does not engage in theft, a full-time gambler does,[21] yet in the *Mishna* Commentary he takes the issue fundamentally, that "it is a principle in our Torah that one should engage in one of two things: either wisdom to perfect the self, or business that will help the subsistence of the world, such as commerce or a trade."[22] In other words, not having a job is in and of itself an unethical way to spend one's time, which removes someone from the class of individuals who have the right to testify.

Does anyone today, besides a full-time professional gambler, fall under this category? Rambam's language suggests that we should invalidate any full-time student whose academic endeavors do not fill either the religious purposes of Torah study or the religious purposes of engaging in a trade.

---

20. One does wonder, however, whether a fulltime student who does not engage in business transactions should be excluded for this reason as well, and whether a student studying Torah but not business should be excluded (or whether the study of the financial law in the *Gemara* suffices).
21. This reading seems to be rejected by the *Gemara*. *Shulchan Arukh* (34:16), copying from Rambam, maintains the same tension.
22. Though not in *Hilkhot Eidut*, the perspective of the *Mishna* Commentary is echoed in *Hilkhot Gezeila Va-Aveida* (6:11). On "wisdom," which appears both here and in the *Mishna* Commentary, See Isadore Twersky, "Some Non-Halakhic Aspects of the *Mishneh Torah*" pp. 95-118 in Alexander Altman Ed., *Jewish Medieval and Renaissance Studies* (Cambridge, Mass.: Harvard University Press, 1967), 100.

Interestingly, these two goals for humanity are the two candidates for what Aristotle meant as the good life: philosophy or politics. There is a debate among Aristotle scholars which is the primary manifestation of a good life; Rambam here includes both.

Imagine a student taking a year off between college and graduate school to complete a master's degree in a topic that is of interest, but not related to a professional career (e.g. in music or history) – would that person be excluded? Or perhaps, we can expand the subjects that fulfill a religious mandate to include the sciences[23] or the humanities[24], thereby allowing most if not all full-time students the ability to testify.

Working for the IRS or a school's tuition committee

Tax collectors are excluded from testifying under Jewish law. It is the general consensus that it is the tax-collector's reliance on an unethical system for setting tax rates that is problematic, not the collection of lawful taxes itself. Thus today, a lawyer or accountant working for the IRS or the Israeli government who collects taxes set through a fair and democratic system of tax collecting would not be excluded from testifying. After all, *Shulchan Arukh* itself (CM 161) has a lengthy discussion of a system for the setting of taxation rates within the Jewish community, recognizing that the need to raise funds from the community to pay for communal needs and public goods that are critical for the functioning of society. Many *poskim* also grant that since the United States and Israeli systems of taxation are both fair and the result of a democratic process, one is likely obligated to participate in it.[25] Likely, someone who engages in illegal tax fraud or tax evasion would be excluded from testifying either as a thief, or through the exclusion of setting a *de facto* unethical taxation system.

---

23. See Rambam *Yesodei Ha-Torah* chapters 2-4.
24. See Rav Aharon Lichtenstein, "Torah and General Culture: Confluence and Conflict," *Judaism's Encounter with Other Cultures: Rejection or Integration*, Ed. Jacob J. Schacter (Lanham, MD: Rowman & Littlefield, 1997), pp. 217-292.
25. *Shulchan Arukh* CM 369:5-11, based on *Bava Kamma* 113. Regarding the United States see *Igrot Moshe* CM 1:88 and 2:62.

It is beyond the scope of this essay to discuss the application of *Dina De-Malkhuta Dina* to taxation systems. Broadly speaking, the three political theories behind governmental authority are echoed in Jewish sources: including social contract (Rashbam *Bava Batra* 54a), Divine right of kings (*Shmu'el Alef* 8:11-17, *Ezra* 1:2), and the king's ownership of the land (Ran *Nedarim* 28); though not all of these arguments apply to modern democratic systems, the halakhic consensus is that *Dina De-Malkhuta* does apply to taxation. See also *Or Zaru'a Bava Kamma* 3:447, *Maggid Mishneh Hilkhot Malveh Ve-Loveh* 7:1, and *Shut Ha-Rashba* 1:895.

Which tax rates are unfair or unethical? To some, the ethical breach is when a Jew engaged in tax-farming collects a greater amount from the population than he is legally required by the government (Tosafot 25b, Or Zaru'a, Rambam 10:4, *Shulchan Arukh* 34:14). Other commentaries and versions of the *Gemara* are of the view that a flat taxation system is unethical because it shifts a larger burden on the poor (Ramah, Maharshal), while others argue the reverse, that a progressive tax system is unethical because it shifts too large a burden on the wealthy (Me'iri). Finally, still others argue that the major concern is a tax-collector who sets individualized rates for specific individuals, based on personal criteria, benefiting some at the expense of others (Rabbeinu Chananel, Rema 34:14). Yet all these commentaries would agree that if the rates were set by the government, and the Jew merely collected those rates, then there is no ethical violation by the Jewish worker (Me'iri). This discussion further highlights that a witness must engage in ethical behavior broadly, in order to be able to testify in a Jewish court, even beyond avoiding formal sin.

Or Zaru'a (and Rema 34:14) cautions that any Jewish leader who sets taxation rates for the community in a way that fails to conform to these principles is also invalidated from testifying. Today, the Jewish community rarely sets its own tax rates, although school tuition committees and synagogue membership committees often set rates that Jews must pay for communal institutions, and often struggle with exactly these questions. Given the large range of opinions on exactly which kinds of taxation system are ethical, one wonders if some of these leaders might lose their ability to testify. It would be impossible to countenance, however, that these volunteers who are *oseik be-tzorkhei tzibbur* would become invalid for taking on the important questions that must be addressed in a fully-functioning Jewish community.

Borrowers or Lenders who used an invalid *Heter Iska*

The relationship between Jews and money has always been complex, and the relationship between Jews and *lending* money has been even more complex. From the time of the *Chumash* and throughout the *Tanakh*,

Jews are warned both that they must lend money to each other, but that they also cannot do so in interest.[26] Yet, basic economics today explains that interest taken as part of a loan is usually nothing more than the sum of the risk of default plus the time value of money lent plus the expected rate of inflation, and thus a money lender essentially takes a loss when making a loan without interest. Yes, at times interest can be predatory and designed to make an undeserved profit, but in many loans it only reflects the opportunity cost of not investing the money in the stock market or in inflation-tracked bonds. The Torah seems to be aware of this reality; interest can be taken or given to gentiles, in recognition that interest is not a moral travesty which would be prohibited even against a gentile. Instead, by not taking interest, the lender extends beyond the conventional moral call of duty; the Torah expects even more when members of a large family, the larger Jewish family, interact with each other (Radak *Tehillim* 15:5). At times, Jews need a work-around or a solution to enable them to loan money with interest, and it was for this reason that the *heter iska* was created.[27] Obviously, in an agrarian economy where small sums of money would be lent for small periods of time, and when the rate of inflation was smaller, the idea of not taking interest would be easier for lenders. However, today, a Jew lending money to another Jew to finance a thirty-year mortgage would be at a significant financial loss if he or she did not take interest, hence the development and proliferation of the *heter iska*.

A Jew using a valid *heter iska* has done nothing wrong, and he can clearly testify. However, a *heter iska* can be used only: [a] for business loans,[28] [b] when the loan only includes an interest rate but not variable

---

26. *Shemot* 22:24, *Vayikra* 25:36-37, *Devarim* 23:20, *Yechezkel* 18:8 and 22:12, *Tehillim* 15:5.
27. For more on the *heter iska*, see *Nachalat Shiva* 40, *Igrot Moshe* YD 2:62-63, and J.D. Bleich, *Contemporary Halachic Problems* Vol. 2 (New York: Ktav, 1983), pp. 376-396. For a discussion of using CPI indexing to correct a loan for inflation, see *Minchat Yitzchak* 6:161 and *Igrot Moshe* YD 2:114.
28. See Yisroel Reisman, *The Laws of Ribbis* (New York: Mesorah Publications, 1995) pp. 249-251 about home purchase loans, based on *Shulchan Arukh Ha-Rav*; pp. 395-398 about personal or education loans.

interest rates, penalty interest, or late payment charges,[29] and [c] when the *heter iska* is used specifically by this lender for this borrower and this loan.[30] Yet, many Jews make loans or attempt to make loans[31] which fail to comply with the conditions of the *heter iska*, either because they are too onerous (such as "c" above), or because they fail to conform to modern-day expectations around loan structuring (such as "b" above). This begs the question whether a Jew who served as borrower or lender in an exchange using an invalid *heter iska* should be permitted to testify.

A ruling on this question may revolve around a debate among the *rishonim* about the testimony of a scribe who wrote a document for an interest-bearing loan. From a legal formal perspective, the scribe violates the same negative commandments as the borrower[32] and lender (*Bava Metzi'a* 75b), yet when considered from the level of his own self-concept, he considers himself to be exempt since he has not benefited at all from the crime. Here, the *rishonim* present different views. One version cited by Ran invalidates him, while Rashi (s.v. *loveh*), Rambam (10:4), *Shulchan Arukh* (34:10), another version of Ran, and Mordekhai (692) argue that the scribe may still testify. If the scribe can testify because his violating of a negative commandment is unbeknownst to himself, then someone unknowingly using an invalidate *heter iska* would surely be of the same status. However, if the scribe is permitted as Mordekhai argues, because he received only

---

29. Late charges and penalty interest charges are included in the prohibition of taking interest (see Reisman, pp. 166-175). The language of the *heter iska*, wherein all charges are stipulated in advance, cannot accommodate a hypothetical situation triggered by a change in circumstances such as late payment. The rate of return can be tied to the CPI or prime rate (Reisman, p. 411), because those situations can be described definitively at the onset and are not tied to the parties action or inaction.
30. Reisman, pp. 415-418, but see *Igrot Moshe* YD 3:41.
31. In 6 years as the director of the Boston Rabbinical Court, I was contacted a half-dozen times about *heter iska* arrangements. None of the cases complied with the principles of *heter iska* above, until the parties were instructed to restructure the loan in order to comply.
32. It is noteworthy that the borrower, who is essentially the victim, is also guilty of a commandment. Evidently, the institution of interest is so damaging that the Torah treats it less as a financial protection (which could be waved by the victim), and more as a larger moral issue, that even the victim can be guilty if his desire for funds causes him to compromise on a moral stand.

minimal benefit, then perhaps the one who uses an invalid *heter iska* would be excluded from testifying, because he receives significant benefit for his morally compromising stance around collecting interest. We will discuss the role of self-concept and self-awareness of unethical behavior further at the close of this essay.

Inter-gender Seclusion

Virtually all the cases in the *Gemara*'s discussion involve a financial component; although to its close, the *Gemara* introduces the category of one who is *chashud al ha-arayot*, suspected of being guilty of forbidden relations, which at first glance speaks of someone who has not committed a crime but has violated the ethical norm of remaining above suspicion.[33] This category poses two major intertwined difficulties; first, to define what is meant by the word '*chashud*,' and if indeed '*chashud*' means someone suspected of a crime without evidence, to justify how someone could be excluded for mere suspicion. Second, even after defining what is meant by the terminology, commentaries further debate what the ruling should be on this matter,[34] and whether this type of person is indeed invalidated.

---

33. The problem with taking this simple reading that there is no financial component to this crime, is that Rava, a later Rabbi, posits that all excluded witnesses must engage in financial crimes. Mordekhai explains that since pleasure is derived from forbidden relations, it is analogous to a financial crime, although this reading greatly expands the bounds of what is meant by 'financial' crimes (Rabbeinu Chananel similarly says the desire is so great that it can lead one to lie in court to get money to achieve this desire, which also expands what is meant by 'financial').

Ran cites this view and rejects it, and instead suggests (based on Ramban in *Milchamot*) that perhaps the debate of the earlier Rabbis was whether to adopt the reasoning later offered by Mordekhai that forbidden relations could be compared to financial crimes. Alternatively, Ran argues that the debate about forbidden relations is sui generis as though it is not a financial crime, its unique severity is so great that even Rava would include it on his list of sins that invalidate. On the other hand, the unique human desire for the sins is so great, and perhaps even Abbayei might not invalidate because the self-concept of being an upstanding member of society who would never commit perjury remains even after forbidden relations.

34. Underlying this debate is whether to consider this case a matter of jurisprudence, when we would follow the lenient Rav Nachman, or a case of prohibited law in which case we would follow the stringent Rav Sheishet.

The Provencal commentaries take the *Gemara* at its simplest reading, that the potential witness is only suspected of forbidden relations, and thus the debate in the *Gemara* is whether engaging in suspicious behavior is a sufficient ethical misstep to invalidate.[35] Ba'al Ha-Ma'or is lenient, thus the *halakha* concludes that we do not invalidate on the basis of mere suspicion,[36] while Ra'avad (in *Katuv Sham*) is stringent, invalidating on the basis of mere suspicion; for example, in the case of a gentleman who regularly secludes himself with a forbidden relation.

On the level of outcome, Rif agrees with Ba'al Ha-Ma'or, but only after disagreeing with him on both of the interpretative challenges discussed above. While Ba'al Ha-Ma'or was lenient, Rif was stringent; yet, while Ba'al Ha-Ma'or felt the debate was focused on suspected perpetrators, Rif believes it was about actual perpetrators of forbidden relations.[37] Thus, both Rif and Ba'al Ha-Ma'or exclude those who engage in forbidden relations, and validate only suspected people, but for opposite reasons; Rif (and Ramban in *Milchamot*) follows the stringent view in one telling of the debate, while Ba'al Ha-Ma'or follows the lenient view within a different telling.

It is not surprising, then, that Rema (CM 34:25; EH 141) rules that someone suspected of forbidden relations may testify; they are only excluded from testifying in matters related to marriage and divorce. Still, Rema does adopt a Ra'avad-esque view at least towards testifying at a

---

35. Though this might seem at first surprising, the *Gemara* and commentaries have numerous examples of punishment on the basis of rumor, often as a social deterrent. See *Kiddushin* 81a, and Rambam *Sanhedrin* 24:4-5.
36. This appears to be the view of Rosh as well, see *Piskei Ha-Rosh* and *Tosafot Ha-Rosh*. Like Ra'avad, he understands being suspect as having seclusion with forbidden relations. Tosafot present both the view of Ba'al Ha-Ma'or and the view of Rif. Rashi's view is hard to determine – he may argue that there were witnesses but not warning to the crime, and so it is more than mere suspicion.
37. Why would anyone think that someone who engaged in forbidden relations would be able to testify? Rif argues that he is not invalidated, because the individual retains the self-concept of keeping the laws of society, and only fails to meet the standard in this one instance, because of the great desire around forbidden relations. Tosafot, Ramban (*Milchamot*), and Or Zaru'a (20) offer echoes of this approach as well. This view, though not accepted halakhically, is a critical one, because it indicates that our focus in this entire topic is less on crimes committed, and more on how the perpetrator sees himself, and what the likelihood is for future negative behavior.

wedding or divorce; an individual can become locally invalidated even on the basis of mere rumor and seclusion alone. Rambam (*Issurei Bi'a* 21:1-4, *Sanhedrin* 19:4:162), writes that anyone who engages in affectionate contact towards the opposite gender is considered "suspect," and this could expand Rema's ruling further such that gentlemen who are not stringent on the prohibitions of both *yichud* and *negi'a* might be automatically excluded from testifying at a wedding. Noda Bi-Yehuda addresses this question at length (*Tinyana* EH 132), and concludes that at least for single Jews, there is a high likelihood that either there is no Biblical prohibition, or at the very least that the individuals erroneously believe there is none – and in that case, there would be grounds to allow them to testify.

The Role of Self-Concept

We have seen that to be qualified to testify, the *Gemara* demands performance of ethical conduct beyond the bare minimum, including minimizing potential *chillul ha-Shem* (charity takers), living productively, contributive lives (gamblers), avoiding suspicion (forbidden relations), and even keeping those laws that require taking a loss (interest). This speaks volumes as to the importance of ethical conduct within Judaism, and to the insistence at times on even supererogatory behavior in order to qualify for the privileges of Jewish society.

Yet, we have also seen that as the ethical demands get greater, the likelihood that the violator be unaware of the ethical norm becomes greater, and we have already seen cases where individuals remain qualified despite their behavior, such as the scribe on an interest document, or, according to some opinions, someone who engages in forbidden relations as a result of passion and not out of rejection of the law entirely.

In essence, these perspectives focus us less on the actions themselves, and more on the role self-concept plays in the development of an individual's ethical profile. Perhaps an individual can remain valid even if he has crossed an ethical red line using objective standards, because he subjectively considers himself ethical in their own mind (because of lack of knowledge or lack of perspective). Is exclusion from testimony

The Ethics of Testimony | 303

a consequence of the action, or is it a concern that the individual might lie, a concern that would only exist if the witnesses' self-concept is one of flexibility around Jewish law?

When discussing the case of individuals who dig graves on *Yom Tov* – violating the Biblical holiday in order to receive financial renumeration – the *Gemara* raises, and according to most authorities concludes,[38] that the fact that "they believe they are doing a positive commandment [burying the dead]" is grounds for them to retain their validation (*Sanhedrin* 26b, *Shulchan Arukh* 34:4). This strongly suggests that it is not the violation of the commandment per se which is problematic, so much as the self-concept of being willing to violate laws that is the issue.[39] This Talmudic logic is also accepted by *Shulchan Arukh* regarding one case of lending money in interest (34:11), in the Responsa of Rav Akiva Eiger (1:96) and in the *Seridei Eish* (3:19=1:88, regarding *Shabbat* desecrators), and is debated further by the commentaries to *Shulchan Arukh* (*Sema* 34:57 and *Netivot* 34:16).

However, the major problem with involving the justification of self-concept is that it could be used theoretically to allow any violation of any kind; so long as the witnesses claims that he felt it was permissible, can he become valid? Tosafot (*Rosh Ha-Shana* 22a, *Sanhedrin* 24b) survey a lengthy list of individuals engaged in theft and argue that since all these individuals don't believe their actions are wrong, they are not invalidated Biblically for theft, only Rabbinically. Ran (loc. cit.) replies that were that

---

38. Rif implies that they remain excluded but Me'iri, Ramah, Rosh (3:15), and *Shulchan Arukh* (34:14) are all lenient (see *Pitchei Teshuva* regarding if they must be interviewed first though, to establish that they made this error). This is an honest mistake because Jews would be permitted to violate the second day of *Yom Tov* to bury the dead (*Beitza* 6b), and so the error from one day to the other is understandable. See also *Shut Ha-Rivash* (311).
39. The *Gemara* also says that a worker who eats a little while working may testify (26b). See Rashi, Ramah, and Me'iri – this may be because no theft has occurred if the owner permits it (Rambam 10:5, *Shulchan Arukh* 34:15), or because the worker has offered a self-justification, again preserving the right to testify because of an erroneous self-justification which serves to insulate the self-concept around ethics. This case may also resemble a situation that is Biblically permitted, the consumption of farm-workers in *Devarim* chapter 23.

true, they should be permitted to testify even if they sinned Biblically, if indeed error can justify unethical conduct![40]

Indeed, Rambam extends the self-concept justification even further (12:1; also *Shulchan Arukh* 34:24) and allows the justification of erroneous behavior to permit even a *rasha* who violates Biblical laws. Yet, once this point has been reached, one questions whether any witness could ever be disqualified for any of the ethical violations discussed in this essay, or whether the doctrine of preservation of self-concept can extend to all of these. Perhaps for this reason, Rav Moshe Feinstein (EH 4:59) is unwilling to apply the self-concept justification to those that violate the entire Torah, because it is in his view impossible to permit a witness just on the basis of a moral self-concept if the individual lacks the commitment to the religious system which gave birth to the rubric of testimony and the imperative for truthful *eidut*. Yet, it is difficult to read this very nuanced position within the case law in the *Gemara*, and so the question of self-concept remains an open one in the validation of witnesses.

In the end, it is my impression that few *Batei Din* and Rabbis invalidate witnesses just for touching members of the opposite gender, just for getting an MA in Music, or for using an invalid *heter iska*, perhaps because all these individuals retain the self-concept that they are strongly observant upstanding Jews. Still, even if in the end there is no potential halakhic ramification to these discussions, the topics force us to consider important ethical issues in Judaism and the high standard within which Jews are asked to conduct themselves.

---

40. For that reason, Ran denies anyone could think these behaviors are justified. But his logical response to Tosafot is telling, and opens the logically possibility that we would extend and allow all these individuals to testify.

Derekh Eretz as Rabbinic Natural Morality

Rabbi Tzvi Sinensky

If asked to translate the phrase *derekh eretz*, many would likely invoke the Yiddish term *mentschlechkeit*, or proper manners. This translation, however, while accurate, is only one of *derekh eretz*'s manifold usages.[1] The striking range of meanings associated with *derekh eretz* leads us to wonder whether or not there is a single, overarching meaning that we can assign this puzzling category.

Alongside the variegated invocations of *derekh eretz*, recent years have seen extensive debate regarding Judaism's view concerning natural law or natural morality, in particular whether we can derive ethics from our human intuitions.[2] Some have claimed that, at least post-Sinai, Judaism is

---

1. For a fairly comprehensive overview of *derekh eretz* in Rabbinic literature, see Safrai, "*Muvano Shel Ha-Munach Derekh Eretz*," *Tarbitz* 60:2 (*Tevet-Adar* 5751), pp. 147-162.
2. The topics of natural morality and natural law (*lex naturalis*) have a long intellectual history that far exceeds the scope of our subject. Still, at the risk of oversimplification, a brief summary follows.

Thinkers have long inquired as to the basis for morality and law, and have explored the following set of questions: Can morality (that which is "right") and even law (that which is required and even enforceable) be deduced without recourse to revelation? If so, can it be observed in the natural world? Or in our own moral intuition? Asked in Aristotelian terms, does humanity have an inherent nature or teleology that ought direct our behaviors? Further, once introduced, does revelation leave room for that human intuition? In a different vein, is law simply an elaboration of natural law? From Aristotle's theory of the teleological nature of mankind, which postulates that humanity was created with an intrinsic nature and purpose, to the Gnostic and Christian *lex naturalis* (natural law) traditions, to the natural law theories of Locke, Hobbes, and America's founding fathers, these questions have been the subject of intense debate for well over two millennia.

exclusively rooted in revelation. In particular, some opponents of Jewish natural law have noted that, as opposed to classical Christian thought (such as that of Aquinas), Judaism appears to have no terminology for natural law. This suggests that this concept is foreign to Judaism. This article seeks to address both questions by suggesting that *derekh eretz* is a Rabbinic variation of natural law. In order to establish this theory on a firm foundation, we begin with a brief examination of *derekh eretz*'s varied appearances in classical sources.

1. Proper Manners

As stated, *derekh eretz* lends itself to this classic usage in numerous contexts. To take one example, in discussing God's visit to Avraham at the beginning of *Parashat Vayeira*, *Bava Metzi'a* 87a expounds, "Why are there dots over the letters *alef-yud-vav* in [the word] *eilav*? The Torah teaches *derekh eretz*, that one should always inquire as to the welfare of his host." Another *midrash* teaches (*Shir Hashirim Rabba* 4:16 and parallels): "Rabbi Yochanan said: The Torah teaches *derekh eretz*, that a groom should not enter the wedding canopy until his bride grants him permission." Indeed,

---

Recent decades have witnessed spirited debate as to where Judaism falls on this controversy. Marvin Fox ("Maimonides and Aquinas on Natural Law," *Dinei Yisrael* 3 (1972), later published with some additions in his "Law of Ethics in Modern Jewish Philosophy: The Case of Moses Mendelsohn," *Proceedings of the American Academy for Jewish Research,* Vol. 43 (1976), pp. 1-13) has advanced the thesis that Judaism emphatically denies natural morality, while R. J. David Bleich ("Judaism and Natural Law," *The Jewish Law Annual* 7 (1988), pp. 5-42) allows for an extremely limited notion of natural law. Dr. Christine Hays presses the case for a minimalist reading of Rabbinic thought in her recent book, *What's Divine about Divine Law*? (2015, Princeton, Princeton University Press).

Others have advocated a more expansive approach, including Rav Aharon Lichtenstein *zt"l* ("Does Judaism Recognize an Ethic Independent of *Halakha*?," *Modern Jewish Ethics*, 1975, Ohio State University Press; reprinted in Leaves of Faith, Vol. 2); Rav Yehuda Amital *zt"l* (*Jewish Values in a Changing World*, ch. 2, pp. 19-43); David Novak (*Natural Law in Judaism*, 1988, Cambridge University Press); and others. Some, prominent among them Rav Lichtenstein, have distinguished between pre-Sinai and post-Sinai, considering the relevance of *lex naturalis* after revelation an open question. It is further possible to claim that Judaism endorses natural morality but not natural law (i.e. an ethical preference without a strict legal mandate).

two entire minor tractates are dedicated to the topic of *mentschlechkeit*: *Derekh Eretz* and *Derekh Eretz Zuta*. One illustrative passage records (*Zuta* 5:1): "One should not take leave of his friend or teacher without first asking permission to leave. And all should learn this lesson from the Omnipresent, who said to Avraham [before leaving], 'Avraham! Avraham!' … One should not suddenly enter his friend's home. Everyone should learn this lesson from the Omnipresent, Who stood on the edge of the garden and called out to Adam, as it says, "And the Lord God called out to Adam and said, 'Where are you?'""

2. Earning a Livelihood

Often, *derekh eretz* is used in reference to earning a livelihood. *Pirkei Avot* (3:5) teaches: "Rabbi Nechunya says, 'Anyone who accepts upon himself the yoke of Torah, we remove from him the yoke of monarchy and the yoke of *derekh eretz*. And anyone who removes from himself the yoke of Torah, we place upon him the yoke of monarchy and the yoke of *derekh eretz*.'" In this context, it is evident that *derekh eretz* refers to garnering a living wage.[3] This usage of the phrase also appears in an oft-cited passage in *Berakhot* (35b), in which Rabbi Yishma'el asserts that the phrase "you shall gather your grain" (*Devarim* 11:14) teaches that one should earn a living ("*hanheg bahen minhag derekh eretz*") and should not spend all day engrossed in Torah study.

3. Intimacy

Perhaps less immediately familiar than the previous two usages, numerous sources invoke *derekh eretz* in reference to sexual intercourse. *Yoma* 74b, cited by the *Haggada Shel Pesach*, teaches: "'And He saw our affliction' – this refers to separation from *derekh eretz* [during the Jews' enslavement]." Similarly, Rabbi Yoshiya in *Mekhilta De-Rabbi Yishma'el* (*Masekhta De-Nezikin Parasha* 3) expounds: "'*she'erah*' – this is her food… '*kesutah*'

---

3. Rambam s.v. *ve-ol*, Rabbeinu Yona ibid., Bartenura s.v. *derekh eretz*, Midrash Shmu'el s.v. *ve-ol* citing Rav Yosef ibn Nachmi'ash, *Chiddushei Ha-Gra* ibid.

[refers to clothing]; 'and her *ona*' – this refers to *derekh eretz* (intimacy)."[4] Indeed, a classic Talmudic passage (*Eiruvin* 100b), in suggesting that, had they not received the Torah, humans could have derived ethical behavior from animals, invokes our phrase in precisely this fashion: "Had the Torah not been given, we would have learned… conjugal manners (*derekh eretz*) from fowl."

As noted by Midrash Shmu'el (*Avot* ibid.), it would appear that this usage has biblical roots. After the destruction of Sedom and its neighboring cities, Lot's elder daughter declares to her sister (*Bereishit* 19:31): "Our father is old, and there is no one on earth to come upon us in the manner of the land (*ke-derekh kol ha-aretz*)." The union of Lot and his daughters, then, is the earliest recorded usage of "*derekh eretz*."[5]

4. Waging War

Here we encounter perhaps the most unexpected connotation. *Berakhot* 32b asserts: "Four activities must be strengthened: Torah, good actions, prayer, and *derekh eretz*." As a support for the latter, the *Gemara* cites a verse from *Shmu'el Bet* (10:12) in which Yo'av, King David's general, urges the nation to join the battle against Ammon: "Be strong and strengthen yourself on behalf of our nation." This verse specifically relates to strengthening one's battlefield resolve. Drawing implicitly upon the proof text, Rashi (*Berakhot* s.v. *derekh eretz*) explains: "If he is a craftsman – for his craft; if he is a merchant – for his merchandise sales; if he is a soldier – for his battle." Whereas Rashi's first two examples return us to *derekh eretz* as earning a livelihood, his final example illustrates this fourth definition.

---

4. Similarly, Midrash Shmu'el to *Avot* 6:5 points to the text of the *ketubba*, in which the husband commits to "bring to you in the way of the entire land" (*me'al levataikhi ke-orach kol ar'a*). The *ketubba* thus obliquely refers to *ona* by invoking the Aramaic equivalent of *derekh eretz*.

5. Based on this source, it might appear that the first reference to *derekh eretz* is sinful in nature. The Rabbis suggest, however, that Lot's daughters were well intentioned, as they were under the impression that the remainder of humanity had been eliminated in the flood. See *Bereishit Rabba* 51, *Pesikta Zutrati* 42, and *Torah Sheleima Vayeira* 19:179-183.

5. Worldly Advice

In yet other scenarios, *derekh eretz* refers to what we colloquially term practical wisdom. *Bereishit Rabba* (*Vayishlach* 76), for example, invokes *derekh eretz* to account for Ya'akov's decision, when faced with the danger posed by Eisav, to split his camp into three: "'And he divided the camp, etc.' Rabbi Chiyya says, The Torah teaches you *derekh eretz*, that one should not place all his money in one corner. From whom do you learn? From Ya'akov." This passage is a variant on the classic aphorism recommending against placing all of one's eggs in a single basket. Along similar lines, while discussing a soldier's various possible exemptions from war, *Sota* 44a teaches: "'One who built [a house], one who planted [a vineyard], one who betrothed [a woman]': The Torah teaches *derekh eretz*, that one should build a house and plant a vineyard, and afterward marry a woman." The *Gemara* is offering practical counsel: one is well-advised to first find shelter and a livelihood, and only then marry. Interestingly, this is the first usage of *derekh eretz* that does not seem to be associated with a positive ethical value.

6. Common Behavior

The opening *midrash* of *Parashat Beshalach* (*Shemot* 13:17) records that "God did not lead the [Jewish people] along the path of the Philistines (*derekh eretz Pelishtim*)." Taken literally, the verse means that God did not lead the Jews through Philistine territory, which would have been the most direct route to *Kena'an*. The Rabbis, however, interpret the phrase metaphorically:

> What is the way of the entire world? One who acquires slaves does so on condition that they bathe him, anoint him, clothe him, load him up, and provide light for him. However, God did not do this for the Israelites; rather, He did not lead them *in the way of the land*. He bathed them… and lit the way for them. (*Tanchuma Yashan* 10a)

In other words, here *derekh eretz* connotes typical behavior – "the way of the entire world." In attending to their personal needs in the desert, God treated His servants in an unusually generous fashion.[6]

7. Worldly Wisdom

Of course, any bird's-eye view of *derekh eretz* would be incomplete without reference to Rav Samson Raphael Hirsch's doctrine of *Torah Im Derekh Eretz*, Torah married to high culture.[7] Oddly, his interpretation does not seem to accord with any of the usages outlined above. This appears to be a significant difficulty, as his understanding seems to outright contradict the range of interpretations proffered in Rabbinic literature.

In light of this striking range of meanings, it is not surprising that we find disputes concerning the meaning of *derekh eretz* in a variety of contexts. This is particularly true in reference to a series of passages in *Pirkei Avot*:

> Rabbi Elazar ben Azarya says: If there is no Torah there is no *derekh eretz*; if there is no *derekh eretz* there is no Torah. (*Avot* 3:17)

The commentators debate the meaning of the phrase *derekh eretz* as it appears in this *mishna*: some understand it to refer to work (Rashi s.v. *im* with Rashi 2:2 s.v. *she-yegi'at*), whereas others understand it to refer to proper character traits (Rabbeinu Yona s.v. *Rabbi Elazar*).

---

6. Significantly, here, for the first time, the phrase is used in a negative sense: God's behavior is positive precisely because his actions are *unlike* those of others. Notably, this pejorative usage of *derekh eretz* also appears in *Avot De-Rabbi Natan* (2:8), which states: "Rabbi Chananya ben Chakhinai said, one who awakens at night and turns his attention to wasteful activities, this is a practice of *derekh eretz*."
7. See Rav Hirsch's article that appeared in the journal *Nachalat Tzvi*, "Religion Allied to Progress," available at http://users.ipfw.edu/bartky/Y200Y401%20 Judaism/Judaism%20Course-Samson%20Raphael%20Hirsch-Religion%20 Allied%20to%20Pr.pdf. For a summary of differing interpretations of the phrase in Rav Hirsch's thought, see Yair Fiksler, "*Ha-Chinnuch Ha-Beiti Be-Mishnato Shel Ha-Rashar Hirsch*," ch. 2, available at http://www.daat.ac.il/daat/chinuch/harashar/2-2.htm.

A similar ambiguity exists in connection with *Avot* 2:2:

> Rabban Gamli'el son of Rabbi Yehuda Ha-Nasi says: "Fine is Torah study with *derekh eretz*, for the struggle in each causes sin to be forgotten. And any Torah that lacks work will ultimately be nullified and cause sin…"

Here too the commentators debate the meaning of *derekh eretz*: Does it refer to work or good character? As the continuation of the *mishna* refers to *sechora*, which in context appears synonymous with work, it seems more likely that *derekh eretz* refers not to work but to proper character. Nevertheless, here too we find a debate among the commentaries: Rashi (s.v. *she-yegi'at*) and Rabbeinu Yona (s.v. *Rabban, she-yegi'at*) adopt the former view, whereas Midrash Shmu'el (s.v. *amar*) claims that *derekh eretz* refers to "making people beloved to one another."

To take one final example – this time from *Perek Kinyan Torah*, a series of teachings appended to *Avot* – the *beraita* (6:5) lists "the diminution of *derekh eretz*" as one of the forty-eight methods for the acquisition of Torah. At first glance it appears likely that the term refers to a reduction of time spent on work, which can dramatically increase one's quantitative Torah study. Alternatively, as Rashi suggests, by diminishing interactions with uncouth individuals found in the marketplace, he is more likely to acquire the traits necessary to study Torah. Tiferet Yisrael (*Yakhin* 83) and Midrash Shmu'el (s.v. *be-mi'ut derekh eretz*), however, translate *derekh eretz* as physical intimacy, which can distract a person from focusing on Torah study. Midrash Shmu'el offers two additional interpretations: a) *derekh eretz* refers to proper manners, meaning that one who is compelled to show deference to an important individual inevitably loses time that could have otherwise been allocated to Torah study; and b) *derekh eretz* refers to the generally desirable characteristic of bashfulness (*busha*). While this is generally an admirable quality, our Rabbis teach that *ein ha-bayshan lamed*, a bashful person fails to ask questions and thereby learn. Thus, one who diminishes *derekh eretz* will ultimately gain more knowledge.

Having reviewed at least seven different renderings of *derekh eretz*, how are we to account for its dizzying range of meanings?

The closing *mishna* of the first chapter of *Kiddushin* offers a direction:

> Anyone engaged with Bible (*Mikra*), *Mishna* and *derekh eretz* will not come to sin quickly, as it says (*Kohelet* 4:12), "And the three-fold cord will not quickly snap." And anyone not invested with Bible, *Mishna*, and *derekh eretz* is not from the settlement. (*Kiddushin* 40b)

By this point we are not surprised to learn that the commentators dispute the meaning of the *mishna*'s usage of *derekh eretz*. Whereas Rambam and Bartenura (s.v. *ve-lo*) understand the term to refer specifically to *mentschlechkeit*, Tiferet Yisrael (*Yakhin* 79) and Maharsha (*Chiddushei Aggadot* s.v. *kol*) understand *derekh eretz* to denote the full gamut of positive character traits.[8] In his commentary to Rav Yitzchak Alfasi in *Sanhedrin* (6a *be-alfas* s.v. *ve-lo*), Rashi writes that the *mishna* refers to one who is not active in the settlement of the world, which suggests one who is not economically productive.

Of particular interest, though, is the *mishna*'s concluding phrase. What does it mean that such an individual "is not from the settlement?" In his commentary to the *mishna*, Rambam suggests that it would be best for the community to expel such an uncouth individual. This reading, however, does not account for the appearance of the phrase in the descriptive form. Had the *mishna* intended to teach that a community ought to dismiss one who behaves dreadfully, the language should have explicitly instructed that the community expel him. Tiferet Yisrael (*Yakhin* 79, 81), after analyzing at length the significance of the *mishna*'s tripartite division of Bible, *Mishna*, and *derekh eretz*, suggests that such an individual ought to inhabit the desert, a place of wild animals, for he is more dangerous to the community than such vermin. Again, Tiferet Yisrael's approach fails to account for the *mishna*'s descriptive formulation.

---

8. Maharsha suggests that Rambam in fact has this broader reading in mind, but this reading seems forced.

Bartenura, on the other hand, states simply *"eino be-yishuvo shel olam,"* he is not participating in the settlement of the world. On this, the *mishna* is not prescribing a particular response, but rather is merely making an observation: one who does not engage with the community in an appropriate fashion has, by definition, excluded himself from the community. *Derekh eretz*, for Bartenura, emerges as a wide-ranging category, denoting one's responsibility to live with civility in accordance with the norms of society.

If Bartenura is correct – and, as we have argued, his reading seems compelling – we can account for the wide range of meanings pregnant within *derekh eretz*, including that of Rav Hirsch, which goes beyond the meanings proffered by Chazal. *Derekh eretz* means that we are mandated to live as civilized citizens. Living as a full member of society encompasses *mentschlechkeit*, earning a livelihood, reproducing, and so much more.

In light of this rendering of *derekh eretz* as commitment to participating in communal life, moreover, the *Gemara*'s (*Berakhot* 32b) identification of *derekh eretz* with going out to war on behalf of one's nation is easily understood. Fighting for the local army is no less an essential part of serving one's community than contributing one's fair share to its moral and economic fabric. Indeed, the proof text from *Shmu'el Bet* – "Be strong and strengthen yourself on behalf of our nation" – highlights precisely this point.

This interpretation of *derekh eretz* accounts for a number of other curious phenomena, such as Rambam's curious allusion to the phrase in his commentary to *Pirkei Avot* (2:5). Generally speaking, *am ha'aretz*, loosely translated as an ignoramus, is a pejorative term. The *mishna*, however, seems to compare an *am ha'aretz* favorably with the *bor*. Rambam explains that while an *am ha'aretz* is ignorant, he is still well-mannered; the *bor*, by contrast, is both ignorant *and* uncivilized. The *am ha'aretz* may know little, but at least he acts with *derekh eretz*. *Derekh eretz*, in other words, as we have postulated, refers not to scholarship but to generally civilized behavior. In this sense, the *am ha'aretz* is lauded as one who acts with proper *derekh eretz*.

This also explains the earliest appearance of *derekh eretz*: bearing children. There is perhaps no contribution more essential to society than helping to ensure its continuity. It is therefore appropriate that this is the earliest appearance of our term.

Indeed, both Rav Avraham Yitzchak Ha-Kohen Kook and Rav Aharon Lichtenstein explicitly associate natural morality with *derekh eretz*, although neither, to the best of my knowledge, elaborates more fully this connection. Rav Kook insists that:

> Every element of Torah must be preceded by *derekh eretz*. If it is something agreeable to natural reason and uprightness, it must pass in a straight path, with the inclination of the heart and consent of the pure will implanted in man, like theft, illicit sexual relations, and modesty which are learned from the ant, the dove, and the cat, and all the more so those things which are derived from the internal cognition of man himself and his spiritual sense… (*Orot Ha-Torah* 12:2-3)[9]

Even more explicit than Rav Kook, as part of a classic analysis of natural morality, Rav Lichtenstein writes:

> The wide-ranging concept of *derekh eretz* – roughly the equivalent of what Coventry Patmore called "the traditions of civility" – points in the same direction. Its importance again, not as descriptively synonymous with conventional conduct but as prescriptive *lex naturalis* should not be underestimated. The *mishna* cites Rabbi Elazar ben Azarya's view that "without Torah, there is no *derekh eretz*, and without *derekh eretz*, there is no Torah"; and the *midrash* goes beyond this dialectical reciprocity, stating that "*derekh eretz* preceded Torah" … Their link reinforces our awareness of the Rabbis' recognition of natural morality. (*Leaves of Faith* Vol. 2 p. 34)

---

9. See also *Orot Ha-Kodesh* 3, *Rosh Davar*, 3:27 and 11; *Orot Ha-Kodesh* 3:318. For a brief discussion, see Yehudah Mirsky, *Mystic in a Time of Revolution*, 109-110. Marc Shapiro has discussed this in a series of blog posts entitled "New Writings From Rav Kook," available at the *Seforim Blog*. Rav Yuval Cherlow addresses Rav Kook's view at: http://shut.moreshet.co.il/shut2.asp?id=18608. See also Yitzchak Blau, "The Implications of a Jewish Virtue Ethic," *The Torah u-Madda Journal* 9 (2000), pp. 34-6.

The identity of *derekh eretz* and natural law, then, offers a compelling framework enabling us to account for the confusingly wide array of meanings associated with the former.

The usage of *derekh eretz* in context of Lot and his daughters, moreover, raises an additional question that our thesis neatly resolves: if *derekh eretz* first appears in relation to gentiles – for despite their relation to Avraham, Lot and his daughters are non-Jews – we might inquire as to whether gentiles are included in the obligation.

A classic *midrash* that appears in *Vayikra Rabba* (9:3; see also 35:6) implicitly addresses this question.[10] The *midrash* recounts that Rabbi Yishma'el invited an individual into his home on the assumption that the guest was a Torah scholar. It quickly became evident, however, that the invitee was anything but. Despite his weak academic credentials the visitor had performed many acts of *derekh eretz* over the course of his life, leading Rabbi Yishma'el to treat the visitor as an honored guest. Echoing the significance of this gesture the *midrash* adds:

> Rabbi Yishma'el said: *Derekh eretz* preceded the Torah by twenty-six generations. This is that which is written (*Bereishit* 3:24): "*lishmor et derekh eitz ha-chayyim*," "to guard the path of the tree of life." '*Derekh*' refers to *derekh eretz*, and afterward the tree of life is Torah.

The *midrash* goes on to suggest that this is one interpretation of the verse in *Tehillim* (50:23): "for the one who sets a proper course, I will show him the salvation of God (*ve-sam derekh, arenu be-yesha Elokim*)." Chazal homiletically interpret the term "*sam*" as "*sham*," meaning to evaluate. The verse thus reads: "If one evaluates the proper *derekh eretz*, I will show him the salvation of God." One who acts with *derekh eretz*, in other words, shall merit salvation.

The *midrash* thus claims that Adam himself was commanded in *derekh eretz*, suggesting that *derekh eretz* is a universal obligation incumbent upon all humanity.

---

10. See also *Tana De-Vei Eliya Rabba* 1.

The *Gemara* (*Bava Kamma* 92a, *Makkot* 9a-b) suggests an additional instance in which *derekh eretz* applies to gentiles, claiming that Avimelekh was liable to death for inquiring as to whether Sara was Avraham's wife or sister. Rashi (*Bava Kamma* s.v. *she-haya*, *Makkot* 9a s.v. *ke-deka*) explains it was due to Avimelekh's lack of *derekh eretz* that he was liable to death. Rashi thus indicates that *derekh eretz* extends to gentiles, and can even generate capital punishment (!).[11]

This universal extension, however, seems difficult. *Derekh eretz* does not appear on the list of seven Noachide commandments listed in *Sanhedrin*. What, then, is the basis for the assumption that both Jews and gentiles were obligated in these practices from the time of Adam? Was there an act of revelation of which we are uninformed?

This suggests that *derekh eretz* is the Jewish version of natural morality. The basis for the obligation of *derekh eretz* is not revelation but human intuition. It is therefore incumbent upon Jew and gentile alike, and was binding long before the Sinaitic revelation. For the Torah, the mandate to act in accordance with the norms of one's civilized community is axiomatic.

This understanding of *derekh eretz* also helps to account for the view of Rabbi Yehuda (*Berakhot* 22a), who permits a *ba'al keri* to the study of the laws of *derekh eretz*. If, as the *Gemara* itself suggests, the prohibition is for a *ba'al keri* to experience Torah study as a reenactment of the Sinaitic revelation, and *derekh eretz* is rooted not in revelation but in natural morality, Rabbi Yehuda's position is easily understood.

Further, our thesis accounts for two Talmudic passages which assign *derekh eretz* the status of biblical law. *Bava Metzi'a* 71a rules that a woman is not able to acquire an indentured servant because it is "not *orach ar'a*," the Aramaic term for *derekh eretz*. (Rashi explains that it is unseemly because they will find themselves in violation of the prohibition of *yichud*.) *Keritot* 10b explains that a poor woman who gives birth may offer an extremely

---

11. Ritva (*Makkot* 9b s.v. *mi-kan*) challenges Rashi, arguing that we cannot hold Avimelekh responsible for his ignorance of *derekh eretz*. Ritva therefore reinterprets the *Gemara* to mean that Avimelekh should not have trusted Avraham's identification of Sara as his sister; he was liable to be killed not for his violation of *derekh eretz* but for the sin of *arayot*. By his own admission, however, Ritva's reading of the *Gemara* is forced.

inexpensive sacrifice, but it must be valued at at least one *peruta* (coin's) worth, for otherwise it is "not *orach ar'a*," disrespectful to God. The context of each *sugya* suggests that both rulings are designated biblical stature. If we see *derekh eretz* as a form of Jewish natural law (and law in the strict sense, not just a moral preference), somewhat analogous to *sevara*, which generates laws that carry the force of biblical law,[12] these *sugyot* are readily understood.

Finally, the identification of *derekh eretz* with natural morality allows us to resolve an additional difficulty. We previously cited *Vayikra Rabba*'s interpretation of the phrase "*lishmor et derekh eitz ha-chayyim*," which renders "*derekh*" as *derekh eretz*. At first glance this is difficult: on what basis does the *midrash* identify "*derekh*" with *derekh eretz* in particular, and not any other path that God calls for mankind to follow? In light of the association between *derekh eretz* and natural morality the answer is clear: *derekh eretz* refers precisely to the "normal" path trodden by upstanding citizens.

For this reason, the Rabbis assert that *derekh eretz* was introduced at the very outset of human experience. *Derekh Eretz* is far-reaching, applicable to Jew and gentile alike, deeply rooted in natural morality, and speaks to our basic ethical obligations toward society. When the *midrash* teaches that *derekh eretz* – in all its manifestations – preceded the giving of the Torah by twenty-six generations, the central place of this cardinal value could not be more crystal clear.

---

12. See *Berakhot* 35a with Penei Yehoshu'a s.v. *sevara*, *Yoma* 82b, *Ketubbot* 22a, *Bava Kamma* 46b, *Sanhedrin* 74a.

If This World is an Anteroom, Why Be This-Worldly?

Rabbi Dr. Aaron Segal

My topic is *Olam Ha-ba*: its place in our value system, our overarching goals, and our religious consciousness.[1] This will surely strike some readers as odd, even antiquated. In his recent book, *Surviving Death*, the Princeton philosopher, Mark Johnston, begins by acknowledging the awkwardness of even raising the topic of the afterlife, in however attenuated a form, when addressing an academic audience (pp. 1-2). "To speak in this kind of academic context about whether we survive death," he notes, "is widely regarded as a form of bad taste." My topic isn't whether there is a World to Come – I take its existence as a given. But I nonetheless find myself in a similarly uncomfortable position. To write for a predominantly Modern Orthodox audience about orienting ourselves toward what lies beyond the grave is at the very least unusual, and quite possibly regarded as bad form. Modern Orthodox thinkers speak with nearly one voice on the matter: halakhic Judaism calls on us to have a this-worldly orientation, to think little if at all about the afterlife and focus our spiritual and religious energies on our earthly existence. The greatest influence on this this-worldly view, or at least its greatest source of support, is the Rav. In *Halakhic Man* he writes:[2]

---

1. This essay is based on a lecture delivered at Yeshiva University on the occasion of Rav Lichtenstein *zt"l*'s first *yahrzeit*. Thanks to Rav Shalom Carmy, Professor Will Lee, and other audience members for their insightful comments and questions. Thanks to Dr. David Shatz for calling my attention to a number of errors and omissions in an earlier draft and offering very helpful suggestions and reformulations.
2. The theme of this-worldliness pervades *Halakhic Man*. See Allan Nadler's

> Halakhic man does not long for superior levels of a "supernal" pristine existence…It is here, in this world, that halakhic man acquires eternal life. (p. 30)
>
> Halakhic man, however, takes up his position in this world and does not move from it…His goal is not flight to another world that is wholly good, but rather bringing down that eternal world into the midst of our world. (p. 41)

The Rav draws out the corollary regarding the proper attitude toward death:

> Judaism abhors death, organic decay, and dissolution…Halakha is devoid of any positive orientation toward death and burial; on the contrary, it views these phenomena from a negative perspective. (*Halakhic Man* p. 31)

One would be hard-pressed to find a prominent Modern Orthodox thinker who explicitly takes issue with the Rav on these points, and it is not difficult to find similar sentiments in the writings of other such figures.[3]

Despite the awkwardness it might engender, I'd like to raise some questions about this wide-ranging modern consensus. The modern view is far from self-evident and even farther from reflecting a broad and historically significant consensus among traditional *ba'alei machshava*. Compare the words with which Ramchal famously begins his *Mesillat Yesharim*:

"Soloveitchik's Halakhic Man: Not a "Mithnagged"," *Modern Judaism* 13(2), pp. 120-26.

3. See, among many others, *Seridei Eish* (v. 4 pp. 365-6) on Rav Shimshon Raphael Hirsch (cited in Rav Elyakim Krumbein's *Musar for Moderns*, Ktav Publishing House and Yeshivat Har Etzion, 2005, pp. 11-13), Rav Norman Lamm's "Attitudes to Life," Sermon delivered on Shabbat Bechukkotai, 1973 (available at https://www.yu.edu/about/lamm-heritage/archives), and Rav Jonathan Sacks's "Defeating Death," in *Lessons in Leadership: A Weekly Reading of the Jewish Bible*, Maggid Press 2015, and his "Rosh Hashana: A Breath of Life," *The Forward* September 23, 2014.

Our Sages of blessed memory have taught us that man was created for the sole purpose of rejoicing in God and deriving pleasure from the splendor of His Presence; for this is true joy and the greatest pleasure that can be found. The place where this joy may truly be derived is the World to Come, which was expressly created to provide for it; but the path to the object of our desires is this world, as our Sages of blessed memory have said (*Avot* 4:16): "This world is like an anteroom to the World to Come." (*Mesillat Yesharim* ch. 1)

Ramchal may have been more emphatic and pointed than others on this issue, but it's hard to deny that his view has deep roots in Chazal, *rishonim*, and *achronim*. Alongside the famed *mishna* that Ramchal quotes, which compares *Olam Ha-zeh* to a mere anteroom and *Olam Ha-ba* to the banquet hall, the frequent Talmudic analogy between *Olam Ha-zeh*/*Olam Ha-ba* and *Erev Shabbat*/*Shabbat* and concomitant admonition to prepare here for the hereafter suggests a clear means-ends structure to human existence, a structure of which we are supposed to be cognizant; our sojourn here is a preparation for an ethereal other-worldly dimension.[4] It's hard to read Rambam's description in *Hilkhot Teshuva* ch. 8 of *Olam Ha-ba* – and his statements that all the *nevi'im* and David Ha-Melekh longed, even pined, for it – or Ramban's discussion in *Torat Ha-Adam*, and not come away with the impression that one ought to have at least one eye on the *yom she-kulo tov*. Even the Rav's "mitnaggedic" predecessors were far more other-worldly than he was.[5] It is no wonder that the Gra identified not with the Rav's wholly negative assessment of death, but with Rabbi Me'ir's famous comment on God's declaration upon completing the creation (*Midrash Aggada Bereishit* ch. 1): "'*Ve-hinnei tov me'od:*' and it is good [that there is] death."[6]

---

4. On the analogy to *Erev Shabbat*/*Shabbat*, see *inter alia*, *Mishna Tamid* 7:4 [6:7], *Bavli Avoda Zara* 3a, and *Mekhilta Ki Tissa parasha* 1.
5. See Nadler ibid.
6. *Aderet Eliyahu al Ha-Torah* ch. 3 v. 21, cited in Nadler ibid. p. 131. I do not know how to reconcile the numerous statements of the Gra collected in Nadler's article with the well-known attestation of Rav Chayyim Volozhin as to the Gra's statement (*Derashat Maharach*, translated and cited by Rav Krumbein ibid.), "What importance does the World to Come have? One cannot serve God with love there, nor do anything to please our Creator and Maker. This world is the main one." Perhaps Rav Chayyim Volozhin's distinction between what is appropriate for the Gra himself and what is appropriate for *us* is useful here.

Its being at odds with a central, maybe even dominant, current in Jewish thought is not a reason to dismiss the modern viewpoint, since, for one thing, there have always been traditional voices with a more this-worldly bent that constituted a counter-current.[7] But it *is* reason to ask whether the modern view is well-motivated, and, relatedly, what it is about modernity or a "modern outlook" that explains its prevalence. This is all the more so given a serious but simple difficulty that the this-worldly view faces: the difficulty is just that *Olam Ha-ba*, whose *existence* is a non-negotiable feature of our religious life and liturgy, seems to serve no significant purpose in the modern outlook. If the Rav is right that it is in *this* world that halakhic man acquires eternal life, what then is the *point* of "more" eternal life? It is hard to believe that the settling of accounts – doling out *sakhar va-onesh* in a just way – exhausts the religious and spiritual significance of *Olam Ha-ba* or justifies our praying at least three times a day for *techiyyat ha-meitim*![8] (Crucially, no analogous difficulty confronts the other-worldly thinkers; as Ramchal and others stress, there is a perfectly good explanation for our this-worldly sojourn that is consistent with an other-worldly *telos*.) There had better be a good reason to reject the traditionally dominant other-worldliness. The trouble is that when we start to look for such reasons, the obvious candidates don't seem to work.

What follows are three obvious candidates and an unavoidably brief discussion of the challenges facing each:

(1) It is tempting to suggest that a demand that we avert our gaze from *Olam Ha-ba*, especially in the course of our *avodat Hashem*, can be rooted in the well-known dictum of Antigonus of *Sokho* in *Avot* 1:3, "Be not like servants who serve their masters in order to [or, on condition that they] receive reward." After quoting this *mishna*, Rav

---

7. See Abarbanel's commentary on *Vayikra* 26, as well as *Kuzari* 1:103-115, cited by Abarbanel.
8. For further discussion, see my "Immortality: Two Models," in *Jewish Philosophy Past and Present: Contemporary Responses to Classical Sources*, eds. Daniel Frank and Aaron Segal, Routledge 2017.

Chasdai Kreskas goes on to say (*Or Hashem* 2:6:1), "Given that this is so, it follows that is to be understood also regarding the eternal compensation. I mean to say that it is not proper that this love [of God] should be for the purpose of the World to Come." To serve God with an eye toward *Olam Ha-ba* is to serve for the wrong reason, or from an improper motive. It bespeaks a failure to appreciate the good that is internal to *avodat Hashem*. Or as C.S. Lewis would put it in his autobiography, *Surprised by Joy*:

> My conversion involved as yet no belief in a future life. I now number it among my greatest mercies that I was permitted for several months, perhaps for a year, to know God and to attempt obedience without even raising that question…I had been brought up to believe that goodness was goodness only if it were disinterested, and that any hope of reward or fear of punishment contaminated the will. (p. 231)

The connection between Antigonus's animating idea and a misplaced focus on *Olam Ha-ba* seems to be made explicit in a passage in the *Sifrei Eikev* 41, which is cited by Rambam:

> "To love the Lord your God": Lest you say, 'I will study Torah in order to become wealthy, in order to be called Rabbi, **in order that I shall receive recompense in the World to Come**,' the verse says: "To love the Lord your God;" all that you do you should do only from love. (*Hilkhot Teshuva* 10:4; emphasis mine)[9]

But contrary to initial appearances, I don't think Antigonus's dictum or the passage from the *Sifrei* can bear the weight it is being asked to

---

9. See also the well-known story told of the Gra's delight in being able to "transfer" his eternal reward for the mitzva of *arba minim* to a Polish noblewoman, so as to ideally fulfill the dictum of Antigonus (*Halakhic Man* p. 30).

bear.¹⁰ In order to justify an exclusively this-worldly focus, one must adopt either a particularly strong compensatory conception of *Olam Ha-ba* – as something given in exchange for proper worship, rather than as its consummation – or a rather austere conception of proper religious motivation. Sure, if the goods of *Olam Ha-ba* are wholly extrinsic to *avodat Hashem* – in the sense that they are not what *avodat Hashem* is *aimed at* or *intrinsically for* – then it is improper or less than ideal to "have one's eye on them" in serving God. But that isn't what's assumed by Ramchal, the Gra, or others with an other-worldly focus. As Ramchal says:

> When you look further into the matter, you will see that true perfection lies only in clinging to God. This is what King David said (*Tehillim* 73:28), "But as for me, closeness to God is my good" and (*Tehillim* 27:4), "One thing I asked from God; that I seek: that I may dwell in God's house all the days of my life, to gaze on the pleasantness of God..." For only this is the good, while anything besides this that people consider good is really emptiness and mistaken worthlessness. (*Mesillat Yesharim* ch. 1)

Kirvat Elokim is, presumably, hardly extrinsic to *avodat Hashem*.¹¹

Of course, if one assumes a conception of proper religious motivation so austere that *avodat Hashem* properly pursued must involve an exclusive focus on the *avoda* itself, then even an *oved Hashem* who seeks nothing *but* to be an *eved Hashem* is somehow defective in his mitzva observance. But I don't know if any serious traditional Jewish thinker held such a conception – even Rambam allows for, and in fact demands, that a person worship out of his understanding, however infirm, of who the Master is (*Hilkhot Teshuva* 10:4) and with

---

10. For a wide-ranging and penetrating discussion of this issue, see Rav Yitzchak Blau, "Purity of Motivation and Desiring the World to Come," *The Torah U-Madda Journal* 14 (2006-2007), pp. 137-56. Of particular relevance is his treatment of Abarbanel's position on Antigonus.

11. See Rav Tzadok, *Divrei Soferim* 4, cited in Blau ibid. pp. 148-49.

a passionate and unceasing desire to come to know Him (ibid. 10:3).[12] In any case it makes *Olam Ha-ba* a red herring: the problem is not so much that one is oriented toward another world; it's that one is oriented at all. The problematic case as far as the *Sifrei* and Rambam are concerned is that of a person who is motivated by the *compensation* awaiting him in the hereafter – by a good that is thought to be extrinsic to the *avoda* itself – not that of a person who, like David Ha-Melekh, is moved by a desire to dwell eternally in God's house.

(2) It might instead be suggested that the trouble with other-worldliness is that it reinforces a bifurcation between the material and the spiritual, a dualism of body and soul, which is supposedly both unhealthy and contrary to the monistic spirit of *Tanakh*. Thus, the Rav:

> Halakhic man is firmly embedded in this world and does not suffer from the pangs of the dualism of the spiritual and the corporeal, of the soul which ascends on high and the body which descends below. (*Halakhic Man* p. 65)

> I have always felt that due to some erroneous conception, we have actually misunderstood the Judaic anthropology and read into the Biblical texts ideas which stem from an alien source… The sooner Biblical texts are placed in their proper setting – namely, the Oral Tradition with its almost endless religious awareness – the clearer and more certain I am that Judaism does not accent unreservedly the theory of man's isolationism and separatism within the natural order of things. (*Emergence of Ethical Man* p. 6)

But even if we set aside the question of whether *Tanakh* is as monistic as these days it is said to be – and there are perhaps reasons to doubt that it is – it's not clear how that monism is supposed to support a

---

12. This interpretation of Rambam is admittedly controversial. Much turns on how we are to understand the phrase "*oseh ha-emet mipenei she-hu emet*," and which of Rambam's writings we focus on: his Introduction to *Chelek* seems more austere.

position according to which *Olam Ha-ba* exists but we are to pay it little attention.[13] According to Ramban's (and others') characterization of *Olam Ha-ba*, human nature will be transformed (or "reformed" to its Edenic state) in crucial ways – having to do with what we can know and what we desire – but in no way that requires a dualism of body and soul.[14] We will continue to exist as embodied agents, just as we are now. And while Rambam's (and others') characterization of *Olam Ha-ba* does indeed require for its realization a pretty thoroughgoing dualism, any objection to dualism (based on *Tanakh* or otherwise) would therefore be an objection to its very *existence*, not merely to our aiming at it. In short: either one accepts a view according to which *Olam Ha-ba* requires no bifurcation or one doesn't. If the former, then it's not clear why an orientation toward *Olam Ha-ba* reinforces a problematic bifurcation, and if the latter then the very existence of *Olam Ha-ba* is jeopardized by an insistence on monism.

(3) One might finally suggest that the problem in other-worldliness lies not in realms of *bein adam la-Makom* or *bein adam le-atzmo*, but in the realm of *bein adam la-chaveiro*. The point can be put in terms of the ethical *dangers* that accompany escapism, as Rav Jonathan Sacks does in a recent essay:

> Why, if we believe the soul is immortal, that there is life after death and that this world is not all there is, do we not say so more often and more loudly? Because since civilization began, heaven has too often been used as an excuse for injustice and violence down here on earth. What evil can you not commit if you believe you will be rewarded for it in the World to Come? That is the logic of the terrorist and the suicide bomber. It is the logic of those who burned "heretics" at the stake in order,

---

13. On whether *Tanakh* is thoroughly monistic in its human ontology, see Richard Steiner's *Disembodied Souls: The Nefesh in Israel and Kindred Spirits in the Ancient Near East, with an Appendix on the Katumuwa Inscription*, SBL Press 2015.

14. See Ramban's commentary on *Devarim* 30:6 and *Torat Ha-Adam* ed. Chavel, pp. 303-6. For further discussion, see my "Immortality: Two Models."

so they said, to save their immortal souls. Against this horrific mindset the whole of Judaism is a protest. ("Rosh Hashana: A Breath of Life")

Or the point can be put more positively, as the Rav does, in terms of the ethical and social *demands* which cannot be satisfied if one averts one's gaze from this world:[15]

> Halakhic man…fights against life's evil and struggles relentlessly with the wicked kingdom…See what many religions have done to this world on account of their yearning to break through the bounds of concrete reality and escape to the sphere of eternity…Had they not desired to unite with infinity and to merge with transcendence, then they might have been able to do something to aid the widow and orphan… (*Halakhic Man* p. 41)

As ethical beings we have to look evil squarely in the face in order to rectify it – and we have to look at our fellow man in order to address his needs – rather than look away from the world in which we live.[16]

But it's not clear what the nature of this difficulty is supposed to be. It might be intended as a conceptual point, as though there is some conceptual barrier to being both concerned for one's fellow man and intent on addressing evil, on the one hand, and oriented toward an other-worldly end, on the other hand. But there seems to be no such conceptual barrier. Ramchal himself, in his *Da'at Tevunot*, sees man as playing an active, (ideally) deliberate, and integral role in the cosmic drama that culminates in God's dominion over all creation in *Olam Ha-ba*. Whether right or wrong, there doesn't seem to be any conceptual incoherence in this view. Why couldn't we have one eye on the evils of this world and the other eye on the ends we are ultimately aiming for?

---

15. See Nadler ibid. pp. 137-9.
16. As David Shatz pointed out to me, it is worth noting in this context that Zionism, a central facet of much of Modern Orthodoxy, might seem hard to square with an other-worldly attitude for the same sort of reason.

The difficulty might instead be meant as a contingent psychological one, the idea being that given human psychology as it is, we will tend to focus less on what needs to be done in the here-and-now if we consciously attend to our ultimate destiny. But this claim about our psychology can be justified only empirically, and I am aware of no empirical justification for it. Indeed, anecdotal evidence suggests otherwise: is the social net in Charedi circles, where there is much less reticence about *Olam Ha-ba*, any weaker than in Modern Orthodox circles? My experience suggests a negative answer.[17]

In light of the challenges just canvassed to the three suggested rationales, one might considerably weaken the modern stance; rather than prescribing a certain *position* or *broad attitude* toward death and the afterlife, it can be understood as expressing a *sensibility*, one endorsed as the *properly human feeling* regarding these matters, to be sure, but nothing more. Rav Lamm astutely notes a subtle difference between Rambam's criticism of one who grieves too much and his criticism of one who grieves too little:

> One should not be excessive in one's grief over the loss of a relative…and one who excessively grieves over [that which is] the way of the world is a fool…and one who does not grieve as the Rabbis have required is merciless. (*Hilkhot Eivel* 13:11-12)

One who grieves too much is a *tipesh*, a fool, while one who grieves too little is an *akhzari*, a merciless person. The former makes a cognitive error, the latter an affective one. One who grieves too much commits a fundamental mistake regarding the nature of the world and our place in it; while one who grieves too little lacks the emotions that make us human, but makes no such philosophical-theological mistake.

Now, it's true that even the assertion of the propriety of such a this-worldly sensibility is controversial, and at least partially characterizes the

---

17. David Shatz, in his "From Anthropology to Metaphysics: David Hartman on Divine Intervention," in *Jewish Thought in Dialogue: Essays on Thinkers, Theologies, and Moral Theories*, Academic Studies Press 2010, pp. 218-9, makes a similar point about an alleged link between an interventionist theology and a dereliction of ethical duty.

modern stance. But it doesn't seem to capture the full force of the position endorsed by the Rav and other Modern Orthodox thinkers. So I'd like to suggest, in light of some themes that were prominent in Rav Lichtenstein *zt"l*'s thought, two ways of justifying the modern consensus that are perhaps more promising than those suggested earlier.[18]

On a number of occasions Rav Lichtenstein suggested that a central point of contention, perhaps *the* central point of contention, between Centrist Orthodoxy and Charedi Orthodoxy is whether our world – in all its natural, social, cultural, and economic aspects – is fundamentally and on the whole *good*. (That this accurately captures an important ideological division between the camps is yet another reason to prefer the term 'Centrist Orthodox' to the term 'Modern Orthodox.' There isn't anything particularly or uniquely modern about a positive outlook on life. There were pre-modern optimists and modern pessimists.) Rav Lichtenstein, aligning himself on this issue with Centrist Orthodoxy, sees the world we inhabit as abounding in spiritual opportunities, as fundamentally good: "*Va-yar Elokim ki tov*" is our mantra. The contrast to Ramchal's outlook couldn't be more stark. As Ramchal claims in his argument for the primacy of *Olam Ha-ba*:

> For what is man's life in this world! Who is truly happy in this world? "The days of our life are seventy years, and, if exceedingly vigorous, eighty years, and their persistence is but labor and foolishness." (*Tehillim* 90:10) How many different kinds of suffering, and sickness, and pains and burdens! And after all this – death! (*Mesillat Yesharim* ch. 1)

---

18. There is another point to keep in mind, which Rav Lichtenstein discussed in an oral presentation that was transcribed by Rav Dov Karoll (available at https://pagesoffaith.wordpress.com/2013/01/10/4-on-the-afterlife): "Modern Orthodox thinkers generally evince less confidence in – and are perhaps even more skeptical of – the details in aggadic passages in general, and those about the afterlife in particular. But as long as *Olam Ha-ba* is taken for granted, skepticism or ignorance about the details wouldn't seem to justify a this-worldly orientation." Thanks to Will Lee for helpful discussion here.

It's no wonder that with such different assessments of man's well-being in this world, they come to different conclusions regarding the relative values of this world and the next. As the Rav claimed – and as was expressed by Abarbanel and Rav Yehuda Ha-Levi before him – there is genuine *chayyei olam* available in this world.[19] Indeed, we might go further. It *is* a distinctively modern view – one denied by classical thinkers, like Aristotle, and embraced by modern thinkers, such as Marx and Nietzsche – that sees a *special* sort of value in the movement from potentiality to actuality, in the process rather than the product.[20] And that is exactly what is available in this world and *unavailable* in the next. As the Rav says:

> It is this world that constitutes the stage for the *halakha*, the setting for halakhic man's life. It is here that the *halakha* can be implemented to a greater or lesser degree. It is here **that it passes from potentiality to actuality**. (*Halakhic Man* p. 30; emphasis mine)

Speaking about productive human activity more broadly, Rav Lichtenstein says:

> Let us be mindful that this applied even in what seemingly had been a perfect world! "And God saw all that He had made and found it very good." (*Bereishit* 1:31) If all is wonderful and perfect, what need is there for *"le-ovdah?"*...indeed the world was created perfect – but part of that perfection, and one of the components within that order, is human activity. Part of "And He found it very good" is man, not existing simply as a biological being enjoying the world, but rather as a functional being who contributes, creates, and works. (*By His Light: Character and Values in the Service of God* ch. 1)

---

19. See note 7.
20. See Thomas Hurka's introduction to Bernard Suits, *The Grasshopper*, Broadview Press 2014, pp. xx-xxiii.

Olam Ha-zeh is therefore good, *and good in a way that Olam Ha-ba couldn't be*. This is, in effect, Rabbeinu Yona's solution to the tension between the two parts of the *mishna* in *Avot* 4:17: "Better is one hour of good deeds and repentance in this world than the whole of the life of the World to Come. Better is one hour of pleasure in the World to Come than the whole life of this world." One naturally wonders: How could both be true?[21] Rabbeinu Yona replies:

> Because in a short amount of time in this world a person is able to earn the next world...and it is with respect to this that it is said [in the *mishna*] "better is one hour of good deeds and repentance"...as they [good deeds and repentance] are effective in this world and not in the World to Come. (Rabbeinu Yona *Avot* 4:17)

It is important to note that this approach is consistent with – indeed, it might well be entailed by – a means-ends conception of the relationship between *Olam Ha-zeh* and *Olam Ha-ba*, thus resolving the quandary about the point of *Olam Ha-ba*, given an infinitely valuable existence that is available in the here-and-now. Our existence in *Olam Ha-zeh* might be a means, even a mere means, to get to *Olam Ha-ba*, and have unique, even infinite value precisely because of that.

But therein lies the difficulty in relying on this approach to justify the modern insistence on turning *away* from the hereafter. It's one thing to suggest that our world has a certain kind of value that is not shared by *Olam Ha-ba*. It's quite another to demand that one not aim at, or even direct one's attention to, *Olam Ha-ba*. That demand makes little sense assuming *Olam Ha-ba* is indeed man's end, for which his present existence is a means.

Unless, that is, it is man's end only in one sense, but not in another. This brings us to a second way in which we might justify the modern attitude. Rav Chasdai Kreskas also addresses the tension in the *mishna* in *Avot* 4:17, and proposes a crucial and beautiful distinction as a resolution:

---

21. For a development of the question, see *Midrash Shmu'el* ad loc. and Tyron Goldschmidt and Aaron Segal, "The Afterlife in Judaism," eds. Benjamin Matheson and Yujin Nagasawa, *Palgrave Handbook of the Afterlife*, Palgrave Macmillan 2017.

> For from the perspective of the commanded, the ultimate purpose is the love [of God] but from the perspective of the Commander, the ultimate purpose is the bestowal of the good and the eternal attachment to the radiance of His Presence. And they indeed implied and explained in their saying in the *mishna*…: "Better is an hour of repentance and good deeds in this world than the whole of the World to Come" – meaning that the ultimate desire of the true servant and lover [of God] is the service [of God], and toward it is the whole orientation [of his life]… [However,] the ultimate purpose for the Commander was what the *mishna* determined about it, in their saying (ibid.): "Better is one hour of spiritual pleasure in the World to Come than the whole life of this world." (*Or Hashem* 2:6:1)

It is mistaken, on this view, to speak of *the* purpose/*telos* of our this-worldly existence. God's purpose for us (in this life, and in general) is that we bask in His radiance, which can only be fully achieved in *Olam Ha-ba*. Our own "chief end" – that which we value or ought to value most – is worshipping God with everything we have, which can only be done in this world. As in a genuinely loving relationship, each party wants only what is best for the other. Speaking theologically, or from the Divine perspective, the arena of *Olam Ha-ba* is where our purpose is primarily realized; speaking anthropologically, or from the human perspective, it is in *Olam Ha-zeh* that our purpose is primarily realized.

The modern consensus therefore derives, or can be derived, from a turn away from theology in general. Yes, we grant that from God's perspective, *Olam Ha-ba* is our ultimate destiny; so the question of the point of *Olam Ha-ba* doesn't arise. But we are not meant to *adopt* God's perspective. Our knowledge of the Divine perspective is so limited as to make it laughable to try to arrogate it for ourselves. As Rav Lichtenstein was wont to quote, the *Gemara* (*Sanhedrin* 105b) mocks Bilam's pompous self-description as a '*yodei'a da'at Elyon:*' "The thoughts of his own animal he didn't know, the thoughts of on High he knows?" What we can and ought to do instead is humbly try to serve God with all our hearts and all our souls, *ve-sof ha-tova lavo*.

Leavings of Sin:
HaRav Aharon Lichtenstein *zt"l* on *Teshuva*[1]

Rabbi Shlomo Zuckier

Introduction

The *yeshiva* "academic year" begins in *Elul*, a heady and intense time leading up to the *Yamim Nora'im* that centers around *teshuva* (repentance) and self-improvement. The mere memory of that season is liable to invoke feelings of Divine longing and spiritual awakening in *yeshiva* alumni. Despite these stirrings, it can be difficult to embrace the *Yamim Nora'im* spirit for those whose lives are structured not around a *yeshiva* schedule but around vocational, familial, and other responsibilities. While classically the *shul* Rabbi's *Shabbat Shuva derasha* (lecture) was meant to break this monotony and inspire spiritual inspiration, the prevalence of the Rabbinic *derasha* nowadays (at least in the US) dulls the intensity of the *derasha* experience. It is perhaps for this reason that the more noteworthy *teshuva derashot* over the past half-century have been offered not by communal Rabbis but by *Rashei Yeshiva*. Most famous among these, at least in the Modern Orthodox world, are the annual *teshuva derashot* of Rav Joseph B. Soloveitchik, offered from 1964 to 1980, and those of Rav Aharon Lichtenstein, offered from 1985 to 2010 at either the Gruss Institute in Jerusalem or a New York synagogue.

While *derashot* are most potent in the moment, with the indelible impression they make upon their listeners, quality lectures of this sort also have the capacity to be of enduring value. To that end, Pinchas Peli collected and published seven *derashot* of Rav Soloveitchik in his journal

---
1. First published on *The Lehrhaus* website.

Panim el Panim and then in a volume, *Al Ha-Teshuva*, which has since been translated into English.[2] Most recently, consumers of *teshuva* literature will be most excited to learn, twelve of Rav Lichtenstein's *teshuva derashot* have been published, by the *Mishnat Ha-Ral* project through Maggid books. *Return and Renewal: Reflections on Teshuva and Spiritual Growth*,[3] adapted and edited by Rav Michael Berger and Rav Reuven Ziegler, affords access to Rav Lichtenstein's teachings on *teshuva* to a general audience. This publication not only allows for the broader public to study and consider Rav Lichtenstein's teachings regarding *teshuva*, but also consolidates his thoughts on *teshuva* for consideration as part of his broader hashkafic and theological writings.

The topics presented in the book have some range, but all are centrally focused on repentance. They include:

1. considerations of certain halakhic issues regarding *teshuva* – whether it is an obligation or not, and gradations of sin and repentance;
2. the timing of *teshuva* – does it stem from a norm or a time of crisis, and *teshuva* at different stages in one's life;
3. the experience of sin and repentance – undoing and rehabilitating a relationship with God, the motivating factor of *teshuva*, experiencing *teshuva* from a place of mediocrity; and
4. the interaction between *teshuva* and other themes, such as truth, integrity, humility, and joy in *avodat Hashem*.

The book's writing style follows Rav Lichtenstein's inimitable fashion, with complex sentences (somewhat attenuated, given the transcribed oral presentation format) drawing upon both traditional Jewish sources and the occasional reference to classical Western literature to support its arguments. The study mixes halakhic analysis with spiritual reflection and includes some consideration of communal concerns as well. As one would expect from Rav Lichtenstein, the analysis relies not on pat generalizations and platitudes, but on a deep and broad consideration of each topic,

---

2. *On Repentance*, Maggid Books (2017).
3. Maggid Books (2018).

establishing the scope of the topic at hand and staking out particular positions on various issues.

In particular, the style in many of the essays utilizes the "mapping out the topic" approach that would be familiar from Rav Lichtenstein's *Gemara shi'urim*. For one representative example, the essay "*La-Kol Zeman: Teshuva* within Four Time Frames of Our Lives" analyzes the temporal aspect of *teshuva* in a variety of ways: is *teshuva occasional*, responding to a particular sin, or *annual*, to be carried out on a yearly basis independent of sin? Is it meant to be *perennial*, drawing upon previously resolved sins as part of the *teshuva* process, or not? And to what extent should *teshuva* be *perpetual*, carried out daily, because today might be one's last opportunity?

Comparing *Return and Renewal* and *On Repentance*
As regards content, given the proximity and similarities between Rav Lichtenstein's and Rav Soloveitchik's *teshuva derashot*, a comparison between *Return and Renewal* and *On Repentance* is in order. It is only reasonable to compare the *teshuva* writings of one great theologian and leader of Modern Orthodoxy with those of his son-in-law and *talmid muvhak*, who occupied a similar position for much of that audience. An analysis will reveal several points of contact, but also several distinctions between the two works.

Many classic Soloveitchikian themes of *teshuva* are noticeable immediately upon consideration of Rav Lichtenstein's study: the heightened role of confession within *teshuva*; the concept of standing before God; the power of free will; *teshuva* in response to a shock; the concept of breaking the covenant; the exclusivity of *avodat Hashem* as servitude to God; *teshuva* as elevating sins; the comparison between seeking out sins and seeking out leaven before Pesach; crisis as a *mechayyev* (obligating force) of *teshuva*; and a future-oriented rather than past-oriented view of spiritual activity. Some of these can be traced further back as classical Maimonidean or *Brisker* themes, while others are more particularly the Rav's contributions. In any event, Rav Lichtenstein engages his father-in-law's *teshuva* discourse by drawing upon these themes, at times citing the Rav. In fact, the volume's central distinction between two types of sin, to be analyzed below, is explicitly attributed to the Rav:

> The Rav z"l used to speak frequently of "sin," meaning specific actions, and "the ways of sin," the whole context of lifestyle and personality out of which sin develops and by which it is sustained. (*Return and Renewal* p. 16)

At the same time, however, Rav Lichtenstein evidences a fairly explicit shift away from certain Soloveitchikian themes. In comparing Rav Lichtenstein's writing on *teshuva* to the Rav's, the argument from silence is instructive – Rav Lichtenstein leaves out almost completely any discussion of the *avodat ha-Mikdash* (Temple service) on Yom Kippur, whose *teshuva*-related themes comprise a core part of the Rav's *On Repentance*. Relatedly, Rav Lichtenstein avoids significant treatment of less prosaic topics such as the nature of the atonement afforded by the day of Yom Kippur itself, the metaphysics of sin and its stain, and the role of suffering in expiating sin. While avoiding these more abstruse metaphysical topics, Rav Lichtenstein substitutes for them more experiential perspectives. Rather than emphasizing the metaphysics of sin and its impact on the broader world, he focuses on the phenomenology of sin, how it impacts upon the sinner and his or her relationship with themselves and with God. Rather than discussing the nature of Yom Kippur in the *Beit Ha-Mikdash* of years past, Rav Lichtenstein turns to contemporary religiosity, considering what sort of introspection might be necessary for various communities. Even among more prosaic areas of *halakha* that appear frequently in his volume, Rav Lichtenstein avoids overly involved discussion of the halakhic nuances. While these appear more frequently in *On Repentance*, *Return and Renewal* prefers to mention or gesture at them and then move on to focus on the more practical upshot from these discussions. For example, while the Rav dwells at length on the question of whether *teshuva* can be commanded (*On Repentance* pp. 15-18), Rav Lichtenstein notes the question quickly (*Return and Renewal* pp. 64-65), and then spends much more time contemplating whether *teshuva*, and *avodat Hashem* more generally, is most spiritually meaningful and effective if commanded or if merely presented as an opportunity (ibid. pp. 65-68).

There would appear to be two ways to explain this divergence between the topical preferences of these two *gedolim*: one based on audience and genre, and the other based on discrepancies between the religious worldviews of the Rav and Rav Lichtenstein.

As regards audience and genre, Rav Soloveitchik's *derashot* from 1962-1974, on which the book is based, were given in Yiddish to an audience presumed to be able to follow some fairly complex halakhic reasoning and attracted Torah scholars outside of Modern Orthodoxy's immediate orbit. By contrast, Rav Lichtenstein's *derashot* were given from 1985 to 2010 in English either at Kehillath Jeshurun in New York, or at the Gruss Institute in Jerusalem, aimed at a general rather than a *yeshiva* audience. The audience's interest would have been best accommodated by minimizing excursions into complex issues of the *avodat ha-Mikdash* of Yom Kippur, and even complex exposition of questions in "*lomdus*" relating to *teshuva*. The use of more familiar textual sources would allow for paying attention to other matters close to the hearts and minds of the audience, including communal and humanistic concerns.

At the same time, however, the discrepancy might also be explained by reflecting on the distinct worldviews of the two presenters. For the Rav, for whom "out of the sources of *halakha*, a new worldview awaits formulation" (*Halakhic Mind* p. 102), halakhic argumentation is necessarily the beginning and end of any discussion about *teshuva*. For Rav Lichtenstein, *halakha* is certainly the core and basis of the entire institution of *teshuva*, but many other sources of insight exist as well. In particular, contributions from humanistic sources, Jewish and otherwise, provide important reflections on how the process and experience of *teshuva* should be viewed. For example, Socrates' aphorism that "the unexamined life is not worth living" is cited approvingly several times in the volume (pp. 16, 71, 147, and 150). While this approach might not be the focus of a *shi'ur* in *Gemara* and "*lomdus*," for a more general reflection on *teshuva*, this broader palette of prooftexts is appropriate for Rav Lichtenstein. In a sense, then, the works on *teshuva* by these two colossi reflect their approach in their disquisitions on Jewish thought more generally; whereas the Rav was more likely to go into extended and often abstruse halakhic discussion than was Rav Lichtenstein, the latter was more likely to take a broader perspective on the topic at hand and to cite humanist thinkers as sources of authority. Parenthetically, one might compare this distinction regarding the Rav's and Rav Lichtenstein's use of non-Jewish sources to their particular approaches to ethics outside of *halakha*, in *Halakhic Morality*[4] and "Does Jewish Tradition Recognize an Ethic Independent of Halakha"[5] respectively, as I may do on another occasion.

The Volume's Key Question: Moral Repentance or Religious Repentance?
As noted above, there is really one primary question (or "*chakira*") that runs through the various essays in *Return and Renewal* – the distinction between *teshuva* as fixing one's sins and *teshuva* as returning to a better relationship with God. In fact, the theme appears so many times that it approaches the point of redundancy. One wonders whether an alternative organizational structure of the volume might have succeeded in integrating this theme, such that it appeared as a single, lengthy essay rather than being presented again and again (albeit from different perspectives) throughout the volume.

Many questions throughout the volume tie into this core question of moral repentance (fixing one's behavior) versus religious repentance (fixing one's relationship with God). Two sources on *teshuva* in the Torah (*Bamidbar* ch. 5 and *Devarim* ch. 30) and two versions of contemporary confession ("*aval anachnu chatanu*" versus the *al chet* listing) each distinguish between a sin-oriented and relationship-oriented *teshuva*. There are at least five aspects to sin, as is laid out several times in this volume (pp. 44-45, 62-63, 90, 122-123), which map onto the two categories.

---

4. Rav Joseph B. Soloveitchik, *Halakhic Morality: Essays on Ethics and Masorah*, Maggid Books (2017).
5. Rav Aharon Lichtenstein, "Does Jewish Tradition Recognize an Ethic Independent of *Halakha*," first appeared in *Modern Jewish Ethics* (1975), pp. 62-88; reprinted in *Leaves of Faith* Vol. 2, Ktav (2004), ch. 2.

The impetus for *teshuva*, whether it is based on a particular sin or on one's situation (whether individual or communal, whether a state of mediocrity or a crisis), also splits among these two questions. Whether combating sin should ideally be a struggle or not, the nature of communal *teshuva*, and even the distinct emphases between Rosh Ha-Shana and Yom Kippur, tie in to this fundamental question pervading the entire volume. As was so often the case for Rav Lichtenstein's *chakirot*, the reader is asked to embrace both sides[6] of the *chakira*, and to strive for *teshuva* to both repair the sin and the human-Divine relationship.

Themes Relating to Rav Lichtenstein's Broader Oeuvre
While this central question dominates many of the essays from their various perspectives, additional perspectives and issues are taken up throughout the volume as well. Many of these integrate well with themes key to Rav Lichtenstein's worldview more generally, as one might have expected. Possibly most prominent among these themes is the close relationship between *teshuva* and *avodat Hashem* in general. If *teshuva* is meant to repair one's religious ways, an understanding of *teshuva* must confront the nature of religiosity overall. Thus, the halakhic Jew's dual focus on the detailed regimen of *mitzvot* and the sweeping relationship with God (pp. 39-40, and addressed at length in Rav Lichtenstein's article on "Law and Spirituality"[7]) correlates well with both the topic of *avodat Hashem* and with the primary question of this volume. The theme of "commandedness," and the related expectation of a strong work ethic, which is so core to Rav Lichtenstein's conception of religiosity (for both Jews and non-Jews), and discussed (among other places) in "To Cultivate and to Guard,"[8] appears several times as well (pp. 8-9, 24, 66-67, 89-90, 114, 134-135).

A good example of Rav Lichtenstein's characteristic nuance appears in the chapter on "Mediocre *Teshuva* and the *Teshuva* of the Mediocre" (pp.

---

6. https://www.yutorah.org/lectures/lecture.cfm/855907/rabbi-shlomo-zuckier/ בזאת-יבא-אהרן-אל-הקודש-חידושו-של-הראל-בתפיסת-קדושת-מקום-המקדש/.
7. Rav Aharon Lichtenstein, "Law and Spirituality: Defining the Terms," in *Jewish Spirituality and Divine Law*, Orthodox Forum, Ktav (2005), pp. 3-33.
8. From Rav Aharon Lichtenstein, *By His Light: Character and Values in the Service of God*, [reprinted by Maggid Books (2016),] ch. 1.

97-120). While noting, on the one hand, that the Torah is less opposed to mediocrity than are certain nineteenth century thinkers, and that there is still value to *teshuva* of this nature, Rav Lichtenstein also argues that such *teshuva* is "grievously inadequate" (p. 110) and that it is the role of the one doing *teshuva* to do everything they can to escape the limitations of mediocrity. Still, if someone does the best he or she can, and yet falls short of a full and perfect *teshuva*, God accepts the *teshuva*, weighing the effort more heavily than the results, and yielding a process attainable by non-elites.

Teshuva and Religious Humanism

Certain cases in the volume would appear to reflect Rav Lichtenstein's broader orientation as a religious humanist[9] as well. One example of this is his nuanced position (noted above) opposing elitism that excludes most religious practitioners, while at the same time having high expectations for the average person in his stirring push against mediocrity. This religious humanist framework allows each individual to pursue religious excellence on their own level.

Additionally, the question as to whether one should have a certain happiness as they go through the process of *teshuva* is resolved with a "personal, intuitive answer" of "an emphatic yes" (p. 217) and only afterwards proven from sources. This position derives primarily not from a halakhic or hashkafic source, but from Rav Lichtenstein's developed religious humanist reflex that spiritual activities, even when difficult, must be attended by joy. A flourishing religious individual, fulfilling his or her telos of serving God, must be happy, even while fulfilling the difficult task of *teshuva*.

Rav Lichtenstein's strong and consistent advocacy of guilt as a healthy religious reaction to sin throughout the volume (see pp. 62-64, 79-81, 89, 93, 110, 131, 208, 215) reflects his religious humanist worldview where what is demanded of a person is more than conforming certain actions and beliefs, but living a life "as ever in my great Taskmaster's eye," where failure of necessity entails a deep-seated guilt.

---

9. See Shlomo Fischer, "The Religious Humanism of R. Aharon Lichtenstein," *Tradition* 47:4 (2015), pp.17-33.

Related to this is the view that "*teshuva*… is itself a crisis" (p. 130), as the religious individual's personality and life is torn apart as they attempt to reform themselves to properly stand before God again. The humanism inherent in the focus on the experience of the person in their religious experience facilitates the development of these novel formulations.

While being understanding of human weakness and not artificially assuming everyone is an elite scholar, and taking the human experience seriously throughout, this volume still strikes a fairly demanding pose (as one might hope for a volume on *teshuva*): It urges people not to accept the mediocre excuses of the "*beinoni*," the mediocre man (p. 105), and strongly rejects an attitude of fatalism in light of free will (e.g. pp. 1-4). The appropriate modulation of expectations for the religious practitioner is yet another expression of Rav Lichtenstein's religious humanism.

Commentary on the Modern Orthodox Community

In addition to the development of *teshuva* themes of general interest, one feature of the volume is the explicit reflection on the Modern Orthodox community, and, at times, its contrast to more Charedi communities. Acolytes of Rav Lichtenstein will be familiar with some of these reflections from his articles "The Future of Centrist Orthodoxy"[10] and "Centrist Orthodoxy: A Spiritual Accounting,"[11] but the added valence of *teshuva* provides for new perspectives and makes these comments pack an additional punch.

As in those articles, a critical angle is often taken towards Modern Orthodox apathy. For example, the community is accused of lacking the proper passion in prayer:

> For the Modern Orthodox Jew and his community in particular, the inclination and the capacity to pray properly and with passion, with a plaintive *cri de coeur* issuing *mi-ma'amakim*, from the depths, is often sadly deficient. (*Return and Renewal* p. 31)

---

10. *Leaves of Faith* Vol. 2 ch. 15.
11. *By His Light* ch. 12.

In his discussion of *timhon levav*, or the role of wondering, Rav Lichtenstein critiques both the Charedi and the Modern Orthodox worlds for failing to find the proper balance between introspection and self-certainty:

> [For the Charedi world] there is no *timhon levav* at all – just passionate certitude, never to walk against your best light, yet never examining what is the nature of that light…. In the Centrist world, by contrast, there is a surfeit of *timhon levav*… While the Charedi world is so certain that it, and it alone, has absolute, comprehensive, detailed truth, the individual in the Religious-Zionist world often doubts its ideals and its ideology, its goals and its methods. Riven by conflicting loyalties, driven by a quest for integration, he finds himself in a state of tension. He likes to see that tension as creative – it has an appealing ring – but on the other hand, he's not quite certain. (Ibid. pp. 155-156)

Certitude can't come at the expense of introspection, nor can an abundance of wondering at the propriety of one's religious community and its goals come at the expense of passion in living that life. This honest reflection on the limitations of both communities in this connection, is developed at length in the essay "Centrist Orthodoxy: A Spiritual Accounting."

The comfortable state of Modern Orthodoxy is representative of the modern era and its relative stability (certainly as compared to the poverty and high mortality rates of years past), which can lead to a sort of calmness and even lack of focus. To that end, Rav Lichtenstein notes the risk of being lulled into a sense of security:

> I need to focus upon the besetting sin, the inherent danger, of the Modern Orthodox community, the danger against which we need to be on our perpetual guard. That danger is, quite clearly, *heise'ach ha-da'at*, spiritual and religious inattentiveness. (Ibid. pp. 73-74)

One notes a similarity in themes to his previous essays, "*Bittachon*: Trust in God"[12] and "When My Soul was Faint Within Me I Remembered God,"[13] as the community is charged to be attentive, to both investigate spiritual deficiencies and do what they can to fix them.

Conclusion

The essays collected in this new volume aim primarily not at an analytical study of *teshuva* but at the phenomenological perspective of a religious humanist. Traditional Jewish sources, studded by references to the Western canon, form the backdrop against which success or failure to live up to one's personal or communal religious obligations must measure up. This volume develops the concept that sin creates a rupture, both on a local level and as it reflects on the relationship between the *oved Hashem* and his God, each of which must be repaired by the penitent. The many insights into *teshuva* included in the volume are deeply nuanced, and are of a piece with Rav Lichtenstein's writings more broadly.

The subtitle of this study by Rav Lichtenstein is "Reflections on *Teshuva* and Spiritual Growth." That description is certainly accurate, but what the volume offers goes beyond that. Each essay contains within it a charge – some more explicit than others, often directed at the individual, at times directed at the community – pushing for growth in *avodat Hashem*. For a religious community that has produced few *mussar* books, this volume's subtle yet powerful religious thrust is significant. Even where the text does not explicitly call upon the individual in the second person, the tone and humanity of its pieces, the piercing ability to reach people on their own level, forces the reader to confront his or her own situation as they read this text.

The presumed readership of this volume is American and English-reading Orthodoxy writ large. To a large extent, this community might be described, with a critical eye, as composed of two groups: those who see Judaism as a mere adornment, embraced primarily to enhance quality of life, on the one hand, and those fully focused on studying Torah (and

---

12. *By His Light* ch. 7.
13. Rav Haim Sabato, *Seeking His Presence: Conversations with Rabbi Aharon Lichtenstein*, Yedioth Books and Chemed Books (2016), pp. 121-133.

facilitating such study), to the absolute exclusion of any other endeavor. This volume, framed by the context of *teshuva*, offers a third way: a Judaism that is based on the Divine command and the imperative of *avodat Hashem* – Divine service and maybe even servitude – but also offers a broad, textured approach to the world, one that values literature and the humanities, eschews religious extremism, and accepts the world's complexity. Of course, this worldview can be gleaned from Rav Lichtenstein's other writings as well, but it is in some ways more powerful to see such an integrative religious worldview come to life in a series of *derashot* on *teshuva*.

Although Rav Lichtenstein has left this world, his enduring legacy – as regards *teshuva* but also about *avodat Hashem* in general – lives on, as this volume furthers the return and renewal of his teachings.

The Obligation to Teach Torah to One's Post-*Bar Mitzva* Child

Rabbi Michael Taubes

- I -

In a section of the Torah that is well known because it is recited twice daily as part of the second paragraph of *Keri'at Shema*, we are told that there is a mitzva incumbent upon a parent to teach his children (*Devarim* 11:19). The *Gemara* in *Kiddushin* (29a) indeed cites this verse as the source for the requirement to teach Torah to one's child; Rambam in his *Sefer Ha-Mitzvot* (positive 11) identifies this obligation as part of the mitzva known as *talmud Torah*, though he initially points to an earlier verse in the Torah (ibid. 6:7), recited as part of the first paragraph of *Keri'at Shema*, as the primary source.[1] He notes, though, as does *Sefer Ha-Chinnukh* (mitzva 419), among others, that this mitzva is in fact alluded to in a number of verses in the Torah and discussed in numerous places throughout the *Gemara*. In his *Mishneh Torah* (*Hilkhot Talmud Torah* 1:1), Rambam codifies this requirement that a father must teach Torah to his child, this time citing the first verse quoted above, and *Shulchan Arukh* (YD 245:1) rules accordingly.

At what age does this obligation begin? The *Gemara* in *Sukka* (42a) states that this obligation to teach Torah to one's child goes into effect as soon as the child learns how to talk (this idea is also found in *Sifrei Devarim* 46), at which time the father should teach him certain famous verses from the Torah (*Devarim* 33:4 and 6:6).[2] *Arukh Ha-Shulchan* (YD 245:1) points

---

1. Rav Achai Ga'on, in *She'iltot Parashat Va'etchanan she'ilta* 142, does so as well; see Netziv's *Ha'amek She'eila* there, no. 1, for an explanation of the differences between the sources.
2. Ra'avya (2:699) and Mordekhai in *Sukka* (no. 763) cite a passage from the *Yerushalmi* (not found in our standard texts) which identifies a verse from *Mishlei* (1:8) to be taught to a child; see also *Or Zaru'a* (2:314).

out that these particular verses serve to implant certain fundamental Jewish principles into the young child's heart. It is clear from *Tosafot* earlier in *Sukka* (28b s.v. *kan*) as well as in *Berakhot* (20a s.v. *u-ktanim*) that the age when the child knows how to speak is indeed the proper age to begin training him in Torah, and Ran (*Sukka* 13a in *Rif* s.v. *heikhi dami*) agrees. Rambam (*Hilkhot Talmud Torah* 1:6) and *Shulchan Arukh* (YD 245:5) thus rule that the requirement to teach Torah to one's child begins as soon as the child starts to talk.

The *Gemara* in *Ketubbot* (50a) presents certain details regarding how to deal with one's child when teaching him Torah, regarding the age at which he should be taught and the style of teaching that is appropriate for each age (as elucidated by Rashi there s.v. *megalgel, yoreid, ve-safei*), and regarding the specific material that should be taught at particular ages. The *rishonim* there, including Tosafot (s.v. *she-yehei, ve-safei, bar*), elaborate on some of these details and in so doing, reconcile them with the ideas presented in the *mishna* in *Avot* (5:21) which also discusses the appropriate ages at which a child should be taught different segments of Torah.

The *Gemara* in *Bava Batra* (21a) calls for Torah teachers to be placed in every district or town at the shared expense (as implied by Rashi s.v. *lo mamtinan*) of the town's residents,[3] an obligation codified by Rambam (*Hilkhot Talmud Torah* 2:1) and in *Shulchan Arukh* (YD 245:7); the precise age at which a child could be sent to those teachers would depend upon the nature of the child, as pointed out by Tosafot there (s.v. *ke-ven, be-vatzir*) and as actually already noted by the above cited *Gemara* in *Ketubbot*.[4] Based upon this, Rambam (ibid. 1:6; see also *Lechem Mishneh* there) writes that one should teach one's child little by little when he is very young until he reaches the proper age to be brought to a teacher, which he details later

---

3. The placement of teachers in these locations served, as explained there by Ritva (s.v. *ve-adayin*), and amplified by Maharsha (*Chiddushei Aggadot* s.v. *she-yihyu*), to enable even young children, who previously could not safely get to the teachers who were further away, to learn Torah because it was now taught closer to home.
4. *Shulchan Arukh Ha-Rav* (*Hilkhot Talmud Torah* 1, *Kunteres Acharon* no. 1) discusses the benefits of having teachers, and asserts that in certain situations, the father's obligation is not necessarily to teach the child himself, but to see to it that he has suitable teachers.

The Obligation to Teach Torah to One's Post-*Bar Mitzva* Child | 347

(ibid. 2:2; see *Hagahot Maimoniyyot* there no. 2). *Shulchan Arukh* (ibid. nos. 5 and 8) codifies this as well, although there are some differences of opinion as to exactly what should be done at what age, depending upon the child, as outlined in the aforementioned sources.[5]

It seems clear, then, that the primary focus of the mitzva of teaching Torah is upon teaching a child when he is quite young, certainly before the age of *Bar Mitzva*. Presumably, this is because when the child reaches the age of *Bar Mitzva*, he becomes obligated on his own to learn Torah, just as he becomes obligated on his own to observe all other *mitzvot*.[6] The question may therefore be raised as to whether or not there is any obligation to teach Torah to one's child, or to see to it that he is taught by someone else, once the child has reached the age of *Bar Mitzva*.

- II -

Bach, in his commentary on *Tur* (YD 245, s.v. *mitzvot*), writes that the aforementioned verse from the second paragraph of *Keri'at Shema*, which, as noted above, is a primary source for the mitzva to teach Torah to one's child, implies that there is an obligation to teach *even* one's young child (who is under the age of *Bar Mitzva*), suggesting that there is certainly an obligation to teach Torah to one's child who is over the age of *Bar Mitzva*. This is despite the fact, or possibly even because of the fact, as indeed may perhaps be inferred from Bach's presentation, that at that age the child has his own independent requirement to study Torah. In other words, it may be that when the child has his own obligation to learn Torah because he

---

5. See *Shakh* there no. 3 and *Bi'ur Ha-Gra* there nos. 17-19.
6. It is true that the *Gemara* in *Bava Batra* cited above does speak of teachers with students who are sixteen and seventeen years old, but that scenario is not mentioned as the ideal; the ideal, as explained by Ritva and Maharsha (quoted in the body) is to have a situation where the younger children are able to be taught Torah. It is also true that the *Gemara* in *Kiddushin* (30a) speaks of a person having control over his child in terms of instructing, directing, and positively influencing him when the child is specifically between the ages of sixteen and twenty-two or eighteen and twenty-four (depending upon two different understandings of the word "youth" in *Mishlei* 22:6, which speaks of training a youth); in either case the child is obviously over the age of *Bar Mitzva*. But the subject there does not appear to be *talmud Torah* but rather, as explained by Rashi (s.v. *a-didakh, mi-shitsar*), either marriage or a kind of general ethical or moral guidance.

is a *Bar Mitzva*, his father is certainly obligated to teach him; the point of the verse is that even when the child has no obligation of his own to learn because he is under the age of *Bar Mitzva*, it is still incumbent upon the father to teach him nonetheless. According to this approach, then, the mitzva to teach one's child applies regardless of the age of the child.

Arukh Ha-Shulchan (quoted above) also states that the implication of the verse is that one is obligated to teach Torah to his child whether the child is old (over the age of *Bar Mitzva*) or young (below the age of *Bar Mitzva*). He too indicates that this is the case even though the child below the age of *Bar Mitzva* is not required to learn, suggesting that it is specifically to such a child, one who is under the age of *Bar Mitzva*, that the verse primarily addresses itself.[7] Apparently, it is more obvious that one must teach Torah to one's child who his past the age of *Bar Mitzva*; there would thus seem to be an obligation to teach Torah to one's child even once the child has become an adult.

Shulchan Arukh Ha-Rav (*Hilkhot Talmud Torah* 1:6) likewise appears to maintain that the verse is talking about teaching Torah to a child under the age of *Bar Mitzva*. He adds, though, seemingly referring to a child of any age, that any time that a child has the capability to involve himself in Torah study but does not do so, if the father has the wherewithal to positively intervene, the father has an obligation to involve his child in Torah study. He further notes, based upon the *Gemara* in *Kiddushin* (30a), that a father must guide his son along the path of *mussar* and *yirat Shamayim* as long as he still has some control over him, meaning, as *Shulchan Arukh Ha-Rav* rules, until the child reaches the age of twenty-four. In his concluding statement, he writes that when the child is past this age, the father should not heavily rebuke or punish him because, as explained by Rashi (*Kiddushin* ibid. s.v. *mi-shitsar*), he may consequently rebel completely. The implication of this statement, though, is that if the father is able to positively influence his child in some other, less threatening manner, it remains his obligation to

---

7. See his citation of the *Gemara* in *Sanhedrin* (68b), which he interprets as understanding that the verse indeed focuses upon a person who is not an adult.

do so, regardless of the child's age.⁸ This certainly seems to be the position of Me'iri (*Beit Ha-Bechira* to *Kiddushin* 30a s.v. *le-olam*), who writes that one must always devote attention to supervising his children and regularly guide them whether they are old or young. He further affirms that the best time to try and exert influence upon the child is when the child is between sixteen and twenty-four, but it is nevertheless important for the father to always try to guide his child in the appropriate fashion.

According to these authorities, although the verse seems to be focusing primarily upon teaching Torah to a younger child, under the age of *Bar Mitzva*, the father's obligation to teach him actually extends well beyond that age. In other words, they assume a broader definition of the obligation than that specifically included in the verse. The Rogatchover Ga'on, however (*Tzafenat Panei'ach* Responsa, Dvinsk Edition 2:10), appears to learn that the verse itself in fact refers to teaching Torah to one who is over the age of *Bar Mitzva* as well, noting that there are different aspects to the mitzva of *talmud Torah* which may apply at different times.⁹ He maintains that the obligation upon a father to teach Torah to his child which is discussed in the *Gemara* in *Kiddushin* (30a) is certainly referring to an adult child, just as the obligation presented earlier there (29a) to marry off one's child is clearly applicable specifically to an adult child.

It is possible that this idea is agreed to by Me'iri in *Kiddushin* (30a s.v. *ein*), who writes that the father's requirement is to teach Torah to his child until the point that the child knows all about the *mitzvot*. Depending upon the aptitude of the particular child and the specific level of knowledge about the *mitzvot* that this obligation demands (which is not made clear), it is certainly conceivable that this obligation to teach one's child about *mitzvot*

---

8. It is noteworthy that *Shulchan Arukh Ha-Rav* there (no. 3, and in *Kunteres Acharon* no. 3) does indicate that the communal obligation to establish Torah teachers in each town, as presented above, applies only to providing teachers for children below the age of *Bar Mitzva*, and he explains the reason for this.

9. His discussion there is about whether a *siyyum* celebrated by a child under the age of *Bar Mitzva* who has completed learning an entire *masekhet* qualifies to exempt adult first-borns from fasting on *Erev* Pesach, when, as summarized by *Mishna Berura* (OC 410:10) and others, it is customary in many places for firstborns to participate in the festive meal associated with a *siyyum* in order to avoid fasting on that day.

extends to a child who is above the age of *Bar Mitzva* as well, especially with regard to teaching him about certain *mitzvot* that a younger child may have difficulty comprehending. It would thus seem that the father's mitzva to teach Torah to his child remains incumbent upon him even after the child has become a *Bar Mitzva*.

It should be pointed out that Rav Aharon Soloveichik, in his commentary on Rambam (*Parach Mattei Aharon* to *Hilkhot Talmud Torah* 1:1), writes explicitly that one should not interpret Rambam, who speaks specifically of a father teaching Torah to his young son, as implying that the obligation to teach Torah to one's child is limited to teaching a child under the age of *Bar Mitzva*. Rather, there is an obligation upon the father to teach Torah to a child who is over the age of *Bar Mitzva* as well. According to this view, then, Rambam too may be numbered among those who hold that one is certainly obligated to teach Torah even to one's older children, despite the fact that he does not expressly say so. In light of the above, it would appear that this position, that it is indeed incumbent upon a father to teach Torah even to his child who is beyond the age of *Bar Mitzva*, reflects the consensus opinion of the commentaries, although they may not all arrive at it in an identical fashion.

- III -

Rav Ya'akov Emden, in his *Sefer Migdal Oz* (*otzar* 6 section 3 no. 29), offers an interesting suggestion as to why a father must see to it that his son is involved in the pursuit of Torah specifically after reaching the age of *Bar Mitzva*. He notes that it is at that age, as he becomes an adult, that the *yetzer ha-ra* begins to try to take over the person and tempt him to do the wrong things. He then quotes a homiletic idea expressed by Chazal which is hinted at by the first *mishna* in *Pesachim* (2a), which speaks of searching for *chametz* by the light of a flame on the eve of the fourteenth (of *Nisan*). The homily teaches that on the eve, or the advent, of the fourteenth year of one's life, that is, when one becomes a *Bar Mitzva*, one should search for and take hold of his *yetzer ha-ra*, which is identified with *chametz* (see, for example, *Berakhot* 17a and Rashi there s.v. *se'or*). To do so, one uses the flame of God, representing the *neshama*, the soul, as stated by the verse in *Mishlei* (20:27), which is fueled by Torah and *mitzvot*. The father of this young man, he continues, must thus specifically at this time, after the boy has become a *Bar Mitzva*, see to it that the child is properly supervised in terms of his Torah growth and placed under the guidance of someone who will ensure that he behaves in accordance with Torah precepts. In short, the obligation to teach one's child Torah begins, in a certain sense, or at least intensifies, when the child reaches the age of *Bar Mitzva*.

This idea may be related to the fact that according to the *beraita* in *Avot De-Rabbi Natan* (16:2) and the *midrash* in *Kohelet Rabba* (4:15), among other places, we learn that the *yetzer ha-tov* first enters a person when he reaches the age of thirteen, a point mentioned as well by Rosh in *Nedarim* (32b s.v. *ish*).[10] This in turn seems to indicate, first, that the *yetzer ha-tov* is associated with the study and knowledge of Torah, in which case it certainly makes sense to say that when the child has his *yetzer ha-tov* implanted within him at the age of thirteen, his involvement in Torah study should increase. Perhaps, then, it is specifically when he reaches that age that his father is obligated to teach him Torah. Second, we may deduce that when the child becomes thirteen and the *yetzer ha-tov* enters in order to do battle with the strengthening *yetzer ha-ra*, as elaborated upon by Chida in his *Midbar Kedimot* (*Ma'arekhet Yod* no. 36), the study of Torah is perhaps more important than ever for this child so that the battle will turn out well. It is thus when he reaches this age that his father must see that he is taught Torah properly.

Along these lines, Rav Pinchas Ha-Levi Horowitz, in the introduction to his *Sefer Hafla'a* on *Ketubbot* (*Pitcha Ze'ira* no. 16), criticizes the apparently then-prevalent practice of teaching one's child as much as possible until he reaches the age of thirteen, presumably in fulfillment of this mitzva to teach Torah to one's child, and then to leave him alone and, in effect, let

---

10. According to *Piskei Tosafot* in *Nedarim* there (no. 62), the *yetzer ha-tov* is initially implanted when the child is still in his mother's womb, at which time he learns the entire Torah, as discussed by the *Gemara* in *Nidda* (30b), and when he is born, the *yetzer ha-ra* immediately enters and chases the *yetzer ha-tov* away until the child becomes intellectually mature (i.e. at age thirteen), and the *yetzer ha-tov* then returns.

him run wild and do as he pleases. On the contrary, he asserts, the arrival of the *yetzer ha-tov* when the child turns thirteen should be a reason to teach him more Torah and inspire him to rise to higher levels of sanctity; it is specifically at that point that the "good" represented by the *yetzer ha-tov* should be accompanied by the "good" represented by *talmud Torah*, and it is thus the obligation of the father to guide the child accordingly.

- IV -

In addition to the above, there is perhaps another reason to suggest that the obligation upon a father to teach Torah to his child continues even after the child becomes a *Bar Mitzva*. Rav Tzvi Pesach Frank, in his *Har Tzvi* on the Torah (*Devarim* 6:6 s.v. *ve-hayu*), presents a question raised by Rav Re'uven Grozovsky as to the nature of the father's mitzva to teach Torah to his son. On the one hand, it could simply be one of the regular obligations of a father regarding his son, similar to his obligation to see to it that his son has a *brit mila* and *pidyon ha-ben*, since the mitzva to teach one's son Torah is recorded together with those other *mitzvot* in the *Gemara* in *Kiddushin* (29a).

On the other hand, though, it could be that the obligation to teach Torah to one's son is part of one's own obligation to learn Torah, meaning that just as one is required to learn Torah himself, as discussed in a number of places in the *Gemara* (see, for example, *Yoma* 35b), and as codified by Rambam (*Hilkhot Talmud Torah* 1:8) and *Shulchan Arukh* (YD 246:1[11]), so too, as an extension of that requirement, one must teach Torah to one's child. He clearly prefers the latter position, and then cites a statement of the Gra (*Bi'ur Ha-Gra* YD 245:7) that the mitzva of *talmud Torah* requiring one to teach Torah to one's child is not parallel to other *mitzvot* such as seeing that one's son has a *brit mila*; it is rather part of the father's own mitzva to learn. He also explains how this may be seen from the *pesukim*. *Birkat Shmu'el* to *Kiddushin* (27:3) also records and elaborates upon this position of the Gra, demonstrating that there are different aspects to the mitzva of *talmud Torah*, and citing a subsequent statement of the Gra there (no. 16) which further shows the direct connection between teaching one's children and learning on one's own.

---

11. See also OC 155:1 and *Bi'ur Halakha* there, s.v. *ve-yikba*.

It is possible that this position relating to learning and teaching one's children is agreed to as well by the aforementioned Rambam (*Sefer Ha-Mitzvot* positive 11), who describes the mitzva of *talmud Torah* as demanding that one must learn and teach, linking the two together as part of the same mitzva, and implying that the obligation to teach Torah is an extension of the obligation to learn Torah. *Sefer Ha-Chinnukh* (mitzva 419) and *Semag* (positive 12) likewise tie together the obligation to teach Torah and the obligation to learn Torah under one mitzva, even though there are those who count learning Torah and teaching Torah as two distinct *mitzvot*.[12] *Shulchan Arukh Ha-Rav* (*Hilkhot Talmud Torah* ibid. no. 7) states explicitly that when a child learns Torah as facilitated by his father, the father fulfills a mitzva *mi-de'oraita* just as he does when he learns by himself, again implying that enabling one's child to study Torah is part of one's own mitzva to learn.

If this is true, it is possible to suggest that inasmuch as one's obligation to learn Torah himself lasts for one's entire lifetime, as implied by the *Gemara* in *Shabbat* (83b), and as stated by Rambam (*Hilkhot Talmud Torah* ibid. no. 10) and *Shulchan Arukh* (YD 246:3), then one's obligation to teach Torah to one's child also lasts for one's entire lifetime, as long as he has a child to teach, regardless of whether the child is over or under the age of *Bar Mitzva*. It is perhaps in consideration of all of the above that the Steipler Ga'on, as reported in *Sefer Orchot Rabbeinu* (vol. 1 p. 190), used to set aside time on a regular basis to learn with his son Rav Chayyim Kanievsky even when the latter was above the age of *Bar Mitzva* and even after he was married (and, we may add, a great *talmid chakham* in his own right). The Steipler followed this practice in order to fulfill this mitzva to teach Torah to one's child, and he did so even when he was weak and suffering with illness and pain until, nearing his death, he was physically unable to continue. The Steipler thus clearly maintains that there is an ongoing obligation to teach one's child, regardless of the child's age.

As an aside, there may be a practical halakhic ramification as to whether or not there exists an obligation upon a father to teach his child once the

---

12. See, among others, Rav Sa'adya Ga'on positive 14-15, *Sefer Halakhot Gedolot kum va-asei* 38-39, *Yerei'im* no. 25-6, and *Semak* no. 105-6.

child is above the age of *Bar Mitzva*, namely, regarding the question of using *tzedaka* money designated as *ma'aser kesafim* for the purpose of paying for one's child to be able to learn Torah. Rambam (*Hilkhot Talmud Torah* ibid. no. 3) and *Shulchan Arukh* (YD 245:4) rule that one must hire someone to teach Torah to the child whose Torah education is his responsibility. Concerning the money that one has set aside for *tzedaka* as *ma'aser kesafim* (constituting one tenth of one's income), Rema (YD 249:1) states that it may not be used for any other mitzva purpose. Although some authorities[13] quote *poskim* who allow using this money for certain *mitzvot*, the consensus, as presented, for example, in *Chokhmat Adam* (144:11), is that one may not use these funds towards the fulfillment of a mitzva in which he is obligated, but one may use them towards the fulfillment of a mitzva which is not obligatory.[14]

If, therefore, teaching Torah to one's child who is above the age of *Bar Mitzva* is indeed obligatory, it would consequently be forbidden to use one's *ma'aser* money to pay for his child to be taught. The situation would thus be the same as with younger children whose Torah education may not be paid for with *ma'aser* funds because the father is obligated to see to this education, as explained by, among others, Rav Moshe Feinstein (*Iggerot Moshe* YD 2:113).[15] Chafetz Chayyim, in his *Ahavat Chesed* (part 2, *Inyan Ma'aser Kesafim* 19:2), rules that one may not use *ma'aser* money to pay for the teaching of one's children because it is the father's obligation to either teach them or hire someone else to do so. Since he makes no mention of the age of these children, Chafetz Chaim seems to be saying that the father's obligation remains in effect even after the children have passed the age of *Bar Mitzva*, and thus at no time may *ma'aser* funds be used for one's children's Torah education. He apparently agrees, then, that the mitzva to teach one's child Torah applies to a child who is over the age of *Bar Mitzva* as well.

---

13. See, for example, *Shakh* (YD ibid. no. 3) and *Taz* (ibid. no. 1), among others.
14. See *Be'er Ha-Gola* (ibid. note "*hei*") and *Pitchei Teshuva* (ibid. no. 2).
15. See, however, Rav Eli'ezer Yehuda Waldenberg, *Tzitz Eli'ezer* (9:1), for a comprehensive discussion of the topic of *ma'aser kesafim*; in chapters 4 and 5 there he explores this issue of using *ma'aser* money for the Torah education of one's children, both young and old.

- V -

In conclusion, it is worthwhile to cite a message from Shelah (*Sha'ar Ha-Otiyyot, Derekh Eretz* s.v. *atta*) regarding teaching Torah to one's child. He writes that in order to fulfill this obligation, one must be willing to invest tremendous personal effort and expense. He should start teaching his child when the child is young,[16] in accordance with his ability, offering rewards that will make the learning attractive to him, and steadily increase those rewards to make them commensurate with what the child wishes as he advances in age, including the "enticement" of an outstanding life, an opportunity to earn a respected title and position, and the ultimate reward in *Olam Ha-ba*. It is obvious from the examples given that Shelah is speaking about teaching not only young children, but also children well beyond the age of *Bar Mitzva*, clearly indicating that the mitzva to teach one's child Torah applies even when the child is older. He also writes there (s.v. *ve-tamid*) that one should always pray for the success of one's children in terms of their Torah learning, righteousness, and general proper behavior; this is certainly appropriate no matter how old the child is.

Since its inception, the particular mission of Yeshivat Har Etzion has been to teach students above the age of *Bar Mitzva* and to inculcate in those young men who fill its *beit midrash* a love and passion for learning Torah at the highest of levels, an uncompromising commitment to *mitzvot*, and a deep and penetrating sense of *yirat Shamayim*; in short – everything that a father should want to teach his son as he grows and matures, and indeed at any age. The unforgettable *Rashei Yeshiva*, HaRav Yehuda Amital *zt"l* and HaRav Aharon Lichtenstein *zt"l*, were living embodiments of the very values they taught and as such were ideal mentors, teaching in the best possible way: by example. As a beneficiary myself of their efforts, I am truly honored to be part of this milestone event in the history of their *yeshiva*.

---

16. *Arukh Ha-Shulchan* (YD 245:5) notes that if a child does not study Torah as a youngster, he will likely go off the proper path as an adult. See also the comments of *Chazon Ish* to *Kiddushin* 30a (s.v. *ve-illu*, in *Even Ha-Ezer, Nashim* no. 148) about teaching one's child Torah as a means of guiding him to keep the ways of God.

The Arrival of Rabbi Akiva[1]

Rabbi Ari Kahn

Rabbi Akiva says, "If you studied Torah in your youth, study in your old age [as well]; if you had students in your youth, take students in your old age [as well]. As it says, 'In the morning plant your seeds, etc. [and in the evening do not withhold your hand; for you do not know which shall prosper, either this or that, or whether they both alike shall be good.]'" It was said that Rabbi Akiva had twelve thousand pairs of disciples, from *Gevat* to *Antipatris*; and all of them died in the same period of time, because they did not treat one another with respect. The world remained desolate until Rabbi Akiva came to our masters in the south and taught the Torah to them. These were Rabbi Me'ir, Rabbi Yehuda, Rabbi Yosei, Rabbi Shimon and Rabbi Elazar ben Shammu'a; and it was they who revived the Torah at that time. A *tanna* taught: "All of them died between Pesach and Shavu'ot." Rabbi Chama bar Abba or, some say, Rabbi Chiyya bar Avin, said: "All of them died a cruel death." What was it? Rav Nachman replied: "Croup."[2] (*Yevamot* 62b)[3]

What Kind of Students?

One of the greatest teachers in the annals of Jewish learning, the unparalleled Rabbi Akiva, suffered many tragic losses. In this passage, the *Gemara* tells us that thousands of his students perished: In one particular period of time, twenty-four thousand victims, or, to be more precise, twelve thousand

---

1. This essay is an excerpt from a forthcoming volume on *aggadot* called *The Crowns on the Letters*.
2. Croup ("*askara*") is specifically associated with slander, the quintessential sin in the realm of interpersonal relations. See *Shabbat* 33a-b.
3. See *Bereishit Rabba* 61:3, *Kohelet Rabba* 11, *Yalkut Shimoni Kohelet* section 989, for parallel sources. Also see *Tana De-Vei Eliyahu Zuta* chapter 22.

"pairs" of his students, died. The fact that they are specifically referred to as "pairs of students," and not as twenty-four thousand individuals, serves to reinforce the explanation for this unthinkable tragedy: They did not treat one another with respect. They died during the *Omer*, the period between Pesach and Shavu'ot that, as a result of this tragedy, was transformed from a time of festive anticipation between two of the highest points in the Jewish calendar, into a period of mourning.[4]

This passage is nothing short of mystifying – on several levels: First and foremost, how can a teacher as great as Rabbi Akiva have raised such a great number of failed students? This nagging incongruity forces us to search other Talmudic passages that refer to students of Rabbi Akiva, and to examine their personal comportment. Alas, there is no dearth of reports of less-than-stellar behavior by students or others in Rabbi Akiva's inner circle.

Love

On the other hand, we find Rabbi Akiva stressing to his students, "Love your neighbor as yourself," (*Vayikra* 19:18) and adding, "This is the great principle of the Torah."

While Rabbi Akiva himself is generally remembered as one of the most saintly, holy, caring individuals in our history, this is an uncomfortable aspect of his biography that gives us pause: the tragic deaths of thousands of his students, deaths which the *Gemara* attributes to a lack of love, honor, and mutual respect among them.

While in general it may be unfair to judge parents for the behavior of their children or teachers for either the failures or accomplishments of their students, the "disconnect" between this particular teacher and these particular students causes us no small degree of wonder, and perhaps even a degree of worry. How could such a great teacher formulate such a great principle, yet fail to transmit the message to his students?

---

4. See Rav Yechi'el Mikhel Epstein in his *Arukh Ha-Shulchan* 493:1, *Chok Ya'akov* (493:3). For more, see Rav Professor Daniel Sperber, *Minhagei Yisrael* vol. 1 (Jerusalem: Mosad Ha-Rav Kook), pp. 18, 98, 117, 179-180; also see Simcha Emanuel, "Customs of Mourning during *Sefirat Ha-Omer*" (Hebrew), *Netu'im* 20, 2016 (Alon Shvut: Herzog College), pp. 101-141, for a different assessment of the origins of the mourning in the Ashkenazic tradition.

We may approach this problem by first examining the reaction of one of Rabbi Akiva's primary students[5] to this principle:

> 'Love your neighbor as yourself.' Rabbi Akiva said, "This is the great principle of the Torah." Ben Azzai said, "'This is the book of the generations of man; [on the day God created man, He made him in the likeness of God]'[6] (*Bereishit* 5:1) – this is an even greater principle." (*Sifra Kedoshim, parasha* 2 chapter 4:12)[7]

For Rabbi Shimon ben Azzai, arguably Rabbi Akiva's greatest and closest student, the larger principle that informs all of Jewish thought is that each and every human being is created in the image of God, and therefore deserving of love, respect, even reverence. In Ben Azzai's view, if we remain cognizant of the image of God inherent in every human being, we will necessarily treat others with love and respect.[8] Thus, in Ben Azzai's opinion, his own principle subsumes that of his teacher and colleague Rabbi Akiva: Loving one's neighbor would be a natural consequence of recognizing the divinity of every other person. Rabbi Akiva's principle becomes redundant if Ben Azzai's principle is scrupulously obeyed.

From Ben Azzai's comment, we begin to understand what at least one of Rabbi Akiva's students thought was an unfortunate limitation of his

---

5. Ben Azzai was a senior student, a *talmid chaver*, of Rabbi Akiva; a more appropriate moniker might be "junior partner." See *Talmud Bavli Bava Batra* 158b, *Talmud Yerushalmi Rosh Ha-Shana* 1:1.
6. The *Gemara* assumes that the reader is familiar with biblical texts, and cites the start of a verse or passage, when the object of interpretation is in fact the second part of the verse which is not expressly quoted.
7. This teaching is found in three places: In the *Sifra*, which is the halakhic *midrash* on *Vayikra*, in *Bereishit Rabba*, and in the *Talmud Yerushalmi Nedarim* 9:4. Only in *Bereishit Rabba* – which comments on the verse in *Bereishit* – does Ben Azzai come first, followed by Rabbi Akiva's position. In the other two instances Rabbi Akiva is cited first, and then Ben Azzai is cited as introducing a greater principle. It is possible that Ben Azzai saw himself as not arguing, but expanding the teaching of his master.
8. It is possible that Rabbi Akiva concurred. In *Pirkei Avot* 3:14, Rabbi Akiva says: "Beloved is man for he was created in [God's] image." It sounds as if the reason we are worthy of love is due to the image of God with which we are endowed.

great teacher's principle: What if a person is an ascetic, and holds himself up to impossible standards of deprivation, self-criticism or harshness? Should he treat others as he treats himself? To phrase this more cynically, does the principle of loving one's neighbor as oneself give the masochist license to be a sadist?[9] Ben Azzai's principle circumvents this problem: Rather than using the individual as the benchmark for how others should be treated, Ben Azzai stressed the need for an objective, Divine benchmark for interpersonal relations.

Until Rabbi Akiva Came
Something had gone terribly wrong; Rabbi Akiva had lost twenty-four thousand students, but he did not despair. He started again, but this time he focused on a much smaller group of disciples – five students, to be precise.[10] It is from these students that Torah spread; it is they who transmitted the legacy of Rabbi Akiva.

> The world remained desolate **until Rabbi Akiva came** to our masters in the south and taught Torah to Rabbi Me'ir, Rabbi Yehuda, Rabbi Yosei, Rabbi Shimon [bar Yochai] and Rabbi Elazar ben Shammu'a; and it was they who revived the Torah at that time. (*Yevamot* 62b)

The phrase "until Rabbi Akiva came" is used many times in Rabbinic literature; in fact, it is used twice as many times in reference to Rabbi Akiva as it is regarding all other sages combined. This is the only instance in which the phrase is descriptive: It is not a general statement, along the lines of "until he came up with the idea;" rather, it describes an actual relocation – he came to the south of Israel and began to teach his new students there. One may theorize that **whenever** this phrase is used, it refers to a teaching Rabbi Akiva imparted to his new students in the south. These particular teachings were aimed at ensuring that his new students would

---

9. This legal lacuna was pointed out by R' Ya'akov of Orleans (a member of the *Tosafot* school who was martyred in London.) See R' Chayyim Palti'el, *Vayikra* 19:18.
10. An alternative source (*Bereishit Rabba* 61:3) states that, in fact, there were seven new students. See below.

be emotionally sophisticated, sensitive and kind, and avoid the mistakes that led to the demise of his earlier followers.

> As it was taught: Shimon *Ha-Amsuni* (others state that it was Nechemya *Ha-Amsuni*) interpreted every '*et*' in the Torah, but when he came to the verse, "You shall fear ['*et*'] the Almighty your God," he desisted. His disciples said to him, "Master, what is to become of all the instances of the word '*et*' which you have interpreted?" He replied: "Just as I received reward for interpreting [them], so will I receive reward for desisting." **Until Rabbi Akiva came** and taught: "'You shall fear ['*et*'] the Lord your God:' [the addition of the word '*et*' teaches us that this fear] includes Torah scholars." (*Kiddushin* 57a)

Rabbi Akiva taught that Torah scholars are deserving of respect, and their honor is part and parcel of the awe and fear we have towards God Himself. We can easily read this as an addendum to his glorious teaching that one must love one's neighbor as oneself. Additionally, we may surmise that this may have been Rabbi Akiva's way of anticipating or responding to the critique that his "great principle of the Torah" leaves a loophole that allows the person who mistreats himself to treat others with disrespect.[11]

A second teaching by Rabbi Akiva may address this issue even more directly:

> This is as it was taught: Two people are travelling on a journey [far from civilization], and one has a pitcher of water. If both drink, they will [both] perish, but if only one drinks, he can reach civilization. Ben Petura taught: "It is better that both should drink and die, rather than that one should witness his companion's death." **Until Rabbi Akiva came** and taught: "[The verse] 'That your brother may live with you' (*Vayikra* 25:36) teaches us: Your life takes precedence over his life." (*Bava Metzi'a* 62a)[12]

---

11. See Rav Pinchas Horowitz's *Sefer Ha-Mikna*, *Kiddushin* 57a.
12. The context of this passage (*Vayikra* 25:35-38) deals with helping someone in financial need, but the language of this verse, "*ve-chei*," suggests a broader application of saving lives.

We must care for others, but when push comes to proverbial shove, one's own life must take precedence. This case uses the extreme situation to teach both sides of Rabbi Akiva's underlying principles: We must love others as we love ourselves, care for them and respect them at all times, but in order to do so, we must love ourselves, and treat ourselves with dignity and care. The fact that Rabbi Akiva had to stress the idea of self-preservation and self-respect indicates that this was not only a law, but a position his students needed to hear. Rabbi Akiva, who believed passionately in the value of life just as he believed passionately in the value of altruism, could not accept the notion that altruism might cause the death of both travelers in the desert.[13] He had seen enough death in his lifetime, and taught his students that if you **can** walk out of the desert[14] alive, it is your **obligation** to do so.[15]

Did Rabbi Akiva succeed in breaking the vicious cycle and raising a different type of student? Close examination of the words and deeds of his new students in the south proves that he most certainly did – but in order to fully appreciate Rabbi Akiva's pedagogic success, we are forced to take a slight detour.

Rabbi Akiva's philosophy regarding interpersonal relationships is perhaps most clearly illustrated in his halakhic rulings regarding marriage. As one of the most important and primary relationships in a person's life,

---

13. The Malbim in his commentary to *Vayikra* 19:18, 45 speculates that Ben Azzai agrees with Ben Petura.
14. Rav Simcha Bunim Bonhart of Peshischa (Przysucha, Poland) (1765–1827), quoted in *Kol Mevaser* (a collection of Rav Simcha Bunim's teachings published by Rav Yehuda Menachem Boim) part 2 *Bava Metzi'a*, and Rav Yitzchak Me'ir Alter (1798-1866, known as the Chiddushei Ha-Rim), say that while it is true that the law is in accordance with the opinion of Rabbi Akiva, in our inner hearts we should feel the altruism of Ben Petura; even when we must value and take care of ourselves, the love for our fellow man should still be strong in our hearts. This teaching is reported by Rav Yitzchak Me'ir Alter's grandson, Pinchas Menachem (Elazar) Yostman, in *Siftei Tzaddik, Parashat Kedoshim* section 11.
15. Rav Ya'akov Emden suggests that as long as one life is preserved, Rabbi Akiva's teaching would be fulfilled. He felt that the owner had the right to keep the water or to give it to the other person, as long as one person was saved. See *Migdal Oz, Even Bohan*, especially 1: 99, 100; also see Rav Avraham Yitzchak Ha-Kohen Kook, *Mishpat Kohen* section 143.

Rabbi Akiva was quite concerned that husband and wife live in tranquility, in harmony, in love. For this reason, Rabbi Akiva's rulings regarding divorce were relatively lenient.

The scholars who preceded him were divided on the question of legitimate grounds for divorce: While Beit Shammai understood that the Torah would only permit divorce in cases of infidelity, Beit Hillel opined that a man may divorce his wife even if she burns his food (and it is my understanding that it is only **his** food, and not hers or anyone else's, which is ruined, indicating aggression, spite, even hatred).[16] We may assume that Beit Hillel's relative leniency is based on the understanding that if this couple is already involved in a contentious relationship, there is no need to wait for the relationship to deteriorate to actual infidelity. And yet, Rabbi Akiva goes one considerable step further, stating that a man may divorce his wife even on the grounds that he has found another woman who is "*na'a mi-mena*" – more beautiful or more pleasant (or perhaps more suitable). While on the one hand it may strike us as outrageous that a wife can be "sent packing" because her lecherous husband has found a newer model with less "mileage," Rabbi Akiva seems exceptionally sensitive to the concern that this relationship should be based on love, mutual respect, and attraction. In fact, in a separate, apparently related teaching, Rabbi Akiva speaks out against the "old time Rabbis" who advocated that wives should refrain from making themselves look attractive during those times that they are forbidden to have marital relations with their husbands. Rabbi Akiva permitted married women to beautify themselves as they saw fit, and did not limit physical attractiveness between spouses as a function of physical intimacy:

---

16. See *Mishna Gittin* 9:10 (found in *Talmud Bavli Gittin* 90a):

> Beit Shammai say: A man should not divorce his wife unless he has found her guilty of unseemly conduct, as it says (*Devarim* 24): "…because he has found some unseemly thing about her." Beit Hillel, however, say [that he may divorce her] even if she has merely spoiled his food, since it says (ibid.): "…because he has found some unseemly thing about her." Rabbi Akiva says, [he may divorce her] even if he finds another woman more beautiful than she is, as it says: "If it comes to pass that if she finds no favor in his eyes."

> The early sages ruled that she must not rouge nor paint nor adorn herself in colorful garments while she is a *nidda*; **until Rabbi Akiva came** and taught: If so, you make her repulsive to her husband, with the result that he will divorce her! (*Shabbat* 64b)

Here is another instance where the phrase "until Rabbi Akiva came" is used. If we are correct in our thesis, this is another instance in which Rabbi Akiva taught his new students to be sensitive to feelings, to legislate in favor of love and attraction. The same Rabbi Akiva who permitted the husband with a straying eye to divorce his wife, spoke out against an earlier Rabbinic ruling that he feared might make wives unattractive to their husbands. Rabbi Akiva spoke boldly, in order to ensure that *halakha* would never provide the reason for a husband's eye to stray.[17]

Rabbi Akiva further stressed the importance of a person marrying an appropriate spouse in order to avoid the pitfalls of a deteriorated relationship:

> A man who marries a woman who is not appropriate for him breaks five different negative commandments of the Torah: "Do not take revenge," (*Vayikra* 19:18) "Do not bear a grudge," (ibid. 18) "Do not hate your fellow man in your heart," (ibid. 17) "Love your neighbor as yourself," (ibid. 18) and "Your fellow man shall live with you." (ibid. 25:36) Because he hates her, he hopes that she will die, and he abstains from procreation. (*Avot De-Rabbi Natan*, version 1, chapter 26)

This very striking passage is, in fact, the only commentary by Rabbi Akiva himself on his "great principle of the Torah." He teaches that in a relationship devoid of love, many other Torah laws are unavoidably trampled upon. The great principle is most evident in this passage, which outlines a destructive progression that begins with a loveless marriage: A cascade of negative emotions leads to hurtful thoughts and, eventually, destructive actions.

---

17. This connection was noted by the Netziv in his commentary *Meromei Sadeh*, *Shabbat* 64b.

The Arrival of Rabbi Akiva | 365

With this information, and against the backdrop of Rabbi Akiva's application of his "great principle of Torah," we may now return to our earlier question: Did Rabbi Akiva succeed in communicating this idea to his students?

Rabbi Yehuda[18], one of Rabbi Akiva's five new students, makes a very similar application of law, and warns of the price to be paid for a relationship that has deteriorated. Both the words and the logic he employs should seem quite familiar:

> 'If a man takes a wife, has relations with her, and comes to hate her...' Rabbi Yehuda says: ... from this we see that if a person breaks an easy commandment, he will eventually break a more serious commandment. If he does not obey the commandment "Love your neighbor as yourself," he will come to violate the commandments "Do not take revenge" and "Do not bear a grudge," (*Vayikra* 19:18) and the commandment "Do not hate your fellow man in your heart," (*Vayikra* 19:17) the commandment "Love your neighbor as yourself," and "Your brother shall live along with you," (*Vayikra* 25:36) and he will eventually reach the point of bloodshed. (*Sifrei Devarim Ki Teitzei* section 235)

Regarding a totally different sort of interpersonal relationship, the *mishna* in *Nedarim* grapples with the problem of a person who made a vow disowning a friend from his assets. The *mishna* discusses the conditions that might annul such a vow (called "opening" the vow), and Rabbi Me'ir's opinion on the matter also strikes a familiar chord:

> Rabbi Me'ir also said: An opening [or annulment of a vow] may be given based on what is written in the Torah, so we say to him: 'Had you known that you were violating [the injunctions] "Do not take

---

18. Rabbi Yehuda bar Rabbi Ilai is often cited as "Rabbi Yehuda." The *Gemara* (*Sanhedrin* 20a) reports that in his generation there was such a strong sense of camaraderie that six students could share one cloak. This seems like quite an improvement over Rabbi Akiva's former students.

revenge," "Do not bear a grudge," "Love your neighbor as yourself," and "Your brother shall live with you," or that he might become poor and you would not be able to provide for him, [would you have made this vow?]' Should he reply, 'Had I known that it would be so, I would not have vowed,' he is absolved. (*Mishna Nedarim* 9:4, found in *Talmud Bavli Nedarim* 65b)

The pattern that emerges is unmistakable: Rabbi Akiva's application of the great principle of "Love your neighbor as yourself" to the area of spousal relationships was applied by two of his new students – first, Rabbi Yehuda in the matter of divorce, and next by Rabbi Me'ir, to help heal a different sort of rift between two people.

The *Sifrei* records a similar teaching in a third area of interpersonal relationships:

"If one person hates another and lies in wait and attacks him": From this we learn that if a person breaks an easy commandment he will eventually break a more serious commandment. If he breaks the commandment "Love your neighbor as yourself" he will eventually come to break the commandments "Do not take revenge" and "Do not bear a grudge," (*Vayikra* 19:18) and the commandment "Do not hate your fellow man in your heart," (*Vayikra* 19:17) and the commandment "Your brother shall live along with you," (*Vayikra* 25:36) until he reaches the point of bloodshed.

This passage deals with hatred that may lead to murder; once again, there is a downward spiral, and along the way commandments are trampled. Again, Rabbi Akiva's teaching is implemented, although this specific teaching is not attributed to a particular scholar. However, the *Gemara* states that anonymous teachings in the *Sifrei* are the work of yet another of Rabbi Akiva's "new" students: Rabbi Shimon bar Yochai:

Rabbi Yochanan said: [The author of] unattributed *Mishna* is Rabbi Me'ir, of unattributed *Tosefta* is Rabbi Nechemya; of an unattributed [dictum in the] *Sifra* is Rabbi Yehuda, and in the *Sifrei*, Rabbi Shimon; and all are taught according to the views of Rabbi Akiva. (*Sanhedrin* 86a)

Thus, we see that three of Rabbi Akiva's new students heard and internalized their teacher's lesson and applied his great principle of Torah regarding the centrality of building and maintaining loving relationships in their own teachings.

A fourth student, Rabbi Elazar ben Shammu'a, taught this same principle of love and respect in a more succinct formulation:

> Rabbi Elazar ben Shammu'a said: Let the honor of your disciple be as dear to you as your own, and the honor of your colleague as [important] as the reverence for your teacher, and the reverence for your teacher as [vital] as your fear of Heaven. (*Mishna Avot* 4:12)

The emphasis Rabbi Elazar places on honoring teachers, colleagues and students reflects Rabbi Akiva's teachings; we may say that this *mishna* is a true expression of Rabbi Akiva's legacy, as it is expressed by one of his new students.[19] Another lengthy *midrash* recounts that Rabbi Elazar ben Shammu'a's kindness and concern extended even to non-Jews, a fact that eventually saved all the Jews of a certain province.[20]

It seems clear that Rabbi Akiva was quite successful with his new students. He taught them sensitivity, he taught them kindness, and he taught them love. He taught them that love of our fellow man is truly

---

19. This emphasis of respect is found in another passage where Rabbi Elazar ben Shammu'a teaches that if one comes late for a lecture they should not awkwardly make their way to their seats if this will cause discomfort to those already seated. See *Sota* 39a and Rashi's comments *ad loc*.

> His disciples asked Rabbi Elazar ben Shammu'a, "How have you prolonged your life?" He replied: Never have I made use of a synagogue as a shortcut, nor stepped over the heads of the holy people, nor lifted up my hands [as a *kohen*] without first uttering a benediction.

20. *Kohelet Rabba* 11:1.

the central teaching in the Torah. Every aspect of Torah law should be impacted by this love; every aspect of our society evolves from the great principle of love.

The Rabbi Akiva who arrived in the south and taught five great students was a Rabbi Akiva who himself had internalized the lesson of his earlier students' tragic deaths. When teaching his new students, he did not leave it to chance that they would understand his message; he drilled it home over and over, and was explicit and specific in teaching them. His pedagogic method, and his diligence in delivering this educational message to his new students, are preserved in another passage that tells the story of the earlier students' deaths, with slight variations:

> Rabbi Akiva said: "If you have raised disciples in your youth, raise disciples in your old age, because you do not know which will survive, these or those, or whether they will be equally successful." Rabbi Akiva had twelve thousand disciples from *Akko* to *Antipatris*, and all died in the same period.[21] Why? Because they looked grudgingly on each other. Eventually he raised seven disciples: Rabbi Me'ir, Rabbi Yehuda, Rabbi Yosei, Rabbi Shimon, Rabbi Elazar ben Shammu'a, Rabbi Yochanan the Cobbler, and Rabbi Eli'ezer ben Ya'akov. Others say: Rabbi Yehuda, Rabbi Nechemya, Rabbi Me'ir, Rabbi Yosei, Rabbi Shimon bar Yochai, Rabbi Chanina ben Chakhinai, and Rabbi Yochanan the Cobbler. [**Rabbi Akiva**] **said to them: My sons, the previous ones died only because they begrudged one another [the knowledge of the Torah];[22] see to it that you do not act as they did**. They arose and filled the whole of the Land of Israel with Torah. (*Bereishit Rabba* 61:3)

---

21. Of note is the lack of a calendric point of reference; the association with the days of the *Omer* is absent. Additionally, here there are "only" 12,000 students, as opposed to the 12,000 **pairs** of students mentioned in the passage in the *Talmud Bavli*.

22. The bracketed words "the knowledge of Torah" are found in a parallel source (*Midrash Rabba* Theodor Albeck edition) and qualify that the begrudging behavior applied to Torah knowledge, which they chose not to share with one another.

Any other man who had lost so many students, whose entire life's work had been eradicated, would have given up. Rabbi Akiva had begun teaching at a relatively late stage of life, and he might easily have felt that all was for naught. Instead, he started again. He found the best minds around, and he filled their hearts with love.

Many generations later, in the holocaust era, another man saw the same type of destruction witnessed by Rabbi Akiva, though multiplied to impossible numbers. He was a young Chassidic *yeshiva* student named Elie Wiesel, and many years later, he wrote about his love for Rabbi Akiva:

> I love Rabbi Akiva. I love him for his humanity, for his passion for study. I love him for his love of the Jewish People. His argument with Ben Petura on the duties and obligations of friendship? His decision teaches us something important. When the surviving friend emerges from the desert, he is no longer alone; he will have to live two lives, his own and that of his dead friend. (Elie Wiesel, *Sages and Dreamers*, p. 240)[23]

---

23. Elie Wiesel, *Sages and Dreamers: Biblical, Talmudic, and Hasidic Portraits and Legends* (New York, NY: Summit Books, 1991). This is a brilliant and original interpretation of the verse, "And your brother shall live with you," taken here to imply "wit**hin** you." The survivor needs to live a dual life: his or her own, and the life of the one who perished.

A Divine Torah Delivered to Human Beings

Rabbi Moshe Taragin

The *Gemara* in *Kiddushin* 32a cites a *machloket* (dispute) about the ability of a *Rebbe* to waive the honor due him from a student (*"limchol al kevodo"*). Rav Yosef allowed this relinquishment just as a parent can waive their honor, whereas, surprisingly, Rav Chisda disallowed this renouncing of *kavod* (honor). Rava analyzed both his and Rav Chisda's respective positions and asserted that the *machloket* surrounded a seminal question: Can the honor or prestige afforded a *Rebbe* who teaches Torah be attributed to the *Rebbe* himself. Perhaps this prestige isn't considered his own personal honor since a teacher is merely conveying *Torat Hashem*, God's Law. As a mere icon representing a system larger than himself, whatever honor is displayed isn't his personal province, and the teacher may not be authorized to waive it, as Rav Chisda suggested. Alternatively, as Rava reasoned, a *Rebbe* does personalize Torah as his own, by studying it and imparting it to others. Perhaps the honor due him may be considered a personal license and may be waived.

This general debate about whether Torah can be personalized, and the related halakhic issue as to whether *kevod ha-Torah*, honor for the Torah, can be waived, stems from an interesting grammatical discrepancy embedded in the second verse of the first chapter of *Tehillim*: "For *Torat Hashem* is his desire, and he will meditate *be-Torato* day and night." The initial clause of this verse portrays Torah as *Torat Hashem*, implying that it can't be possessed by a human being and, by extension, whatever honor accrues from teaching Torah cannot be personalized and certainly can't be waived. By contrast, the concluding clause of the verse defines Torah as *Torato*, the Torah of the *ish*, or person, referenced in the previous verse. This phrase implies that Torah is, indeed, possessed by the person studying and ultimately imparting it to others. As Torah is designated as *Torat ish*, the Torah of man, it can be personalized and the honor due a teacher can be personally renounced.

This duality in the verse and the consequential halakhic debate about *mechilat kavod*, forgoing honor, showcases a fundamental paradox regarding our interface with Torah. As a distillation of God's infinite will, Torah is likewise infinite, just as it is immortal and celestial. It belongs to a different world and originates in a different sphere. The version of Torah delivered to humans isn't the only "version" of Torah – it is merely *our* version of Torah; Torah itself supersedes human cognition and experience. Even our version of Torah had to be snatched from Heaven by Moshe while fending off angels who opposed its delivery to a terrestrial sphere. *Tehillim* 68:19 states: "*Alita la-Marom, shavita shevi*" – Moshe ascended to the Heavens and seized Torah; this verse captures the unnatural nature of this delivery. Moshe ultimately descends with his "plunder" in the form of two tablets, the *luchot*, upon which *devar Hashem* (the word of God) is engraved. Yet even this humanized Torah lies beyond human comprehension: the script upon the *luchot* was unlike any other form of composition and its letters were suspended in supernatural fashion. Or, as Chazal comment, the Torah fonts were formatted as "*eish shechora al gabbei eish levana*" – black fire upon white fire. The text of the Torah and the engraved letters upon the *luchot* were unlike any human handwriting! These Divinely authored Torah items reflected a world beyond human experience.

Yet despite its expanse, Torah was formatted specifically for human experience and, inevitably, addresses all conditions of human experience. The *midrash* discusses a Heavenly argument about the notion of delivering Torah to humans and the objection of many angels is recorded. Ultimately, these protests were defeated by reminding these angels that only humans give birth, decease and exhibit the life-cycles that the Torah addresses.

Despite human limitations and failures, Torah is earmarked for humans as it provides a guide for human life. Though Torah is rooted in a sphere beyond the ken of human experience, it is meant to pervade and elevate human experience and mustn't remain distant and detached in Heaven.

This paradox – whether Torah *matches* or *transcends* the human realm – actually impacts several important aspects of the experience of *talmud Torah* (Torah study).

1. Decorum while Studying Torah

This balance between the awe of Torah and the attempt to humanize Torah is reflected in the question of what physical state is appropriate for the study of Torah. The *Gemara* in *Megilla* 21a documents that until the era of Rabban Gamli'el, Torah was studied only while standing. In part, this posture mirrored the manner in which the Torah was delivered at *Har Sinai*, but it also captured the gravitas of the overall experience of studying Torah. How can *devar Hashem* be studied while sitting casually or reclining in a relaxed state? Unfortunately, this demand wasn't sustainable – the *Gemara* comments that in the period of Rabban Gamli'el human nature weakened and Torah was subsequently studied even in a seated position. Fundamentally though, Torah should be studied while standing to capture the transcendence of the experience. How can the word of God be absorbed in any state other than one of coiled attention? However, human nature is weak, and both the human body and spirit cannot sustain fulltime standing. Had this flexibility not been allowed, Torah study itself would have wilted. Many still adopt the practice of standing during public *Keri'at ha-Torah* to retain a residue of this original practice. When *Har Sinai* is more directly recreated during *Keri'at Ha-Torah*, the awe of Torah study can be sustained by remaining standing. However, in a general sense, by allowing Torah study while sitting, the "awe" of *Torat Hashem* was compromised to enable greater achievements of *Torat ha-adam*, the Torah of man.

In truth, the shift from standing to sitting while learning should not be seen as purely pragmatic – to enable continued Torah study for a physically weakened population. Beyond the practical issue of sitting or standing lies a deeper question about whether Torah should be performed while "standing to attention" or in a more casual manner. The Torah's description of *talmud Torah* suggests a more informal and thereby more integrated experience: "When you sit in your home and when you travel, and when you lie down and when you rise up." Torah is framed within the totality of the human experience – while relaxing at home, while traveling, **while reclining**, and while arising. *Talmud Torah* is specifically cast within the domestic residence and within bedrooms and leisure rooms. If Torah is limited to the "spaces of awe" and "reverential settings" it can become compartmentalized and lose its ability to thread the total sweep of the human condition. The danger of bifurcation – "what happens in the *Beit Midrash* stays in the *Beit Midrash*" – can become magnified if Torah is experienced as something apart and distant. By infusing Torah study in the home, Torah can be internalized more deeply within human identity. To insert *talmud Torah* and its values into the core of human experience, some of the transcendence may be conceded. If Torah is studied only while standing it will not "sit" deeply embedded within the human heart.

The same tension about retaining the transcendence of Torah while still humanizing it can be sensed in the oscillations about whether a *ba'al keri* (one who had a seminal emission) can study Torah. The *Gemara* in *Berakhot* 21a-b narrates that Ezra instituted a prohibition for a *ba'al keri* to study Torah without prior *mikveh* immersion. Indeed, it is certainly odd to imagine a seamless transition from the bedroom into the *Beit Midrash*. Additionally, the timing of Ezra's *takana* (decree) is crucial. Ezra "*Ha-Sofer*" sought to refresh Torah for a generation returning from exile outside the Land of Israel. In addition to reformatting the fonts of the Hebrew language (into *Ketav Ashuri*) and restructuring *Keri'at Ha-Torah* (institutionalizing the *aliya* protocols and adding *Targum*), he also stressed the transcendence of Torah by creating distance between marital life and the study of Torah. It is also noteworthy that Ezra was facing a phenomenon of severe intermarriage and sought to restore a healthier approach to sexuality and marriage. His *takana* to require a *mikveh* transition between marital activity and Torah study accomplished both agendas!

Either way, the *takana* backfired. The imposition of *mikveh*, which was intended to augment the luster of Torah, only diminished the actual study of Torah as people delayed *mikveh* and thereby reduced their Torah study. Eventually, the *takana* was repealed for the sake of a greater spread of Torah study. Once again, the ideal attitude regarding the transcendence of Torah was flexed to enable a more successful human experience of *talmud Torah*. Ultimately, to enable Torah study for frail humans, we were allowed to sit, just as we were permitted to study Torah within typical married life.

2. Authorization to Study Torah?

In some ways this tension can be detected in the nature of the *berakha* (blessing) – or, more precisely, the multiple *berakhot* – recited prior to studying Torah. Though each classic mitzva prompts a *birkat ha-mitzva*, the *berakhot* prior to *talmud Torah* are obviously far more iconic and their embellished language reflects this symbolism. Reciting a *berakha* upon Torah study is the only *berakha rishona* (*berakha* recited *prior* to the act) which is Biblically mandated, based upon the verse "*Ki Sheim Hashem ekra, havu godel l-Elokeinu*" – when I call the Name of the Lord, attribute greatness to our God. A well-known *midrash* attributed the destruction of the *Beit Ha-Mikdash* to the omission of *birkat ha-Torah* prior to *talmud Torah*. Furthermore, there was great debate (*Berakhot* 11b) about which of the three suggested *berakhot* should be included, and ultimately Rav Hamnuna mandated that all three be recited. Evidently this *berakha* carries deep symbolism.

On the surface, the essence of a *berakha* prior to Torah study appears to be a classic *birkat ha-shevach* – a *berakha* recited to praise God during moments of enjoyment or emotional elation. Presumably, the latter two *berakhot* that describe, among other issues, the sweetness of Torah, the hope that we will deliver it to future generations and the pride in our selection, all reflect the *shevach* or praise component of *birkat ha-Torah*. What experience causes greater jubilation than *talmud* Torah, and what experience warrants this type of *birkat ha-shevach* more so than the study of Torah.

In addition to the classic function of *birkat ha-shevach*, Rav Soloveitchik claimed that a *birkat ha-Torah* serves as a *"mattir"* – an authorization to permit the erstwhile forbidden study of Torah. As such, the *berakha* prior to Torah study may be modeled upon a *birkat ha-nehenin* blessing recited prior to consuming food. Prior to reciting a *berakha*, food doesn't belong to a human and its consumption would be considered theft. Similarly, prior to a *berakha*, Torah doesn't belong to a human being but instead is Divine province. The *berakha* is crucial in authorizing human entry into a realm beyond human experience. The *berakha* reinforces the sense that Torah isn't a human-sized entity and that, when we study, we are merely visitors in a different world. A *berakha* upon Torah study isn't merely a response to joy of study but functions as a *mattir* to allow us to enter the hallowed realm of Torah.

Ultimately, *birkat ha-Torah* functions as both a *shevach* as well as a *mattir*, and certainly the diversity of *berakhot* suggest that it can serve multiple functions. If the final *berakhot* evoke the joy of study and of national selection, the initial *berakha* is more generic and describes our labor and toil in Torah (*"la'asok be-divrei Torah"*). Perhaps the initial *berakha* functions as a *mattir* or legalization of engagement with Torah, while the latter two voice the *shevach* or joy of this experience. The variety of *berakhot* for Torah captures the dichotomy of the experience. While we recite praise at the joy of this experience, we also recite a *berakha* to remind us that we are entering a transcendent realm.

3. Systemizing *Halakha*

This built-in dichotomy regarding our view of Torah and its study also impacts the degree of personal creativity expressed when processing Torah and achieving halakhic conclusions. In the 16th century, recognizing the destabilizing influence of continued exile upon the integrity of the halakhic tradition, Rav Yosef Karo attempted to systematize halakhic procedure. No longer would halakhic verdicts be a personal journey of the individual *posek* but, instead, halakhic conclusions would become standardized based on a universal calculus. He asserted that *halakha* should follow a majority of a three-person panel – Rif, Rambam, and Rosh. Where a *machloket* existed, the *halakha* would be decided by the majority of opinions. This would stabilize the process by providing a universal formula for halakhic development. In his generation, Rav Yosef Karo's attempt to institutionalize Torah study came under great fire. Rav Shlomo Luria – otherwise known as Maharshal – deeply opposed any attempt to systematize Torah as an "organized table" – as the name *Shulchan Arukh* suggested. Torah was too broad and uncontrollable to be tamed by any particular human mind or even a quorum of great scholars. Each path through the labyrinth of Torah is unique and each *talmid chakham* (Torah scholar) must navigate this maze independently while arriving at a more personal halakhic verdict. *Devar Hashem* can't be fully conquered and organized by human beings. To accentuate the vast Divine sweep of Torah, Maharshal entitled his own book "*Yam Shel Shlomo*" (The Sea of Solomon), recalling the outsized *mikveh* in Shlomo *Ha-Melekh*'s *Beit Ha-Mikdash* that, to the onlookers, resembled a massive ocean. Just as the oceans lie beyond human restriction, so is Torah unaccommodating of institutionalized human logic. History has certainly sided with Rav Yosef Karo's very practical measures. However, the conceptual issue of whether Torah lends itself to human processing, or resists and defies human command, is certainly a built-in dualism that governs the way we engage in Torah study.

4. The Challenge of the *Brisker Derekh*
In many ways, this challenge has been reformulated in the modern Torah world with the rise and popularization of the *Brisker derekh*. Rav Chayyim's strategy, of cataloging and categorizing thereby creating networked categories based upon the endless stream of Talmudic detail, has captured most of the Torah world. Some *yeshivot* are more overtly pedagogic and methodological in applying the *Brisker derekh* while others are less didactic but no less engaged in this process. At the core of this analytical process is the premise that the system can be tamed and cataloged. The methodology assumes that the vast enormity of Torah can be distilled into categories that enable more deft navigation through the entire body of Talmudic

logic. Prior to Rav Chayyim's revolution, Torah study was more osmotic – enormous volumes of Torah were studied until a system and a logical template emerged from the sheer volume of associated ideas. However, Torah remained a humbling process and the notion of conquering the system was elusive to many and, to others, entirely unimaginable. Rav Chayyim's approach implies that the system can – with enough effort and diligence – be organized and systematized.

If Rav Chayyim's logical strategy invited this aspiration, Rav Lichtenstein's weekly Talmudic methodology *shi'urim* loudly announced: the system exhibits repeating patterns that can be traced across vastly different *sugyot* (topics) and can then assist in decoding other *sugyot*. The very term "Talmudic methodology" has become popular in many *yeshivot* (including the virtual branch of Yeshivat Har Etzion known as the VBM!).

It is legitimate and important to question whether this this process has compromised the enormity of Torah or eroded the awe of *devar Hashem*. Without question, this approach to Torah study bridges between man and God as we are granted a deeper insight into the Divine logic at a structural level. We don't merely study random details but construct images of larger systems that God willed. However, does this empowering form of learning blind us to the overwhelming force of Torah as *devar Hashem*? Too often, the skills to conquer Torah efface the mystery of an uncontainable word of God. When Chazal repeatedly conclude a *sugya* with the verdict of *"teiku"* (the matter is inconclusive), are they merely voicing inability to advance further argument? Or, are they acknowledging human inadequacy in capturing Torah and reinforcing the mystery and insolvability of Torah? In our own learning, are we just as capable of attitudinally achieving *"teiku"* as we are in creating the sophistries of a *Brisker chakira*? The debate of the 16th century between Rav Yosef Karo and Maharshal is deeply resonant 400 years later and streams through the *Brisker derekh* and its dominance in today's contemporary Torah world.

5. Surrendering to the Infinity of Torah

Recognizing the infinity of Torah must also invite human surrender. The ability to surrender to the mystery of Torah was captured very eloquently by Shimon *Ha-Amsuni* (cited by the *Gemara* in *Pesachim* 22b). He was quite deft at extracting lessons from extra letters and words in the Torah. In fact, he drew novel ideas every time the Torah inserted the seemingly redundant preposition of "*et*." For example, he inferred the mitzva of honoring an older sibling from the word "*et*" in the Torah's iteration of "*kabbeid et avikha ve-et imekha* (honor your father and mother)." However, the process stalled with his inability to interpret "*et*" in the phrase "*et Hashem Elokekha tira* (you shall fear the Lord your God)": what other being should be awed in a manner similar to God? Unable to proceed, he surrendered rather than fabricating an incorrect extension of *yirat Shamayim* to mortal beings. When asked about his surrender and the connotations for the entire body of his previous *derashot*, he responded "*ke-sheim she-kibbalti sekhar al ha-derisha, kakh kibbalti sekhar al ha-perisha*" – just as I have received reward for my logical ingenuity, I will be rewarded for my retreat. This phrase delicately calibrated his ability to master the system along with his abiding recognition that the system of Torah is indominable. Without the final withdrawal, the earlier creativity would have been dishonest and impudent. The final surrender reinforced the sense of infinite and unattainable sweep of Torah. Just the same, without attempts of innovative "*derisha*" and without the attempt to conquer the system, the surrender of "*perisha*" would have been hollow. Only by struggling to master the system can a person sufficiently appreciate its unobtainability; *derisha* and *perisha* walk hand in hand. The process of *derisha* should pave the route toward the surrender of *perisha* while the embrace of *perisha* should preserve the magnificence of *derisha*.

Not incidentally, he experienced the surrender of *perisha* while considering the verse that is the conceptual root of *perisha* and the reason that, ultimately, every Torah laborer encounters *perisha*. Shimon *Ha-Amsuni* was unable to extend the verse of "*et Hashem Elokekha tira*." Our awe of God stems from His magnificence and our inability to grasp that enormity. It is a singular experience reserved for God and unexportable to any other realm or subject. The moment of *perisha* for Shimon *Ha-Amsuni* didn't occur during any random analysis. While contemplating the unknowability of God, Shimon *Ha-Amsuni* more deeply understood the consequential unknowability of Torah and embraced *perisha* as a vital attitudinal element in maintaining the balance between *Torat Hashem* and *Torat ha-adam*.

6. Acknowledging *Siyyata Di-Shmaya*

This balancing between *derisha* and *perisha* isn't just a theoretical or attitudinal issue but should affect the emotional fabric of *talmud Torah*. Torah is primarily a cognitive experience, or at least its core methodology is cognitive. Indeed, it must be sparked by emotional drive and it can certainly generate passion, but the experience itself consists of cognitive analysis and intellectual creativity. It is perhaps the greatest and most challenging human artistic endeavor – wedding human intellect to the Divine word. The attempt to decode the vast and unlimited will of God challenges the human mind far beyond any other discipline. Systemic approaches to Torah – such as the *Brisker derekh* for one – equip us with skills and tools to detect the inner networked logic of Torah. Humans naturally possess the brain power to attempt the acquisition of Torah and our developed systems of analysis have empowered us with the strategies and approaches to succeed in this ambitious project. However, mastery of Torah can be acquired only through *siyyata di-Shmaya*, or Divine assistance – for both theological as well as intellectual reasons. As Torah is a reflection of the Divine will, it can be authentically obtained only through Divine allowance. Perhaps the raw "knowledge" or "data" of Torah can be studied as any other discipline can be learned, but the acquisition of Torah's inner *chokhma*, or wisdom, is dependent upon Divine delivery. God ultimately determines who is privy to understand Him and His word. From a theological standpoint, God must admit humans who wish to enter His inner realm of Torah and thereby grasp His essence.

Beyond the theological basis for *siyyata di-Shmaya*, there is a purely logical basis: the sheer vastness and overwhelming nature of Torah logic also mandates that success in Torah is dependent upon Divine assistance. From a purely logistical standpoint, humans cannot acquire the depth and vastness of Torah without Divine aid. Describing the conclusion of Moshe's forty days atop *Har Sinai* studying God's will, the Torah announces, "*Va-yittein el Moshe ke-khalloto ledabber itto*," stressing that God *gifted* Torah ("*va-yittein*") to Moshe. Sensing the redundancy of this phrase, the *midrash* narrates that after forty days of relentless effort Moshe acknowledged his own inadequacy and was disappointed at how little he had retained. Whether this was factually true or merely Moshe's self-impression doesn't change the fact that Moshe believed his fortyday heroic effort to be futile. At this point, God acknowledged his effort and responded, "I will now deliver the Torah to you as a gift." Through direct Divine delivery, Moshe acquired, in an instant, the sweep of Torah that evaded him for forty days!

Moshe's experience provides a template for appreciating the role and necessity of *siyyata di-Shmaya* – particularly for those who do apply tools and methodologies toward Torah study. Some study Torah in a completely "receptive" or "reactive" manner. Without attempting to systematize Torah, they strive to absorb its data and grasp its logic osmotically; by traversing large terrains of a logically integrated Torah, the logic will necessarily emerge. As massive Torah information flows through our imagination, the elements of Torah information begin to merge into larger units and, ultimately, patterns emerge even without frontally articulating them or developing them. This approach to Torah study more easily acknowledges the authorial role of God in allotting Torah wisdom. In the absence of frontal attempts to analytically "master" the system, it is obvious that God's decisions and His Divine allocation determine the degree of success. By contrast, those who do attempt to schematize, identify and apply patterns may allow their own intellectual empowerment to obscure the Divine role in enabling the process. By asserting the prospect of conquering Torah through human strategies and methodologies, the study of Torah may come to resemble the pursuit of finite non-Torah disciplines. For those who do frontally attempt to "patternize" Torah and generate systematized approaches, the role of *siyyata di-Shmaya* mustn't be obscured just as the identity of Torah as the Divine realm mustn't be ignored.

7. Modern Forms of *Tanakh* Study

With our return to our ancient homeland and the land of history, the study of the book of history has been reinvigorated. For various reasons, in certain circles, *Tanakh* study declined over the past millennia, but over the past 150 years has been revitalized. Additionally, new methodologies have been employed to better grasp *Tanakh*'s messages and apply them to our own prophetic reality. Chief among these new methodologies is the literal reading of *Tanakh* – known in Israel as "*Tanakh be-govah ha-einayim*" (at eye level). Much of the traditional treatment of *Tanakh* may be described as "deconstructionist" – disassembling larger units of text (*parshiyyot*, *pesukim* (verses), or even phrases) into smaller units and carefully extracting meaning from even very minute elements. The *Gemara* in *Eiruvin* (21b) asserts that mounds of *halakhot* can be culled from otherwise trivial textual features such as the tail of the letter *yud*. This approach dominated Chazal's comments and became the paradigm for much of *Tanakh* study throughout the ages. Recently, more holistic approaches have been popularized in which tracts of text aren't deconstructed into smaller units but read in a complete and undivided fashion and compared to other parallel segments. Ideally, this can complement traditional methods of studying *Tanakh*, in providing macro-analysis to assist in tracing textual patterns that can emerge only from these macro-reads. In, and of itself, it is an extremely valuable approach toward a better understanding of the multi-layered *devar Hashem*. Despite the dominance of deconstructivist approaches to *Tanakh*, these more macro-analytical approaches can certainly be sensed in many *rishonim* (Ramban and Abarbanel), as well as in Chazal themselves.

Yet, undoubtedly, these approaches don't dominate or characterize Chazal's primary *Tanakh* analyses. Chazal primarily dealt with textual nuances rather than broader "thematics." Furthermore, the premise of these newfound approaches (about which many disagree) is that *Tanakh* can be read narratively, as a story, and not just as a collection of assembled letters and phrases that are mere hieroglyphs to deeper coded-meanings that only Chazal can unlock. These more rational forms of processing the narratives of *Tanakh* can be extremely empowering as a complement to the traditional coded-meanings that Chazal deciphered. However, these practices should not lead to the depreciation or even belittling of traditional forms of studying *Tanakh*. Potentially, the rational/literalist reading may appear more textually based while the coded readings may feel more synthetic as they can be grasped only by overlaying a non-literal system of codes. However, as *Tanakh* is part of God's infinite word, human comprehension can't serve as the baseline for determining authenticity. Indeed, *Tanakh* was delivered to humans and we can draw inspiration by applying our "human" reads. However, *Tanakh* is Divine province and our human literary expectations cannot serve as yardsticks to determine full meaning.

8. The Emotions of Torah Study

Finally, this duality of Torah must also govern the emotions that underwrite the process of Torah study. As emotional beings, we are expected to approach Torah study with heightened emotions. Furthermore, the process of encountering *devar Hashem* should generate deep-seated spirituality. Without question, one of the deepest, if not the most profound, human emotion is the state of joy and happiness. What function should *simcha*, or joy, play within the learning experience? As joy is so primal, the elation we sense during Torah study can potentially anchor it to our deepest layers of identity. Chazal mention that Torah can be studied only during *simcha* and they certainly rally against the unhealthy gloom and sadness that sometimes frames religious devotion and piety. Additionally, prophetic experience was induced by music and joy. Prophecy isn't primarily a cognitive experience but demands full existential investment. Joy awakened these emotional reservoirs and enabled the emission of prophecy. This potent emotion may play a similar role in catalyzing a deeply spiritual and profoundly existential process of Torah study. Alternatively, and given the fact that joy is essential to initiate prophetic or Torah-study process, it may compromise the gravitas of the experience while also amplifying the human voice in what many would feel should be a Divinely-dominated experience. Perhaps, some would argue, a human should be more emotionally passive during the Torah experience, allowing the word of God, and not the heart of man, to flavor the moment. *Iglei Tal* (Rav Avraham Bornsztain, a 19th century Talmudic scholar) famously defended the value of *simcha* during learning as a mechanism for internalizing Torah "into our blood." However, this approach was far from the only attitude toward the role of joy in Torah study. The very fact that he was so forceful is justifying *simcha* in Torah study (and even a bit disdainful to those who questioned its value) is reflective of how suspicious some were about the potential function of joy within the reverential process of Torah study. After all, if Torah was delivered with fear and awe, how can it be studied with joy and exultation? Of course, the most comprehensive and religious healthy form of Torah study is through a distillation of these two competing emotions of joy and gravitas – recognizing Torah as a personal gift while still maintaining the transcendent "otherness" of Torah.

Conclusion
Rav Chisda and Rav Yosef debated the halakhic ability of a Torah *Rebbe* to relinquish the honor due him from a student. Their debate centered around whether Torah can be legitimately personalized. This localized issue reflects a broader duality that is built-in to the nature of Torah as a Divine and infinite system delivered to finite and frail human beings. It should affect our experience and attitudes toward learning just as it should help us balance between human-scripted methodologies for Torah study and the recognition of Torah's unattainability.

One of David *Ha-Melekh*'s generals was always escorted by the *kereiti u-fleiti*, which literally refers to a military unit in the royal army. However, the *Gemara* in *Sanhedrin* (16a) views this term as a nickname for the *Urim Ve-Tumim* – the gemstones on the breastplate of the *kohen gadol* (high priest) through which Torah information flowed. The term "*kereiti*" connotes a dissected and anatomized Torah, while the term "*peleiti*" (stemming from the root *peleh*, or wondrous,) implies a mysterious and baffling Torah. This dual term, describing the conduit of Torah from God to man, captures the fundamental dichotomy of Torah. This paradox isn't meant to be resolved but rather to be sustained to ensure that Torah remains transcendent just as it becomes acquired and personalized.

Soul Food: The Profound Impact of *Talmud Torah*

Rabbi Nasanayl Braun

This Book of the Torah shall not depart from your mouth; but you shall meditate on it day and night. (*Yehoshu'a* 1:8)

Shammai used to say: Make your Torah study a matter of established regularity. (*Mishna Avot* 1:15)

Talmud Torah is meant to be constant and continual. It is how we connect to God and a central component of our *avodat Hashem*.[1]

Yet, there are two instances where we encounter a prohibition to learn Torah: when one is an *avel* (mourner) during the *shiva* period, and on the day of Tisha Be-Av. Through the prism of these prohibitions we can gain new insight into the nature of *talmud Torah*.

Specifically, let us address the following questions:

1. What is the rationale for these prohibitions? Are they the same or different?
2. What is the scope of these prohibitions? If allowances are made, what does that tell us about the nature of *talmud Torah*?

The Sources

The prohibitions of *talmud Torah* both for an *avel* and on Tisha Be-Av are recorded in the *Gemara*:

---

1. *Mishna Avot* (1:2): "The world stands on three pillars: Torah…"

> A mourner is forbidden [to engage] in the words of the Torah, because the All-Merciful said to Yechezkel: Sigh in silence. (*Mo'ed Katan* 15a)

> Our Rabbis have taught: All the restrictions that apply to the mourner apply on Tisha Be-Av. Eating, drinking, bathing, anointing, the wearing of shoes and marital relations are forbidden thereon. It is also forbidden [thereon] to read Torah, *Nevi'im* and *Ketuvim* or to study *Mishna, Gemara, Midrash, halakhot,* or *aggadot*; he may, however, read such parts of Scripture which he does not usually read and study such parts of *Mishna* which he usually does not study; and he may also read *Eikha, Iyov* and the sad parts of *Yirmeya*; and the school children are free from school, for it is said "The precepts of the Lord are right, rejoicing the heart." Rabbi Yehuda said: Even such parts of Scripture which he does not usually read he may not read, nor study parts of the *Mishna* which he does not usually study, but he may read *Iyov, Eikha* and the sad parts of *Yirmeya*; and the school children are free [from school], for it is said: "The precepts of the Lord are right, rejoicing the heart." (*Ta'anit* 30a)

At first glance, the rationales for these two prohibitions are different: One cannot learn on Tisha Be-Av because learning is a joyous activity and joy and Tisha Be-Av are incongruous, whereas the *avel* cannot learn because the *avel* is meant to be silent. Me'iri says just that in his commentary to *Mo'ed Katan*: "Regarding the *avel* the matter is dependent upon silence, and on Tisha Be-Av it is dependent only upon pain."

Further investigation, however, proves that it is not that simple. The opening line of the *Gemara* cited above (*Ta'anit* 30a) suggests a comparison between the two: "all the restrictions that apply to the mourner apply on Tisha Be-Av [as well]." This apparent inconsistency in rationale is noted by Ritva who writes (*Mo'ed Katan* 21a): "the Rabbis were unsure if they should merge the two *Gemarot*."

Elsewhere (ibid. 15a), Ritva injects the element of *simcha*, joy, as a reason to prohibit learning during *aveilut*. The *Gemara* in *Sukka* states that an *avel* is obligated in every mitzva except for *tefillin*, seemingly implying that they are allowed to learn Torah – a clear contradiction to the *Gemara* in *Mo'ed Katan*. To solve this, Ritva suggests two answers. His second answer maintains there is an obligation for the *avel* to learn. However, he fulfills this obligation by reciting *Shema* morning and evening. After he fulfills that obligation then he cannot learn any more, thus the prohibition codified in *Mo'ed Katan*.

Ritva's first answer maintains that one should not read all that much into the "general rule" in *Sukka*. It was not meant to be a complete and exclusive statement. An *avel* is certainly prohibited from learning, he states, because Torah brings joy to the heart! Thus, Ritva inserts the element of *simcha* from Tisha Be-Av into the world of *aveilut*.[2]

Lastly, both Ritva (*Mo'ed Katan* 21a) and Me'iri (ibid. 15a) discuss whether the permission given to learn the sad texts regarding Tisha Be-Av (listed in the *Gemara* above) is to be extended to *aveilut* as well. Such an extension is not obvious. In fact, Tosafot[3] record that Rabbeinu Tam in his youth prohibited *aveilim* from learning anything, including the sad texts, but changed his mind in his later years and permitted *aveilim* to learn those items.

To recap, there are two possible reasons to prohibit *talmud Torah* on Tisha Be-Av and during *aveilut* in the *shiva* period:

1. *Talmud Torah* is a joyous activity that will conflict with the sadness that we are meant to experience on these two occasions.
2. *Talmud Torah* is meant to be an engrossing and all-encompassing

---

2. Interestingly, Maharsha (*Ta'anit* 30a) tries to do exactly the opposite. He suggests that were it not for the commentary of Rashi, one could argue that the aspect of *simcha* is only being used to explain why children do not learn on Tisha Be-Av. He explains that the general prohibition of learning Torah on Tisha Be-Av is not because of *simcha*, rather it is so that one does not forget the mourning of the day. In this way, Maharsha injects the element of silence into Tisha Be-Av – the opposite of Ritva.
3. *Mo'ed Katan* 21a s.v. *ve-asur*.

activity that will distract us from the loss that we are meant to focus on.[4]

Some believe that the first option explains the prohibition on Tisha Be-Av and the second applies to *aveilut*. Others believe that there is only one reason for the prohibition that applies to both cases, and disagree regarding that primary reason.

Defining the Element of *Simcha* within *Talmud Torah*

What *simcha* is there in learning Torah? When I give a *shi'ur*, I hope that it will be interesting and that it will capture the attention of the people present. I hope that they will leave having learned something new and on a really good day maybe they will be inspired to learn more. Joy and happiness are neither expected outcomes, nor are they usually present.

Let us attempt to define that element by asking two questions:

1. Why are we allowed to learn the sad texts on Tisha Be-Av (and possibly during *aveilut*)?
2. Why can children not learn?

Permission to Learn the Sad Texts

Arukh Ha-Shulchan (OC 554:3-4) implicitly raises the following question: All *talmud Torah* brings joy to a *talmid chakham*. One who delves into the laws of *aveilut* in *Mo'ed Katan* and develops innovative ideas certainly experiences *simcha* in that learning, just as they would learning *Pesachim* or *Berakhot*. If so, why are we allowed to learn anything at all on Tisha Be-Av?

He explains that there are two elements inherent in *talmud Torah*: *simcha* and the pain of toiling in Torah. That pain exists even for the most learned as there is no end to the depths of the Torah. Nevertheless, despite the exertion that must be devoted, the activity of *talmud Torah* is one that primarily gladdens the Jewish soul.

---

4. Thus, the call for silence to allow us to focus upon the loss/tragedy. Alternatively, "silence" can be understood as an expression of surrender to the Divine will.

The joy of *talmud Torah* is not akin to the joy experienced at a ball game when your team scores or wins. It is not a euphoric sense of joy. Rather, it resembles an internal spiritual satisfaction. Learning Torah provides *simcha* to the soul, not to the body.

The Rav[5] raises a similar question from the opposite perspective of *Arukh Ha-Shulchan*. What if one hates learning Torah? What if someone does not enjoy learning at all? Even worse, what if it brings back painful memories of torturous high school classes? Can such a person learn even things that are not included the *Gemara*'s list of sad texts on Tisha Be-Av? It certainly will not bring them any *simcha*!

A possible answer is simply "*lo plug*": once codified as *halakha*, exceptions are not made based on the reason behind that *halakha*. The Rav, however, suggests that this person cannot learn because *talmud Torah* is considered, as a matter of law, an item of joy, even though in this case the body does not experience happiness or pleasure.[6] Once it is classified as such, it must be avoided on Tisha Be-Av.

One could suggest a third possibility, namely that even if one doesn't enjoy the learning per se, the act of *talmud Torah* nonetheless makes an impression upon the soul and brings *simcha* to the soul. And it is that *simchat ha-nefesh*, joy of the soul, that we are meant to avoid on Tisha Be-Av.

If so, we remain with our previous question. If learning is, by definition, *simchat hanefesh* and this can be attained even through learning *Mo'ed Katan* and *Iyov*, how can we learn anything at all on Tisha Be-Av?

Arukh Ha-Shulchan acknowledges that the sweetness of Torah exists even in the sad texts. The permission to learn them is due to the fact that the *tza'ar*, pain, of learning them will negate the *simcha*, even if new Torah insights are created in this learning.

What is the nature of this *tza'ar*? Clearly it cannot be the toil and frustration referred to before that is inherent in all *talmud Torah*. If that were the case, the sad texts would be identical to all forms of Torah and prohibited. Rather, this is an internal *tza'ar*, a pain caused by internalizing

---

5. *Shi'urei Ha-Rav, Tisha Be-Av* p. 44.
6. Rav Elyakim Koenigsberg, footnote 2, suggests that the Rav means that this is *simchat ha-nefesh* without *simchat ha-guf*, joy of the soul without physical joy.

what we have learned. In this case, both the *simcha* and the *tza'ar* are internal, with the latter neutralizing the former.

The Rav[7] is bothered by the same question: given that all *talmud Torah* is objectively joyful, how can one learn the sad texts on Tisha Be-Av? He suggests that while this is true, and learning these things brings the same type of *simcha* as the rest of the Torah, there is a special exception made on Tisha Be-Av for *inyanei de-yoma*, items that relate to the day. He draws support from *Kolbo* cited in *Beit Yosef* which states that on Tisha Be-Av one can learn *Eikha*, *kinot* and the like in order to remember the destruction of the *Beit Ha-Mikdash*. That last clause is unnecessary. Why the need to state, "in order to remember the destruction of the *Beit Ha-Mikdash*?" If one can learn these things because they are not joyous, or because the requisite pain of their contents cancels out the *simcha* of learning them, surely no other reason is necessary. *Kolbo* must believe that permission to learn these things is given, not because learning these portions of Torah are less joyous, rather because learning about the destruction and suffering of our people is part of the obligation of the day that must be performed, despite the *simcha* involved.

The permission granted by both *Arukh Ha-Shulchan* and the Rav to learn in depth on Tisha Be-Av opposes the opinion of *Taz* and *Magen Avraham* who allow only cursory reading and not in-depth learning. In a beautiful piece, *Arukh Ha-Shulchan* notes how hard that would be for a *talmid chakham* who will inevitably ("*ba'al korcho*") come to questioning and answering any piece of Torah read. The Rav allows such learning because that is part of the *inyanei de-yoma*, while *Arukh Ha-Shulchan* seems to believe that the deeper the learning of those sad texts, the more internalized the pain will be.

Beit Rabban

The *Gemara* (*Ta'anit* 30a) cited above implies that both according to Chakhamim and Rabbi Yehuda children do not learn on Tisha Be-Av. Their regular lessons are cancelled; the only argument between them is regarding learning texts that one is not familiar with, a topic not addressed in this article.

---

7. *Harerei Kedem* 2:292.

Rif[8] and Rid[9] attribute the opposite position to Rabbi Me'ir and maintain that he believes that the children in *Beit Rabban*, elementary school, do not stop learning on Tisha Be-Av.

Rabbi Me'ir's position would seem to be the intuitive position. Children in *Beit Rabban* are learning how to learn and have not yet developed the skills or mental capacity to achieve joy in learning or *simchat ha-nefesh*. If so, there is no reason for them to stop.[10]

This, in fact, is the rationale of *Taz* (OC 554:1). It is not the children who achieve *simcha* while learning but the teacher. It is the teacher's *simcha* that prevents the children from learning. *Magen Avraham* (ibid. 2) disagrees with this premise: The children do have *simcha* in their school learning. They rejoice in learning to read even if they do not understand what they are reading. The children's *simcha*, perhaps reflective of a profound feeling of accomplishment, is not quite the same as the one envisioned by *Arukh Ha-Shulchan* or the Rav.

Arukh Ha-Shulchan (OC 554) rejects both *Magen Avraham* and *Taz*. He rejects *Taz* because there is no *simcha* in teaching kids. Furthermore, even if the teacher did experience *simcha*, Tisha Be-Av should not be sufficient reason to absolve the teaching of children. After all, an *avel* is required to teach children (YD 384).[11] He also rejects *Magen Avraham* because he does not agree that the *simcha* of accomplishment is that which is forbidden on Tisha Be-Av. Amazingly, he writes, "Rabbi Yehuda believes that despite the inherent challenges in learning and teaching, it pales in comparison to

---

8. *Ta'anit* 10a in the *alfas*.
9. *Piskei Ha-Rid Ta'anit* 30a.
10. *Sha'agat Aryeh* (*Gevurot Ari Ta'anit* 30a) suggests that Rabbi Me'ir's position might have nothing to do with the presence or lack of *simcha*. He writes that teaching children is something that contains no sin, and *Yerushalayim* was destroyed because the children stopped learning. Thus, specifically on Tisha Be-Av we should teach the children Torah! Rav Chayyim of *Brisk* suggests that Rabbi Yehuda's position might have nothing to do with *simcha* as well. *Mo'ed Katan* 22b records, "when a *chakham* dies, his *Beit Midrash* is cancelled." Certainly, then, the destruction of the *Beit Ha-Mikdash* and the murder of so many Jews should lead to cancelling school.
11. That is not explicit in *Shulchan Arukh* there; *Shakh* there (note 2) argues that a teacher of children is equivalent to "*rabbim tzerikhim lo*," someone who the public require, while *Taz* there (note 1) allows it only after the third day.

the joy of the soul when it learns the Torah of God; even though there is no physical joy, nonetheless the soul of the Jew is happy when one learns Torah." According to *Arukh Ha-Shulchan*, the encounter with Torah at any age impacts and impresses the soul.[12]

In a similar vein, *Sefat Emet* (*Ta'anit* 30a) writes that even if one does not understand what they are reading, the words of Torah nevertheless are "*mesammechei lev*," bring joy the heart. Although that seems difficult to accept, he too understands that there is something inherent in the encounter with Torah that is joyous.

An Exception

Although the prohibition to learn Torah as an *avel* and on Tisha Be-Av seems non-negotiable, the *Yerushalmi* (*Mo'ed Katan* 3:5, 16a) records a possible exception. It teaches us, "One who burns after the Torah is permitted [to learn it]."

Rav Elyashiv[13] notes that this position is not recorded in any of the *poskim* because today we do not have people who truly burn after the Torah. We do not have people whose souls are alit with the fire of Torah and simply cannot live without it.

There is a possibly apocryphal story which claims that the Rogatchover learned Torah during his *aveilut* in the *shiva* period because he was a *mitzta'er*, one who is suffering, and simply could not function without learning Torah. Rav Elyashiv is unsure if we should believe the story, because the Rogatchover could have learned the sad texts or *Mo'ed Katan*.

Ideally, we should all strive to burn after the Torah. We should feel a constant need to be learning Torah and engaged with the Torah. Minimally, we should have a constant and continual encounter with God's Torah that yields the *simchat ha-nefesh* and its attendant impact upon us.

---

12. The Rav (*Harerei Kedem* 2:291) argues that children do not learn because learning is an objective act of *simcha*, very much like a wedding. Even if one does not enjoy the wedding, a wedding is inherently a joyous occasion.
13. He'arot to *Mo'ed Katan* 21a.

Our Founding *Rashei Yeshiva zt"l*

It is that encounter with the Torah, that special *simchat ha-nefesh* attained via *talmud Torah*, that each *talmid* in Yeshivat Har Etzion experiences. Its impact lasts well beyond the years spent in *Yeshiva*. The importance of *talmud Torah* and the centrality of the encounter with Torah is one of the core messages of the *Yeshiva* and one that each of the *Rashei Yeshiva* stressed and taught.

Rav Amital *zt"l* taught:

> A person who studies Torah "takes" God with him and creates a bond with Him. Even if we are unable to explain exactly how this bond is created, history proves that without intensive Torah study, nothing will remain. Jewish communities in which there was no Torah study, no occupation with the intricate discussions of Abbayei and Rava, did not survive. Go and look at all the curricular experiments that have been conducted to this day, go and visit all the various *Batei Midrash*, and you will see that the only institutions to survive are those where *Gemara* was and continues to be studied.[14]

Rav Lichtenstein *zt"l* taught that "*aseh Toratekha keva*" (*Mishna Avot* 1:15) means:

> There are things to which a person is committed to the degree that he wants them to be a part of him. When he has that kind of experience, he wants it to be internalized, not to remain ephemeral. This is what the *beraita* tells us that with regard to Torah. "*Aseh Toratekha keva*" – see to it that it is ingrained and absorbed, that it becomes a part of you. This, of course, has implications for the nature of the experience at the time.[15]

---

14. https://www.etzion.org.il/en/kol-yehuda.
15. *By His Light*, [reprinted by Maggid Books (2016),] p. 60.

It is that bond, that internalization of Torah, which brings about the *simchat ha-nefesh* described by *Arukh Ha-Shulchan*.

These quotes constitute but one of so many examples. The centrality of the experience of *talmud Torah* was one of the *Rashei Yeshiva zt"l*'s most repeated themes. I chose these teachings because both were found in the context of the layman, or the ordinary person, and not the professional *talmid chakham*.

Rav Lichtenstein writes:

> In certain respects, this is an extraordinary demand, because one might have thought, "You can ask an ordinary person to engage in *talmud Torah* or to be in touch with Torah; but you cannot ask the average person to internalize his learning into something which is permanent." In other areas, we assume that there is a great difference between professional scholars and those who have a dilettantish interest… However, regarding *talmud Torah*, the demand on the average person really is to make it a permanent part of himself. He cannot simply attend a *shi'ur* and think, "Fine, I'll hear the *shi'ur* – it will be a nice experience, he's a good speaker. I'll enjoy it. I'll be enlightened. And I'll go home."[16]

Rav Amital succinctly teaches us:

> There is no room for the statement, "I'm not a *lamdan* (studious one)." If you aren't a *lamdan*, if you don't engage in Torah study, you'll end up engaging in worthless matters.[17]

May the *Yeshiva* continue to instill within its *talmidim* a deep and abiding connection to the Torah, and inculcate within them the *simchat ha-nefesh* that results from that encounter!

---

16. Ibid. p. 62.
17. https://www.etzion.org.il/en/kol-yehuda.

The 48 *Kinyenei Torah*: An Introduction[1]

Rabbi Dovid Gottlieb

I.

Torah is the purpose and blueprint for creation,[2] and, as a result, it is the foundation of our religious life. Not surprisingly, therefore, there is no shortage of statements in Chazal which extol the virtues and importance of Torah study. While most of the teachings can be found as individual statements, spread throughout the writings of Chazal, one of the most extensive and cohesive treatments is the chapter popularly known as *Kinyan Torah*. This chapter, which discusses the beauty of Torah and serves as a primer for how to be successful in one's Torah study, is well-known as the sixth and final chapter of *Avot*.[3] It consists, strictly speaking, of *beraitot*, not *mishnayot*, and although it was not originally included with *Avot*, all later editions include this sixth chapter.

The addition of *Kinyan Torah* evidently came as a result of the popular custom to study a chapter of *Avot* each week during the period in between Pesach and Shavu'ot; as a result, there are now six chapters to study on the six *shabbatot* in between these holidays. The earliest references to this custom, such as by Rav Amram Ga'on in the 9th century, explicitly mention the practice to study "*Avot* and *Kinyan Torah*."[4]

---

1. This article is intended as an introduction to a series of articles which I hope to present in the future which will analyze each of the 48 *Kinyenei Torah* individually and, at the same time, identify common themes which run through many of the *kinyanim*.
2. See *Bereishit Rabba* 1:1 and *Zohar Parashat Teruma* p. 161a.
3. The *beraitot* also appear together in *Tana De-Vei Eliyahu Zuta* ch. 17, and *Kalla Rabbati* ch. 9.
4. *Seder Rav Amram Ga'on, Mincha Shel Shabbat*. See also *Siddur Rashi* section 516.

It is evident that the reason that this chapter, specifically, was chosen, was because the focus on Torah is a most appropriate topic to be studied in advance of Shavu'ot, the holiday that celebrates the giving of the Torah.[5] The *Sefer Ha-Chinnukh* mitzva 306 explains that the ultimate purpose of *Sefirat Ha-Omer* is to demonstrate – and build – our excitement for receiving the Torah.[6] In this spirit, the custom of studying *Avot* in between Pesach and Shavu'ot emerged out of a recognition that proper ethical behavior and character refinement – the essential themes of *Avot* – are an ideal, and perhaps even necessary, preparation for the holiday of Shavu'ot and the celebration of *Mattan Torah*.[7] Given this background, it was fitting that "*derekh eretz kadema la-Torah*," namely, after the study of *Avot* and proper character, we then study *Kinyan Torah* and learn about the glory of Torah. This six-week course of study is, thus, most appropriate for the period of *Sefirat Ha-Omer* and serves as ideal preparation for Shavu'ot.[8]

II.

Perhaps the most famous component of *Kinyan Torah* is the *beraita*'s list of 48 attributes which are necessary to "acquire Torah." Before enumerating the specific attributes, the *beraita* begins by comparing Torah to two other points of prestige:

> Torah is greater than the priesthood and the monarchy, for the monarchy is acquired with 30 attributes (*ma'alot*) and the priesthood [is acquired] with 24 [attributes], but the Torah is acquired with 48 things (*devarim*). (*Avot* 6:6)

---

5. See Rashi *Avot* 6:1, s.v. *shanu Chakhamim*.
6. See, also, *Tzeror Ha-Ma'or Devarim* 15:12, *Levush* OC 489:1, *Sefat Emet Emor* 5644 s.v. *bi-sefirat ha-omer*. For further elaboration of this idea and how it fits into the general philosophy of the *Chinnukh*, see Gersion Appel, *A Philosophy of Mitzvot*, revised edition 2008, ch. 3, and especially pp. 50-51.
7. Avudraham *Tefillot Ha-Pesach* s.v. *arba'a kosot*, *Ha-Chasid Ya'aveitz Avot* 6:1 s.v. *shanu Chakhamim*. The Ya'aveitz is also quoted in *Midrash Shmu'el Avot* 6:1 s.v. *veha-chasid z"l*. See also *Chiddushei Ha-Rim* p. 162 and *Oheiv Yisrael* pp.283-284.
8. *Ha-Chasid Ya'aveitz* and *Midrash Shmu'el*. Regarding the broader principle that refined character traits – *mentschlechkeit* – is a prerequisite for Torah, see *Vayikra Rabba* 9:3, *Avot* 3:17, Rabbeinu Yona ad loc. s.v. *im ein derekh eretz ein Torah*, Rav Chayyim Vital *Sha'arei Kedusha chelek* 1 *sha'ar* 2 s.v. *ve-hinnei inyan ha-middot*.

The 48 *Kinyenei Torah*: An Introduction | 397

The attributes of monarchy referred to are the rights and prerogatives enjoyed by the *melekh*, known as the "*mishpat ha-melekh*," introduced in *Shmu'el Alef* 8:11-21 and expanded upon by the *Gemara* in the second chapter of *Sanhedrin*.[9] Similarly, the attributes of the priesthood refer to 24 gifts that the *kohen* receives, which are mainly enumerated in *Bamidbar* 18:9-19, 28.[10] In fact, then, the *beraita* does not mean that the monarchy and priesthood are actually acquired through the enumerated attributes, but rather, that these are the ways the elevated status of the *melekh* and *kohen*, respectively, are manifest and demonstrated. With respect to Torah, however, the 48 qualities which are listed in the continuation of the *beraita* are actually the means used to acquire Torah; they are not the benefits of a certain status but the method to succeed in Torah study.[11] In other words, for the *melekh* or *kohen* these characteristics are a *siman*, a sign of the person's exalted station, whereas for a *talmid chakham* these qualities are the *siba*, a catalyst for the elevated status.[12]

Some commentators go even further and explain that the delineated *kinyanim* are not just beneficial or even recommended, but are, in fact, the *only* way to acquire Torah. While Torah can be learned and knowledge can be obtained even without these 48 attributes, to truly "own" Torah – to have a "*kinyan* in Torah" – a person must possess these traits. Similar to other objects of acquisition – real or movable property – where the proper mode of *kinyan* must be used, otherwise the transaction is invalid, Torah, as well,

---

9. Rashi *Avot* 6:6 s.v. *sheha-malkhut nikneit bi-shloshim ma'alot*, *Machzor Vitri* ch. 429 s.v. *sheha-malkhut bi-shloshim ma'alot*, *Tiferet Yisrael Avot* ch. 6 *Yakhin* n. 66.
10. Rashi ad loc., *Tiferet Yisrael Avot* ch. 6 *Yakhin* n. 67. See, however, *Machzor Vitri* ad loc., who suggests that the reference is to 24 special laws that govern the lives and Temple service of the *kohen*.
11. See *Derekh Chayyim, Avot* 6:7 s.v. *gedola Torah*. In fact, *Ha-Chasid Ya'aveitz* s.v. *sheha-malkhut bi-shloshim* deletes the word "*nikneit*," acquired, with regards to kingship and priesthood.
12. See, however, Rav Tzvi Yehuda Ha-Kohen Kook, *Kinyan Torah* p. 33, who understands that the honor and tributes offered by the nation actually "create" the special and elevated status of the *melekh* and *kohen*; that is to say, these positions are only fully realized by the honor shown to them by the people, and, as such, "*nikneit*" is understood as a *siba* for the monarchy and priesthood, just as it is for Torah.

can only be acquired by someone who possesses these characteristics.[13] Nevertheless, it is not "all or nothing" – even possession of only some of the attributes enables a person to acquire a partial "*kinyan* in Torah." But the more the better, obviously, and only someone who possesses all 48 attributes can master the entire Torah in its full breadth and depth.[14]

Some commentators suggest, additionally, that this difference explains the discrepancy in terminology used in the *beraita*. The attributes associated with the monarchy and, by implication, the priesthood, are referred to as "*ma'alot*," whereas the 48 traits connected to Torah are referred to as "*devarim*." Regarding the monarchy and priesthood, the term "*ma'alot*" is used because these attributes serve to demonstrate the elevated – *na'aleh* – status of those who possess them. However, this phrase is abjured when discussing Torah, because in that context the enumerated characteristics do not indicate superiority but are simply those characteristics – *devarim* – which are required of a person who wishes to achieve mastery of Torah.[15]

III.

The *beraita*'s comparison of Torah to the monarchy and priesthood echoes the earlier *mishna* in Avot 4:13, which famously refers to these elevated statuses as "*shelosha ketarim heim*," the three crowns. The term "crown" is used to allude to the fact that we are required to honor anyone who "wears the crown" of monarchy, the priesthood, or Torah.[16] The *Gemara* (*Yoma* 72b) also compares the priesthood, Torah, and the monarchy to each other, associating them with the *mizbei'ach*, *aron*, and *shulchan* respectively,

---

13. *Or Ha-Chayyim Vayikra* 26:3 #9, *Koveitz Iggerot Chazon Ish* v. 1 n. 2, Rav Yerucham Leivovitz, *Da'at Torah* v. 3 p. 107 (see also v. 4 pp. 167-168), and Rav Aharon Kotler, *Mishnat Rebbe Aharon* v. 1 p. 65 and v. 3 p. 13. See, also, *Shir Hashirim Rabba* 4:15 with the commentary of Radal ad loc. s.v. *hada hu di-khtiv*, as well as the interpretation of the *midrash* in *Sefat Emet Chukkat* 5652 s.v. *be-inyan shirat ha-be'er*.
14. *Sefat Emet Avot* 6:5 s.v. *veha-Torah nikneit*, *Lev Eliyahu* v. 3 p. 58, *Koveitz Iggerot Chazon Ish* ad loc. n. 4. See, also, Rav Yosef Zundel *Mi-Salant*, quoted in *Yerach Le-Mo'adim, Sefirat Ha-Omer-Shavu'ot* v. 2 p. 45.
15. *Derekh Chayyim* ad loc., *Tiferet Yisrael* ad loc. n. 68. See, also, *Barukh She-amar Avot* 6:5 s.v. *sheha-malkhut bi-shloshim ma'alot*.
16. Rav Ovadya *Mi-Bartenura Avot* 4:13 s.v. *shelosha ketarim heim*. *Magein Avot*, Avot 4:13 s.v. *shelosha ketarim heim*.

each of which is distinguished by having a *zer*, a decorative rim, which surrounds it like a crown.[17]

The repeated grouping of these stations of prestige underscores their commonality, on the one hand, but, on the other hand, also raises the question of why the *beraita* considers Torah greater than the other two. If all three are honored positions, then on what basis is Torah superior? If anything, one might argue that the *beraita* itself implies the opposite: the *melekh* and *kohen* are bestowed many privileges while the student of Torah is just described as requiring many prerequisites to achieve a *kinyan*, true mastery of the material. Why does the *beraita* declare that "Torah is greater than the priesthood and the monarchy?"

An answer to this question can be found in the continuation of the *Gemara*, which similarly asserts that the "crown of Torah" is superior to the others. The basis of this conclusion is the verse in *Mishlei* 8:15, which indicates that even kings are only successful if they are imbued with Torah; in essence, then, it is the Torah that "appoints" the *melekh* and, therefore, Torah is the true source of prestige and honor.[18] In other words, we should not be distracted by the numerous benefits bestowed upon the *melekh* or *kohen*; the ultimate source of respect is Torah.

Another approach to this question relates to the relative accessibility of the various "crowns." The *Gemara*, in the course of its discussion, notes that while priesthood is reserved for the descendants of Aharon *Ha-Kohen* and the monarchy is reserved for descendants of David *Ha-Melekh*, Torah is not reserved for anyone; rather, "*kol ha-rotzeh likach yavo ve-yikach*," it is accessible to anyone – from any tribe or family – who wants to study. While it initially viewed the non-exclusivity of Torah as a sign of inferiority, the *Gemara* concludes, based on the aforementioned verse from *Mishlei*, that Torah is nevertheless superior to the monarchy and priesthood.

---

17. See Rashi *Yoma* 72b s.v. *shelosha zeirin*.
18. Rashi ad loc. s.v. *bi melakhim yimlokhu* and Rambam *Hilkhot Talmud Torah* 3:1. The *Gemara* only addresses the superiority of Torah over the monarchy, but never directly mentions that – or why – Torah is superior to the priesthood. The commentators, however, assume this to be the case and offer different rationales for the basis of Torah's preeminence. See *Maharsha* and *Sefat Emet Yoma* ad loc., and *Lechem Mishneh Hilkhot Talmud Torah* 3:1.

Rashi, however, states emphatically that Torah's preeminence is not *despite*, but *because* of its universality. Commenting on the *mishna* in *Avot* 4:13 which presents the "three crowns," Rashi notes this discrepancy of accessibility and then adds, "*le-khakh gadol kitrah shel Torah mi-shenayim halalu*," this – the universal accessibility of Torah – is the reason for the primacy of Torah over the monarchy and priesthood. The very fact that that the Torah is *not* exclusive and that anyone can "wear the crown" is the basis of Torah's superiority.[19]

Rather than searching for a source for the preeminence of Torah from somewhere else – an earlier *mishna* in *Avot* or a selection from the *Gemara* – some of commentators to *Kinyan Torah* suggest that evidence is actually found in the *beraita*'s own words.

Midrash Shmu'el and Derekh Chayyim point out that the very fact that Torah requires 48 characteristics to acquire it, whereas the monarchy is "acquired" with 30 attributes and the priesthood is "acquired" with 24, is itself an indication of the superiority of Torah.[20] As we are familiar with from other areas of life, the more worthwhile a goal is the more effort one must expend to accomplish it, and the more valuable an object is the more expensive it is to purchase. So too, the greater number of requirements necessary to acquire Torah indicates its supremacy.[21]

Alternatively, some commentators focus on the qualitative – and not just quantitative – difference between the different attributes as the key to Torah's exalted status. Seforno notes that the privileges and prerogatives (*ma'alot*) granted to both the *melekh* and *kohen* are all material, and focused on "*kavod be-chayyei sha'a*," granting honor in this, impermanent, world. The attributes required for Torah, however, are "*be-hefekh zeh*," the opposite of those of the monarchy and priesthood: they are not prerogatives but rather virtues that separate a person from material pleasures and worldly honor; the benefits from Torah will enable a person "*lehaknot kavod le-chayyei olam*," to acquire eternal honor in the World to Come.[22]

---

19. Rashi *Avot* 4:13 s.v. *shelosha ketarim heim*.
20. *Midrash Shmu'el* 6:7 s.v. *tzarikh le'ahavin*, *Derekh Chayyim* 6:7 s.v. *gedola Torah, uve-ulai yiksheh lekha*.
21. *Yachel Yisrael Avot* v. 6 p. 111.
22. Seforno *Avot* 6:5.

In a similar vein, Midrash Shmu'el notes that while the "*ma'alot*" elevate the *melekh* and *kohen*, providing authority and importance, nevertheless they do so through privileges which are superficial and external to the person, and which were not achieved "*be-hishtaddeluto ve-charitzuto*," through genuine effort and personal accomplishment. But the "crown of Torah" is just the opposite: it is not in any way external to the person, but rather it is something that becomes part of the person's essence ("*kinyan gamur be-nafsho*"). Moreover, the attributes necessary to acquire Torah are not called "*ma'alot*" because they do not "elevate" the person or secure privileges; on the contrary, they demand humility and subservience.[23]

Another distinction suggested is that "*ma'alot*" implies that what is important is the elevated position of the *melekh* and *kohen* – the result – which is evidenced by these characteristics. And when it comes to the position, either you are or you are not – there is no in between – and if you are, you receive all of the attendant benefits; there is no *melekh* without all 30 of the royal privileges and there is no *kohen* without all 24 of the priestly gifts. However, "*devarim*" suggests a process, as the aspiring scholar masters each trait, one by one. In addition, while the goal is – obviously – to move from one trait to the next, each one is not just a rung on the ladder, but possesses independent value.[24] As such, the journey towards obtaining the "crown of Torah" is itself important and the spiritual benefits obtained from each trait accrue whether or not the ultimate goal is achieved.[25]

The common denominator of these explanations – whether highlighting the spiritual dimension, the effort demanded, or the inherent value of the process – is that there is a qualitative and fundamental distinction between the "*devarim*" of Torah and the "*ma'alot*" of monarchy and priesthood, and that these differences reflect the inherent superiority of Torah and, thus,

---

23. *Midrash Shmu'el* ad loc. s.v. *tzarikh le'ahavin*.
24. *Yachel Yisrael Avot* v. 6 pp. 109, 114.
25. *Magein Avot* (Kluger) *Avot* 6:6 s.v. *gedola Torah*. This explanation is reminiscent of the well-known interpretation of the words we recite at a *siyum*, "*anu ameilim ve-heim ameilim, anu ameilim u-mekabbelim sakhar ve-heim ameilim ve-einam mekabbelim sakhar*," that with regards to the study of Torah, we are rewarded for the effort we exert even if we do not achieve the ultimate success of understanding. See *Chafetz Chayyim Al Ha-Torah Vayikra* 26:3, p. 179.

support the *beraita*'s contention that, "Torah is greater than the priesthood and the monarchy."

IV.

Lastly, a number of commentators have suggested that the 48 *kinyenei Torah* correspond to the 49 days of the *Omer*. In other words, not only is there natural relationship between *Avot-Kinyan Torah* and the weeks preceding Shavu'ot, but this relationship is further highlighted by focusing, specifically, on the *beraita*'s list of attributes and the number of days leading up to *Mattan Torah*.[26] Some – such as the early students of Rav Yisrael Mi-Salant – actually put this insight "into action" and spent each day of the *Omer* period working on a different one of the *kinyanim*, so that all of the traits would be acquired in time for Shavu'ot.

The problem with this insight, obviously, is that the numbers do not match up. If the days of the *Omer* are intended to focus on the *beraita*'s list, why aren't there 49 attributes? If we are one attribute short, what is the extra day intended for?

Most assume that – as a practical matter – the "missing" day is the final one and, as a result, suggest various explanations for what to do once the 48 *kinyanim* have been completed. One suggestion is that the final day should be used to review and reinforce all the characteristics. The importance of *chazara*, reviewing one's learning, is often emphasized by Chazal,[27] and certainly if these characteristics are to be truly actualized, review is essential.[28]

The Alter of *Kelm* maintains that the last day should be used not just to review, but to integrate all of the various characteristics into a harmonious whole. To truly maximize the impact of these characteristics they cannot remain disjunct, in which case the whole might turn out to be less than the sum of its parts. But if all 48 of the *kinyanim* are harmonized in a balanced way then a spiritually potent personality – worthy of the "crown of Torah" – will be forged.[29]

---

26. Maharal *Netivot Olam, Netiv Ha-Torah* ch. 12 s.v. *uva-perek ha-ba*.
27. See, for example, *Chagiga* 9b, *Sanhedrin* 99a.
28. *Chiddushei Ha-Rim* p. 163, *Lev Eliyahu* v. 3 p. 58.
29. *Chokhma U-Mussar* v. 1 ch. 236.

Others suggest that what is needed is not more work on the characteristics themselves – review or integration – but rather an additional step. Rav Asher Weiss explains that the final day is needed so that we can pray to God for success in this spiritual endeavor. The preceding 48 days are necessary for *hishtaddelut*, for us to put in the effort of studying and internalizing these characteristics. But all human effort – material or spiritual – requires *hashgacha*, Divine blessing and munificence, to be successful.

The need for a combination of prayer and diligent effort, specifically with regards to Torah study, is evident from the story described in *Nidda* 70b. Rabbi Yehoshu'a ben Chananya was asked what a person should do to obtain the wisdom of Torah. His initial answer was, "*yarbeh bi-yshiva vi-yma'et bi-schora*," that it required hard work and single-minded dedication. But, his petitioners responded, many have put in the effort and still not been successful; what else is needed? Rabbi Yehoshu'a ben Chananya then replied: "*yevakshu rachamim mi-mi sheha-chokhma shelo*," your efforts must be followed by devout prayer, asking God to share "His Torah" with you. Thus, explains Rav Weiss, after completing this 48-day course of study – "*yarbeh bi-yshiva*" – on the final day we turn to God and pray – "*yevakshu rachamim*" – that He bless our efforts.[30]

Additionally, Rav Aharon Kotler maintained that the final day is needed so that we do not "lose sight of the forest for the trees" and we can prepare for Shavu'ot. After 48 days of running, as it were, from *kinyan* to *kinyan*, the extra day allows us to pause and fully contemplate of holiness and significance of *Kabbalat Ha-Torah*.[31]

Unlike the previous explanations, some have suggested that the extra day is not the last day of the *Omer*, but the *first*; there is a step that is necessary before we even begin the process of acquiring the different

---

30. *Sichot Minchat Asher Al Ha-Mo'adim* v. 3 ch. 43, and Rav Asher Weiss, "*Kinyenei Ha-Torah: Hakhana Le-Mattan Torah*" in *Kinyan Torah Ha-Shaleim*, pp. 235-240. See there, as well, for additional sources highlighting the broader idea that the unique nature of Torah means that our efforts alone are not sufficient and, as a result, it is necessary for God to gift the Torah to us. Regarding the specific idea of praying for success in Torah study, see also Ibn Ezra *Devarim* 4:7 and *Koveitz Iggerot Chazon Ish* v. 1 ch. 2.
31. *Mishnat Rebbe Aharon* v. 3 p. 13.

kinyanim. Maharal contends that the first day is dedicated to praying to God – not for spiritual success, but for material sustenance. The *mishna* famously teaches that "*im ein kemach, ein Torah*," without sufficient financial resources serious Torah scholarship will remain forever elusive.[32] Chazal were painfully realistic in their assertion that sustained dedication to Torah study is simply impossible if it is not accompanied by at least minimal financial security. As such, it makes sense that we first address this precondition and pray for material blessing – we focus on the *kemach* – and only thereafter do we begin the long and arduous journey of working towards the "crown of Torah."[33]

Rav Asher Weiss offers an additional explanation for why we need an extra day before we even begin studying the 48 *kinyanim*. Prior to undertaking any difficult mission, it is necessary to understand its importance and to appreciate how essential the success of the mission is. It is inevitable that there will be difficulties and even setbacks and only one who truly understands how crucial the mission is will persevere despite the obstacles. Similarly, maintains Rav Weiss, before a person begins the challenging task of mastering the many character traits enumerated in the *beraita*, it is critical to appreciate the importance of Torah. Only one who understands the cosmic significance of Torah – the world could not exist without constant Torah study[34] – and the transformative power of Torah in the lives of those who study her words – it is the "Tree of Life" (*Mishlei* 3:18) and the source of countless other blessings[35] – will muster the requisite fortitude to internalize the many different and difficult *kinyanim*. Thus, the first day of the *Omer* is dedicated to contemplating the significance of the goal and only afterwards, on the second day, does the process of achieving the goal begin.[36]

In a slightly different vein, we can suggest that the importance of appreciating the value of Torah is not only to enhance a person's motivation

---

32. *Avot* 3:17 with commentaries of Rabbeinu Yona and Rav Ovadya *Mi-Bartenura*.
33. Maharal *Derush Al Ha-Torah* p. 22.
34. *Nefesh Ha-Chayyim* 4:11.
35. *Avot* 6:1, "*kol ha-oseik ba-Torah li-shmah zokheh li-dvarim harbeh.*"
36. *Sichot Minchat Asher Al Ha-Mo'adim* ad loc. ch. 44, and Rav Asher Weiss, "*Kinyenei Ha-Torah: Hakhana Le-Mattan Torah*" ad loc.

and resilience, but also because without such an appreciation it may be impossible to acquire Torah. With regards to commercial transactions, there is a fascinating law that a person only acquires an object to the extent that he values the object, even if in truth the item is more valuable. For example, if a person possesses a piece of metal which he then sells for the market price of metal and then, after the sale, becomes aware that it is in fact silver, he cannot undo the sale or demand payment for the differential price of silver. The rationale for this law is that since the seller thought it was metal and had not previously realized it was silver he never truly "owned" the silver. In other words, you only own an object to the extent that you are aware of its value.[37] Similarly, it can be argued, even if you "make a *kinyan*" on Torah, the *kinyan* is only effective to the extent that you appreciate the value of Torah. Even if you acquire all 48 traits, if you think Torah is merely "metal" then that will compromise your acquisition.[38] It is crucially important, therefore, that you first spend a day contemplating the value of Torah, and only after you realize its true value as "silver" start the process of studying the 48 *kinyanim*.[39]

V.

Kinyan Torah is one of Chazal's most concentrated presentations regarding the importance and beauty of Torah. The significance of the material is evident from the long-standing practice of appending this chapter to *Avot* and the popular custom of studying it, annually, the week before Shavu'ot. At the heart of this chapter is the famous *beraita* which associates the greatness of Torah – even greater than the monarchy or priesthood – with

---

37. *Hagahot Ashri Bava Metzi'a* 2:9, Rema CM 232:18.
38. See *Sod Yesharim – Sukkot, Simchat Torah* p.66 and *Mevaser Tov – Ko'ach Kiyyum Yisrael* pp. 346-347 who make this general point about Torah, although not in connection with the 48 *kinyanim*. See, as well, this idea – that you only acquire something to the extent that you appreciate its value – in *Beit Ya'akov Vayikra* p. 58, regarding mitzva performance, and *Mei Marom* v. 6 "*Mi-Ma'ayanei Yeshu'a*," p. 293 regarding the Land of Israel.
39. Compare to Ran *Nedarim* 81a s.v. *davar zeh*, citing Rabbeinu Yona, who explains that studying Torah without proper appreciation and respect is tantamount to abandoning Torah (*Yirmeyahu* 9:12, "*al ozvam et Torati*").

48 "*devarim*," attributes, necessary to acquire Torah. As we have seen, the scope, nature and challenge of internalizing these attributes is itself ample tribute to the value of Torah. The "crown of Torah" is available to anyone willing to put in the necessary effort, and a prerequisite to that effort is the acquisition of these 48 traits. Every trait helps and each one gets us one step closer to the final goal, but a full "*kinyan* Torah" can only be achieved by someone who internalizes all of these "*kinyanim*." Lastly, as noted, the "missing" day during the customary *Omer* study period itself highlights, among other ideas, the necessity of reviewing the material and integrating the many ideas into a balanced whole, the importance of praying for success, and the need to fully appreciate the importance of Torah. Each of the 48 *kinyenei Torah* deserves serious study and contemplation, and the unit, as a whole, presents an inspiring text for study and an instructive guide for life.

Berakhot and Bilam

Rabbi Dr. Michael S. Berger

The story of Bilam, taking up three chapters in *Bamidbar*, elicits extensive commentary for the many problems it poses, both in terms of its own plot, including God's seemingly changing His mind, the ass's miraculous speech, Bilam's true intent, and that of its inclusion in the Torah at this point in the narrative flow of *Bamidbar*. Irrespective of these significantly thorny issues, on three separate occasions the *Tanakh* finds God's intervention noteworthy:

1) With reference to the prohibition against marrying an Ammonite or Moabite (*Devarim* 23:5-6): "Because they hired against you Bilam the son of Be'or of *Aram Naharayyim* to curse you, yet the Lord your God refused to heed (*lo ava…lishmo'a*) Bilam, and for your sake the Lord your God turned the curse into a blessing."
2) In Yehoshu'a's valedictory (*Yehoshu'a* 24:9-10): "Then Balak…arose and fought against Israel, and he sent and called for Bilam son of Be'or to curse you, but I refused to heed Bilam; instead he blessed you, and I delivered you from his hand."[1]
3) In the final chapter of *Nechemya*, in which the people learn that marriage to Ammonites and Moabites is prohibited based on the reasons in the injunction in *Devarim*, including God's having changed Bilam's curse into a blessing.

---

1. *Metzudat David* (ad loc.) understands "his hand" as referring to Balak's, not that of Bilam, since it was Balak who sought to wage war against Benei Yisrael via Bilam's words.

Thus, in each of the *Tanakh*'s three sections – Torah, *Nevi'im* and *Ketuvim* – we have a reference to the episode of Bilam, with special emphasis in the first two on God having transformed Bilam's curse into a blessing. Indeed, in Yehoshu'a's final speech, he mentions only three episodes of God's protection and redemption of the Jewish people in the wilderness (crossing the *Yam Suf*, conquering the Amorites, and Balak's hiring of Bilam to curse), suggesting that Bilam possessed some genuine maledictive power that required Divine intervention to thwart its aims. This framing, which seems to grant Bilam quasi-demonic powers, only compounds the bewilderment: what is the source of his capacity to bless or curse?

What is more, this begs the larger question as to the basis for the human capacity to deliver blessings and curses throughout *Tanakh*, including prior to the Bilam story. The book of *Bereishit* is replete with this power, from No'ach's curse of Kena'an (9:25), to Ya'akov's blessings, first of Pharaoh (47:10), then of Yosef and his sons (ch. 48) and finally of Ya'akov's sons (ch. 49) near the end of the book. In between, Malki-Tzedek (14:18-20), Rivka's mother and brother (24:60), Yitzchak (ch. 27 and 28), and the *ish* in the nocturnal struggle with Ya'akov (32:30) all display this capacity. When the Jews leave Egypt, Pharaoh asks Moshe and Aharon "to bless me as well" (*Shemot* 12:32). While we are inclined to see the blessings of prophets, that is, people with whom God communicates directly, as a unique endowment,[2] the other cases of blessings present a difficulty. Did Malki-Tzedek and Rivka's relatives possess magical powers? Or were their pronouncements simply invocations, benevolent expressions of a hoped-for reality but enjoying no special status?[3]

---

2. Rashi on *Bereishit* 12:2, s.v. *ve-hyei berakha*, quoting *Bereishit Rabba*, clearly reflects this view: "The blessings are given into your hand; until now they were in My hand – I blessed Adam and No'ach – but from now on you will bless whomever you want."
3. This is the presumed intention of other expressions in *Bereishit*, such as "*ve-hitbarekhu ve-zarakha*" (26:4). As Rashi spells out ad loc.:

> A person says to his son, "Your descendants should be like the descendants of Yitzchak," and similarly in all of Scripture. And this [passage] is the archetype for all of them, [e.g.] "in you will Israel bless, saying 'may Elokim make you [like Efra'im and Menasheh]'" (*Bereishit* 48:20). And

To resolve these difficulties, I will examine the subject of human blessings and curses through the prism of the Bilam story and suggest a broader understanding of this activity that is seemingly given over to flesh-and-blood individuals. Finally, I will consider whether this understanding might shed light even on Divine blessings which appear hundreds of times throughout *Tanakh*.

The Meaning of Curses

One way of entering the analysis is by taking a closer look at imprecations. As we know, Balak sent for Bilam not to bless, but to curse. The initial delegation came to Bilam with the following request:

> Now, please come and curse (*ara*) this people for me, for it is mightier than me –perhaps I will be able to smite them and drive them from the land. For I know that he whom you bless, is blessed, (*eit asher tevarekh mevorakh*) and he whom you curse, is cursed (*va-asher ta'or yu'ar*). (*Bamidbar* 22:6)

The root *a.r.r.* in multiple Semitic languages clearly means to "curse," but it is also related to "to disgrace."[4] Its frequent use with respect to limiting fecundity, both natural (e.g. *Bereshit* 3:17, 5:29, *Devarim* 28:17-18) and human (*Devarim* 28:16-19), often in explicit juxtaposition with *berakha* (e.g. *Devarim* 28), implies fruitlessness and infertility.[5] Such a definition of *a.r.r.* fits well with its being the contrast to *b.r.kh.*: blessing is about fertility, productivity, potency and abundance. In other words, Balak wants Bilam to curse Benei Yisrael so that, unlike in their victorious campaigns against

---

even for curses we find a similar approach: "And the woman will be for a curse" (*Bamidbar* 5:27) – one who curses one whom he hates says, "You should be like that woman…"

4. See the entry *a.r.r.* in *The Hebrew and Aramaic Lexicon of the Old Testament*, Trans. and ed. by M.E.J. Richardson (Leiden: E.J. Brill, 1996), I:91.
5. Rav Shimshon Raphael Hirsch, on *Bereshit* 3:17, sees it related lexically to *ariri* (the *alef* and *ayyin* being interchangeable) – i.e. "barren" or "desolate." The contrast of the two possible outcomes of the *sota* drinking the *mayyim ha-me'arerim* (*Bamidbar* 5:24; 27-28) supports this idea of *a.r.r.* implying barrenness.

Sichon and Og, they will be unsuccessful (or possibly disgraced) in their efforts to conquer *Mo'av*.

That cursing seeks to impose some sort of reduction, limitation, sterility and failure on another object or person is corroborated by other terms used in *Tanakh* for "curse." Thus, *k.l.l.* is related to "*kal*" – light, insignificant, of minor importance – and *k.l.h.*, which in the *nifal* form means lightly esteemed and dishonored, as in "*ve-nikla achikha le-einekha*" (*Devarim* 23:3).[6] This is in contrast to "*kaved*," heavy, significant, bringing in its wake respect (*kavod*) of others. Similarly, a *kal* can be discounted, whereas someone who is *chashuv* must be reckoned with. Finally, the other term for "curse," *k.v.h.* (or *k.v.v.*), used frequently in the Bilam story,[7] is related in Semitic languages to chopping or cutting off, as well as despising, abusing or ignoring, and in Hebrew, the boring of a hole, especially in wood.[8] While there may be distinct, nuanced usages for these three terms, all convey the notion of rendering something or someone unproductive, trivial and impotent.

Accordingly, while many curses anticipate harmful events, the verbs used for "curse" all seem to point to an important psychological dimension of the curse: causing its target to feel vulnerable, exposed, of limited capacity in warding off or overcoming a future danger. Thus, for those inclined towards a more rationalist, non-magical line of interpretation, the failure brought about by a curse may come not from an external force that objectively overpowers an individual or group, but from the victim's lack of self-confidence and intensifying self-doubt engendered by the curse. The listener comes to believe that she or he will not be able to repel an attack that will soon arrive.

If this psychological view of cursing is correct – entirely so, for the rationalist, and perhaps as an additional component to those inclined to

---

6. See also *The Brown-Driver-Briggs Hebrew and English Lexicon*, p. 885, s.v. *II k.l.h.*
7. *Bamidbar* 22:11, 16; 23:8, 11, 13, 25, 27; 24:10.
8. One is tempted to identify *kav*, the dry measure mentioned in Rabbinic literature, with this same root, but in his dictionary (VI: 5667, n. 1), Eli'ezer Ben-Yehuda identifies that word with an ancient measurement, whose lexical source is likely not Hebrew. See the entry *kav: ?I* in *The Hebrew and Aramaic Lexicon of the Old Testament*, Trans. and ed. by M.E.J. Richardson (Leiden: E.J. Brill, 1996), III:1060.

grant them mystical power – then the curse, in fact, involves *two* aspects: an imaginative dimension and a motivational one. First, a different reality must be imagined, deemed to be a genuine possibility rather than an implausible dream. In a curse, a vision of success must be replaced by a portrait of failure; excitement for a bright future must give way to anticipation of inadequacy, the concept, as we have seen, with which the Biblical roots for cursing are associated. That vision, in turn, motivates people to act in certain ways – or, in the case of a curse, perhaps to not act. In the grip of a dark vision, accursed people are less likely to muster courage, train themselves or be resourceful; setbacks are seen as self-fulfilling prophecies, and failure begets failure. By the same token, those in the orbit of such accursed individuals, or who are engaged in conflict with them, may hear of the anticipated defeat and become motivated to mount a challenge to the already-vulnerable opponent. Imagined vulnerability – what many psychologists now call "a fixed mindset"[9] – demoralizes one side but may stimulate the opposition to resist and overcome.

Returning to the Bilam narrative, this may be precisely what Balak hoped for. In the initial invitation, Balak lays out his plan:

> Now, please come and curse this people for me... perhaps I will be able to smite them and drive them from the land. (*Bamidbar* 22:66)

Were the curse to take the form of some fatal event, such as a plague or natural disaster, the hoped-for outcome would simply be the disappearance of the Israelite threat, such as Sancheiriv's army abandoning its siege of Jerusalem without Chizkiyahu lifting a finger (*Melakhim Bet* 19:35-36). Surely that would be most desirable. In fact, however, Balak articulates his anticipated goal – that *his* Moabite forces will be able to repel Benei Yisrael and send them out of his land – not decimate or defeat them, but merely to fend off the expected Israelite incursion into Balak's territory.[10]

---

9. See the work of Carol Dweck, especially her original *Self-theories: Their role in Motivation, Personality and Development* (Philadelphia: Psychology Press, 1999). Dweck has since published several, more popular books about "mindset," relating it to fulfilling one's potential and success.

10. Abarbanel underscores the Moabite people's trepidation and fear, which was more intense and all-consuming than Balak's own concerns. See his answers to the first four questions in *Parashat Balak*.

One may say, then, that the psychological impact of a curse, at least in certain circumstances, exerts itself no less on the audience than on the target – and perhaps exclusively on the audience, given that the Jews could not hear Bilam's curse. This helps explain an interesting, often unnoticed fact about the story. While we might mistakenly imagine that two men standing alone in different locations as Bilam sought to curse the Jewish people, the Torah makes it clear that, at least on the first two occasions, there is an audience:

> And he [Bilam] returned to him [Balak], and behold he was standing over his offering – he, and all the officers of Mo'av. (23:6)

> And he [Bilam] came to him [Balak], and behold he was standing over his offering, and the officers of Mo'av with him, and Balak said to him, "what did God speak?" (23:17)

At the initial attempt to curse, all Mo'av's officers were present; it seems Balak wanted to impress them, thereby emboldening them to lead the people in repelling Benei Yisrael's anticipated incursion into their territory. Strikingly, by the second attempt, we do not see the word "all," indicating that some of the attendees were no longer present, Rashi[11] suggests, feeling that the Midianite seer was a vain source of hope. If so, the absence of any mention of others being present at the third attempt (23:27 - 24:13) may imply that the entire audience had left! In sum, curses can psychologically impact both their targets as well as others. In this case, the intended target was the leaders of Mo'av, who were terrified of the threat Benei Yisrael posed.

Understanding Blessing

In this light, we may approach the notion of blessing differently. Human blessings comprise the same two psychological dimensions involved in

---

Of course, one cannot rule out that Balak's request was that Bilam curse Benei Yisrael merely to weaken them rather than destroy them – *tafasta meruba, lo tafasta* – making it possible for Balak's forces to repel them.

11. On v. 17, s.v. *ve-sarei Mo'av itto*.

cursing: first, they activate the recipients' imaginative faculty, painting a picture that enables them to imagine a brighter future within their reach. And like curses, blessings can motivate such people to act differently, inspiring them to pursue dreams and make them a reality. In contrast to curses, however, blessings focus on fecundity, both material and spiritual.[12]

Furthermore, parallel to what we explained with respect to curses, blessings may have an impact not only on their intended objects, but also on those in their orbit, such as colleagues, neighbors, and observers. This is the method by which the impact of both blessings and curses grows, pithily captured in God's promise to Avraham at the beginning of his odyssey: "I will bless those who bless you and those who curse you I will curse" – a phrase closely resembling language Bilam himself invokes as he completes his third blessing (24:9). Because both blessings and curses change people's attitudes and motivations, they intrinsically have exponential potential. As we noted, Bilam's blessings brought Balak and his military leaders to the realization that armed resistance against the Jews was pointless, and so they abandon that idea: there is no evidence that the Moabites threatened the Jews militarily as did the Edomites (*Bamidbar* 20:20-21), to keep them from entering their territory.[13]

---

12. See above, n. 3.
13. Since the Torah (*Devarim* 2:9) records that God insisted that Benei Yisrael not encroach on *Mo'av*'s territory, it raises another possibility as to why God intervened in Bilam's plan. Let us assume Bilam did as Balak asked and cursed the Jews. Seeing Benei Yisrael circumvent his territory, Balak would have interpreted the behavior as a result of Bilam's imprecation, not the Divine instruction to not challenge *Mo'av* or *Ammon*. Since it was God's intention that Benei Yisrael approach the Land in a way that would instill fear in its inhabitants (e.g., *Devarim* 2:25, *Yehoshua* 2:10), Benei Yisrael avoiding *Mo'av* after Bilam's curse would have led the nations to perceive the Jewish people as vulnerable, encouraging others to offer fiercer resistance. By forcing Bilam to offer Benei Yisrael multiple blessings, God thus prevented such an interpretation, leaving the fear engendered by the defeat of Sichon and Og in place. [Is this the Abarbanel's approach?] This understanding of the episode highlights the psychological effects of blessings and curses.

Admittedly, Yiftach (*Shoftim* 11:17) offers a slightly different portrayal of Benei Yisrael's encounters with other nations as they neared the Land, wherein the Jews were denied permission to pass through both *Edom* and *Mo'av*, and so circumvented those territories. And though Balak is mentioned by name (v. 25), no reference is made to God changing Bilam's curses to blessings. However, since

This may help us understand why Moshe and Yehoshu'a informed Benei Yisrael of what God did for them in turning Bilam's curses into blessings. In the fortieth year, while still on the eastern side of the Jordan River, Moshe wanted the people to know what happened so that they would be encouraged as they embark on conquering the Land. Indeed, demoralizing Israel's enemies is a major theme in *Shirat Ha-Yam*, in which *Edom* and *Mo'av* are among those singled out for being instilled with fear upon hearing of the splitting of the sea.[14] Now that they are on the threshold of entering the Land, having a record of what recently happened involving a nation they circumvented and a person whom they killed in the war with *Midyan* (*Bamidbar* 31:8) reassures them that they will not be deterred by enemies, and that God is helping ensure their success. This is consistent with the thrust of Yehoshu'a's valedictory which underscores that, with God's assistance, Benei Yisrael has been able to overcome formidable foes, from Egypt and the Amorites to the nations of *Kena'an* – and they therefore owe Him their allegiance.

"*Va-Yissa Meshalo*" – Bilam's Muse

Our approach helps explain a rather unique phrase that occurs no less than seven times in the saga of Bilam: "*va-yissa meshalo*." The English translation of this idiom is hard to render, as is the individual word "*mashal*."[15] It is clearly some sort of poetic construct, since in recounting the immediately prior episode, the victory over Sichon, the Torah records what the *moshelim* – poets or bards[16] – sung about Sichon's military victories. Whatever the precise translation, the key seems to be that the *mashal* is not a historical chronicle but rather a literary form. Whatever Balak wants to accomplish, Bilam will achieve it with the inspiration of a muse.

---

the account is part of Yiftach's appeal to the king of *Ammon* justifying Israel's claim to the territory in an effort to avoid war, including this part of the story may have been a tactical decision.

14. *Shemot* 15:15. See also Rashi ad loc. s.v. *alufei Edom eilei Mo'av*, who suggests that these nations were aggrieved over Israel's success.

15. "Parable" (JPS, 1917; Stone Chumash; Everett Fox); "theme" (JPS, 1985; Robert Alter); "oracle" (Kaplan).

16. Alter's "rhapsodes" and Kaplan's "minstrels" similarly convey the artistic nature of the work.

This should come as no surprise. If, as we have explained, blessings and curses call upon us to imagine another set of possibilities and reach deeply within ourselves for untapped capacities and potential, then poetry is the most appropriate literary device to help us do that. Of course, prose can be imaginative, even fanciful. But by its very nature, verse forces us to be creative, to interpret symbols and decipher metaphors, to draw analogies and flesh out brief references and allusions. The brevity and suggestiveness of poetry call upon us to look past simple meanings and search for deeper, less obvious senses of the words before us. Curses and blessings thus employ poetry precisely because they want to activate and inspire our own imaginations regarding our world and our roles in it, whether for good or ill. Literalness plants us firmly in reality, appealing to our rational selves as we are. Poetry, on the other hand, pushes us out of the present into futures as yet unknown.

In fact, the episodes in *Parashat Chukkat* that precede our story actually offer one, and possibly two, other uses of poetry or song. In appreciation for a well, the people compose a song (21:17-20), and, just a few verses prior, at least according to Ibn Ezra and Ramban,[17] a fragment of an anthology of songs describing Israel's battles ("*Sefer Milchamot Hashem*") is used to describe the people's travels through the Transjordan. In other words, leading up to the Bilam story, the Torah employs poetry, incorporating an aesthetic tool that alerts us to the potential of the *mashal*. As Benei Yisrael are making their way to *Eretz Kena'an*, the increasing use of poetry makes sense: the people must now imagine a future, pull themselves out of the monotony and predictability of forty years of wandering, and visualize the society they seek to build. In the space of only a few chapters, we hear extensively about *shir* and *mashal*/*moshelim* because we are in the mental zone of imagining the future, an activity precipitated and enhanced not by prose, but by the unique literary forms of poetry.

Blessing the Divine

In the final section of this paper, I would like to apply this approach of curses and blessings to our daily recitation of *berakhot* to God. Rav Soloveitchik, in

---

17. On *Bamidbar* 21:14, *s.v. be-sefer milchamot Hashem*.

an essay "*Ha-Berakhot Ba-Yahadut*,"[18] powerfully develops the idea, based on *Kabbala*, that despite the unbridgeable metaphysical gap between God and humans, at times God willingly contracts Himself and makes Himself hidden, concealed, and thus, as it were, in need of human involvement to have the Divine Presence revealed. For the Rav, our recitation of *berakhot* achieves the paradoxical aim of aiding God and adding holiness to the world by bringing His Presence to light in every natural phenomenon such as the sunrise and sunset, the vast seas and the verdant fields, and in every morsel of food we eat. This is the compelling image of *berakhot* that Rav Soloveitchik draws.

We can integrate our explanation of curses and blessings into the Rav's idea. As noted above, audiences are no less essential to the act of blessing and cursing as the ones who utter them, or the ones about whom they are uttered. Indeed, the instances of blessing and cursing God in the Torah demonstrate precisely this idea.

The most obvious example is the account of the *nokev Shem Hashem*, the man who curses God's Name (*Vayikra* 24:10-23). While the commentators struggle to elaborate what exactly this person said or did, the focus of the Torah's account is on what should be done to him punitively. In the only instance in *Chumash*, those who heard the curse – not merely the witnesses, but presumably all those who heard the curse uttered – must place their hands on the convicted person's head before his stoning, which is completed by *kol ha-eida*, the entire congregation. This individual did not commit a personal or private offense. What he did was an act that would reduce God's reputation, as it were, "diminishing" the Divine's potential to be seen as the world's sovereign. The "ripple effect" of, first, those in earshot, followed by the entire congregation, accounts for the severity of his punishment.[19] The participation of "the audience" in the punishment is because a curse, by its nature, inherently implicates those who hear it.

---

18. In *Yemei Zikkaron*, transl. Moshe Krone (Jerusalem: Rav Joseph B. Soloveitchik, 1986), pp. 29-57.
19. In a slightly different vein, *Chizkuni* (*Vayikra* 24:14) takes "those who heard it" to be the witnesses; since, in the course of the court proceedings, they must repeat what they heard (*cf. Mishna Sanhedrin* 7:5), the witnesses were forced to utter an ineffable phrase, involving them to some degree in the same sin. Therefore, they must use this expiatory gesture, whereby the blasphemer's death atones for their sin, as if he or she were an atoning sacrifice.

The first instance of blessing in the Torah is Malki-Tzedek's blessing of Avram and God after Avram's victory over the four kings (*Bereishit* 14:18-20). While the *mise en scene* is not explicit, the simplest understanding of the story has the king of *Shalem* bringing food out for Avram and his tired troops,[20] in the presence of the king of *Sedom*, who already came out to greet Avram (14:17).[21] There are thus hundreds of people present when Malki-Tzedek blesses Avram and God for the miraculous outcome of the battle, underscoring that blessings aim not only at the blessed, but also at the audience. In this case, the dedication of Avram's troops to his vision of serving God would be reinforced by hearing a local king-priest praise God and even the king of *Sedom* might come to appreciate the significance of Avram and his vision for a God-fearing society.

The final example is the mitzva to bless God upon eating from the Land's yield to the point of satiety: "*ve-akhalta ve-savata u-veirakhta et Hashem Elokekha*" (*Devarim* 8:10). Of course, Chazal understood this as a personal mitzva, yet its collective context is unmistakable: Moshe is exhorting the people not to abandon God and His laws, something which enjoying the Land's abundance might promote. The blessing of God in this context is presented not as a formal, personal act, but as an effort to ensure that the nation never forgets that their good fortune derives from God, and not from themselves. Similar to Rav Soloveitchik's argument, *berakhot* are meant to enhance awareness and appreciation of God's providence in the world, specifically with respect to the Jewish people and their history. On this basis, the institution of *birkat ha-zimmun*, creating an "eating fellowship" in order to hear the *berakha*,[22] makes eminent sense, since the goal is not merely to bless God oneself, but to have others hear it, thus affecting their receptivity to appreciating God's influence in the world.[23]

---

20. See *Bekhor Shor* ad loc.
21. See Rav David Z. Hoffman ad loc., who lays out in detail the sequence of the dialogue in this episode.
22. I take this term from Joel Wolowelsky, "The Eating Fellowship: An Exploration," *Tradition* 16:2 (1977): 75-82.
23. See *Shulchan Arukh* OC 183:7, and *Mishna Berura* ad loc., no. 27, stating that the original custom was to have the leader recite the entire *birkat ha-mazon* and have all the assembled listen to the leader and thereby fulfill their obligation. However, due to the difficulty for many to pay attention for the entire time, the custom developed to have each person recite all the blessings along with the leader, in an undertone.

This may also help to explain Chazal's institution of different levels of *birkat ha-zimmun* based on the size of the assembly (*Mishna Berakhot* 7:3). In no other context, liturgical or otherwise, do we find gradated levels for the formulation of the blessing based on the size of the audience. This distinctive feature of *zimmun* is consistent with our presentation above.

* * *

As in most *yeshivot*, the time spent in Yeshivat Har Etzion contributes significantly to the acquisition of skills in *talmud Torah*. For thousands of *talmidim*, daily *shi'ur*, *chavruta*, and *shi'ur kelali* helped them develop the tools to analyze a *sugya*, understand *rishonim* and organize the different *shittot*, becoming serious *benei Torah* in the process. However, the founding *Rashei Yeshiva*, HaRav Amital *zt"l* and HaRav Lichtenstein *zt"l*, infused the Yeshiva with the gift of being a *berakha* in both its dimensions, inspiring us to imagine ourselves and the world around us differently, and encouraging us to go out and make a difference. Their "blessings" came through most powerfully in their *sichot*: who heard Rav Lichtenstein's Ta'anit Esther *sicha* and was not moved to consider, if not to decide on, a life dedicated to helping Am Yisrael through *chinnukh*, *rabbanut* or *shelichut*? Who was able to listen to Rav Amital's pre-*Ne'ila sicha* and not believe that genuine *teshuva* was within reach? These are just two of myriad instances in which the *Yeshiva* blessed us, igniting our imaginations and insisting that the power to actualize the vision lay within us.

Over the last fifty years, thousands of us, each in his own way, have been privileged to receive the *Yeshiva*'s blessing. We saw the potential in ourselves and in the world around us – whether in Israel or in the diaspora – and tried to make a difference. While some may view a *yeshiva* as a metaphoric Noah's ark, saving the fortunate few from an all-engulfing, devastating flood, Yeshivat Har Etzion modeled itself on the life of Avraham, believing in the possibility – no matter how small the odds – of a greater personal and collective future, and then empowering its students, one at a time, to influence others and bring the promised world into reality. This is "*va-avarekha mevarekhekha*" – blessing those who bless.

May this remarkable institution be blessed to continue spreading its *berakhot* for decades to come.

Success Is Hard-Fought, For Our Greatest

Gidon Rothstein

At the urging of Rav Daniel Rhein and Eli Weber, I joined the first *shacharit* at the *shiva* house for *Moreinu ve-Rabbeinu* HaRav Aharon Lichtenstein *zt"l*, and thus I was present when Rabbanit Amital *tbd"l* came to pay a *shiva* call. After a weighted moment of silence, Dr. Tovah Lichtenstein *tbd"l* said to her, "*hitzlachnu*" – we succeeded.

The word put a whole new light on the videos I had always seen of the early days of the *Yeshiva*, the caravans positioned atop a cold, windswept mountain in newly reconquered territory. By the time I arrived in 1982, the campus was already dotted with beautiful buildings and well-kept grounds, but Dr. Lichtenstein's word reminded me it didn't start that way, didn't spring fully formed from the ground, and didn't come with any assurances of success.

When she and her husband *zt"l* came, lured (as Rav Lichtenstein always said) by the warm personality of Rav Amital *zt"l*, they were partnering in a startup in the fullest sense of the word, with all the potential for failure which comes with the territory.

This is a theme I have also come to realize over years of reciting the paragraph in *selichot* which starts "*Mi she-ana le-Avraham Avinu*," where we call out to God who answered the prayers of Avraham at *Har Ha-Moriyya*, as he was about to bind and (he thought) sacrifice his son. Avraham prayed to God, the *selicha* seems to me to assume, because he was hoping against hope for a different outcome.

The prayer expands and alters a series of six added blessings *Ta'anit* 15a tells us were recited on fast days, gives us nineteen examples of great figures from *Tanakh* who called out to Hashem, and each time has us ask the One who answered them to answer us. The stories of five of those figures will help us remember the worry and fear of failure which led these greatest of our forebears to cry out to God.

Only when we fully appreciate how reasonable their fear was, and thus what a salvation they would have experienced when God responded positively to their prayers, can we also fully appreciate and admire the greatness of their success.

Avraham *Avinu*, Leading Up to and At *Har Ha-Moriyya*
We might think only atop *Har Ha-Moriyya*, about to sacrifice his long-awaited son, did Avraham pause to ask God to revoke or change the decree. A step back to look at other incidents of his life shows it to have been full of moments of such fear and uncertainty.

First, his discovery of monotheism seems to be a foregone conclusion only in retrospect. Some *midrashim* do portray Avraham's coming to recognize God as an event of his childhood. In that version (which many of us hear in our own childhoods), Avraham decided one day there had to be a power which ran the world, spent a day or two to dismiss the sun and moon as candidates, and settled on God.

My teacher, Prof. Isadore Twersky *zt"l*, used to highlight Rambam's alternate picture (*Hilkhot Avoda Zara* 1:3). In *Bereishit Rabba*, Reish Lakish says the Patriarch found God at age three, while Rabbi Yochanan and Rabbi Chanina say he was forty-eight (Rambam's text apparently reads forty). Rambam himself combines the two claims, says Avraham started searching as soon as he was weaned, and only found the answer at forty.

I think he wants us to understand monotheism is not intuitive or obvious to people in a polytheistic society. It's not child's play. No one, not even Avraham *Avinu*, takes on the most serious theological question in the universe and solves it in a few days, especially not as a three-year-old.

For our purposes, Rambam also teaches us to look at Avraham as someone who grew in his comprehension of how God deals with the world, who improved himself gradually over a sustained period of time, after harder work than we might stop to notice.

The *Brit Bein Ha-Betarim* and Circumcision

Rashi to *Bereishit* 15:5 points us to the next milestone in Avraham's journey, God's omnipotence even in the face of destiny. During the *Brit Bein Ha-Betarim*, the Covenant between the Parts, God told Avraham his descendants would be like the stars of the sky. When Avraham protested that he had no descendants or heirs, God told him to go outside (to see the stars, as uncountable as which would be his descendants).

The *midrash* thinks Avraham had previously consulted the stars, and found he was destined not to have children. God took him outside, the *midrash* thinks, to teach Avraham God can overcome or override what is written in our stars. Note that the *midrash* does not deny the prediction; it says God can overcome it. For us, the parallel might be if a doctor had told Avraham and Sara they would never be able to have children as a matter of absolute biological fact. God was telling Avraham all such incontrovertible facts cannot stand in the face of God's omnipotence.

Twenty-four years later, God introduces *mila* (circumcision) by telling Avraham (17:1), "walk before Me and be *tamim*," whole or complete. The Torah does not tell us in what way *mila* completes Avraham, but Rambam (*Hilkhot Mila* 3:8) chooses to incorporate the Torah's not considering Avraham whole until he had undergone circumcision as a way the uncircumcised are clearly lesser. If so, Avraham was still making progress in self-improvement at age ninety-nine.

Being Answered on *Moriyya*

Fast-forward one final time to the *Akeida* (Binding of Yitzchak), which Rashi times to when Yitzchak was thirty-seven (Ibn Ezra thinks Yitzchak was a child, so Avraham may have been as young as 105). After Avraham showed his full readiness to obey even such a difficult Divine command, the angel told him (on behalf of God, 22:12), "*atta yadati*," now I know, Avraham truly feared God.

The moment the *selicha* singled out, Avraham thought he was being asked to sacrifice more than his long hoped-for son. The death of Yitzchak would have been the death of a lifetime of efforts. The God he found after decades of painstaking work, in whose Name he had rejected the best science of the day (astrology), for whom he had undergone a painful physical procedure which others surely saw as needless self-mutilation, was asking him to put an end to his central hope (the one which had led to the *Brit Bein Ha-Betarim* in the first place), an heir and successor.

The prayer which the author of the *selicha* assumes Avraham offered was the prayer of a man who had given everything, repeatedly, and was being asked to throw it all away. He was about to, but in desperation asked God for salvation.

The *Akeida*: Brilliant Success or Narrow Escape?

I once heard that the Rav, Rav Joseph B. Soloveitchik *zt"l*, suggested Avraham might not have seen the *Akeida* as a moment of crowning success. Right after the *Akeida*, the end of *Parashat Vayeira* tells us Avraham received word of all the children his brother Nachor's wife and concubine had borne him. Rashi gives a simple reason for us to hear the information: it tells us (and Avraham) Yitzchak's intended, Rivka, has been born.

But Rashi also thinks Avraham left the *Akeida* berating himself for leaving Yitzchak unmarried, which made him vulnerable to the extinguishing of the line. In response, God sent word of the birth of Rivka.

The Rav, perhaps because the Torah names all of Nachor's children, which is unnecessary if Rivka and her father Betu'el are the only ones who interest us, said the Torah is sending a message about success. At this relatively late point in Avraham's life, observers would have been within their rights to see Nachor as the success in the family – he was rich, ensconced in his ancestral land, surrounded by family, with many children and grandchildren. Avraham had money, perhaps, but was a stranger in a new land, without even a burial plot for his wife, and only narrowly avoided sacrificing the son on whom he had pinned all his hopes of continuity. We cannot judge success even by success, the Rav said; we cannot be sure what looks to us like success is in fact how God sees it.

To me, this idea frames how the Torah presents Avraham: a colossus, but whose life took him on a slow and uncertain journey to understanding God, to lasting impact on human history, to real, enduring success.

Moshe *Rabbeinu* on *Chorev*

The *paytan*, the liturgical poet, does not tell us when during Benei Yisrael's time at *Sinai* he assumes Moshe prayed. Likely, it was after the sin of the Golden Calf, when Moshe searched for a way to save the people from their deserved fate. How he managed the feat, and what God taught him to do in the future, deserve independent discussion; here, I want to note other places where Moshe is less sure of himself than we might have expected.

Most obviously, Moshe did not believe he was the right man for the job, and argued against being chosen lengthily enough to earn God's "*charon af*," flaring anger. We might reasonably chalk that up to the newness of the experience, perhaps not indicative of any general characteristic. I find more interesting Rashi's reading of *Bamidbar* 16:15, when Moshe reacts to Datan and Aviram's rejection of his invitation to meet and discuss their part in Korach's rebellion.

Rashi to verse 14 says they refused to go, partially because they said Moshe had failed them. He had promised to take them to a land flowing in milk and honey and instead doomed them to death in the desert. The timing matters, since Datan and Aviram are reacting this way after the sin of the spies, the tenth time the Jewish people mishandled their relationship with God.

Upset, Moshe asks God not to pay attention to their sacrifice, and reminds God he has always done his best for the people. I often wonder why Moshe felt the need to make the request. He had by this point served as God's messenger to confront Pharaoh, bring the plagues, lead Benei Yisrael out of *Mitzrayim*, split the Sea, bring down *man*, draw water from a rock, and be the mouthpiece of the *Aseret Ha-Dibberot*, the Ten Commandments. He had saved Benei Yisrael from destruction, convinced God to teach him the *Yud-Gimmel Middot*, the Thirteen Attributes, as a more assured way of securing atonement, and was about to summon a new kind of earthquake on demand.

Yet he was unsure God would reject Datan and Aviram's sacrifice. His lack of self-assurance, at one of the last points we will see him for thirty-eight years, puts the moment on *Sinai* in a new light. Ever since the burning bush, Moshe has been positive he's not right for this job and has been asked to do what was beyond him. Immediately after the sin of the Golden Calf, he does not possess the *Yud-Gimmel Middot*, must stand up for a people who have committed one of the worst sins barely forty days after the greatest mass revelation in history.

He turns to God, asking Him to forgive the people, and prays for assistance, not at all confident he'll be up to the task.

Pinchas: Worries of a Zealot
The Torah itself tells us of some of Avraham and Moshe's fears, so the *paytan*'s listing them among those who prayed for salvation does not ask us to change or adjust our view of them. The example of Pinchas as he arose from among the people shows the *paytan* inferring concern or fear where we could have read the text to indicate unreflective self-confidence. *Bamidbar* 25:7-8 tells us Pinchas saw Zimri take Kozbi, followed them into the tent, and slew them both, nothing more.

(The *paytan* may have been building off of *Tehillim* 106:30, which says Pinchas stood "*va-yefallel*," but the commentators to *Tehillim* uniformly take the word to mean "judged" rather than "prayed." A *paytan* certainly has poetic license, but we should notice the view of the incident he suggests.)

Rashi inserts a first element of hesitation in Pinchas. He says Pinchas checked with Moshe before he acted, to be sure he was correct in his understanding of *halakha*, he did have the right to kill Zimri.

Ramban gives a richer context. He thinks God told Moshe to have judges try those who had sinned with the Moabite women. Unless they did, Hashem would bring a plague, which kills more indiscriminately than a court. Zimri challenged Moshe, either of his own volition or (as *Sanhedrin* 82a has it) because his tribe accosted him, angered by his quiescence in the face of the capital punishments they were suffering.

Either way, Ramban thinks a large retinue of allies and followers backed up Zimri as he accosted Moshe. Pinchas stood to kill Zimri, then, with no reason to expect he would escape the experience alive. Assassins rarely get away with their crimes, certainly not when the victim's followers are right there.

As he stood to perform his zealous act, with every reason to think he was at death's door, the *paytan* thinks he prayed to God and was answered.

Eliyahu Brings Down Fire
Eliyahu is the first of the characters we are discussing whose prayer for assistance is recorded in *Tanakh*. In *Melakhim Alef* 18:36-37, Eliyahu asks God to help him show the people God is the true and only Deity, by sending fire from heaven to burn his sacrifice. The fire comes, and Eliyahu succeeds. Tosafot in two places (the more explicit is *Sanhedrin* 89b) say Eliyahu came up with the test on his own, and did not ask God's advice or consent until *Har Karmel*. In Tosafot's view, Eliyahu came to believe the people needed to see a public contest between God and Ba'al, and set it in motion based only on his own assessment. This would become the paradigmatic example of a "*hora'at sha'a*," the right of a *Beit Din* (court) or *navi* (prophet) to temporarily suspend *halakha* (in this case, offering a sacrifice outside of the *Beit Ha-Mikdash*), and Tosafot think Eliyahu acted of his own accord, without first checking or securing God's promise to cooperate.

The prayer becomes more significant once we know the background. Calling fire down from heaven upon command might be challenging enough, but to do it with no certainty God agreed with his decision to break the ordinary bounds of *halakha* would cow many a lesser man.

The words of the prayer *Tanakh* records do not carry any obvious desperation or fear. I am suggesting the *paytan* detected tension and worry over the very real possibility God would decide not to go along. Eliyahu did pull it off, with great success, but the *paytan* reminds us how close a call it could have been.

Chananya, Misha'el, Azarya
The third chapter of *Daniel* tells the story of the one time in *Tanakh* we see God save people from a fiery furnace: Chananya, Misha'el and Azarya, courtiers of Nevukhadnetzar's, peers and colleagues of Daniel's (Avraham's experience, which we know from the *midrash*, does not appear in *Tanakh*).

Their words to Nevukhadnetzar before he throws them into the furnace support my point.

In 3:17-18, they assure Nevukhadnetzar God *could* save them, but are equally clear they do not expect to be saved. They still will not bow to his statue (some sources suggest it was not even an item of worship, a discussion we need not enter here).

Rashi to *Vayikra* 22:32 points to these three as prime examples of the need to be ready to sacrifice one's life *al kiddush ha-Shem*, for the sanctity of God's Name. Sanctifying God's Name by refusing to transgress the Torah on pain of death means the Jew knows he or she will have to forfeit his or her life.

While God could easily save all Jews put in such situations, we are not allowed to expect a miracle, Rashi says. We must accept death, as did the three, without the danger freeing us of the need to do what's right.

Yirmeyahu Does Not Know He Will Survive
The *selicha* does not mention Yirmeyahu, but he is another great Jew who had no expectation of extraordinary protection or salvation. At the outset of his career, in the first chapter of the book, God promised him protection from all who would attack him. Forty years later, as the destruction of *Yerushalayim* approached, events unfolded which made him feel no longer immune.

Chapter 37 tells us some government officials accused him (falsely) of planning to surrender to the Babylonians, and threw him in jail for "*yamim rabbim*," many days. At some point thereafter, the king, Tzidkiyahu, sends for him in secret, to hear if God has any message.

Yirmeyahu delivers the sad news of Benei Yisrael's impending defeat and conquest, reminding the king he now has proof all the *nevi'im*, prophets, who assured him of victory had been wrong. Then, in verse 20, the *navi* asks the king not to send him back to jail, "so he not die there." In the next chapter, Yirmeyahu is thrown in a pit, saved from starvation only because Eved-Melekh, one of the king's servants, intervenes.

After the dreaded destruction arrived, and the Babylonian general gave him various privileges, chapter 44 has Yirmeyahu in *Mitzrayim*, still trying to convince Benei Yisrael to forego their idolatry, yet they still brazenly repudiate his views.

In a difficult life marked by few external successes, Yirmeyahu became who he was, a figure whose prophecies we still study, from whom we still learn. But he did not have it easy, and had no assurance of any form of detectable success.

Success on the Road Not Taken
I conclude by applying these lessons back to the edifying context that framed our study from the outset: as we celebrate the fiftieth anniversary of our beloved *Yeshiva*, part of the celebration is encapsulated in Dr. Tovah Lichtenstein's one word, "*hitzlachnu*" – all because two remarkable families, the Amitals and the Lichtensteins, decided to take the road not taken, the less secure path, with no guarantees.

Succeed they did, to the benefit of those who merited learning from them, and the benefit of the Jewish community at large.

Father Knows Best?
Understanding Yitzchak's Love of Eisav[1]

Rabbi Dr. Ezra Frazer

When a young child first hears the story of Ya'akov and Eisav, the characters are typically presented as caricatures – Ya'akov *Avinu* (Our Father) and Eisav *Ha-Rasha* (the Wicked). The story is often embellished with *midrashim* that support the extreme characterizations of Ya'akov as saintly hero and Eisav as nefarious villain.

When these images of Ya'akov and Eisav are ingrained in one's mind from a young age, it becomes difficult to respect Yitzchak's initial choice of Eisav to receive the birthright. Upon reading the narrative, one is tempted to repeatedly pause and scold Yitzchak, who appears to make a glaringly foolish decision in favoring Eisav.

In this essay, I propose that if one reads the story as Yitzchak would have experienced it, following the *peshat* (plain sense) of the narrative without *midrashim* that were composed with the benefit of hindsight, Yitzchak's preference for Eisav is entirely reasonable. After explaining

---

1. This essay is dedicated in honor of my many *rebbe'im* in Yeshivat Har Etzion. The six years that I spent in Yeshivat Har Etzion gave me a deeper appreciation of the profundity of the *Tanakh* when studied on both *peshat* and *derash* levels. I chose to focus on this particular narrative because many of my thoughts about it were formed by *sichot* and *shi'urim* during my years in *yeshiva*. I fondly remember HaRav Lichtenstein *zt"l* commenting on a student's *devar Torah* that he felt didn't do justice to Ya'akov's character, HaRav Amital *zt"l* cautioning against engaging in deception and unethical behavior merely because one claims to know God's plan, HaRav Medan and HaRav Mosheh Lichtenstein exchanging perspectives on Eisav's character, and Rav Menachem Leibtag discussing *berakha*, *bechira*, and *bekhora*. I hope this essay represents a modest contribution toward appreciating the richness of the characters of *Sefer Bereishit*, and a fitting tribute to the *yeshiva*'s legacy of revitalizing the intensive study of *Tanakh*.

Yitzchak's initial perspective, I examine how his view evolved until he ultimately determined that only Ya'akov would be a "chosen" member of the covenant that God made with Avraham.

Our first indication that God favors Ya'akov comes during Rivka's pregnancy. She is told (*Bereishit* 25:23)[2] "*ve-rav ya'avod tza'ir*," which is typically understood to mean that "the older [brother] shall serve the younger." However, several commentators (e.g. Radak, Rav Yosef Ibn Kaspi) observe that the phrase in question is technically ambiguous. While the prophecy is ultimately fulfilled according to the aforementioned translation, the rules of Hebrew syntax permit the words to be read as: "The older brother – the younger brother shall serve [him]." What is more, beyond the syntactic ambiguity, while Rivka clearly understood the prophecy to favor Ya'akov, the text never informs us whether she communicated this prophecy to Yitzchak. And even if she did convey its words to him, Yitzchak could have responded that the words of the prophecy are ambiguous and do not necessarily favor Ya'akov.

Once the children are born, the *peshat* of the text tells us relatively little about them. Eisav was a hunter, Ya'akov a shepherd, and each son was favored by one parent (25:27-28). The Torah does not state which parent had better judgment, nor does it explicitly pass judgment on either son's profession.[3] Instead, the Torah proceeds to recount how Ya'akov bought the birthright. Eisav is a somewhat sympathetic character in this narrative, since he is starving and tired, yet his ultimate scorn for the birthright does not reflect well upon him. Regardless, there is no reason to assume that Yitzchak knew of this transaction, so neither Ya'akov's purchase nor Eisav's scorn would have influenced his eventual decision to bless Eisav.

After an unrelated narrative concerning Yitzchak in Gerar (26:1-33), in which his sons are not mentioned, the Torah informs us that Eisav married Chittite women. The text (26:34-35) adds that these marriages were "a source of bitterness (*morat ru'ach*)" for his parents.

---

2. All references are to *Bereishit* unless indicated otherwise.
3. One might argue that by explaining why Yitzchak liked Eisav ("because he ate of his hunting," 25:28, as interpreted by Onkelos) but making no particular attempt to justify Rivka's love of Ya'akov, the text implies that the default choice would have been to favor Ya'akov.

The text then proceeds to the story of the blessings (ch. 27). In order to appreciate Yitzchak's behavior in this story, it is important to observe that the blessing that he intends for Eisav is one of prosperity and leadership.[4] It does not determine who is included or excluded from the "chosen" family. This fact's significance becomes clear when one contrasts this blessing with the blessing that Yitzchak gives Ya'akov later (28:3-4). The later blessing is labeled "the blessing of Avraham" and closely parallels the language of the blessing that Avraham received as part of the covenant of circumcision (17:1-8). Accordingly, it appears that at some later time, Yitzchak decided to include only one son in the family's covenant with God. But at the start of chapter 27, Yitzchak was under the impression that both of his sons would carry on his and Avraham's spiritual legacy as one nation. Through his blessing, he sought to select one of these brothers as the leader of that nation. He therefore chose Eisav because he believed that Eisav had better leadership potential, but he had no intention of expelling Ya'akov from the family or its covenant with God.

To summarize the considerations that drove Yitzchak's decision, in seeking a leader for the chosen nation, he had to decide on the basis of the following evidence:

Eisav	Ya'akov
Was the older twin	Was the younger twin
Was a hunter, which served the constructive purpose of obtaining food, but might also indicate an inclination toward aggression	Was a shepherd, which had been the family profession for at least two generations
Married at the same age as his father (40), but married Canaanite women, which greatly upset his parents (26:34-35)	Did not marry, perhaps because he did not want to marry a Canaanite (Radak ad loc.)

---

4. In the NJPS translation, the blessing reads (27:28-29): "May God give you of the dew of heaven and the fat of the earth, abundance of new grain and wine. Let peoples serve you, and nations bow to you; be master over your brothers, and let your mother's sons bow to you. Cursed be they who curse you, blessed they who bless you."

As readers, we further know two pieces of information that favor blessing Ya'akov:

1. Rivka received a prophecy that she understood to mean that the older brother would serve the younger, although that prophecy may have been ambiguous.
2. The sale of the birthright (25:29-34) indicates that:
   a. Ya'akov acquired the birthright, albeit in a transaction in which Eisav was under duress.
   b. Eisav put his immediate needs and desires ahead of the long-term benefit of the birthright, perhaps indicating the negative character trait of impulsivity.

As mentioned above, however, the text never states whether Rivka shared her prophecy with Yitzchak, nor whether Ya'akov told his father of his purchase. Hence, Yitzchak's decision was limited to the information in the chart above. Eisav's status as the older twin would have made him the default choice for the blessing. One might therefore frame the issue as whether Eisav's profession and marriages were sufficiently problematic to deny him the blessing.

In truth, however, Eisav's profession was likely part and parcel of Yitzchak's desire to bless him. When the Torah first presents Yitzchak's love of Eisav, it explains that Yitzchak loved him "*ki tzayyid be-fiv*," translated by Onkelos as "because he ate of his hunting (*mi-tzideih hava akhil*)."[5] From Yitzchak's perspective, Eisav's profession provided him with food and may have further demonstrated Eisav's strength and fitness for leadership. As readers, we will eventually learn that Eisav's violent tendencies lead him to threaten Ya'akov's life (27:41), but Yitzchak has not seen evidence to this point that Eisav would use his hunting skills against a human being.[6]

In order to better appreciate Yitzchak's hopes for Eisav as a leader, it is instructive to examine the character of Yehuda, whose talents as a leader

---

5. Onkelos' interpretation is accepted by many commentators as the text's plain sense (e.g., Rashi, Rashbam, Ibn Ezra), although Rashi also cites a widespread midrashic interpretation that Eisav's mouth deceived Yitzchak.
6. Rashi to 25:29 alludes to a midrashic view that Eisav murdered Nimrod.

are repeatedly recognized by Ya'akov (43:8-14, 46:28, 49:8-12). Earlier, we characterized Eisav as an impulsive, aggressive character, who additionally committed the sin of marrying a Canaanite. Strikingly, the same could be said of Yehuda in *Bereishit* 38. The chapter begins with Yehuda marrying the daughter of a man named Shu'a whom the text describes as a Canaanite. Most commentators interpret "Canaanite" in this verse as a merchant,[7] due to the difficulty of ascribing such a sin to Yehuda. Nevertheless, Ibn Ezra and Malbim observe that the *peshat* of the text is that Yehuda indeed married an ethnic Canaanite.[8] His sinful marriage is consistent with a pattern of disturbing behaviors that Yehuda performs in that chapter, including his deception of Tamar (38:11), his fornication with a woman he believed to be a prostitute (38:15-18), and his swift condemnation of Tamar to death (38:24).[9] Simply put, in *Bereishit* 38, Yehuda looks a lot like Eisav: an impulsive, aggressive character who betrays his father's values by marrying a Canaanite.

Yet we all know that following Yehuda's confession and apology to Tamar (38:26), he emerges as a hero and leader by confronting Yosef on behalf of Binyamin (44:18-34), and subsequently earns the blessing of future leadership from his father (49:8-12). One might argue that the passionate, fiery spirit that contributed to Yehuda's earlier negative behaviors is the same set of character traits that make him a strong, forceful leader after his repentance.

---

7. This interpretation is based on *Zekhariya* 14:21, where "Canaanite" indeed refers to a merchant. However, an obvious difference exists between *Bereishit* and *Zekhariya* in that literal Canaanites no longer inhabited *Eretz Yisrael* in Zekhariya's time.

8. Ibn Ezra's comments to this verse are somewhat circumspect regarding his personal view, perhaps because they recognized that their interpretation could generate controversy. Nevertheless, it is clear from his comments to 46:10-12 and from Malbim's comments to *Divrei Hayamim Alef* (2:3) that they both considered Yehuda's wife to be a Canaanite.

9. One might add to that list his suggestion to sell Yosef in the previous chapter (37:26-27), which likely precipitated his departure from his family in chapter 37. The relevance of that incident to our discussion is not entirely clear, however, due to disputes among commentators regarding how to assess the decision to sell Yosef – a seemingly immoral action that nonetheless saved his life – and how to reconcile certain chronological difficulties with placing chapter 38 after chapter 37.

If our analysis is correct, one can understand Yitzchak's hopes for Eisav. He saw in Eisav many of the same qualities that we later find in Yehuda. Since he was thinking in terms of choosing a leader for a nation that would include both sons, it was logical to prefer the bold hunter over the soft-spoken shepherd.

Indeed, on his deathbed, Ya'akov appears to recognize that Yehuda became what Eisav could have become. Ya'akov blesses Yehuda that his "father's sons" (=his brothers) will bow down to him ("*yishtachavu lekha benei avikha*"), paralleling the blessing that Yitzchak had intended for Eisav, that his "mother's sons" would bow down to him ("*ve-yishtachavu lekha benei immekha*").[10] Later in *Tanakh*, the author of *Divrei Hayamim* similarly implies that Yehuda achieved what Yitzchak had intended for Eisav. The text of *Divrei Hayamim Alef* (5:2) remarks that Yehuda "became more powerful than his brothers (*gavar be'echav*)," echoing the blessing to be "master over your brothers (*hevei gevir le-achekha*)" that Yitzchak intended for Eisav.

Having argued that Yitzchak's decision to bless Eisav was reasonable from his perspective, I now examine Yitzchak's development over the course of chapter 27. Rather than experiencing one specific "aha moment," Yitzchak appears to gradually recognize his error in judgment.

First, in 27:20–22, Yitzchak is stunned by Ya'akov's explanation that God assisted him in obtaining food so quickly. That comment arouses Yitzchak's suspicion, prompting him to again feel his son to check whether it truly is Eisav. He then observes that this son sounds like Ya'akov despite having the hairy hands of Eisav. Undoubtedly, hearing Ya'akov acknowledge God prompted Yitzchak to contemplate the fact that Eisav did not speak that way, even as he was still prepared to bless Eisav.

Subsequently, when the real Eisav appears and, fearing that he has blessed the wrong son, Yitzchak begins to tremble, he asserts that Ya'akov, too, shall be blessed. At this point, Yitzchak still hopes to bless Eisav with a blessing comparable to the one he had just given to Ya'akov. However, in 27:36, Eisav exclaims that, given the purchase of the birthright, Ya'akov has

---

10. Ya'akov presumably switched from "mother's sons" to "father's sons" because he had multiple wives, so Yehuda had brothers who were not his mother's sons.

now supplanted him twice. Assuming that Yitzchak did not previously know of that sale, this new revelation surely prompted him to consider that perhaps it was divinely ordained that Ya'akov had received the blessing rather than Eisav. Accordingly, in his next response to Eisav (26:37), he no longer suffices with the assertion that Ya'akov will "also" be blessed. Instead, he explains that he has already made Ya'akov the "master," and cannot give Eisav an equivalent blessing. He therefore gives Eisav a superficially similar blessing of (27:39) "the fat of the land" and the "dew of the earth," but the meaningful part of the blessing makes it clear that Eisav will "serve" his brother (27:40), knowingly or unknowingly echoing Rivka's understanding of her prophecy that (25:23): "the older brother shall serve the younger brother."

Were the narrative to end here, Yitzchak would have concluded that although he thought Eisav was better suited to lead a nation of his two sons, in fact Ya'akov was destined to lead such a nation. Until now, Yitzchak has shown no indication that losing out on the blessing will cost Eisav his membership in the covenant. However, Rivka intervenes in 27:46.

Upon hearing that Eisav wishes to kill Ya'akov once their father dies, we would expect Rivka to tell Yitzchak that Eisav is threatening to kill Ya'akov. Instead, she brilliantly calls Yitzchak's attention to the one thing that she knows Yitzchak already dislikes about Eisav: his marriages. Without mentioning Eisav by name, she cautions that Ya'akov is liable to marry "a Chittite woman like these, from among the native women." By alluding to "these women," she reminds Yitzchak of Eisav's marriages without mentioning Eisav by name. Having recently come to terms with the fact that his physical blindness allowed him to be deceived, having heard the way in which Ya'akov – but not Eisav – mentioned God when feeding him, and having just learned from Eisav's own mouth that Ya'akov had already acquired the birthright, Rivka's subtle jab at "these women" comes at just the right moment for Yitzchak to finally realize that Eisav has no place at all in the covenant of Avraham. Consequently, Yitzchak summons Ya'akov, commands him to marry a member of Rivka's family, and bestows the "blessing of Avraham," i.e. of "chosenness," upon him (28:1-4).

By the time the reader reaches the end of this narrative, it is possible to understand how each twin evolved into the character that is familiar to young children. Ya'akov is now the chosen son, on his way to find a wife from the covenantal family, while Eisav's aggressive, violent nature has brought him to the point of longing to commit murder. However, a careful reading of the text's *peshat* is critical to understanding how each character reached this point. Moreover, this careful reading also enables the reader to appreciate how the story unfolded from the vantage point of Yitzchak, who was attempting to make the best decisions for his family without the benefit of hindsight and without being privy to certain key pieces of information. From his perspective of a father, one can hardly fault Yitzchak for hoping that his fiery, impulsive son would mature into the same caliber of leader that his grandson, Yehuda, would eventually become.

The Days and Nights of *Shir Hashirim*

Rabbi Elie Weissman

"Swear not by the moon," a stricken Juliet commands her Romeo who has proclaimed his love beneath her balcony. "The inconstant moon, / That monthly changes with her circled orb, / Lest thy love prove likewise variable" (2:2). Romeo and Juliet's love longed to break free from mutable time, exist in its pristine ideal, never subject to the natural world and its changes. Juliet laments the arrival of the morning after their wedding night. Romeo curses Juliet's lateness to their planned meeting. Time, the "star-crossed lovers" discover, plays the antagonist as much as any Montague or Capulet.

The metaphorical *Shir Hashirim*, Song of Songs, casts a shepherd boy, or *dod*, as its Romeo, and an orphaned vineyard girl, or *ra'aya*, as its Juliet. More profoundly, the *dod* represents God, the *ra'aya* His nation, and their drama the ups and downs of our destiny. This imagery-filled drama is meant, Rashi suggests in his introduction, to inspire a nation in exile to transcend its struggles and recall God's youthful love. God's love for His people remains as powerful as ever. It is timeless. Still, like Romeo and Juliet, *Shir Hashirim*'s eternal lovers contend with time and its influence. Lurking behind the engaging thrust and parry of their courtship exists a complex relationship with time. Morning, afternoon, and night not only set the scenes of this Divine drama but reflect and frame the couple's interactions. Being a model for the relationship between man and God, *Shir Hashirim* highlights the power of time within *Tanakh* and our overall spiritual experience.

The first chapter of *Shir Hashirim* depicts the *ra'aya* defending her beauty and self-worth against the criticisms of the daughters of Jerusalem. "I am dark but desirable" (1:5), she insists. The reference to the glaring sun (1:6) seems to indicate that this scene takes place at the heat of the day. It is here that she meets the *dod*, who stands just outside the vineyard lattice. "Tell me, whom I love so," she wonders, "where you pasture your flock in the afternoon" (1:7)? Her inquiry, a suggestive request for an afternoon rendezvous, bolsters the notion that this initial meeting takes place when the sun is high in the sky. The *ra'aya* impulsively reaches out to the *dod* and he responds in kind: "Your cheeks are lovely with looped earrings, your neck with beads" (1:10). In the heat of the day, the *dod* and *ra'aya* both desire to be with one another.

In chapter two, the *ra'aya* retreats. The *dod* pleads for his "dove, hiding in the crevices of the rock" (2:14), to appear and run off with him carelessly into the fields. "The fig tree has put forth its green fruit and the vines in blossom waft fragrance. Arise and go, my friend, my fair one, go forth!" (2:13) The *ra'aya*, however, sends her lover away: "Until the day's breeze blows, and the shadows flee, turn around, be like a deer, my love, or like a gazelle on the cloven mountains" (2:17). The reference to fleeing shadows suggests that it's the afternoon when the shade disappears and blends into the encroaching night. The *ra'aya*, we can conclude, missed the appointed date and has now turned down the beloved that has sought her out. In the afternoon, unlike the boldness of midday, the *ra'aya* is reluctant.

The heroine's desire returns in the night at the start of chapter three. She searches for her beloved "in the street and in the square" (3:2) with the promise that once she finds him, she will bring him to her mother's home and the room where she was conceived." With the *dod* and *ra'aya* locked in a private embrace, it is tempting to point to the night as the time of requited love. Careful textual reading, however, proves otherwise. The chapter begins with the *ra'aya* "lying on her couch" at night (3:1). She says to herself, "Let me rise and go round the town… let me seek whom I love so" (3:2). The narrative never describes her actually getting up from the bed; the passionate seeking and emotional union take place only in her imagination as she continues to lie in bed. It is no more than a vivid dream. She is still in her room and in the presence of the daughters of Jerusalem (3:5), not her beloved. Unlike her boldness and impulsiveness during the day, at night the *ra'aya* is timid; though she yearns for her beloved, dreams of meeting him, she is, nonetheless, paralyzed by her own fears.

In chapter three the scene turns from the pastoral to the urban. No longer complacent, the *ra'aya* rises out of the desert "like a pillar of smoke" (3:6) and is greeted in the city by a monarch riding a palanquin on his wedding day. According to HaRav Yaakov Medan,[1] the heavily-guarded king is none other than the *dod*, who has shed his shepherd robes to don princely garments while being fawned upon by a multitude of eager young women. As chapter three turns to four, the *dod* is ebullient in his praises only for the *ra'aya*, complimenting her hair, teeth and lips. From among the *dod*'s many admirers, only the *ra'aya* has captured his heart. This meeting, like that of chapter two, takes place in the afternoon or twilight. The *ra'aya* again refers to the day's waning breeze and the fleeing shadows (4:6). In chapter two, also set at twilight, the *ra'aya* had sent an eager *dod* fleeing into the woods. Here again, displaying similar reservations and anxieties, the *ra'aya* wishes to run back to her "mountain" (4:6). The *dod* calls her "a locked well, a sealed spring" (4:12). The *ra'aya*'s reluctance in the face of an eager *dod*, like in chapter two, occurs in the late afternoon.

"A strange, stubborn indolence," to quote Rav Joseph B. Soloveitchik (*Fate and Destiny* p. 24), overtakes the *ra'aya* at the start of chapter five. Though her beloved knocks, she refuses to rise from her bed. It is not from lack of desire. Indeed, her heart is woke with aspiration (5:2). The *dod*'s incessant knocking, and the *ra'aya*'s refusal to rise, take place at night. Eventually she rises, only to miss the moment: "I opened the door for my beloved, but my beloved had slipped off, was gone" (6:6). This nighttime scene mirrors chapter three, when the *ra'aya* had also lain in bed, desired to get up, but did nothing more than dream. Her refusal to respond to the beloved's knock confirms the nighttime setting as the time of yearning without action.

Chapter six refers to morning for the first time in the narrative and harkens a drastic shift in mood. The coyness that had separated the two

---

1. https://etzion.org.il/he/שלמה-השם-למשמעות/.

lovers throughout this story disappears into reunion. "Who is this espied like the dawn, fair as the moon, dazzling as the sun, daunting as what looms on high" (6:10)? The daughters of Jerusalem marvel at the *ra'aya* as she paces toward her *dod*, effusive with compliments. "Come, my lover," the *ra'aya* says to the *dod*, "let us go out into the field, spend the night in henna. Let us rise early in the vineyard" (7:12-13). No longer does she recoil, bashful in the face of her lover's advances as she had in the afternoon, nor does she yearn for him but refuse to act, as she had at night. With the sun high in the sky, in chapter one, she had reached out to her *dod*, who responded with affection. Now again, as night turns into day with the rising sun, desire and emotion turn to action. The *ra'aya* walks hand in hand beside her *dod*.

The position of the sun, then, highlights three distinct experiences. The afternoon, with its setting sun and shadows receding into darkness, makes the *ra'aya* reticent even as the *dod* pleads for her hand. At night, the sun is absent and the *ra'aya* dreams in bed. Desire churns deep inside her heart, but the foreboding darkness paralyzes her, preventing her from acting. In the morning, with the sun casting its bright rays across the vineyard, the *ra'aya* acts boldly, maximizes her opportunity, and reaches for the hand of her beloved.

Morning, afternoon, and night frame not only the story of the *dod* and *ra'aya*, but a number of stories in *Tanakh*. Recall that the *Brit Bein Ha-Betarim* (Covenant Between the Parts) between Avraham and God takes place at dusk (*Bereishit* 15:12). Avraham worries over an uncertain future and God comforts him with a commitment, embraced by the shadows of the setting sun. Later, following Avraham's circumcision and with his future more certain due to the birth of his son Yitzchak, God appears to him in the heat of the day (*Bereishit* 18:1), an expression of clarity and certitude about his relationship with God. So certain is Avraham of God's commitment that he boldly argues over the fate of *Sedom*.

The timing is again relevant in the story of *Yetzi'at Mitzrayim*, the Exodus from Egypt. The final night of slavery represents the danger not only for the firstborn Egyptians, but for *Benei Yisrael* as well, who find themselves in need of God's protection. True freedom takes place "*be-*

etzem ha-yom," midday (*Shemot* 12:51, *see Torah Temima*), when God's guidance and protection is in abundance. The most anxious moments of *Yetzi'at Mitzrayim*, when the Egyptians trap Benei Yisrael on the shore of the *Yam Suf*, take place in the dead of night. Benei Yisrael, like the *ra'aya*, are fearful and yearning for Divine intervention. The Sea opens to salvation, "*lifnot boker*," just as the sun rises in the morning (*Shemot* 14:27), representing God's abundant care for His people. The Exodus reaches its culmination when God reveals Himself to the Jewish people at *Sinai*. This revelation takes place on the third day, "*bi-hyot ha-boker*," in the morning (ibid. 19:16). The singular relationship formed with the giving of the Torah on that morning recalls the *ra'aya*'s confident embrace of her *dod* in the morning (*Shir Hashirim* ch. 7). The rising sun expresses the confidence and optimism of a burgeoning relationship.

Rav Soloveitchik begins his eloquent recounting of *Shir Hashirim* by setting a scene:

> As the setting sun of the Sabbath eve ignites the western horizon, and the Sabbath Queen, delicate, pleasing, and grateful as a bride, emerges from the rosy blaze of sunset, the strains of the Song of Songs course into a world becoming pure and sanctified, wrapped in the serenity of calmness and rest. (*And From There You Shall Seek* p. 5)

The moving introduction places the recitation of *Shir Hashirim* in a particular moment in time, attesting to the power of context within the religious experience.

The days and nights of *Shir Hashirim* inject another level of meaning into the spiritual fluctuations of the Jewish soul. In the bright light of the sun, morning and midday, the *ra'aya* acts boldly, reaching out to her beloved, as we, in the *berakhot* of *Keri'at Shema* in *shacharit*, reflect upon overt miracles, *Yetzi'at Mitzrayim*, and celebrate the clarity of God's guidance. *Tefillin* and *tzitzit*, marks of majesty, can be worn only during the day, when God's abundance is clear. The afternoon, with its slow transition toward darkness, leaves us, like the *ra'aya*, still drawing from the clarity and warmth of the sun though reticent about its setting. We pray *mincha* still invigorated by the brightness of the day while acknowledging the encroaching darkness. The night, with its thick darkness and confusion, is ripe for anxiety and yearning, similar to the *ra'aya* who dreams of her beloved's companionship. Indeed, the *berakha* of "*hashkiveinu*" in *arvit*, with its references to the looming power of the Satan and our desire for God's sheltering protections, reflects our own nocturnal fears that correspond to the *ra'aya*'s. *Shir Hashirim*, "poem of the creation and the Creator" (ibid.), represents the model for the complex interaction between God and man in *Tanakh* and in our lives. Through its scenes, the drama highlights the role that light and dark play within that exceptional relationship.

In the Presence of the Almighty[1]
The Compromise Between Moshe and the Tribes of Gad and Re'uven

Rabbi Daniel Fridman

The Biblical narrative[2] concerning the tribes of Gad[3] and Re'uven and their desire to receive their tribal portions in the Transjordan, the eastern bank of the Jordan river, is a particularly challenging episode to understand.

First and foremost, one wonders how such an audacious proposal[4] could have been made on the part of these two tribes. As Moshe immediately responds, this does appear to be a rejection of *Eretz Yisrael* proper, as

---

1. I would like to dedicate this essay, with its focus on both the national and spiritual dimensions of *Eretz Yisrael*, and, in particular, the capacity to radiate spirituality outwards from Zion, to the memories of our beloved and revered *Rashei Yeshiva*, HaRav Yehuda Amital *zt"l*, and HaRav Aharon Lichtenstein *zt"l*. In their many *shi'urim* and *sichot*, and even more so in their shared life's work, in creating Yeshivat Har Etzion, they educated toward the spiritual opportunities intrinsic to *Eretz Yisrael*, per se, as well as its capacity to project and radiate ideals outward from that *sanctus terra* (*Yeshaya* 2:3): "For out of Zion will go forth the law."
2. *Bamidbar* 32:1-34.
3. The ordering is intentional. The consensus view amongst the commentaries is that the tribe of Gad, somewhat counterintuitively relative to both their birth order and birth mother, was primary relative to Re'uven. See Ibn Ezra (*Bamidbar* 32:2), Chizkuni (ibid.), and Ramban (32:1-2), who all subscribe to this notion. I will maintain this order, of Gad, and then Re'uven, throughout this brief essay.
4. See Rashi 32:19 s.v. *ki va'a nachalateinu*, who understands that Gad and Re'uven are not merely making a request, but presenting a *fait accompli*. See Ramban (ibid.), who finds this, at least in his first response, a bridge too far to cross. Remarkably, however, in his second interpretation, he may render their actions far more radical even than Rashi's presentation, as they are essentially telling Moshe that there is nothing he can do to stop them from eventually abandoning *Eretz Yisrael*.

delineated by the geographic boundaries recorded just a few chapters later in the Torah.[5]

Given the very tragic history involved with respect to a failure to appreciate *Eretz Yisrael*, duly noted by Moshe as the undoing of the previous generation in the context of the spies, it seems almost unfathomable that two entire tribes could even contemplate making such a request, notwithstanding the material benefits that they hope to accrue in this land that is so suitable for cattle grazing. How, exactly, did Gad and Re'uven *think* that Moshe would react?

Secondly, in light of the end of the story, in which Moshe does arrive at a compromise with these tribes, one wonders how Moshe's attitude could have changed so drastically from a point of total opposition to one of acceptance. Initially, Moshe accuses these tribes of being as insidious as the spies were in the previous generation, literally leading the Jewish people down the path of annihilation.[6] How is Moshe able to make peace with this proposal? Not only does Moshe seem to accept, on the conditions described below, Gad and Re'uven's presence in the Transjordan, but he even initiates the entry of another tribe into the equation, as a portion of the tribe of Menasheh is sent to the northern portion of the land in question.[7] One can hardly conjure up an analog in the entirety of the *Chumash* in terms of the degree of Moshe's apparent *volte-face*, especially one concerning such a crucial issue.

It seems to me that to fully appreciate the dynamic in this compromise, which according to Rabbi Me'ir[8] becomes the halakhic template for all conditional agreements governing future events, we need to thoroughly investigate the particular formulations in the text of this chapter in the Torah.

First, it is abundantly clear that Gad and Re'uven had no premeditated intention of seeking out the conquered lands of Sichon and Og as their eternal

---

5. *Bamidbar* 34:10-12, which details the eastern boundary of *Eretz Yisrael*. It clearly does not include the Transjordan.
6. *Bamidbar* 32:14-15: "And so you will destroy all this people."
7. *Bamidbar* 32:33. The precise reason why Menasheh was chosen is subject to dispute. See Ramban (ibid.) who conjectures that they too were cattle herders, while the Chizkuni (ibid.) has a gloomier point of view concerning the tribe of Menasheh being split into two portions.
8. *Kiddushin* 61a.

inheritance. They could not possibly have, as the battle against Sichon and Og was not initiated by the Jewish people altogether. As is recorded both in *Bamidbar* (chapter 21) as well as recounted in *Devarim* (chapter 2), Moshe sent a peace delegation to Sichon, which he summarily rejected.

Indeed, if one looks carefully at the text of this chapter, it is clear that Re'uven and Gad make an *ex post facto* calculation concerning their acquisition of this land. The Torah opens the chapter by observing that these tribes had an enormous amount of cattle, and then notes (*Bamidbar* 32:1), "When they saw the land of *Yazer* and the land of *Gilad*, that, behold, the place was a place for cattle." In other words, only upon assessing the conquered lands did this idea even occur to these tribes. There was clearly no premeditated rejection of *Eretz Yisrael* here as some have attributed to the spies.[9]

Secondly, and more importantly, these two tribes immediately attribute the victories over the Amorite kings Sichon and Og to Divine assistance (*Bamidbar* 32:4), "the land that God smote before the congregation of Israel;" it is the land that God has delivered into the hands of the Jewish people. This statement on the part of Gad and Re'uven is significant on two levels. First, it quite explicitly demonstrates that these tribes, unlike the spies, had not lost their faith in the power of the Almighty. Secondly, it provides a *prima facie* rationale for these tribes to have believed that there was a chance that their request, made in clearly respectful terms (*Bamidbar* 32:5), "if we have found favor in your sight," of Moshe, Elazar, and the rest of the tribal princes, might be accepted. After all, if God had delivered this land to the Jewish people in a stunning and surprise victory, perhaps it might be construed as God's own desire for the Jewish people to annex this territory to the land west of the Jordan.

The respectful nature of this spontaneous request, along with their attribution of victory to God, is nonetheless not nearly enough for Moshe. Why not? Why does Moshe compare these tribes to the spies?[10]

---

9. See Rashi to *Bamidbar* 13:26 s.v. *va-yeilekhu va-yavo'u*.
10. Onkelos' formulation (ibid. 32:14) is particularly striking, rendering "*tarbut anashim chatta'im* (a brood of sinful men)" as "*talmidei guvraya chayavaya* (students of the guilty men)," as if Gad and Re'uven had actually studied the insidious plot of the spies.

The answer, it seems from the text, is threefold: First, Moshe notes that there is something fundamentally unacceptable, on the fraternal level, for members of the Jewish people to sit comfortably at home while their brothers are exposed to mortal danger on the field of battle, as Moshe says, incredulously (*Bamidbar* 32:6), "Shall your brothers go to the war, and shall you sit here?"[11]

Secondly, given the fearful prospect[12] that the rest of the Jewish people are facing, that of having to conquer all of the city states of *Kena'an*, surely Gad and Re'uven's decision to accept the Transjordan as their eternal portion would have seemed quite attractive to the rest of the Jewish people, who might similarly eschew crossing the Jordan river entirely.

Thirdly, and finally, Moshe expresses a concern that the stated desire not to enter (*Devarim* 11:12) "a land that God cares for," the land where God's presence is most intensely felt, is actually a rejection of the Almighty himself, as Moshe says (*Bamidbar* 32:15), "for if you turn away from after Him," you are not merely retreating from *Eretz Yisrael*, but from the God of Israel.

We can now well appreciate how Gad and Re'uven's offer to serve as the vanguard of the Jewish army, and not to return 'home,' as it were, until the Jewish people, aided in no small measure by their own frontline service, had conquered *Eretz Yisrael*, addresses the first two of Moshe's objections. Surely, Gad and Re'uven's commitment to not only enlist in the

---

11. Seforno (32:6 s.v. *ha-acheikhem yavo'u*) takes the position that Moshe considered this proposition, that of Re'uven and Gad sitting in the Transjordan while the rest of the Jewish people fought for *Eretz Yisrael*, so outlandish that Moshe concluded that there simply was no way that these tribes could seriously have imagined such a scenario occurring. Rather, Moshe concluded, knowing that the rest of the Jewish people would never accept such a blatant abandonment of national responsibility, Re'uven and Gad must deviously have made such a request so as to influence the entire nation not to cross the Jordan altogether. In essence, Seforno collapses the first two reasons for Moshe's objections, which I have presented as distinct, into a singular point of resistance.

12. It is important to bear in mind that the Jewish people had conquered only two kings, in Sichon and Og, and nothing on the scale of the dozens that they would have to battle in *Eretz Yisrael*. Moreover, the Jewish people had never achieved any victory without Moshe, which is precisely the scenario that the Jewish people were facing at this historical juncture. Simply put, there was good reason for them to be concerned, and by extension, for Moshe to be concerned about their fragile psychology.

armed forces, but to serve in the frontlines, would be sufficient to mitigate any charges of abdication of national duty. Secondly, their willingness to confront even greater danger than the rest of the Jewish people in the battle for *Eretz Yisrael* would have substantially mitigated Moshe's second concern, namely that of these two tribes influencing the rest of the Jewish people not to bother with the conquest of *Eretz Yisrael*.

Yet, Moshe's third concern, that of Re'uven and Gad, in effect, turning their back on proximity to the Almighty, remains unaddressed. After all, they will, at some point, cross back over to the eastern side of the Jordan, and return home.[13] Is this not, then, to some degree, a rejection of the Almighty Himself?[14]

---

13. While the imperative to reside in *Eretz Yisrael* in Rambam's view has been the subject of enormous controversy, given his omission of a specific mitzva in *Sefer Ha-mitzvot*, contra Ramban's celebrated position affirming such a command (see both his commentary to *Bamidbar* 33:53 as well as his glosses to *Sefer Ha-mitzvot*, *shikhechat ha-asin* 4), there is no question whatsoever regarding the severity with which Rambam treated what he deemed an unjustified exit of *Eretz Yisrael*, once one had established residence there. See *Hilkhot Melakhim* 5:9. It is absolutely striking to note that Rambam, in seeming affirmation of a mitzva to live in *Eretz Yisrael*, writes that "One should always live in *Eretz Yisrael* even in a city with a majority of idol worshippers..." (ibid. 5:12) only some three *halakhot* after he has established a prohibition to leave *Eretz Yisrael*, and in the latter context, where Rambam does utilize the affirmative formulation of the importance of residing in *Eretz Yisrael*, he twice repeats the earlier, negative formulation concerning leaving *Eretz Yisrael*. It may very well be for Rambam that there is a particular stigma attached to actively withdrawing from the spiritual opportunities presented by *Eretz Yisrael*, over and above the mandate to seek out those spiritual opportunities. As such, the proposed maneuver of the tribes of Re'uven and Gad, to leave *Eretz Yisrael* after nearly a decade and a half of uninterrupted residence, might be perceived of as particularly problematic from Rambam's vantage point.

14. At the very moment in *Yehoshu'a* (chapter 22 especially verses 15-19) when Re'uven and Gad (as well as elements of Menasheh) do return home, and erect a monument that reflects their commitment to the entirely of the Jewish people and the God of Israel, they are suspected by the rest of the Jewish people of having constructed an idolatrous altar. A civil war is only narrowly averted. It is striking that the Jewish people, in accusing these three tribes of idolatry, use precisely the same language that Moshe utilized, "to turn away this day from following (*me-acharei*, opp. *lifnei*) God," as well as "that you must turn away this day from following (*me-acharei*) God," (*Yehoshu'a* 22:16,18) in describing their actions. In other words, Moshe's third concern was never fully alleviated, and continued to lurk in the hearts of the Jewish people for another generation.

In consideration of Moshe's ongoing concern regarding the long-term commitment of these tribes to their relationship with God, it is extremely illuminating to study Moshe's response to the offer of Gad and Re'uven to serve as the vanguard of the Jewish people.

The tribes of Gad and Re'uven had offered to travel in front of the Jewish people (*Bamidbar* 32:17): "But we ourselves will be ready armed to go before (*lifnei*) the Children of Israel". Moshe, though, has something completely different in mind:

> And Moshe said to them: If you will do this thing, if you will arm yourselves to go before (*lifnei*) God to the war, and every armed man of you will pass over the Jordan before (*lifnei*) God, until He has driven out His enemies from before Him, and the land be subdued before (*lifnei*) God, and you return afterward, then you shall be clear before God and before Israel, and this land shall be for you a possession before (*lifnei*) God. But if you will not do so, behold, you have sinned against God, and know that your sin will find you. (*Bamidbar* 32:20-23)

Four times Moshe uses the expression "*lifnei Hashem*," to come before God. Moshe is prepared to accept Gad and Re'uven's proposal, only in so far as entering *Eretz Yisrael* is an act of coming *lifnei Hashem*. It is not sufficient for Gad and Re'uven to fight in front of the Jewish people, "*lifnei Benei Yisrael*," but they must perceive of themselves as being *lifnei Hashem*. Moshe trusts that this experience will have the necessary transformative impact on these tribes of establishing the long-term bond that will keep them in the fold generations hence, even after they return to the far side of the Jordan.

As Moshe continues, if these two tribes enter and fight for the land west of the Jordan, the land that is *lifnei Hashem*, then they will be able to extend that sense of *lifnei Hashem* to the eastern bank of the Jordan,[15] and this land

---

15. The idea that the sanctity of *Eretz Yisrael* must extend and radiate outwards from *Eretz Yisrael* proper is well established in *halakha*. See Rambam *Terumot* 1:2-3, regarding David's conquests. In this connection, it is important to note that Re'uven and Gad returned home only following the distribution of the land,

shall be for you a possession *lifnei Hashem*. In context, this is perhaps what Moshe meant when he uttered what became one of Chazal's most celebrated phrases[16] (*Bamidbar* 32:22), "then you shall be clear before God and before Israel." It is not sufficient for you, the tribes of Gad and Re'uven, to do right by the Jewish people. You must, first and foremost, ensure that you are doing right vis-à-vis your relationship with the Almighty, and not allowing your own material self-interest to come at the expense of something of far greater, non-quantifiable value, your relationship with the Almighty. As Moshe concludes, this sin would transcend the national-fraternal realm, but would directly impact their relationship with the Almighty, "But if you will not do so, behold, you have sinned against God."

The tribes of Gad and Re'uven get the message. In amending their previous statement,[17] these tribes no longer describe their future mission as being merely in front of the people, "*lifnei Benei Yisrael*," but rather, on two separate occasions as *lifnei Hashem* (*Bamidbar* 32:27, 32:32).

As such, one may indeed re-conceptualize the nature of Gad and Re'uven's serving as a vanguard in the battle for *Eretz Yisrael* proper. True, there was a national-fraternal dimension, one meant to ensure that they were not shirking their responsibilities to the Jewish people, a direct response to Moshe's charge, "Shall your brothers go to the war, and shall you sit here?" Secondly, in so doing, these tribes would prevent the catastrophic scenario first envisioned by Moshe, of an entire nation dwelling in the

---

which, according to Rambam (ibid.), was the decisive moment in determining the status of *Eretz Yisrael*. While according to Seforno (*Bamidbar* 32:28, 32:33) Re'uven and Gad actually took formal title during Moshe's lifetime, which would run contrary to this line of argument, Ramban appears to disagree on precisely this point (ibid. 32:29).

16. See, for example, *Mishna Shekalim* 3:2, *Yoma* 38a, *Pesachim* 13a. Ironically, in all of those instances, Chazal utilize the expression in precisely the opposite sense in which it is meant in the Torah, namely as a mandate to do the right thing not only in God's eyes, but in the eyes of people as well.

17. It is interesting to note that Yehoshu'a, both when first addressing the tribes of Gad, Re'uven, and Menasheh, as well as upon sending them home, refers to their fighting *lifnei acheikhem*, before your brothers (*Yehoshu'a* 1:14, 22:3). In fairness, however, Yehoshu'a is unequivocal in issuing precisely the same warning as Moshe, namely, that the geographic distance not create spiritual attrition, See *Yehoshu'a* 22:5, in which Yehoshu'a urges not only fidelity to the commandments, but, all importantly, a sense of love and a feeling of cleaving to God as well.

Transjordan (*Bamidbar* 32:7): "And why will you turn away the heart of the children of Israel?" To satisfy these two purposes, however, there really would have been no need for these tribes to remain for an additional seven years during the distribution of the conquered territory.

Thus, one might conclude, entering *Eretz Yisrael* not only for the conquest but remaining for the distribution[18] was essential for Gad and Re'uven themselves. Only by first entering *Eretz Yisrael*, experiencing "*dukhta de-Moshe ve-Aharon lo zakhu lah* (a place that Moshe and Aharon did not merit to enter),"[19] imbibing the proximity to the Divine presence captured in those inimitable words (*Devarim* 11:12), "the eyes of God are always upon it," and specifically, by waiting for the sanctity of *Eretz Yisrael* to be fully activated after its distribution to the tribes,[20] could Gad and Re'uven turn around and project a certain degree of that quality into the Transjordan,[21] what had heretofore been nothing more than *Chutz La-Aretz*.

Moshe, in hearing that these tribes internalized his message that they must not allow the narrow waters of the Jordan to create a far greater distance between themselves and the Almighty, accedes to their request. He is now confident that the Transjordan, as a projection of the sanctity of *Eretz Yisrael* proper, could truly be a possession that is *lifnei Hashem*, an eternal portion in the presence of the Almighty.

---

18. See Malbim to *Yehoshu'a* 1:15.
19. *Ketubbot* 112a.
20. While the mitzva of *hafrashat challa* began immediately with the crossing of the Jordan, the rest of this genre of *mitzvot*, which are contingent upon the land itself, were activated only after the fourteen years of conquest and division.
21. The precise halakhic status of the Transjordan, both with respect to being part of *Eretz Yisrael* (*sheim Eretz Yisrael*) and whether it has the sanctity of *Eretz Yisrael* (*kedushat Eretz Yisrael*), is beyond the scope of this essay.

About the Authors

HaRav Yehuda Amital *zt"l* and HaRav Aharon Lichtenstein *zt"l* were the founding *Rashei Yeshiva* of Yeshivat Har Etzion.

HaRav Baruch Gigi '75, HaRav Mosheh Lichtenstein '78, and HaRav Yaakov Medan '68 are *Rashei Yeshiva* at Yeshivat Har Etzion.

Rabbi Dr. Michael Rosensweig '73 is a *Rosh Yeshiva* at Yeshiva University.

Rabbi Michael Taubes '77 is a *Rosh Yeshiva* at Yeshiva University.

Rabbi Dr. Michael Berger '80 is a Professor of Jewish Studies at Emory University.

Rabbi Ari Kahn '80 is a Professor of Jewish Studies at Bar-Ilan University and the Rabbi of Mishkan Etrog in Givat Ze'ev.

Terry Novetsky '80 is the former Chairman of the Etzion Foundation and a Partner at King & Spalding LLP.

Rabbi Joel Finkelstein '81 is the Rabbi of the Anshei Sphard-Beth El Emeth Congregation in Memphis, TN.

Rabbi Nathaniel Helfgot '81 is the Head of the Talmud Department at SAR High School.

Gidon Rothstein '82 is a *talmid*.

Rabbi Yitzchak Etshalom '83 is the *Rosh Beit Midrash* at YULA High Schools.

Rabbi Moshe Taragin '83 is a *Rebbe* at Yeshivat Har Etzion.

Rabbi Dr. Yossef Slotnik '83 is Director of the Overseas Program at Yeshivat Maale Gilboa.

Rabbi Reuven Ziegler '86 is Editor-in-Chief at Koren Publishers.

Rabbi Mark Smilowitz '88 is a Teacher at YTA Girls High School.

Rabbi David Brofsky '90 is a *Rebbe* at Midreshet Lindenbaum.

Rabbi Nasanayl Braun '92 is the Rabbi of Congregation Brothers of Israel in Long Branch, NJ.

Rabbi Dr. Moti Novick '92 is a Lecturer in Mathematics at Machon Lev and Herzog College.

Rabbi Dr. Shlomo Dov Rosen '93 is the Rabbi of Yakar in Jerusalem.

Rabbi Yehoshua Grunstein '95 is the Director of Training and Placement at the Straus-Amiel Institute.

Rabbi Dr. Ezra Frazer '96 is a *Rebbe* at the Ramaz Upper School.

Rabbi David Nachbar '96 is a *Rebbe* at TABC and teaches in GPATS at Stern College.

Rabbi Elie Weissman '96 is the Rabbi of the Young Israel of Plainview, NY.

Rabbi Dr. Shlomo Brody '98 is the Director of the Tikvah Overseas Students Institute.

Rabbi Rafi Eis '98 is the Director of the *Semikha* Program at Yeshivat Har Etzion.

Rabbi Dr. Yaakov Jaffe '98 is the Rabbi of the Maimonides Kehillah and Dean of Judaic Studies at Maimonides School.

Rabbi Tzvi Sinensky '98 is the Director of Interdisciplinary Learning and Educational Outreach at Rae Kushner Yeshiva High School.

Rabbi Dr. Aaron Segal '99 is a Lecturer in Philosophy at Hebrew University.

Rabbi Daniel Fridman '02 is *Sgan Rosh Yeshiva* at TABC and Rabbi at the Jewish Center of Teaneck.

Rabbi Shlomo Zuckier '05 is a member of Yeshiva University's *Kollel Elyon*, a PhD candidate at Yale University, and Founding Editor of *The Lehrhaus*.

Rabbi Dovid Gottlieb '09 is the Rav of Ganei HaEla in Ramat Beit Shemesh and a *Rebbe* at Yeshivat Har Etzion.

www.ingramcontent.com/pod-product-compliance
Lightning Source LLC
Chambersburg PA
CBHW070045230426
43661CB00005B/764